W9-AMB-771

Success Skills

Strategies for Study and Lifelong Learning

third edition

Abby Marks Beale

Corporate Learning Specialist

Founder, The Corporate Educator

SOUTH-WESTERN
CENGAGE Learning™

Australia • Brazil • Japan • Korea • Mexico • Singapore • Spain • United Kingdom • United States

SOUTH-WESTERN
CENGAGE Learning

Success Skills: Strategies for Study and Lifelong Learning, Third Edition

Abby Marks Beale

VP/Editorial Development:
Jack W. Calhoun

VP/Editor-in-Chief:
Karen Schmohe

Executive Editor:
Eve Lewis

Senior Developmental Editor:
Penny Shank

Consulting Editor:
Laurie Wendell

Marketing Manager:
Courtney Schulz

Senior Marketing Coordinator:
Linda Kuper

Marketing Communication Manager:
Terron Sanders

Production Manager:
Patricia Matthews Boies

Senior Content Project Manager:
Kim Kusnerak

Director of Technology:
Tim Butz

Manager Production Process Development:
Peggy Buskey

Technology Project Editor:
Chris Wittmer

Manufacturing Coordinator:
Kevin Kluck

Production House:
Interactive Composition Corporation

Printer:
Edwards Brothers
Ann Arbor, MI

Art Director:
Tippy McIntosh

Cover and Internal Designer:
Lou Ann Thesing

Cover Image:
© John Berry/Images.com

Photo and Permissions Editor:
Darren Wright

COPYRIGHT © 2007 by South-Western,
a part of Cengage Learning.

Printed in the United States of America
2 3 4 5 6 10 09 08

ISBN-13: 978-0-538-72963-5
ISBN-10: 0-538-72963-5

ALL RIGHTS RESERVED.
No part of this work covered by the
copyright hereon may be reproduced or
used in any form or by any means—
graphic, electronic, or mechanical,
including photocopying, recording,
taping, Web distribution or information
storage and retrieval systems, or in any
other manner—without the written
permission of the publisher.

For permission to use material from this
text or product, submit a request online
at www.cengage.com/permissions.

For more information about our products,
contact us at:
South-Western Cengage Learning
5191 Natorp Boulevard
Mason, Ohio 45040
USA

REVIEWERS

Jacqueline Andresen
Business Teacher
Marquette Senior High School
Marquette, MI

Jeanne M. Derryberry
Marketing Teacher
Diamond Oaks Institute of Technology and
    Career Development
Cincinnati, OH

Patricia Hartley
Business Technology Teacher
Hoover High School
Hoover, AL

Dana Hoeffner
Business Career Prep Coordinator
Monterey High School
Lubbock, TX

Delores Lawrie-Higgins
Assistant Superintendent
Cape May County Technical School District
Cape May Court House, NJ

Rebecca A. Lindhorst
Career Connection Facilitator
Mainland High School
Daytona Beach, FL

Patricia Morgigno
Business Education Teacher
West Islip High School
West Islip, NY

Pamela Mullan
Assistant Professor, Reading
Onondaga Community College
Syracuse, NY

Katrina M. Ryan
Business Department Chair
Shafter High School
Shafter, CA

Sherrie Stuessy
Business and Information Technology
    Teacher
Belleville High School
Belleville, WI

ABOUT THE AUTHOR

Abby Marks Beale is the founder of The Corporate Educator (formerly The Reading Edge), a speaking, training, and consulting business that specializes in helping busy professionals work smarter, faster, and just plain better. Her extensive client list includes Fortune 500 companies, small businesses, schools, universities, associations, and individuals. In addition to her corporate training, she offers professional development workshops to educators in the areas of study skills, learning styles, motivating learners, and revving up reading. Abby holds a B.A. in Spanish from Boston University and an M.S. in Adult Learning from Southern Connecticut State University.

CONTENTS

Chapter 3
Creating Concentration 58

Chapter 4
Learning Time Management. 78

Chapter 5
Studying Smart. 114

Chapter 9
Revving Up Your Reading 230

Chapter 10
Mastering Tests 262

Chapter 11
Using Your Critical and Creative Mind . . 296

Chapter 12
Reading and Researching Online 323

Chapter 13
Writing in the Real World **354**

ENGAGE STUDENT INTEREST

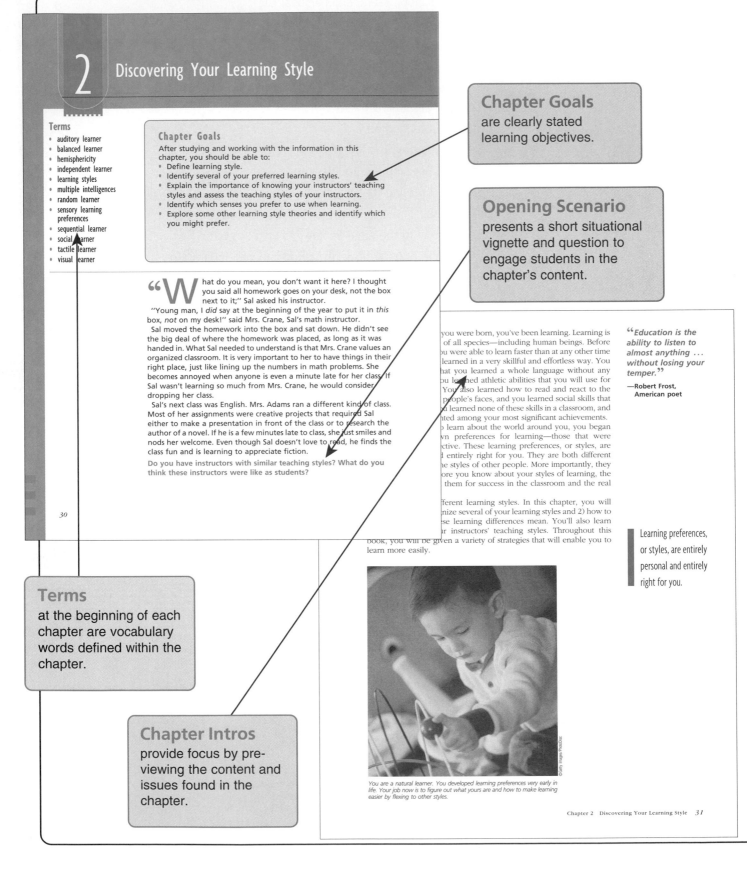

2 Discovering Your Learning Style

Terms
- auditory learner
- balanced learner
- hemisphericity
- independent learner
- learning styles
- multiple intelligences
- random learner
- sensory learning preferences
- sequential learner
- social learner
- tactile learner
- visual learner

Chapter Goals
After studying and working with the information in this chapter, you should be able to:
- Define learning style.
- Identify several of your preferred learning styles.
- Explain the importance of knowing your instructors' teaching styles and assess the teaching styles of your instructors.
- Identify which senses you prefer to use when learning.
- Explore some other learning style theories and identify which you might prefer.

"What do you mean, you don't want it here? I thought you said all homework goes on your desk, not the box next to it;" Sal asked his instructor.

"Young man, I *did* say at the beginning of the year to put it in *this* box, *not* on my desk!" said Mrs. Crane, Sal's math instructor.

Sal moved the homework into the box and sat down. He didn't see the big deal of where the homework was placed, as long as it was handed in. What Sal needed to understand is that Mrs. Crane values an organized classroom. It is very important to her to have things in their right place, just like lining up the numbers in math problems. She becomes annoyed when anyone is even a minute late for her class. If Sal wasn't learning so much from Mrs. Crane, he would consider dropping her class.

Sal's next class was English. Mrs. Adams ran a different kind of class. Most of her assignments were creative projects that required Sal either to make a presentation in front of the class or to research the author of a novel. If he is a few minutes late to class, she just smiles and nods her welcome. Even though Sal doesn't love to read, he finds the class fun and is learning to appreciate fiction.

Do you have instructors with similar teaching styles? What do you think these instructors were like as students?

30

...you were born, you've been learning. Learning is ... of all species—including human beings. Before ...ou were able to learn faster than at any other time ...learned in a very skillful and effortless way. You ...hat you learned a whole language without any ...ou learned athletic abilities that you will use for ... You also learned how to read and react to the ... people's faces, and you learned social skills that ...u learned none of these skills in a classroom, and ...ted among your most significant achievements.

...o learn about the world around you, you began ...wn preferences for learning—those that were ...ctive. These learning preferences, or styles, are ...d entirely right for you. They are both different ...he styles of other people. More importantly, they ...ore you know about your styles of learning, the ...them for success in the classroom and the real ...

...ferent learning styles. In this chapter, you will ...nize several of your learning styles and 2) how to ...se learning differences mean. You'll also learn ...r instructors' teaching styles. Throughout this book, you will be given a variety of strategies that will enable you to learn more easily.

"*Education is the ability to listen to almost anything ... without losing your temper.*"
—Robert Frost, American poet

Learning preferences, or styles, are entirely personal and entirely right for you.

You are a natural learner. You developed learning preferences very early in life. Your job now is to figure out what yours are and how to make learning easier by flexing to other styles.

©Getty Images/PhotoDisc

Chapter Goals are clearly stated learning objectives.

Opening Scenario presents a short situational vignette and question to engage students in the chapter's content.

Terms at the beginning of each chapter are vocabulary words defined within the chapter.

Chapter Intros provide focus by pre-viewing the content and issues found in the chapter.

"To furnish the means of acquiring knowledge is... the greatest benefit that can be conferred upon mankind."

—John Quincy Adams, Sixth President of the United States

Distinguishing between Active and Passive Learning

The terms *active* and *passive* are opposites of each other. Being **active** simply means *doing something* or *being* **conscious and mindful**, while being **passive** means *doing nothing* or *being* **unconscious** and **mindless**. Though you can sometimes learn mindlessly and unconsciously, those who are mindful and conscious are far more effective and successful in their learning.

The process of *osmosis* is a helpful example in demonstrating the difference between active and passive learning. **Osmosis** is a passive process by which a person learns information or ideas *without conscious effort*. As an example, you might have learned how bees make honey simply by tuning into a program on television.

If, however, you place a book under your pillow before going to sleep, the information contained in the book obviously will not be absorbed into the pillow nor into your head. In this case, the passive process of osmosis doesn't work, so you must become more active in your learning process to absorb the material in the book.

ACTIVITY 1

Read the following list of learning habits. Put a "P" on the line next to those habits that you think are Passive and an "A" next to those you think are Active. At the bottom of the list, add three more passive and three more active habits. Feel free to work with a partner.

_____ Frequently daydreaming about a non-related topic

_____ Mentally relating what you know to the new information

_____ Doing a half-hearted job

_____ Ignoring deadlines

_____ Comparing notes with someone else

_____ Taking notes from written material

_____ Not asking for help (or knowing when to ask)

_____ Sharing with others what you are learning

_____ Not participating in discussions

_____ Sitting far away from the instructor

_____ Waiting until the last minute to do the work

_____ Listening carefully and/or taking notes

_____ Reading at a time of day when you are most tired

_____ Learning from mistakes

P _____

P _____

P _____

_____

A _____

_____

A _____

A _____

4   Success Skills

Activities challenge students to recall information, think critically about chapter concepts, and analyze their own study habits.

Think about different jobs people do, for example, a professional athlete. Does an athlete need to be more active or passive in the way he or she approaches training? Certainly, to get and stay in shape and be ready for the season, the athlete must work out actively and consistently. Sure, you can build some muscle by passively and mindlessly lifting weights, but you will build more muscle if you actively and mindfully engage your mind with your body while working out.

Consider servers in a restaurant. Their basic job is to take food and drink orders, deliver them to the kitchen, and then deliver meals to the patrons when they are prepared. However, consider the server who does this job and also returns to the table often to ask if patrons need more of anything like water, drinks, or napkins. This server will probably make more money and be viewed as better than the one who just does the basic job.

Throughout this book, more detailed explanations will be given about active habits. Each explanation will help you better understand how and why being more active in the learning process is better than being passive. As you attend classes or meetings, read and take notes, and perform other learning functions, be aware of how active or passive you are. Think about the internal and external conditions— what you are thinking about and what is happening around you—that affect your ability to be more active at certain times and more passive at others. The more active you are, the better!

What other professions can you think of where you can compare active versus passive behaviors?

Checkpoint

1 Do you think most people are passive or active learners? Why?

_____

_____

_____

2 Do you think you are mostly an active or passive learner? What active or passive behaviors do you exhibit?

_____

_____

_____

3 What do you want to learn from this chapter?

_____

_____

_____

Chapter 1   Learning by Doing   5

Checkpoints found at the end of each main topic assist with review and comprehension of key concepts.

SPECIAL FEATURES ENHANCE LEARNING

Quotes from authors, leaders, and celebrities add relevance, humor, and motivational thoughts.

Success Tips highlight helpful tips for succeeding in the areas of reading, studying, and lifelong learning.

Becoming an active learner is a simple and rewarding way to gain knowledge without wasting valuable time and money. The information in this chapter will provide specific steps you can take to become more involved in your learning process.

Why Learning Skills Are So Important

Developing learning skills is essential in this technological age because businesses continue to use advanced technologies that require a high level of learning skill from their employees. More and more, employees are required to work in teams and pool their knowledge. Software is constantly being added and updated, and new products are constantly being developed, which we have to learn how to use.

All this requires a work force that is highly adaptable to gaining new knowledge. A company is considered successful when it has an abundance of **intellectual capital**, or a smart work force that is able to continuously learn and improve.

Learning How to Learn

Learning-how-to-learn skills are the keys to your success in life. Possessing and using effective and efficient learning skills means 1) you feel confident in your ability to learn and 2) you spend less time learning more. Not only do these skills help you achieve academic success, but also they lead to career and family success.

You may wonder how all of this relates to your future. In Figure 1-1 on page 8, you will see chapter by chapter how each of the learning skills discussed in this textbook can be used in the future.

> "The people who get on in this world are the people who get up and look for the circumstances they want, and, if they can't find them, make them."
> —George Bernard Shaw, Playwright

Success tip

Learn from ALL the intelligences. Just because you may not be as talented as your musical friend, you may be better at math. You may be able to debate strongly while your friend is better at sports.

Feel proud about the intelligences you are naturally strong in and appreciate others who may have strengths other than yours. You can learn much from each other!

3. **Body/Kinesthetic**—relates to physical movement

4. **Musical/Rhythmic**—based on the recognition of tonal patterns and sensitivity to rhythm, beats,

5. **Interpersonal**—relies primarily on socia to-person relationships and communicatio

6. **Intrapersonal**—relates to being alone a being, self-reflection, metacognition (or t thinking), and awareness of spiritual reali

7. **Verbal/Linguistic**—relates to words and written and spoken

8. **Naturalist**—relates to the recognition, a understanding of the natural world aroun

With a partner or in a small group, make a lis people who are strong in each of these ei combination of the areas). For example, Oprah V talk show host and producer is strong in interpe Albert Einstein, the Father of Physics, was stro matical intelligence. Ballet dancer Mikhail Barys body/kinesthetic intelligence. Author and conserv Thoreau was probably strong in both the nat linguistic intelligence. You can locate names on th key words "multiple intelligences."

Checkpoint

1 Name the three learning theories discussed in this section.

_____

_____

_____

2 Do you think you are a social or independent learner? Why?

_____

_____

_____

3 Which of the multiple intelligences are your strongest?

_____

_____

ence between an observer and a participant? Which are you?

successfully on a comfortable couch. Be aware of room temperature. Many libraries are overly warm, which can make you feel sluggish or sleepy.

2. MANAGE YOUR CLUTTER. Your desktop or tabletop should be clear of clutter, except for the materials you need for studying. You should have enough room for your elbows, reading material, a notebook, and any other necessary items. If your desk or table is cluttered, try the **arm-swing rule**; that is, gently sweep a semicircle of clear space in front of you using the length of space from your elbow to your fingertips. You may end up with a clutter fortress piled up around the semicircle, but nothing directly in front of you. When you have learning to do, clutter is a distraction.

3. ENSURE GOOD LIGHTING. Some people require a bright space, while others prefer a dimmer environment. It is easier to learn when the lighting is just right for your eyes. For example, if fluorescent lights bother you, place a lamp on your table, or sit by natural sunlight. If outside light bothers you, draw the curtains.

4. FEED YOUR BODY RIGHT. What you eat plays an important role in how well or how poorly you concentrate. Protein foods (such as cheese, meat, fish) and vegetables keep the mind alert, while carbohydrates (such as pasta, bread, and processed white sugars), make you sleepy. Caffeine (commonly found in coffee, tea, soft drinks, and chocolate) acts as a stimulant in low doses. In high doses, it can cause jitters, heart palpitations, diarrhea, and sleeplessness. So when you want to concentrate, eat more protein in relation to your carbohydrates, and limit your caffeine.

5. AVOID FOOD. Food and serious learning don't mix well. Think about it. When you try to eat and study at the same time, which gets more of your attention? The food, of course! You will be more effective if you eat first, then study. If you want to study while you eat, review material or read background information that requires less concentration.

6. CREATE ROOM TEMPERATURE COMFORT. Room temperature is also important. An overly hot room makes you sleepy, while an overly cold one makes you think about getting warm. You end up focusing more on how warm or cold you are than on your learning. Getting

■ Focus on Ethics

You're taking an online course with people you don't know, and you've been assigned to work on a team project. You have been given the responsibility to write the final report, but your mother is sick and you have taken on a lot more responsibilities around the house. You are under a lot of pressure, but don't want to let your teammates down, so you don't say anything.

You keep putting off getting started and you tell your teammates you're working on it. On the day before the course ends, you send an e-mail to your teammates telling them that you're very sorry but you were not able to get the work done.

Where did you go wrong? What could you have done differently to avoid this situation? Would you have acted differently if it was a traditional face-to-face class rather than an online course?

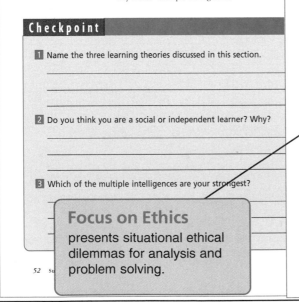

Focus on Ethics presents situational ethical dilemmas for analysis and problem solving.

Becoming aware of what you do and how it relates to your goals is a valuable step toward reaching your goals and getting what you want out of life.

Choices for Spending Time

Knowing what is important to you helps you plan your time according to *your* needs, not someone else's. Becoming aware of how you currently spend your time is the next step to planning how best to spend your time in the future. There are basically two ways to spend time: productively and unproductively. Spending **productive time** involves engaging in some activity that gets you closer to your goal(s). If learning a new computer program is one of your goals, then spending time at your computer trying out the program is a productive use of your time. If you intend to keep a clean house, then doing dishes and vacuuming is a good use of your time.

On the other hand, spending **unproductive time** is when you are *not* engaged in an activity that carries you toward your goal(s). Spending time at your computer aimlessly surfing the Web will not help you learn the new program and is an unproductive use of your time. (But surfing the Web for a project or for the answer to a question is a productive use of your time.) If you decide to watch TV or read the paper instead of cleaning the house, you are using your time unproductively. (However, if your intent is to relax, then those activities are a good use of your time.) In the end, what is considered productive depends entirely upon your goals and intentions.

Achieving a balance between the time you spend on productive versus unproductive activities is a daily challenge. We all know how easy it would be to ignore an alarm clock, get up when we want, and do only what we please all day. But reality dictates that we go to work or school and take care of our families and ourselves. Becoming aware of how what you do relates to your goals is a productive step in reaching your goals and getting what you want out of life.

Margin Notes
include tips and quips to increase interest and relevancy.

Focus on Technology
presents different technologies and software that aid or are relevant to learning.

You can use your academic calendar to make out a schedule for completing papers and projects. Typically, you need a lot of time to complete papers and projects. For example, if today is Tuesday and you have a paper due six weeks from today, you can plan each of the steps you must do to complete the assignment.

Week 1: By Friday   Decide on a topic
Week 2: Tuesday   Start research
Week 3: Tuesday   Continue research
        Thursday   Con
Week 4: Tuesday   Writ
Week 5: Tuesday   Writ
Week 6: Sunday   Rev
        Tuesday   Han

Now that you have a calendar f dates and social events, you still assignments and responsibilities.

Using a Weekly Project Pla

A **weekly project planner** is like a a to-do list specific to one day. It into 5 one-day periods with plenty way to keep track of assignments school calendar.

When you were in grade scho notepad to write your assignments

NETBookmark

Many Internet sites offer free web-based calendars on which you can record your personal schedule. Look at one or two web calendars to find a calendar with features useful for you. Some even let you share your calendar with others, which is especially useful for families, school projects, and work teams. You can also do a web search using the key words "free web calendar."
For links to sites that provide web calendars, go to:

http://sskills.swlearning.com

inside
Nov
hav
stud
Or
sho
rep
nee
for
you
con
nee
Ma
pro
little
divi
If I
meeting on Monday, October 15, weekly project planner on Wed

NETBookmark
provides web-search activities for learners to go beyond the book.

---

10. HOLD ALL CALLS AND IM'S. Receiving telephone calls or engaging in IM conversations during your study time is both distracting and time consuming. Thanks to other human beings and answering devices, you have the ability to hold your calls until you complete your work. If you choose to study between 7:00 and 8:30 in the evening, you can leave a message on your answering machine, or you can tell the person answering the phone for you to let your callers know that you will return their calls after 8:30. If you don't respond to your friends' text messages, they will think you are away from your computer, which you are, and they will get back to you later. Both ideas will provide uninterrupted time for studying.

11. LET E-MAIL WAIT. Checking e-mail is just like answering the phone. If you choose to wait until you are finished with your work, your concentration will stay on track.

12. MOVE TO A QUIETER PLACE. Reading or working when other people are around can make concentrating difficult. If you do your reading or working in a public place such as a library, it may be quiet, but other people will always be moving around. If you read or work at home, your family may interrupt you more often than necessary. If you read at work, your boss or coworkers will inevitably interrupt you. In all cases, you have the ability to prevent these distractions. At the library, find a quiet corner of the building where few people go. At home, explain to your family your need for uninterrupted time, and move to a place where you can close the door. At work, move to a place where no one will find you, such as an empty conference room or the cafeteria during off-hours. These options provide more uninterrupted work time and a better chance of increasing your concentration.

13. DUMP YOUR TO-DO LIST. If while you are reading or working, you find yourself thinking of other things you need to be doing, try writing them on a piece of paper. At inappropriate times your mind will almost always wander to things you need to do. Keeping track of your thoughts on paper and referring to the paper from time to time can be very effective for clearing your mind and focusing on your work in front of you.

Focus on Technology

While reading from a computer screen can sometimes seem daunting and slow, there are certain features that can make the process better than reading paper documents. When you use eBook software like Microsoft® Reader you may find that having a search function, post-it note capabilities, and the ability to easily carry hundreds of thousands of pages of text with you is well worth the few drawbacks.
To get started reading eBooks go to Microsoft's web site (search online for "Microsoft Reader") and download Microsoft's Reader software. There are versions for desktop, laptop, tablet, and pocket PCs. Once you have downloaded the software you will have access to thousands of eBook titles—many of which are available free.

REVIEW AND ASSESSMENT

Self-Check ✓

The following self-evaluation will give you an idea of how familiar, or unfamiliar, you are with some of the topics and terms discussed in this chapter. After reading each statement, circle the letter Y, S, or N to indicate the answer that is most appropriate for you. Answer honestly. Rate yourself at the end; then complete the information on your Self-Check Progress Chart.

Y = yes; frequently   S = sometimes   N = no; never

1. I gen
   while

2. I sit n
   leade

3. I activ
   in dis

4. I liste

5. I wor
   envir

6. I take
   quest

7. I am
   on tir

8. I keep
   a sch

9. I ask

10. I lear

Rate Y

Numb

Numb

Numb

> ### Self-Check
> provides self-assessment of individual learning habits.

CHAPTER SUMMARY

1. The terms *active* and *passive* are opposites. Being an active learner means you do something conscious and mindful to make learning happen, while being a passive learner means you do nothing to make learning happen. Though you can sometimes learn from doing nothing, doing something makes learning more effective and successful.

2. Advantages of becoming an active learner include learning more in less time and knowing how to learn anything you want. Active learners also possess feelings of self-confidence and high self-esteem as a result of their involvement in learning.

3. Learning-how-to-learn skills can help you succeed in school, at work, and at home.

4. With every learning task, you have a purpose and a responsibility. By giving yourself a reason to begin working (your purpose) as well as a point at which you are finished (your responsibility), you will concentrate better and learn and remember more of what you are working on.

5. If you believe in your ability to learn, you will possess the confidence necessary to succeed in any area of your life. You can begin to gain this c
   success words and negative attitudes with p

6. This chapter describes many ways to be active
   it, sitting close to the action, fearlessly asking
   and learning from your mistakes.

7. Every school and every workplace has resourc
   solving problems. These resources include pe

8. Your health, or lack of it, greatly influences yo
   prepared you are, the easier it is to learn.
   difficult.

> ### Chapter Summary
> provides a review of the key points from the chapter.

CHAPTER ASSESSMENT

Terms Review
Match the following terms to their definitions.

___active   a. The end result of wh
___body language   b. Feeling capable and
___conscious   c. A smart work force
___empowered   d. Those who prefer to
___5Ws and H   e. Postures, gestures, an
___intellectual capital   f. Doing something mi
___observers   g. Learning information
___osmosis   h. Believing in somethi
___participants   i. Being aware and mi
___persistence   j. The five questions to
___purpose   k. Those who prefer to
___responsibility l. The reason you do s
___unconscious   m. Mindless and passiv

> ### Chapter Assessment
> evaluates mastery of chapter terms and concepts and identifies ways students can apply the concepts to their own studying, reading, and learning practices.

Review
Based on the information you learned in this chapter, answer the following questions using your own words and thoughts.

1. What is a passive learner?

_____

_____

_____

_____

2. What is an active learner?

_____

_____

_____

_____

3. Name at least 5 things you can do to become more active in your learning.
   1. _____
   2. _____
   3. _____
   4. _____
   5. _____

4. Why do you think being an active learner is smarter than being a passive one?

_____

_____

_____

_____

5. Given one of your recent reading assignments, what was (is) your purpose and responsibility? How do you go about identifying these?

_____

_____

_____

_____

6. Why is knowing your purpose and responsibility helpful before reading?

_____

_____

_____

26 Success Skills

CASE STUDIES

for Creative and Critical Thinking

ACADEMIC CASE—Connecting to Science Lab

Lab partners Trisha and Maria entered their freshman biology lab and sat at their bench prior to starting their assignment entitled "Earthworm Dissection." Trisha said to Maria, "When I was looking over the procedure for this lab, I didn't quite understand Part II in the instruction manual. Did you?"

"No," Maria replied, "I didn't even read it, but I'm sure we will figure it out."

Trisha sought the help of the lab instructor before picking up the scalpel and starting the dissection. About halfway through the assignment, Trisha asked Maria if she would like to take over. "You are doing such a great job," Maria responded. "I think I'll just keep watching you and taking notes."

1. Which lab partner was the active learner? What specifically did she do to be considered an active learner?

   _____
   _____
   _____
   _____

2. Which lab partner was the passive learner? What specifically did she do to be considered a passive learner?

   _____
   _____
   _____
   _____

3. What do you see as the possible problem(s) here for Trish

   _____
   _____
   _____
   _____

4. In this case, what are the advantages of being the active

   _____
   _____
   _____
   _____

Case Studies present thought-provoking situations that require critical and creative thinking about studying and learning dilemmas in both academic and workplace environments.

WORKPLACE CASE—Connecting to Job Orientation

John and Miranda are newly hired employees at a local computer store. They were attending an orientation seminar designed to introduce them to the store and the company. An agenda was distributed to all the new hires before the orientation started. It outlined the topics of the seminar, which included benefit options, company guidelines, basic work procedures, the performance evaluation process, and other useful information.

John read through the agenda and on a pad he brought with him jotted down questions about several of the topics. He wanted to know when his health insurance would take effect and how many weeks of vacation he would be allowed. John took a seat in the second row, which he saved for himself when he arrived 15 minutes earlier. He made sure to ask his questions. At the end of the meeting, he felt satisfied that he had all the information he needed.

Miranda spent the time before the seminar talking on her cell phone. When it was time to go into the seminar, Miranda was the last one into the room and had to sit in the back because all the seats were taken. She sat quietly, saying nothing. When the session was over, Miranda complained to John that the presenter didn't tell her what she needed to know about automatic deposit of her paycheck and whom to call if she is going to be late.

1. Which of the two was more actively involved in their learning? Why do you think so?

   _____
   _____
   _____
   _____

2. What specific things did John do that secured a positive experience for him?

   _____
   _____
   _____
   _____

3. Whose responsibility is it to secure the information that Miranda wants to know? What more could she have done?

   _____
   _____
   _____
   _____

4. Based on this situation, which employee do you think might do a better job? Why do you think so?

   _____
   _____
   _____
   _____

WELCOME TO YOUR SOURCE FOR LIFELONG LEARNING

Success Skills: Strategies for Study and Lifelong Learning equips users with the learning and study skills required in today's academic and workplace environments. With a focus on learning *how* to learn, critical thinking, reading comprehension, and managing information, this text-workbook prepares users to make successful learning an ongoing part of their academic and career development.

This totally new edition of Abby Marks Beale's *Success Skills: Strategies for Study and Lifelong Learning* emphasizes key areas that are vital to successful lifelong learning:

- learning *how* to learn

- managing time and tasks

- building reading speed and comprehension

- effective listening for note taking

- improving memory and concentration

- successful test taking

- reading and researching online

- thinking critically and creatively

- gathering information and writing effectively

Features

The thirteen newly designed chapters offer a fresh look with engaging instructional features:

- **Academic** and **workplace scenarios** introduce each chapter and have been updated to engage students in the importance of lifelong learning in both academic and work environments.

- **Self-Checks**, **Checkpoints**, **Activities**, and **Review** exercises challenge learners to recall information, think critically about chapter concepts, and analyze their own study habits.

- New **Focus on Technology** and **NET Bookmark** features apply technology to learning processes and suggest key words for conducting web searches for additional information on lifelong learning subjects.

- **Focus on Ethics** features have been updated and present ethical dilemmas for analysis and problem solving. These features consider the ethical implications in managing time, using technology, and working with others at school or at work.

- **Success Tips** and **Quotes** in the margins highlight interesting facts, findings, and trends in the areas of reading, studying, and lifelong learning.

- End-of-chapter **Case Studies** have been updated and present thought-provoking situations that require critical and creative thinking about studying and learning dilemmas. These cases illustrate the importance of good learning habits both in school and at work.

Supplementary Materials

Success Skills: Strategies for Study and Lifelong Learning is supported by extensive tools that make instruction easier:

- The new **Annotated Instructor's Edition** provides solutions and general guidelines for instruction along with specific suggestions pertaining to each chapter. Also included are suggestions for guiding discussion, facilitating activities, and working through case problems.

- A new **Instructor Resource CD** provides these teaching resources for each chapter:

  - Course management tools

  - PowerPoint presentations

  - Transparency masters and form masters/handouts

  - Self-checks and progress charts

  - Links to helpful web sites

  - Additional readings, activities, and study scenarios

  - ExamView® electronic test banks with questions for comprehensive review and assessment. The software allows for easy generation of tests and editing of individual questions.

  - A free trial version of Ace Reader software for improving reading speed and comprehension.

- Visit the companion **web site** for this text (*sskills.swlearning.com*) for links to suggested web resources for each chapter, printable worksheets and handouts, additional vocabulary activities and games, and teaching resources.

A Word from the Author

CONGRATULATIONS! By picking up this book, you have expressed a desire to discover how to make your learning easier. This third edition is the best edition yet, as it is now current with technology and provides useful strategies for managing it.

You may have this book because an instructor required it, or you may have picked it up out of curiosity. For whatever reason, you probably have a very personal need to learn from this book. Think about what you want to know or do as a result of working with this book, what you want from your formal education, and the kinds of jobs or careers you envision yourself having. You might want to write your thoughts down and keep them in a safe place to refer back to from time to time while you go through this book. They will remind you of your personal desire for learning more about *how* to learn.

This book is intended to honor and identify who you are currently as a learner. It is also geared to provide you with the awareness, knowledge, and tools you need to build the skills for lifelong learning. Ultimately, it will guide you in understanding what you can do to be a more efficient and effective learner.

The learning strategies discussed in this book are meant to be used for learning tasks in school, at work, and in your personal life. If you can learn to use it for school, you can learn to use it in life and work.

Because I know there is no one best way to learn, I have provided you with a buffet of learning strategies from which to choose. Your job is to try them all and find those that work best for *you*.

Keep in mind that the road to knowledge begins with the turn of a page. Enjoy learning!

Abby Marks Beale

How to Use the Self-Check Feature

The Self-Check in each chapter, provided it is answered honestly and accurately, is one of the most important tools of this text. You will use it to evaluate your learning habits at the beginning of every chapter and then to reevaluate them at the end of your course in the Final Self-Check provided by your instructor. The objective of the exercise is to assess your current skills and habits and then see improvement based on what you learned.

After each chapter introduction, in a box labeled, "Self-Check," there are ten statements. You are asked to respond with one of the three choices: "yes; frequently," "sometimes," or "no; never." Your response should be based on your current knowledge, experience, and habits. The following Self-Check for Chapter 1 includes one student's sample responses.

After responding to all ten statements, first count the number of Ys you have circled and place that number in the appropriate blank in the "Rate Yourself" section located at the end of the exercise box. Then do the same for the Ss and then the Ns. Now multiply the number of responses by the number next to it.

> **"Success has always been easy to measure. It is the distance between one's origins and one's final achievements."**
>
> —**Michael Korda, Contemporary author**

Sample Response to Chapter One Self-Check

Self-Check ✔

The following self-evaluation will give you an idea of how familiar, or unfamiliar, you are with some of the topics and terms discussed in this chapter. After reading each statement, circle the letter Y, S, or N to indicate the answer that is most appropriate for you. Answer honestly. Rate yourself at the end; then complete the information on your Self-Check Progress Chart.

Y = yes; frequently   S = sometimes   N = no; never

1. I generally have a positive attitude while learning.	**(Y)**	S	N
2. I sit near the instructor or meeting leader.	Y	**(S)**	N
3. I actively and confidently participate in discussions.	Y	S	**(N)**
4. I listen carefully and take good notes.	Y	**(S)**	N
5. I work or study in an appropriate environment for learning.	Y	**(S)**	N
6. I take good notes and write my questions while reading.	Y	**(S)**	N
7. I am prepared and complete my work on time.	Y	**(S)**	N
8. I keep a calendar and follow a schedule.	Y	S	**(N)**
9. I ask for and get help when needed.	Y	**(S)**	N
10. I learn from my mistakes.	**(Y)**	S	N

Rate Yourself:

Number of Ys __2__ × 100 = __200__

Number of Ss __6__ × 50 = __300__

Number of Ns __2__ × 0 = __0__   **Total** __500__

"Rate Yourself" Sample

The highest number you can have is 1,000 (10 × 100), and the lowest is 0 (0 × 10). Getting the highest number is NOT the objective here—showing honest improvement from beginning to end is the goal.

Once you have completed the Rate Yourself section, fill in the Self-Check Progress Chart provided by your instructor. Take your total number of points and fill in the bar graph above "Begin" for Chapter 1 as shown in the sample.

Sometime during your course of study, depending on your instructor's syllabus, you may be asked to complete all or parts of the Final Self-Check provided by your instructor. The Final Self-Check is all of the self-check statements from all 13 chapters, separated by chapter number and name. There are 130 statements in all. If you have completed all of the chapters, then you may eventually be responding to all of the statements. If you have not worked with all of the chapters, then you will only be responding to those chapter statements that you have completed.

After you have finished responding to the statements in the Final Self-Check, you follow the same procedure for completing the bar graph except this time fill in the bar graph above "End" for each chapter. See sample on the right.

Compare your beginning and ending bar graphs. Hopefully, you will see a rise in your graph from beginning to end. The more Ys you have, the more efficient and effective learner you have become. The Ss are habits you are working on and put to use as needed. The Ns that remain are areas you need to pay attention to and continue to work on.

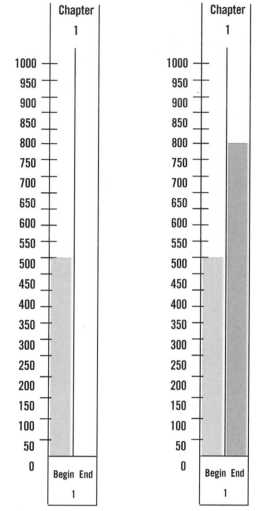

Sample Self–Check Bar Graph (Beginning)

Sample Self–Check Bar Graph (Final)

Chapter Goals

After studying and working with the information in this chapter, you should be able to:

* Distinguish between active and passive learning.
* Recognize the advantages of becoming an active learner and understand why learning skills are so important.
* Identify ways to become a more positive and active learner, engage in your learning, and find the support you need.

Terms

* active
* body language
* conscious
* coping attitude
* empowered
* 5Ws and H
* intellectual capital
* mindful
* mindless
* observers
* osmosis
* participants
* passive
* persistence
* purpose
* responsibility
* unconscious

Rachel is a recent high school graduate. All through high school, she worked part-time at a clothing store at the local mall and was finally able to save enough money for a used car by the time she graduated.

In order to pay the car payments and insurance and still have gas and spending money, she realized she needed to earn more money than her mall job was paying. She began looking for a full-time job. She could work more hours as a store clerk, but she soon realized that in order to make more money per hour, she needed to have more education than a high school diploma.

Even though Rachel wasn't a strong academic student in high school, her family reassured her that she was a hard worker, and they suggested that she should try taking a few courses at a nearby college.

Instead, she took a job waiting tables at a local restaurant where the tips were good. Rachel spent the next six months thinking about trying college and struggling to make her car payments.

Her biggest worry is all the work she has heard college students have to do, and she wonders how she would ever be able to do it all—especially the reading! She is paralyzed by a lack of confidence and fear of the unknown, and her fears are blocking her ability to make a decision.

What advice do you have for Rachel? What would you do?

Your first exposure to independent work and studying was some time around the first grade. You were probably instructed to go home, complete your work, and bring it back the next day. As the years progressed, your assignments became more challenging in both scope and content. Out of necessity, you probably figured out on your own how to complete the work.

Some learners are more successful with their self-taught learning skills than others. They seem to finish their assignments in a reasonable amount of time and do the reading without staying up all night. They haven't been formally taught how to do this; they have just figured out how to do it on their own. There are others of us, however, who take much longer to do the same assignments and many times don't do any better. So, if time spent isn't the issue, what is? Study skills!

When people continue formal learning beyond high school, many find that their self-taught learning skills are not enough. Whether in college or on the job, they work hard to learn what they need to know. Just as a car's engine may run for years with little maintenance, so, too, can some people make it through high school while giving little attention to learning skills. Learning in college or the workplace, however, proves to be quite a different story!

Only when a car gets a tune-up and a person acquires effective learning skills do they function efficiently. Any learning *is* work, but learning can be a lot easier when the proper skills are applied. *Working harder or longer is not the same as working smarter.*

This chapter 1) identifies the differences between active and passive learning, 2) provides simple ideas and strategies for you to become a more active learner, and 3) encourages you to create your own action plan for learning success.

Feeling confident in your ability to learn how to learn ANYTHING is vital to success in life, work, and school. What can you do to feel more confident?

Finding serious study buddies is great for sharing info and learning from one another. It is certainly more fun than studying alone!

The following self-evaluation will give you an idea of how familiar, or unfamiliar, you are with some of the topics and terms discussed in this chapter. After reading each statement, circle the letter Y, S, or N to indicate the answer that is most appropriate for you. Answer honestly. Rate yourself at the end; then complete the information on your Self-Check Progress Chart.

Y = yes; frequently   S = sometimes   N = no; never

1. I generally have a positive attitude while learning.   Y   (S)   N

2. I sit near the instructor or meeting leader.   (Y)   S   N

3. I actively and confidently participate in discussions.   Y   (S)   N

4. I listen carefully and take good notes.   Y   (S)   N

5. I work or study in an appropriate environment for learning.   Y   S   (N)

6. I take good notes and write my questions while reading.   Y   S   (N)

7. I am prepared and complete my work on time.   Y   (S)   N

8. I keep a calendar and follow a schedule.   Y   S   (N)

9. I ask for and get help when needed.   Y   S   (N)

10. I learn from my mistakes.   Y   (S)   N

Rate Yourself:

Number of Ys __1__ × 100 = _100_

Number of Ss __5__ × 50 = _250_

Number of Ns __4__ × 0 = _0_   Total _350_

"To furnish the means of acquiring knowledge is... the greatest benefit that can be conferred upon mankind."

—John Quincy Adams, Sixth President of the United States

Distinguishing between Active and Passive Learning

The terms *active* and *passive* are opposites of each other. Being **active** simply means *doing something* or *being* **conscious** *and* **mindful**, while being **passive** means *doing nothing* or *being* **unconscious** and **mindless**. Though you can sometimes learn mindlessly and unconsciously, those who are mindful and conscious are far more effective and successful in their learning.

The process of *osmosis* is a helpful example in demonstrating the difference between active and passive learning. **Osmosis** is a passive process by which a person learns information or ideas *without conscious effort*. As an example, you might have learned how bees make honey simply by tuning into a program on television.

If, however, you place a book under your pillow before going to sleep, the information contained in the book obviously will not be absorbed into the pillow nor into your head. In this case, the passive process of osmosis doesn't work, so you must become more active in your learning process to absorb the material in the book.

ACTIVITY 1

Read the following list of learning habits. Put a "P" on the line next to those habits that you think are Passive and an "A" next to those you think are Active. At the bottom of the list, add three more passive and three more active habits. Feel free to work with a partner.

P	Frequently daydreaming about a non-related topic	P	Waiting until the last minute to do the work
A	Mentally relating what you know to the new information	A	Listening carefully and/or taking notes
P	Doing a half-hearted job	P	Reading at a time of day when you are most tired
P	Ignoring deadlines	A	Learning from mistakes
A	Comparing notes with someone else	P	Not listening to instructions
A	Taking notes from written material	P	Never doing Homework
P	Not asking for help (or knowing when to ask)	P	Never participating in class
A	Sharing with others what you are learning	A	Always passing work in on time
P	Not participating in discussions	A	Paying attention to the teacher
P	Sitting far away from the instructor	A	Participating in a study group

Think about different jobs people do, for example, a professional athlete. Does an athlete need to be more active or passive in the way he or she approaches training? Certainly, to get and stay in shape and be ready for the season, the athlete must work out actively and consistently. Sure, you can build some muscle by passively and mind-lessly lifting weights, but you will build more muscle if you actively and mindfully engage your mind with your body while working out.

Consider servers in a restaurant. Their basic job is to take food and drink orders, deliver them to the kitchen, and then deliver meals to the patrons when they are prepared. However, consider the server who does this job and also returns to the table often to ask if patrons need more of anything like water, drinks, or napkins. This server will probably make more money and be viewed as better than the one who just does the basic job.

Throughout this book, more detailed explanations will be given about active habits. Each explanation will help you better understand how and why being more active in the learning process is better than being passive. As you attend classes or meetings, read and take notes, and perform other learning functions, be aware of how active or passive you are. Think about the internal and external conditions—what you are thinking about and what is happening around you—that affect your ability to be more active at certain times and more passive at others. The more active you are, the better!

> What other professions can you think of where you can compare active versus passive behaviors?

Checkpoint

1 Do you think most people are passive or active learners? Why?

_____

_____

_____

2 Do you think you are mostly an active or passive learner? What active or passive behaviors do you exhibit?

_____

_____

_____

3 What do you want to learn from this chapter?

_____

_____

_____

"*Tell me and I will forget; show me and I may remember; involve me and I will understand.*"

—**Chinese proverb**

Advantages of Active Learning

Most of us make it through school with self-taught learning skills. Some of us are *observers* while others are *participants* in the learning process. **Observers** learn by paying careful attention to what they see, while **participants** learn by getting involved in the process.

Beginning electricians can learn by observing someone with more experience install a light switch, but that does not necessarily mean they will be able to perform the same task successfully the first time on their own. If, however, they participate in the installation, instead of simply observing it, they will probably be more successful when they try it on their own. Similarly, new computer programs are learned faster and understood more thoroughly if the user is able to work directly with the program while learning it.

Because active learners are involved in their learning process, they understand more when new information is introduced. As a result, they learn more with less effort and in less time. The information in this chapter will provide specific steps you can take to become more involved in your learning process.

ACTIVITY 2

Think about a task you recently learned. Some examples include downloading music files onto an MP3 player, programming a cell phone, or trying a recipe. Answer the following questions.

What did you learn to do? _____

How did you learn it? _____

Which learning method(s) was used: *telling, showing,* or *involving the learner in the process?*

_____

In your opinion, what are the differences between each type of learning method?

Telling: _____

_____

Showing: _____

_____

Involving: _____

_____

Which methods do you prefer for learning? Why? _____

_____

Becoming an active learner is a simple and rewarding way to gain knowledge without wasting valuable time and money. The information in this chapter will provide specific steps you can take to become more involved in your learning process.

Why Learning Skills Are So Important

Developing learning skills is essential in this technological age because businesses continue to use advanced technologies that require a high level of learning skill from their employees. More and more, employees are required to work in teams and pool their knowledge. Software is constantly being added and updated, and new products are constantly being developed, which we have to learn how to use.

All this requires a work force that is highly adaptable to gaining new knowledge. A company is considered successful when it has an abundance of **intellectual capital**, or a smart work force that is able to continuously learn and improve.

Learning How to Learn

Learning-how-to-learn skills are the keys to your success in life. Possessing and using effective and efficient learning skills means 1) you feel confident in your ability to learn and 2) you spend less time learning more. Not only do these skills help you achieve academic success, but also they lead to career and family success.

You may wonder how all of this relates to your future. In Figure 1-1 on page 8, you will see chapter by chapter how each of the learning skills discussed in this textbook can be used in the future.

> **"The people who get on in this world are the people who get up and look for the circumstances they want, and, if they can't find them, make them."**
>
> **—George Bernard Shaw, Playwright**

Checkpoint

1 What is the difference between an observer and a participant? Which are you?

_____

_____

2 Based on the Chinese proverb in the margin on the previous page, describe the best way to learn to change a tire.

_____

_____

3 If we matched the terms "passive" with "observer" and "active" with "participant," would that mean that observers are *not* active? Think about it and explain your point of view.

_____

_____

_____

FIGURE 1-1

How Learning-How-to-Learn Skills Relate to the Future

No.	Chapter Title	Relationship to the Future
1	Learning by Doing	Active learning is useful for all types of life activities, including job hunting, career development, taking care of your health, and raising a family.
2	Discovering Your Learning Style	Understanding that people learn differently enables you to (1) understand your learning abilities and (2) adapt better to others.
3	Creating Concentration	In order to read or learn effectively, you need concentration. This involves gaining control over your work environment to keep your mind focused.
4	Learning Time Management	Effective and efficient people use some form of time management system, most commonly a calendar, to schedule time for school, work, and family activities. Without it, important tasks might not be accomplished.
5	Studying Smart	Knowing how to study smart means you know the factors necessary for success in the real world, such as being prepared and learning from your mistakes.
6	Taking Notes in Class	Organizing information on paper is a useful skill for school and business activities, such as lectures, meetings, and training workshops.
7	Taking Notes from Reading Material	Organizing information on paper is a useful skill for school and business activities including report writing, and project tracking.
8	Improving Reading Comprehension	Reading professional journals, newspapers, magazines, and textbooks will increase your reading comprehension and retention. Having a good vocabulary helps you read, speak, and write better, making you a more desirable candidate for many professions.
9	Revving Up Your Reading	Knowing how to read effectively and faster will enable you to read more in less time.
10	Mastering Tests	Tests are not only taken in a school setting. Many professions offer certificate programs that require passing a series of tests. Other types of tests are necessary for gaining or keeping employment.
11	Using Your Creative and Critical Mind	Using your creative mind allows you to unleash possibilities for better problem solving and global thinking. Using your critical mind is important for all the decisions you will ever make, including those for your career, your family, and yourself.
12	Reading and Researching Online	In this technological age, using computers is essential to locating information on the Web. You can also use computers to research schools and career opportunities.
13	Writing in the Real World	Writing is a part of most careers. Becoming good at it will help you to perform any job more effectively.

Becoming an Active Learner

Active learners can be described as people who are **empowered**. They feel capable and confident in their ability to learn anything they want, know what they have to do in order to learn, ask questions when they don't know, and then proceed to learn. Active learners continually seek ways to make learning easy and rewarding. They want to learn as much as they can in the least amount of time. Most importantly, active learners possess a feeling of self-confidence and high self-esteem as a result of their involvement in learning. Any learners can become active learners once they know how.

Next time you have the opportunity to peek into a class or meeting in session, look around. Can you spot the active learners? What are they doing? How about the passive learners? What are they doing?

The easiest place to start becoming more active in your learning is to be aware of your **body language**. *Body language* consists of the postures, gestures, and expressions we use to communicate without words. Without saying a word, your body communicates whether you are passively or actively learning. Are you slouched in your chair or sitting up? Are you leaning your head into your hands or holding your head up without help? Where are your eyes—staring into space or looking at the instructor? Do you have an empty desk on which to lay your head or a notebook and pen ready for writing?

If you use passive learner body language, try looking like an active learner, even if you don't feel like it. Your body will fool your mind and you will start to become more engaged with the learning.

> Body language consists of the postures, gestures, and expressions we use to communicate without words. Active learners have specific body language. Do you know what it looks like?

Know Your Purpose and Responsibility

For every reading assignment, you have a purpose and a responsibility. Your **purpose** is the reason *why you are* doing it and your **responsibility** is *how* you are accountable for it. For example, let's say your instructor assigns 15 pages of a chapter to read and 10 questions to answer. What is the purpose? Why are you reading it? Here are several possible responses:

- Because the reading was assigned.
- Because you want to learn about the topic.
- Because you know you are going to discuss the material in class tomorrow and you want to be prepared.

Your responsibility, besides being ready for the discussion, is to answer the 10 assigned questions. It might help to take notes so you can review the information for a test later in the term.

By taking a few moments to prepare yourself mentally for the work, you are identifying a reason to begin (your purpose) as well as identifying a point at which you are finished (your responsibility). People who keep their purpose and responsibility in mind while doing any learning activity find that they not only concentrate better but also learn and retain more.

In your job at a retail store, you are asked to learn a new procedure for documenting refunds. You have been given a five-page memo to read, which gives you the details for performing this new procedure.

What is your *purpose* for reading the memo? _____

_____

What is your *responsibility?* _____

_____

You just bought an ear thermometer to use in taking your child's temperature. Before using it, you need to read the instructional brochure enclosed with the thermometer.

What is your *purpose* for reading the brochure? _____

_____

What is your *responsibility?* _____

_____

Think of a learning activity you have to do for school or work, and consider your purpose and responsibility. Fill in your answers to each of the following questions.

Learning Activity 1 _____

_____

What is your *purpose?*_____

_____

What is your *responsibility?*_____

_____

Learning Activity 2_____

What is your *purpose?* _____

_____

What is your *responsibility?*_____

_____

Writing down your purpose and responsibility is not necessary once you have trained yourself to ask the questions mentally.

Work in a Conducive Environment

In Chapter 3, the ingredients of a good learning environment for improving concentration are discussed in detail. For now, start thinking about how you set up your own learning environment. Does it include any of the following?

- A place with lots of noise and distractions or a quiet, distraction-free place?
- An uncomfortable or too-comfortable chair?
- A room that is too hot or too cold?
- Lighting that is too bright or too dim?
- Not enough learning tools like pens, highlighters, reading materials, or notepaper?

Start thinking about the place where you do your reading or learning. Can you work uninterrupted, or are you constantly being interrupted by external noises or physical needs? Sometimes working outside your regular work area (such as in a school library, an empty office or classroom, or a conference room) can greatly improve your concentration.

Develop a Positive Belief in Yourself

You may not be aware of it, but every time you need to learn something new, you begin with a predetermined attitude or belief in your ability to do the activity. Do you feel confident in your ability to learn, or do you feel uncertain?

If you are confident in your ability to learn, it makes your learning easier. If you believe the work is easy and you can do it, then it will be easy. A positive attitude encourages you to persist.

On the other hand, if you feel uncertain or skeptical about your learning abilities, it makes learning challenging. If you believe the work is too hard or that you can't do it, then it will be hard. A negative attitude encourages you to give up.

If, however, you are determined to learn as much as you can, no matter how hard the work or how much of it there is, you will learn more easily. A positive attitude provides you with the **persistence** you need to continue until you succeed.

If you believe in yourself—in the fact that you CAN learn anything you want—you will possess the confidence necessary to succeed in all aspects of life.

You may have heard of Colonel Sanders, the founder of Kentucky Fried Chicken. He was living on his small Social Security income when he decided to try to sell his chicken to make money. He believed in it so much that he traveled by car across the country from restaurant to restaurant, cooking batches of chicken for restaurant owners and their employees. Within 10 years, Colonel Sanders had more than 600 chicken franchises in the United States and Canada. Now that's a positive attitude!

> "Success consists of going from failure to failure without losing your enthusiasm."
>
> —Winston Churchill, British statesman and author

One way to gain learning confidence is to replace failure words with success words. Provide the success word that means the opposite of each failure word below.

Failure Words	Success Words
1. can't	1. _____
2. fail	2. _____
3. impossible	3. _____
4. no	4. _____

Now think of a typical statement you might say or hear others say using each of the failure words; then rewrite the statement using the success word. For example, "I can't read that much in a night," becomes "I can read that much in a night."

1. _____

_____

2. _____

_____

3. _____

_____

4. _____

_____

Are positive words part of your vocabulary? If so, good for you! If not, why not start using them now?

A middle step on the way to a more positive attitude is to use a coping attitude. A **coping attitude** is neither positive nor negative, but one that helps you deal with the work or situation.

With any attitude, be aware that *you* make the choice to think either positively or negatively about your abilities and work load.

If you find that you didn't do as well on a test as you had hoped, which of the following statements is closest to your attitude?

- **Positive:** This is a great opportunity to learn from my mistakes.
- **Coping:** How can I do better next time?
- **Negative:** I'm a failure. The test was too hard.

Developing a more positive attitude overnight may not be realistic. However, by the time you complete this textbook, you will have new approaches to all kinds of learning tasks that will make it easier to think positively about your abilities as a student. Think about the difference between each negative and positive statement you wrote.

What attitude do you think they have (or should have!) at this moment?

Which is a more typical statement for you? Are positive words part of your vocabulary? If so, good for you! If not, why not start using them now?

The late Earl Nightingale, a popular speaker on personal development said, "You go in the direction of your most dominant thoughts." This means that if you think negatively, you will more likely end up with negative results. If you think positively, you will more likely end up with positive results. Remember, the choice is yours.

> **"The illiterate of the future are not those who can't read or write, but those who cannot learn, un-learn, and relearn."**
>
> **—Alvin Toffler, Futurist**

ACTIVITY 6

Think about or discuss with others the differences each attitude brings to your ability to learn. In the first column, some negative attitude statements are listed with spaces for you to list more. In the second column, rewrite the negative statements into positive or coping statements.

Negative Attitude Statements	Positive or Coping Attitude Statements
I can't do it.	I can do it. I can deal with it.
I have too much work to do.	I need to set aside more time today to do my work.
I dislike my instructor or boss.	_____
The work is too hard.	_____
I don't have time to study.	_____
_____	_____
_____	_____

In reaction to each of the following situations, create a positive, coping, and negative response:

You find out a week in advance that you have two tests in one day.

Positive: _____

Coping: _____

Negative: _____

Your boss gives you an extra project on top of your already heavy workload.

Positive: _____

Coping: _____

Negative: _____

You have trouble learning a new computer program.

Positive: _____

Coping: _____

Negative: _____

You have to write a resume, but you are not sure how to do it.

Positive: _____

Coping: _____

Negative: _____

You feel nervous about going to your first job interview.

Positive: _____

Coping: _____

Negative: _____

You have been given the opportunity to retake a test you failed.

Positive: _____

Coping: _____

Negative: _____

Engage in Your Learning Process

Most people have mastered "the look"—with which you stare blankly at someone while trying to act interested. In reality, your mind is wandering more than listening or learning. It could be that the person speaking is not very interesting or that you are just tired or unmotivated that day.

No matter the situation, it is your responsibility to understand what the person is saying. In a learning situation, the key is to engage with the speaker. To engage means to get either mentally or physically involved and to participate actively. Active participation 1) increases concentration, 2) improves listening, 3) seems to make the time go quicker, and 4) positively affects overall learning.

How can you actively take part in a learning situation? Five key ways to engage in the learning process are discussed in the following sections.

BE THERE AND DO IT. One obvious way to increase your potential for learning is to be physically and mentally present.

Whether you are learning in a classroom or lab or searching the Internet, learning sessions are a very important part of the learning process.

Since learning is an individual activity, there is no substitute for being there. In every learning situation, you have the choice of acting like a sponge or a rock.

Learners who act like sponges soak up the information through active participation, demonstrate a positive learning attitude, and possess an eagerness to learn. On the other hand, learners who act like rocks generally have a negative learning attitude and are, in effect, just occupying space. It should be no surprise that sponges learn more than rocks.

Who are you? Are you an active learner, like the sponge who soaks up knowledge, or a passive learner, like the rock who expects knowledge to come to it?

SIT CLOSE TO THE ACTION. This is an easy way to ensure your participation in the learning process. Sitting up front limits distractions from others and gives you a clear view of the instructor and the instructor a clear view of you. Learners in front usually sit up taller than those in the back and thus appear more eager and ready to learn. Though you may feel a little uncomfortable at first, try sitting in front in your next class. You just might find yourself concentrating better and learning more.

Every trade has tools. Carpenters use hammers; plumbers use plungers. What are all the tools *you* use for learning?

FEARLESSLY ASK AND ANSWER QUESTIONS. To ask an intelligent question and to respond intelligently, you have to be listening and concentrating. Too many learners feel that asking questions makes them look stupid. Actually, learners who don't ask questions don't learn nearly as much or as easily as those who do.

■ Focus on Technology

Online learning has become one of the biggest growth areas in education in the last decade. Just about any course imaginable can be taught online. With the help of video and audio technology, even language, public communication, and health and first aid courses are being taught online.

Taking courses online has obvious advantages: you can access your course any time, you don't have to leave your house, you can attend class in your pajamas, you don't have to turn off your cell phone, etc. It also has its disadvantages: you often have more work than in a traditional classroom, you don't have the personal interaction with your peers or with an instructor, and you usually have to type everything you want to say.

Check out Barnes & Noble's Online University for free online courses or look for degree programs by using your favorite search engine using the key words "free online courses."

Remember that you aren't expected to know it all; that's why you are studying—to learn. Your job as a student is to ask questions so you can learn more. Though you may feel a little uncomfortable asking questions in front of others, many times, they are happy the question was asked, as they themselves had the same question in mind but were afraid to ask. In the workplace, active questioning is essential for clarifying work tasks and communicating efficiently with others.

Questions can be asked during instruction, after class, during office hours, or in a scheduled appointment. As long as the question is answered, it doesn't matter where or when it is asked. Remember to keep an ongoing list of the questions you have so you don't forget them.

Not all questions need to be asked aloud. When you are curious about a topic, write down your questions. Decide which ones someone else can answer and which ones you can research yourself. Asking questions and working to find the answers will help you learn even more.

Questions are easy to ask when you use the **5Ws and H**: who, what, when, where, why, and how. For example, if you are taking a computer course and the day's topic is "Font Styles and When to Use Them," you might think about the following questions:

1. Who uses the fonts?
2. What are the font styles?
3. When should the font be changed?
4. Where do I get fonts?
5. Why should fonts be used?
6. How many fonts are available?

Think of yourself as a young child, a curious student of the entire world. By learning to ask questions, you will understand the world better while learning more in less time.

If you are taking an electronics course and the day's topic is "Measuring with an Oscilloscope," what questions might you ask? Remember to use the 5Ws and H on the previous page to help you come up with your questions.

1. _____
2. _____
3. _____
4. _____
5. _____
6. _____
7. _____
8. _____

If you are taking a travel or tourism course and the day's topic is "Handling Cancellations," what questions might you ask? Remember to use the 5Ws and H to help you come up with your questions.

1. _____
2. _____
3. _____
4. _____
5. _____
6. _____
7. _____
8. _____

If you are taking a learning skills course and the day's topic is "Active Participation for More Learning," what questions might you ask? Remember to use the 5Ws and H to help you come up with your questions.

1. _____
2. _____
3. _____
4. _____
5. _____
6. _____

NETBookmark

The Web is an amazing resource for getting academic help. Many instructors post their class notes, past tests, diagrams, projects, and learning resources for all the world to see—for free!
Using a search engine, like Google or Yahoo, enter the name of any one of your courses, such as "biology." From your results, look for those web sites that will give you the help you need. You are sure to find a great deal of information about what other instructors are doing, and more importantly, what more you can learn. For links to some helpful sites, go to:

http://sskills.swlearning.com

More concentration means less mind wandering. Less mind wandering means more learning in less time.

TAKE NOTES. Taking effective notes is like taking a picture for later reference of anything you see, hear, or read. Learners who take notes are more focused, have information to study from, and—most importantly—daydream less. Even if you are not required to take notes, creating your own notes will help you learn more. Knowing how to take good notes will transform the act of reading—which for many is a passive activity—into an active process. Note taking while reading forces you to concentrate because you are actively seeking out important information. *More concentration means less mind wandering. Less mind wandering means more learning in less time.*

An example of notes from part of a chapter of the text *Civil Litigation for the Paralegal* is shown at the bottom of this page. Notice that the notes are written in an easy-to-read format and in the learner's own words. When it comes time to study, the learner will not have to reread the chapter, but only refer back to the notes. In Chapters 6 and 7, how to take effective notes will be discussed in more detail. In the meantime, take notes as best you can to promote active participation in learning.

GET HELP. Even the most active learners need some help sometime. Assistance can come from your instructor, boss, or fellow learners. The time to ask for help is *not* the day of or the day before an exam or a project deadline. Starting to prepare at least a week ahead will ensure that the help you need is available when you want it. Classroom instructors generally do not have a lot of sympathy for students who wait until the last minute to ask for help. Bosses have even less tolerance for employees who wait to ask for help.

		9/24/06
pp 3-22	1-1 _What Civil Litigation Is_	
Civil Litigation	=	resolving private disputes thru courtesy
Trial or hearing	=	parties present evidence to judge
		or jury
Litigation attys &		
assts.	=	gather & analyze facts/research law
		— legal doc's prep'd & filed
		— witnesses interviewed
		— other evidence identified & located

Where to Look for Help

Though it may seem like you are all alone in your quest for learning success, know that you are not. There are many people you can talk to, places you can go, and materials you can read to help you reach your goals.

PEOPLE YOU CAN TALK TO. There are plenty of people who will be able to provide you with the information you need regarding school-related issues, work-related issues, and personal issues. In Figure 1-2, you will see a list of these people and descriptions of how they can help you. Most are specialists whose job is to give you assistance and advice. Visit them in person, on the phone or via e-mail. They are there to help!

FIGURE 1-2

People You Can Go to for Help

People You Can Talk to	How They Can Help You
Course Instructor	- Answers questions about the course - Helps you manage course requirements
Other students in class	- Help with homework and projects - Provide a network of friends
Academic Advisor or Guidance Counselor	- Helps you select courses you need to graduate - Helps you decide on a major area of study - Lends support for personal problems
Career Counselor	- Evaluates where your interests lie - Provides information about careers - Assesses your employment opportunities - Sets up internships - Provides information on available jobs
Tutor	- Provides extra academic assistance
Librarian	- Helps you find answers to questions - Guides you to appropriate research materials
Head of Department	- Assists with problems related to a course
Department Secretary	- Answers questions about department requirements and course offerings
Boss	- Provides feedback on skills you can improve upon for career growth
Resident Assistant (if you live on campus)	- Advises on campus services and student activities - Lends support for academic problems
Athletic Coach (if you are on an athletic team)	- Lends support for personal issues

PLACES YOU CAN GO. There will probably be times when you have a question or problem and you don't know where to go for help. Know that there are many places available to help you; you just need to find them. Every school or business has a staff of knowledgeable people who are there to assist you.

To find the specific locations and contact information, look in a school or company catalog, in a campus directory, on a web site, or in a telephone directory. Figure 1-3 lists several places students and employees can go for information and shows how these resources can be helpful.

FIGURE 1-3

Places You Can Go for Information

Places You Can Go	How They Can Help You
Learning Skills Center	- Assists in the development of reading, writing, math, or study skills that help you meet course requirements
Tutoring Center	- Provides assistance for your course work
Library	- Provides you with resources to find answers to your questions
Student Activities Office	- Provides information about what is happening on campus
Student Government Office	- Provides information about campus events, clubs, and organizations
Career Development Center	- Provides information on careers; also evaluates your interests and skills
Computer Lab	- Assists with computer course work and learning software
Academic Advising/Guidance Office	- Helps you choose your courses and manage your academic life
Registrar's Office	- Handles applications, registrations, grades, and transcripts of the courses you have taken
Financial Aid, Academic Assistance Office, or Bank	- Assists with money matters
Health Office/Infirmary	- Provides medical advice and help
Human Resources Department	- Provides advice about career growth and development - Provides information on jobs available within a company
Training Department	- Gives information on training programs available for further education

MATERIALS YOU CAN READ. In addition to people you can talk to and places you can go, there are also materials you can read to find the information you seek. A school or company handbook will contain a wealth of information about policies, programs, services, and requirements. The school catalog usually contains a calendar that lets you know when classes begin and end, when holidays occur, when drop and add periods end, and when final exams are scheduled. The company handbook usually contains the company's mission statement, policies and services, department phone numbers and e-mail addresses and a list of training workshops or courses.

A course catalog, usually found in the admissions or registrar's office of a school or college or the training department of a company, will list all the information you need to register for a course, including dates, times, and the instructor. A school newspaper or company newsletter will provide you with information about coming events and other news. Bulletin boards and web sites are the best source for the most current information.

Learn from Your Mistakes

If you get everything right all the time, then you should wonder why you are in school! School is where you solidify what you know, but more importantly, is where you go to learn what you don't know. Many times, the "I don't know's" are looked at as mistakes, but when looked at as learning experiences, you realize they are part of the learning process. The next time you get a 78% on a test, think "Wow! I got 78% correct. Now what do I need to learn to get the remaining 22%?"

If you ask most successful people you know how they gained their success, they will most likely tell you that while they did a lot of things right, they also made *many* mistakes along the way. Mistakes are a necessary part of becoming successful, as long as you learn from your experiences.

Have you ever made the "mistake" of being unprepared for a class or a meeting? To prevent this from happening again, you can use a calendar to keep track of your responsibilities (see Chapter 4 for more information) or maybe find a working partner who can be relied upon. Have you ever stayed up too late the night before an important test causing you to do poorly? Hopefully, next time, you will get more sleep. People can and do make mistakes, but the key is to recognize that you have made a mistake and then act to prevent it from happening again.

■ Focus on Ethics

What is ethics? According to *Webster's* dictionary, ethics is "the system or code of morals of a particular person, religion, group, or profession."

At school and in the workplace, ethics are subject to personal interpretation. Two people may not view the same issue the same way. For instance, one person may think that another person's behavior is unethical, but someone else may not think that the person is acting unethically at all. Ethical issues and legal issues are not the same thing. Legal issues have specific definitions (laws) with consequences if the laws are broken. Ethical issues are guidelines with no real definitions of what is right and what is wrong. Laws must be followed—ethical guidelines do not have the same authority.

Give three examples of behaviors you consider to be ethical and unethical. Explain your answers.

Success tip

Though reading about active learning may be interesting, doing something with it is more rewarding.

On page 24, complete the Awareness and Action Plan to start to build awareness toward active learning. This plan is meant to help you become aware of what you do, or do not do, in your own learning process. The idea is to encourage changes in your habits so you can move from passive to active learning. Copy the page as needed to complete one for each learning activity.

©Getty Images/PhotoDisc

Challenging your body is just as important as challenging your mind. Find ways to add movement into your days.

Take Good Care of Yourself

Your health, or lack of it, greatly influences your ability to learn. The more mentally and physically ready you are, the easier it is to learn. The more tired and stressed out you are, the harder it is to learn. You have the ability to control how well and how easily you learn by getting enough sleep, eating nutrition-packed meals, and exercising. Health problems increase with habits such as smoking and drinking alcohol, so understandably, it is advisable to avoid them. If you don't take good care of yourself, no one else will. (See Chapter 3 for more information.)

ACTIVITY 9

List *at least* five common mistakes that you have made as a student. By being aware of them, you can prevent them!

_____

_____

_____

_____

_____

_____

_____

Checkpoint

1 Without looking back, list five active learning habits.

_____

_____

_____

_____

_____

2 Which active learning habits do you practice regularly?

_____

_____

_____

_____

3 Which active learning habits do you need to improve?

_____

_____

_____

_____

©CORBIS

Learning how to play a musical instrument means you WILL make mistakes. By learning from those mistakes and with more experience, you will come to appreciate the skills you learn.

Awareness and Action Plan

Name _____ Date _____

Learning Activity _____ Instructor's Name _____

Topic(s) of Discussion _____ Meeting Time: From _____ To _____

Today's Format (check those that apply)

_____Lecture _____Discussion _____AV Presentation _____Internet Class _____Other _____

1. Did I sit close to the action? (circle one)   Yes   No

   If yes, what did I notice about my learning? _____

   If no, what did I notice about my learning? _____

2. Did I actively participate in the discussion? (circle one)   Yes   No

   If yes, what did I do? _____

   What did I notice about my learning? _____

   If no, what did I notice about my learning? _____

3. Did I take notes? (circle one)   Yes   No

   If yes, what did I notice about my learning? _____

   If no, what did I notice about my learning? _____

4. Was I prepared (e.g., doing the work as assigned)? (circle one)   Yes   No

   If yes, what did I do to be prepared? _____

   What did I notice about my learning? _____

   If no, what did I notice about my learning? _____

5. Did I have a positive attitude about learning? (circle one)   Yes   No

   If yes, why did I have this attitude? _____

   What did I notice about my learning? _____

   If no, why did I have this attitude? _____

   What did I notice about my learning? _____

6. Did I make any mistakes? (circle one)   Yes   No

   If yes, what happened?_____

   What did I learn from it?_____

After the Learning Activity

7. Did I choose an appropriate working environment? (circle one)   Yes   No

   If yes, what did I notice about my learning?_____

   If no, what did I notice about my learning?_____

8. While reading, did I take notes or write down questions? (circle one)   Yes   No

   If yes, what did I notice about my learning?_____

   If no, what did I notice about my learning?_____

9. In general, as a learner today, I was_____

10. Next time I plan to_____

CHAPTER SUMMARY ✴

1. The terms *active* and *passive* are opposites. Being an active learner means you do something conscious and mindful to make learning happen, while being a passive learner means you do nothing to make learning happen. Though you can sometimes learn from doing nothing, doing something makes learning more effective and successful.

2. Advantages of becoming an active learner include learning more in less time and knowing how to learn anything you want. Active learners also possess feelings of self-confidence and high self-esteem as a result of their involvement in learning.

3. Learning-how-to-learn skills can help you succeed in school, at work, and at home.

4. With every learning task, you have a purpose and a responsibility. By giving yourself a reason to begin working (your purpose) as well as a point at which you are finished (your responsibility), you will concentrate better and learn and remember more of what you are working on.

5. If you believe in your ability to learn, you will possess the confidence necessary to succeed in any area of your life. You can begin to gain this confidence in yourself by replacing failure words with success words and negative attitudes with positive and coping attitudes.

6. This chapter describes many ways to be active in your learning. They include being there and doing it, sitting close to the action, fearlessly asking and answering questions, taking notes, getting help, and learning from your mistakes.

7. Every school and every workplace has resources you can turn to for help in answering questions or solving problems. These resources include people, places, and reading materials.

8. Your health, or lack of it, greatly influences your ability to learn. The more mentally and physically prepared you are, the easier it is to learn. Being tired and stressed out makes learning more difficult.

CHAPTER ASSESSMENT ✴

Terms Review

Match the following terms to their definitions.

F active
E body language
I conscious
B empowered
J 5Ws and H
C intellectual capital
D observers
G osmosis
K participants
H persistence
L purpose
A responsibility
M unconscious

a. The end result of what you are doing
b. Feeling capable and confident in the ability to learn anything
c. A smart work force that is able to continuously learn and improve
d. Those who prefer to learn by paying careful attention to what they see
e. Postures, gestures, and expressions we use to communicate without words
f. Doing something mindful and conscious to aid in learning
g. Learning information or ideas *without conscious effort*
h. Believing in something so much you refuse to quit
i. Being aware and mindful
j. The five questions to ask when learning anything
k. Those who prefer to learn by getting involved
l. The reason you do something
m. Mindless and passive

✳ Review ✳

Based on the information you learned in this chapter, answer the following questions using your own words and thoughts.

1. What is a passive learner?

   Someone who is lazy and doesn't participate in class

2. What is an active learner?

   Someone who participates in class and asks questions and always turns things in ontime + takes notes

3. Name at least 5 things you can do to become more active in your learning.

   1. _Work in a good learning enviornment_
   2. _Believe in yourself_
   3. _Participate in class discussion_
   4. _Ask questions_
   5. _____

4. Why do you think being an active learner is smarter than being a passive one?

   Because you learn more when you're an active learner

5. Given one of your recent reading assignments, what was (is) your purpose and responsibility? How do you go about identifying these?

   to understand what the story is about and wright a response to it.

6. Why is knowing your purpose and responsibility helpful before reading?

John and Miranda are newly hired employees at a local computer store. They were attending an orientation seminar designed to introduce them to the store and the company. An agenda was distributed to all the new hires before the orientation started. It outlined the topics of the seminar, which included benefit options, company guidelines, basic work procedures, the performance evaluation process, and other useful information.

John read through the agenda and on a pad he brought with him jotted down questions about several of the topics. He wanted to know when his health insurance would take effect and how many weeks of vacation he would be allowed. John took a seat in the second row, which he saved for himself when he arrived 15 minutes earlier. He made sure to ask his questions. At the end of the meeting, he felt satisfied that he had all the information he needed.

Miranda spent the time before the seminar talking on her cell phone. When it was time to go into the seminar, Miranda was the last one into the room and had to sit in the back because all the seats were taken. She sat quietly, saying nothing. When the session was over, Miranda complained to John that the presenter didn't tell her what she needed to know about automatic deposit of her paycheck and whom to call if she is going to be late.

1. Which of the two was more actively involved in their learning? Why do you think so?

   _____

   _____

   _____

   _____

2. What specific things did John do that secured a positive experience for him?

   _____

   _____

   _____

   _____

3. Whose responsibility is it to secure the information that Miranda wants to know? What more could she have done?

   _____

   _____

   _____

   _____

4. Based on this situation, which employee do you think might do a better job? Why do you think so?

   _____

   _____

   _____

   _____

2 Discovering Your Learning Style

Terms

- auditory learner
- balanced learner
- hemisphericity
- independent learner
- learning styles
- multiple intelligences
- random learner
- sensory learning preferences
- sequential learner
- social learner
- tactile learner
- visual learner

Chapter Goals

After studying and working with the information in this chapter, you should be able to:

- Define learning style.
- Identify several of your preferred learning styles.
- Explain the importance of knowing your instructors' teaching styles and assess the teaching styles of your instructors.
- Identify which senses you prefer to use when learning.
- Explore some other learning style theories and identify which you might prefer.

"What do you mean, you don't want it here? I thought you said all homework goes on your desk, not the box next to it;" Sal asked his instructor.

"Young man, I *did* say at the beginning of the year to put it in *this* box, *not* on my desk!" said Mrs. Crane, Sal's math instructor.

Sal moved the homework into the box and sat down. He didn't see the big deal of where the homework was placed, as long as it was handed in. What Sal needed to understand is that Mrs. Crane values an organized classroom. It is very important to her to have things in their right place, just like lining up the numbers in math problems. She becomes annoyed when anyone is even a minute late for her class. If Sal wasn't learning so much from Mrs. Crane, he would consider dropping her class.

Sal's next class was English. Mrs. Adams ran a different kind of class. Most of her assignments were creative projects that required Sal either to make a presentation in front of the class or to research the author of a novel. If he is a few minutes late to class, she just smiles and nods her welcome. Even though Sal doesn't love to read, he finds the class fun and is learning to appreciate fiction.

Do you have instructors with similar teaching styles? What do you think these instructors were like as students?

From the moment you were born, you've been learning. Learning is a natural process of all species—including human beings. Before the age of five, you were able to learn faster than at any other time in your life. And you learned in a very skillful and effortless way. You were so successful that you learned a whole language without any formal instruction. You learned athletic abilities that you will use for the rest of your life. You also learned how to read and react to the expressions on other people's faces, and you learned social skills that you still use today. You learned none of these skills in a classroom, and yet they may be counted among your most significant achievements.

As you continued to learn about the world around you, you began to develop your own preferences for learning—those that were comfortable and effective. These learning preferences, or styles, are entirely personal and entirely right for you. They are both different from and similar to the styles of other people. More importantly, they are yours, and the more you know about your styles of learning, the better you can adapt them for success in the classroom and the real world.

There are many different learning styles. In this chapter, you will learn 1) how to recognize several of your learning styles and 2) how to understand what these learning differences mean. You'll also learn how to identify your instructors' teaching styles. Throughout this book, you will be given a variety of strategies that will enable you to learn more easily.

"*Education is the ability to listen to almost anything ... without losing your temper.*"

—Robert Frost, American poet

Learning preferences, or styles, are entirely personal and entirely right for you.

©Getty Images/PhotoDisc

You are a natural learner. You developed learning preferences very early in life. Your job now is to figure out what yours are and how to make learning easier by flexing to other styles.

The following self-evaluation will give you an idea of how familiar, or unfamiliar, you are with some of the topics and terms discussed in this chapter. After reading each statement, circle the letter Y or N to indicate the answer that is most appropriate for you. Answer honestly. Rate yourself at the end; then complete the information on your Self-Check Progress Chart.

Y = yes; frequently   N = no; never

1. I know what learning styles are.   (Y)   N

2. I know my learning style preferences.   (Y)   N

3. I am familiar with how a sequential learner prefers to learn.   Y   (N)

4. I am familiar with how a sequential instructor prefers to teach.   (Y)   N

5. I am familiar with how a random learner prefers to learn.   (Y)   N

6. I am familiar with how a random instructor prefers to teach.   (Y)   N

7. I know if I am a more visual, auditory, or tactile learner.   (Y)   N

8. I know several learning strategies that will help me learn best.   Y   (N)

9. I am aware of other learning styles.   Y   (N)

10. I know how to adjust my learning styles to the teaching styles of my instructors.   Y   (N)

Rate Yourself:

Number of Ys ___6___ × 100 = ___600___

Number of Ns ___4___ × 0 = ___0___   **Total**___600___

What Are Learning Styles?

Learning is a natural and constant process of gathering and processing information. The term **learning styles** refers to how you prefer to gather information and then what you do with the information. How you do a lot of things in life—such as where you live, how you dress, what you do for a living, and how you arrange your home—is a reflection of your learning styles.

Observers and participants are two kinds of learners with different learning styles. The observer, or more thoughtful learner, prefers to think about what is being taught, while the participant, or more involved learner, prefers to experience learning firsthand. For example, in a driver's education course, the observer would be content to listen to a lecture or watch a movie. The participant would prefer to sit in the car, play with the radio and wiper controls, and begin driving as soon as possible.

You have probably been aware of differences in people for as long as you can remember. You may have a friend who is "neat as a pin" and who keeps a very orderly apartment or bedroom. On the other hand, your house or bedroom may look like a violent storm just hit it. For you, this may be comfortable, but for others who live with you, this disorderliness may be annoying and result in tension and friction. People who are untidy cannot seem to figure out the concern for neatness.

How you approach the matter of neatness is, to some extent, a reflection of your learning style. Your learning style is a reflection of how you absorb information from your world and how you process that information. Your way of dealing with your course work, work life, and living space quite naturally reflects that style.

If you are an instructor, teaching either in a formal classroom or in an informal setting, your teaching style will match your preferred learning style. As a student, if you know your preferred learning style and recognize your instructor's teaching style, you can adjust your learning skills to meet that instructor's demands. This ensures greater learning success.

If, however, you have an instructor who you think is unusually hard to learn from or seems unfair, it may be because he or she does not match your learning style preferences. This makes learning and classroom success more challenging. In spite of this, if you try to adapt to his or her preferences, even though it seems unnatural for you, you will find the class easier and success more attainable.

The same holds true in the workplace. If you know your boss's and coworkers' preferences and know how to flex to their styles, you will be looked at more favorably than someone who sticks to his or her own ways. If you provide your sequential boss with the detailed report he wants (even though you may dislike all the specifics) or help a colleague brainstorm ideas for a new project (even though you might be secretly worried about how much time it will take), you will be more successful working with them. It doesn't mean giving up who

Success tip

What do comedians Abbott and Costello, muppets Bert and Ernie, and the Odd Couple Felix and Oscar have in common? Each one of the pair has a distinct learning style that is opposite of the other.

Many successful relationships, be they marriages or friendships, are successful when two people with opposite styles get together. In effect, they "balance" each other out. If your friend is too much like you, you might drive each other crazy! So, when looking for new friends, business partners or a significant other, consider looking for someone with some opposite preferences!

you are. It means to know your natural strengths and then work on the areas you're not as good at!

Learning styles are only preferences for the way people learn. One preference is no better or worse than any other. You can consider your preferred learning style as your comfort zone for learning.

Checkpoint

1 What is meant by "learning styles"?

_____

_____

2 Why do you think it would be helpful to know about learning styles?

_____

_____

_____

3 Why might you want to determine the learning styles of your instructors?

_____

_____

_____

©Getty Images/PhotoDisc

Some instructors are easy to learn from; others are more challenging. By understanding your own learning style and how it compares to your instructors, you will have a better chance of matching their style for classroom success.

Sequential or Random: Which Are You?

The learning styles assessment that follows will help you understand whether you prefer the sequential or random learning style. If you have a higher number on the left side, you are a sequential-preferenced learner. A higher number on the right means you are a random-preferenced learner. If your numbers are the same, you are an equal-preferenced, or balanced, learner. Both styles will be further explained after the exercise. Remember that one style is not better than another.

ACTIVITY 1

As you read the two lists below, notice that the quality on the left is opposite the quality on the right. Compare the first quality on the left and the first quality on the right; then place a check mark (✓) next to the one that sounds most like you. If both qualities honestly sound like you, mark both sides. Mark a response for *all* of the qualities. Go with your first impression. Try not to think too much about each response, as there are no right or wrong answers. When you are done, count the number of check marks you have on the left and on the right. Place each total at the bottom of the column.

Sequential Preferences	Random Preferences
_____ Organized	✓ Disorganized
✓ Enjoy learning and testing theories	✓ Enjoy comparisons and examples
_____ Want order and structure in life	✓ Like creativity and dislike authority
✓ Want details	✓ Want big picture (first)
_____ See play as a waste of time	✓ Enjoy play
✓ Want intellectual recognition	✓ Want personal attention and feedback
✓ Have difficulty with improvisation	_____ Enjoy improvisation
_____ Find speculation difficult	✓ Have vivid imagination
✓ Prefer math	✓ Prefer art, music, sports
_____ Show high regard for time	✓ Show little regard for time
✓ Good at making decisions	✓ Good at considering possibilities
✓ Prefer to work on one project at a time	_____ Prefer to work on several projects at a time
✓ Like one correct answer	_____ Like several possible answers
✓ Like routine	✓ Like impulsive activities
_____ Prefer reading and lecture	✓ Prefer role-playing, open discussion, and small group work
✓ Learn well independently	✓ Learn well through discussion, collaboration, and participation
10 **Total check marks**	**12** **Total check marks**

Can you think of careers where sequential preferences would be valued?

The Sequential Learner

If you possess several of the qualities listed on the left in Activity 1, you have the preferences of a **sequential learner**. You probably also possess some random qualities from the right that tone down your sequential nature.

High sequential-preferenced learners tend toward a more logical, step-by-step approach to solving problems and taking in information. If this is your type, you most likely enjoy theory and want order in all things, including your living area, your study area, and even your notebooks. You take pride in submitting neat papers and projects. You are a planner and require structure in your life. When you are under stress, you stick firmly to your sequential learning preference because it is most comfortable for you.

So what might this mean in real life? If a friend tells you about a recent party, you probably want all the details—a complete description of who was there, what they were wearing, what time everyone left—and you want the description delivered in an orderly, sequential way. You might feel impatient if your friend rambles, telling you a little of this and a little of that. Most likely, to keep things on track and in your sense of order, you'll start asking questions that guide and control the conversation. At work, when discussing a project with a coworker, you might feel you are wasting time if the person does not "get to the point" as quickly as you would like.

Sequential learners tend to think in one-two-three order. They find formal school structure and traditional instruction comfortable. Many successful American businesses also place a high value on sequential thinking. Can you think of careers where sequential preferences would be valued?

The Random Learner

If you possess many of the qualities listed on the right side in Activity 1, then you have the preferences of a **random learner**. You probably also possess some sequential qualities that tone down your random nature. Random learners tend to learn better in a less structured manner. This means that math may not have been one of your favorite subjects in school, since it is a sequential subject. Your English papers may have been returned with comments such as "lacks organization," "good ideas, but you fail to order them or develop them fully," and "you didn't follow the assignment." At work, you are probably involved in discussions of current events and sports.

As a random learner, you need examples and comparisons to make the facts stick in your mind (and if the analogy or example is in story form, so much the better). You often have a gut sense as to when something is right but are unable to support your feelings with details or facts. When you read, you frequently study and remember the illustrations. When you are under stress, you stick firmly to this preference because it is most comfortable for you.

Random learners frequently go off in many directions at once and are accused of being disorganized. If, as a random learner, you describe

Can you think of careers where random preferences would be valued?

the party in the earlier example to a sequential-preferenced friend, your friend may get annoyed when you jump around from this that happened to that. The sequential-preferenced friend will probably ask you for factual details, preferably in time order.

Random learners tend to skip around in their thinking. They are not as comfortable as sequential learners with formal school structure and traditional instruction. To be successful in a sequential-demanding world, they must force themselves to act disciplined and orderly. After a while, however, acting sequential becomes easier. Some people are surprised to discover they are random-preferenced learners because they have adapted so well to the demands of a sequential world. Sequentially preferred learners often can be identified by their neat, organized desks, while random preferred learners can often be identified by their less organized workspace.

Research shows that you can change or adjust your learning style for different tasks. More importantly, doing so expands your thinking capability. (Random learners, in fact, are well ahead of the sequential ones who didn't have to adjust so much in high school.) Imagine what it's like for sequential learners when they enter a random classroom!

The Balanced Learner

If you have close to the same number of check marks in each of the two columns of Activity 1, you can consider yourself an equal-preferenced, or **balanced learner**. You are balanced between the two styles and possess both sequential and random preferences.

You are able to adapt to either style and can do it better and more easily than individuals who definitively fall into one of the two preferences. You probably get along well with others because you can match their styles as needed. When under stress, you tend to become unbalanced and lean toward one or the other preference. If you can identify which preference you lean toward, you might be able to figure out your true learning style preference.

What type of learning preferences do you think are shown in the photo? Why do you think so?

> **"I desire that there be as many different persons in the world as possible; I would have each one be very careful to find out and preserve his own way."**
>
> **—Henry David Thoreau, American author and poet**

The most challenging part of flexing to other styles is overcoming the discomfort of thinking differently. The more you do it, the easier it becomes!

Learning to Flex to Other Styles

In addition to sequential and random, we use many other styles of thinking and learning. Several of them will be explained later in this chapter. Being aware of your preferences and learning to adapt to others makes you think and recall more efficiently. In fact, *using both styles benefits memory and thinking*. The most challenging part of flexing to other styles is overcoming the discomfort of thinking differently. The more you do it, the easier it becomes! Practicing a style that is not your preference is like learning to use your non-dominant hand. On a sheet of paper, write your full name. Now, write your full name using your other hand.

Chances are, when you wrote with your dominant hand—your natural hand—the writing was easy. When you wrote with your non-dominant hand, the writing probably felt awkward, unnatural, and may not have looked as neat. Though you prefer writing with your dominant hand, with practice, you would be able to adapt and get comfortable with your non-dominant one. Learning to adapt to your non-dominant learning style preference helps you become a more balanced learner. You will always retain your natural preferences, but you can stretch your mind by understanding and experiencing the styles of others. Practicing a style that is not your own allows you to develop the ability to face all styles with equal success.

Checkpoint

1 Identify someone you know who you think possesses sequential preferences. What do you think makes them sequential?

_____

_____

_____

2 Identify someone you know who you think possesses random preferences. What do you think makes them random?

_____

_____

_____

3 Based on your preferred learning style, which behavior of the other style seems most challenging for you?

_____

_____

Identifying Teaching Styles

Whether you are learning at work, in class, or at home, it should not matter who instructs you. The fact remains that it is *your* job to learn and succeed in every learning situation. Every person teaches differently. Some will be easy to understand, while others will be difficult. Some will be likeable, others not. The best strategy is to first observe your instructors, learn as much as possible about their teaching styles and habits, and then find ways to adapt to each style.

Understanding Your "Other" Teachers

Think about the other "teachers" in your life—like your parents, guardians, grandparents, bosses, friends. There are probably some things you naturally do, or don't do, when dealing with each one to make the communication successful. For example, when your grandmother shares her favorite cookie recipe, you decide you need to write down the procedure, not just watch her. Or, when your boss gives you a piece of paper describing how to ring up a cash sale, you ask her to show you exactly what it looks like on the cash register.

Understanding Your Instructor

While it is your instructor's responsibility to understand you, it is also your responsibility to understand your instructor. Think of a current learning situation you are involved in. Is your instructor's information organized or disorganized? Is information presented verbally, on handouts, or on the board? Are you only given theories, or are you able to get first-hand experience with the subject matter? Are the work assignments useful for class discussions and group projects, or are they just preparation for tests? How are you evaluated? What are your instructors' expectations of you? Answers to these and other questions can help you gather information about your instructors. It is important to realize that instructors' teaching styles are mostly an extension of their learning styles. *Most instructors teach the same way they prefer to learn.*

Understanding Your Past Instructors

Think about your past instructors. Recall one or two with whom you really felt in tune. Did you always know exactly what they wanted? Did you enjoy their teaching? What did they do to make their classes enjoyable? When they asked questions, did they want just one correct answer, or did they want your thoughts and opinions? Think also of one or two instructors with whom you felt at odds, never knowing exactly what they wanted or never being able to give them quite what they expected. What made their teaching difficult to understand? In addition, think about your "other" teachers—parents, guardians, grandparents, bosses, friends, etc. Which ones did you understand best and feel most in tune with? With which ones did you feel at odds? Is it possible that their preferred learning styles either matched, or didn't match, yours?

"If you don't go after what you want, you'll never have it. If you don't ask, the answer is always no. If you don't step forward, you're always in the same place."

—Nora Roberts, Author

Descriptions of the two types of instructors are given on pages 41 and 42. If you are a sequential learner, you may prefer to skip this activity and get right to the descriptions. Don't! Complete the activity; it is good practice for getting into a random mode of thinking—imagining, recalling how a class felt, having a gut sense of information. Go with it—go random for a moment to improve your thinking skills.

A past instructor to whom I could relate was _____

This instructor used presentation methods like _____

_____

_____

This instructor asked questions like _____

_____

_____

This instructor did things like _____

_____

_____

This instructor dressed like _____

_____

A past instructor to whom I could *not* relate was _____

This instructor used presentation methods like _____

_____

_____

This instructor asked questions like _____

_____

_____

This instructor did things like _____

_____

_____

This instructor dressed like _____

_____

My worst memory of this instructor was _____

_____

My favorite memory of this instructor was _____

_____

The Sequential Instructor

Characteristics of a sequential instructor, quite naturally, are similar to those of a sequential learner. These instructors may also demonstrate several random characteristics, but they are clearly more sequential. From the list of sequential characteristics below, see if you recognize an instructor, a coworker, a parent, or a boss.

- Is idealistic, systematic, and organized
- Likes facts and details
- Values sequential thinking
- Shows more interest in data than in people
- Prefers informational forms of instruction, such as reading or a lecture
- Can sometimes be completely unaware of the emotional climate in a room
- Seeks efficiency
- Is a decision maker
- Typically teaches subjects that require sequential thinking such as math or computers
- Has well-planned learning activities
- Tends to be a firm disciplinarian
- Grades answers as right or wrong (no partial credit); stresses correctness and facts

The Random Instructor

Characteristics of the random instructor, as you can surely guess, are similar to those of the random learner. These instructors may also demonstrate several sequential characteristics, but they are clearly more random. See if you recognize an instructor, a coworker, a parent, or a boss with these random characteristics.

- Enjoys people
- Is non-judgmental and supportive (values others' opinions)
- Prefers role-playing, open discussion, and small group work
- Will often individualize instruction
- Prefers to create own course of study
- Gives imaginative assignments
- Assumes learning is a function of interest
- Prefers self-discovery, experience, and a variety of instructional modes
- Tends to follow what he or she feels like doing rather than a structured lesson plan
- Typically teaches subjects that require random thinking like art, music, or physical education

- Displays a learning environment that sequential instructors may view as disorderly
- Stresses concepts and conclusions

The Balanced Instructor

Characteristics of a balanced instructor show an equal mix from the sequential and the random preferences. These instructors are generally well liked because they attract both styles. Because the traditional role model for teaching is a sequential instructor, the balanced instructor may tend more toward the sequential style than the random style.

Balanced instructors are challenging to both the sequential and random learner because they require each type of learner to adapt to the other style while providing some comfort in his or her preferred style. Can you guess with some certainty the styles of the two instructors you described in Activity 2? You will most likely relate to an instructor with the same preference as you.

Quick Ways to Assess Your Instructor's Style

The following four guidelines may also help you identify the preferred learning style, and teaching styles, of your instructors. Apply them to several instructors in your life. Do you get a clearer picture of these people?

1. Listen for clues in how they present their material.

2. Determine what kinds of questions they ask.

3. Observe their behavior.

4. Look at how they are dressed.

LISTEN FOR CLUES IN HOW YOUR INSTRUCTOR PRESENTS THE MATERIAL. The way instructors deliver content in the classroom can provide clues to their preferred teaching and learning styles. As you read the following descriptions, try to think of examples from your current and past instructors. Recall some of the techniques they have used to teach their classes and guess what those techniques may reveal about their styles.

Sequential-preferred instructors generally deliver content in a lecture format in a very specific order. They probably use a lot of outlined notes, detailed PowerPoint slides, and/or handouts, and they rarely deviate from their established outlines. Because they are likely to view fun and play as wasteful, they probably use very little humor in the classroom. These instructors may have a serious and formal tone and may even speak in a monotone voice, showing very little emotion or personality. They always stick to the topic and rarely take time out for interesting or entertaining diversions. They make clear connections to relevant topics and do not allow the class to wander very far off the topic.

> " ... Dominance is part and parcel of the normal human condition .. as a result, we are handed, footed, eyed and—in a general sense— brained."
>
> —Ned Herrmann, Contemporary author and educator on brain dominance

Random-preferred instructors tell stories, use metaphors, analogies and humor, and allow for "wanderings" during a lecture. During a computer lesson, they might tell the "story of computers" and describe and develop its characters. Such a lesson may sound more like a conversation than a lecture.

Instructors who are balanced in their learning preferences tend to use both styles of delivery. However, since most of the teaching models in traditional education are sequential, balanced instructors may lean in that direction.

In some subjects, you can take an educated guess as to your instructor's preferred style. For instance, a math teacher might be sequential, and an art teacher might be random. However, you *will* come across random math teachers and sequential art teachers, so don't automatically judge your instructors just by the topic they teach!

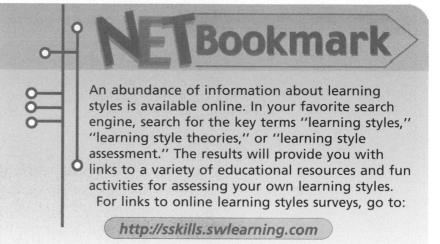

An abundance of information about learning styles is available online. In your favorite search engine, search for the key terms "learning styles," "learning style theories," or "learning style assessment." The results will provide you with links to a variety of educational resources and fun activities for assessing your own learning styles. For links to online learning styles surveys, go to:

http://sskills.swlearning.com

DETERMINE WHAT KINDS OF QUESTIONS YOUR INSTRUCTOR ASKS. Sequentials ask questions that require you to recall and recite facts, data, and specific theories. They tend not to ask for your opinion, especially if they are the type of sequential who is comfortable with only one correct answer. The test formats they prefer are those that require you to pick one correct answer (such as multiple choice, true or false, and matching).

Randoms ask questions that ask you to interpret, give an opinion, suggest an application, form a connection to some other subject area, and provide for multiple answers.

The test formats they prefer include more writing (such as short answer and essay), in which you have to provide your thoughts and opinions.

Those who are balanced in their learning preferences tend to use both styles of questioning.

OBSERVE YOUR INSTRUCTOR'S BEHAVIOR. Highly-preferred sequentials are formal and will stand behind a lectern or table. Their notes on PowerPoint or the overhead are in outline form. They use few abbreviations and are in the color black only. Their lecture delivery tone will be restrained and, at the worst, will consist of one-word utterances. They will have a low tolerance for students who want to sit anywhere but at desks or tables in straight rows—"classroom style."

Highly-preferred randoms will wander around the room and gaze out the window—or better yet, sit on the windowsill and play with the venetian blind cord. They will scribble fragments of ideas on the board, use arrows to connect one fragment to another, and use abbreviations or even pictures to illustrate ideas. They may use an overhead or PowerPoint, but it is generally used only for demonstrating an idea or showing a picture, not word-for-word lecturing. Randoms will gesture with their hands, and their vocal tones will vary from soft to animated. They might even tolerate students sitting on the floor or propping their feet up.

Those who are balanced in their learning preferences tend to use both styles of behavior. They sprinkle their organization of content (e.g., an outline) with some imaginative creativity (e.g., a personal story). Their PowerPoint and overhead use is sometimes supplemental and sometimes essential. They are naturally good at mixing both preferences.

LOOK AT HOW YOUR INSTRUCTOR IS DRESSED. Looking at how an instructor usually puts a wardrobe together can give you a clue to his or her preferred style. However, don't rely just on dress to assess preferences, as this can sometimes fool you. Here are some guidelines to consider:

Sequentials are more inclined to wear muted colors that blend and match with every part of their outfit. They dress in "sets," or outfits, and one outfit usually doesn't get mixed with another. They look organized and put together.

Randoms, too, look put together but tend to wear more relaxed, colorful, and casual clothing. Women might wear dangling jewelry while the men might wear colorful ties. Randoms don't like boredom.

Those who are balanced in their learning preferences tend to mix both styles. They may dress more formally on the days they are feeling sequential and more casually on the days they are feeling random.

What might you guess about the styles of these two? Looking at how they dress is one strong clue, though sometimes not what we might think!

All three teaching styles have a place in instructional settings. More than likely, you will not encounter any one instructor who is purely sequential or random. As you read the previous descriptions, you could probably recall past teachers who demonstrated each style. Use these descriptions to help you identify individual teaching styles so you can plan your learning strategy now and in the future.

Learning from Style Differences

Though you may not initially think so, it can be to your advantage if your instructor teaches in a style different from your preference. For example, a random instructor can help a sequential learner develop creativity through imaginative assignments that ask for concept development and conclusion. Research shows creativity is part of the truly successful learning experience.

Sequential instructors can help a random learner develop the discipline to get a job done more easily and quickly, thereby reducing the unnecessary work that results when the random learner wanders off.

The same is true for the bosses who may prefer to do things differently than you. Though you may have a more challenging time working for those whose preferences are different than yours, you can learn to flex to their style, making you look good and fostering successful work relationships.

Experiencing and adapting to both styles will definitely help your learning and thinking and will instill in you a tolerance for and appreciation of differences. The more you are able to adjust your style to that of your instructor (or boss, parent, etc.), the more success you will have as a learner (or employee, son/daughter, etc.).

Checkpoint

1 Why is it important to identify the learning styles of your instructors?

_____

_____

2 What can you do to identify your instructor's preferred learning styles?

_____

_____

3 Would it be a good idea to try to find instructors who match your learning style? Why or why not?

_____

_____

Your Senses and Learning

You possess yet another set of personal learning preferences called **sensory learning preferences**. These are visual, auditory, and tactile. John Grinder and Richard Bandler have researched and written about this theory.

Visual learners prefer to use their eyes to learn. They learn best by seeing information, either through demonstration, visual aids, or in their mind's eye. They prefer to see information on the board, and they like to write things down—otherwise, they tend to forget. Visual learners tend to use statements such as, "I see what you mean," "Show it to me," or "I get the picture."

Auditory learners prefer to use their ears to learn. They learn best by hearing information, either by listening or speaking. They do not have a great need to write things down because they tend to be comfortable relying on what they hear. They also work well in partners and teams. Auditory learners tend to use statements such as, "I hear you," "That sounds good to me," or "I'm glad you mentioned that."

Kinesthetic or **tactile learners** prefer to use their bodies to learn. They prefer to be involved physically in their learning. Being comfortable is important to tactile learners. As a result, they tend to move around a lot, fidgeting and slouching in their chairs. Tactile learners express themselves through their body language. They tend to use statements such as, "I grasp what you mean," "You're on the right track," or "That really tickles my funny bone."

Knowing your preferences can help you learn more easily in and out of the classroom. Most teachers use a combination of all three styles when they teach. Can you identify which you like best? Do you like the Power-Point slides or writing on the blackboard because you can see it? Do you prefer to hear the stories your teacher tells or listen closely to lectures to understand? Or do you prefer to doodle and take notes so you can keep your body busy while your mind is focusing on the subject?

Many people have a combination of more than one of these preferences. For example, a visual-tactile learner learns best by watching and experiencing, while an auditory-tactile learner learns best by listening and experiencing. If you had to pick one of these three to identify yourself, which would you be? Use Activity 3 to guide you. Remember, as with any learning style preference, one preference is not better than another.

▪ Focus on Ethics

You have a teacher that you just can't get along with. You have tried, but you don't see eye to eye on anything. You feel like the teacher picks on you and you can't do anything right in class. You're embarrassed by the constant negative attention.

You have met privately with her and asked her to stop singling you out in class, but she keeps doing it. You are so frustrated that you are feeling spiteful and considering how you can get back at her. What could be the result of taking this type of action? What might be the source of your differences with this teacher? What are your best options for handling the situation?

A quick way to assess your sensory learning preferences is shown below. Read each statement and, if it sounds like you, place a checkmark (✓) on the line to the left. If the statement doesn't sound like you, leave the line blank. Total your checkmarks for each section.

Visual

__✓__ I prefer reading more than listening or doing.

__✓__ I learn more easily when I see a demonstration of what is being discussed.

__✓__ I learn how to spell better by seeing words written on paper or in my mind's eye.

__✓__ Seeing my notes is helpful for recalling what was discussed in class or a meeting.

_____ I would rather read a newspaper than watch the news on television.

__✓__ I remember people's faces better than their names.

_____ I remember telephone numbers or e-mail addresses after seeing them once or twice.

__5__ **Total Visual Preferences**

Auditory

_____ I prefer listening more than reading or doing.

__✓__ I learn how to spell by saying words aloud before writing them down.

_____ I remember better when I explain what I am learning to someone else.

_____ I learn best when I study with other people.

__✓__ I learn more when I watch the news than when I read about it.

_____ I remember better when I am told something.

_____ I remember people's names better than their faces.

__2__ **Total Auditory Preferences**

Tactile (or Kinesthetic)

_____ I prefer doing more than reading or listening.

__✓__ I prefer to learn through real-life experiences.

__✓__ I have a hard time sitting still while working independently.

__✓__ I take notes to help me concentrate and remember.

__✓__ Rewriting my notes helps me learn.

__✓__ If given a choice, I'd rather complete a project than write a report.

__✓__ I like to doodle pictures in my notes.

__6__ **Total Tactile (or Kinesthetic) Preferences**

Total each sensory learning preference section so you can see which preferences are stronger and weaker. You will probably find that you have some preferences in each of the three areas. You can apply many learning strategies to accommodate your different sensory learning preferences.

Using strategies from all of the preferences will help you learn more. Read the list of strategies in Figure 2-1 below, then create your own "Master List of Personal Learning Strategies." If you think of other strategies that work for you, add them to your list.

FIGURE 2-1

Sensory Learning Strategies

Visual Strategies *Need to Know 5 of each*

- Take good notes for reference later.
- Read notes and use flash cards repeatedly.
- Read instructions rather than listen to someone describe how to do something.
- Review the reading material to be covered in class the next day.
- Write reminders to yourself on sticky notes.
- Look up new vocabulary in a dictionary or glossary, and then write the words.
- Visualize the spelling of people's names when you meet them, and match the names to their faces.
- Write the names of people you meet, documenting where and when you met them.
- Set up and use a calendar and assignment planner.
- Sit close to the action so you can see more easily.
- Close your eyes and "see" what you need to remember.
- Watch educational TV on topics related to the content you are learning.
- Reduce test anxiety by picturing yourself in control of the information.
- Reduce your learning anxiety by picturing yourself mastering the information.
- Color code your notes and files for visual remembering.
- Keep a separate notebook or file for each topic area.
- Figure numbers by visualizing them in your head (when possible).

Auditory Strategies

- Read aloud when possible. (This will take longer than silent reading.)
- Listen to a tape of yourself reviewing the material you are learning.
- Work and review material with a partner or small study group.
- Ask the meaning of something when you don't understand.
- When recalling information, create a rhythm or song.

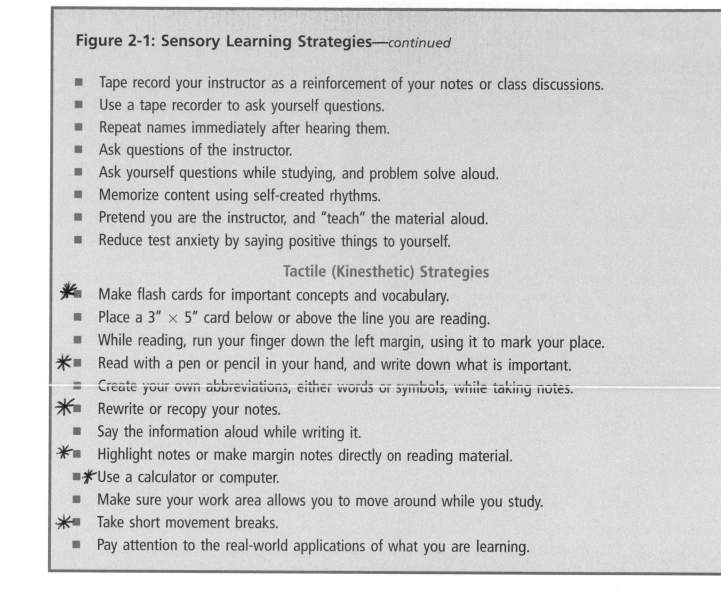

Figure 2-1: Sensory Learning Strategies—continued

- Tape record your instructor as a reinforcement of your notes or class discussions.
- Use a tape recorder to ask yourself questions.
- Repeat names immediately after hearing them.
- Ask questions of the instructor.
- Ask yourself questions while studying, and problem solve aloud.
- Memorize content using self-created rhythms.
- Pretend you are the instructor, and "teach" the material aloud.
- Reduce test anxiety by saying positive things to yourself.

Tactile (Kinesthetic) Strategies

- Make flash cards for important concepts and vocabulary.
- Place a 3" × 5" card below or above the line you are reading.
- While reading, run your finger down the left margin, using it to mark your place.
- Read with a pen or pencil in your hand, and write down what is important.
- Create your own abbreviations, either words or symbols, while taking notes.
- Rewrite or recopy your notes.
- Say the information aloud while writing it.
- Highlight notes or make margin notes directly on reading material.
- Use a calculator or computer.
- Make sure your work area allows you to move around while you study.
- Take short movement breaks.
- Pay attention to the real-world applications of what you are learning.

Learning Style Preferences and the Computer

Whether fair or not, computers are heavily biased toward visual and tactile learners. Using a computer is a hands-on and eyes-on experience where you learn by seeing and doing. No matter how many formal classes about computers you take, you will not learn to use a computer unless you actually put your hands on it and work with it. Connecting to a computer is also a highly tactile experience. Unless you are working with an interactive or multimedia CD-ROM, which plays sound, auditory learners are not accommodated at all.

There are few rules when surfing the Web and researching on the Internet, which delights the random learner but frustrates the sequential learner. Randoms love to explore the Web and patiently search for information. Sequentials want efficiency and prefer to go to the one site that will help them. Randoms may enjoy searching many related sites to answer one question, but sequentials tend to feel

Save a tree; read on-screen! Although we won't likely ever be a paperless society, it is a good idea to strive to be a "less paper" society. Not only does excessive printing waste natural resources, but it also wastes your time and resources. Save time and resources by using the following printing habits:

Set a page limit for printing and stick to it. If you currently print anything over two pages, double that and say to yourself that you will only print documents over four pages in length.

Don't print just because you CAN. Think about what you are printing and why you are printing it, and then decide if it is truly necessary. Print only what you need printed. Recycle your paper by printing on both sides when possible.

overwhelmed. Sequentials do, however, enjoy the step-by-step process in programming or following a well-thought-out set of links.

More and more, people are using the Internet to take courses because of its convenience and availability. The ability to take a course at any time and at any place a computer is located appeals to busy people. Online courses at present, however, are usually visual and tactile, not auditory. They require the learner to read a sequence of screens (just like a book on screen) and then interact with an instructor or expert by keying questions and reading the answers. Streaming video with sight and sound is one way auditory learners are accommodated on the computer. Be aware that many auditory and sequential learners learn well with computers. They have figured out how to adapt their styles to manage the technology.

Checkpoint

1 What are some learning preferences of a visual-auditory learner?

_____

_____

2 What are some learning preferences of an auditory-tactile learner?

_____

_____

_____

3 Which of the three sensory preferences would you guess is the most common? Why?

_____

_____

Other Learning Styles

In addition to sequential and random styles of learning, there are several other learning styles worth mentioning. If you would like more information about any of these learning style theories, search the Web using the theory name or any of the people's names listed. Also, look under the keywords "psychology," "the brain," or "learning styles."

Left Brain/Right Brain Theory

Left brain/right brain theory, also known as **hemisphericity**, is closely related to the sequential and random learning theories previously discussed. This theory says that the brain has two hemispheres, a left side and a right side. Each side represents certain qualities. In effect, a left-brain person tends to resemble a sequential learner, while a right-brain person tends to resemble a random learner.

Roger Sperry, Kenneth and Rita Dunn, Ned Herrmann, Betty Edwards and others have researched and written about this theory.

There are some who are trying to prove that if you are right-handed, you are left-brained, and if you are left-handed, you are right-brained. However, instead of definitively proving this opposite relationship between handedness and brain dominance, research just shows that the majority of people process language (including writing) on the left side of the brain. So left-handers are not as right-brained as originally thought.

Social and Independent Learning Theories

Social and independent learning theories say that some people prefer to learn independently while others prefer to learn in a group. If you prefer to learn independently, you are called an **independent learner**. It is possible you are also introverted and prefer to rely on your own thoughts and feelings. If you prefer to learn in a group, you are called a **social learner**. It is possible you are also extroverted and prefer to rely on others' thoughts and feelings.

Multiple Intelligences

Howard Gardner of Harvard University has identified eight natural intelligences, also called **multiple intelligences**. People can be strong in one or more of these areas. Many schools have begun using his model to enhance students' learning. The eight intelligences are listed below with brief descriptions of each. See if you can identify your type of intelligence.

1. **Logical/Mathematical**—deals with inductive and deductive thinking, questioning and reasoning, numbers, and the recognition of abstract patterns

2. **Visual/Spatial**—relies on the sense of sight and being able to visualize an object or a picture

Learn from ALL the intelligences. Just because you may not be as talented as your musical friend, you may be better at math. You may be able to debate strongly while your friend is better at sports.

Feel proud about the intelligences you are naturally strong in and appreciate others who may have strengths other than yours. You can learn much from each other!

3. **Body/Kinesthetic**—relates to physical movement

4. **Musical/Rhythmic**—based on the recognition of tonal patterns and sensitivity to rhythm, beats, and music

5. **Interpersonal**—relies primarily on socializing and person-to-person relationships and communication

6. **Intrapersonal**—relates to being alone and inner states of being, self-reflection, metacognition (or thinking about thinking), and awareness of spiritual realities

7. **Verbal/Linguistic**—relates to words and language, both written and spoken

8. **Naturalist**—relates to the recognition, appreciation, and understanding of the natural world around us

With a partner or in a small group, make a list of several famous people who are strong in each of these eight areas (or any combination of the areas). For example, Oprah Winfrey, a successful talk show host and producer is strong in interpersonal intelligence. Albert Einstein, the Father of Physics, was strong in logical mathematical intelligence. Ballet dancer Mikhail Baryshnikov is strong in body/kinesthetic intelligence. Author and conservationist Henry David Thoreau was probably strong in both the naturalist and verbal/linguistic intelligence. You can locate names on the Internet using the key words "multiple intelligences."

Checkpoint

1 Name the three learning theories discussed in this section.

_____

_____

_____

2 Do you think you are a social or independent learner? Why?

_____

_____

_____

3 Which of the multiple intelligences are your strongest?

_____

_____

_____

CHAPTER SUMMARY

1. Learning styles are a reflection of how you absorb and process information.

2. Your preferred learning styles are considered your comfort zones for learning.

3. A preference for sequential learning means you tend toward a logical, step-by-step approach for taking in information. A preference for random learning means you tend toward a less structured means of taking in information.

4. No strong preference for either sequential or random indicates you are a balanced learner, most able to adapt to either style.

5. Your preferred learning style does not mean you are any better or worse at learning than anyone else. It only means you have a preference for a certain way of learning.

6. Learning to adapt to other styles will make learning easier in any situation.

7. Instructors' teaching styles are generally a reflection of their preferred learning styles. By discovering instructors' learning styles and flexing to them, you can make learning easier.

8. To assess the teaching style of your instructors, listen for clues in how they present their material, determine what types of questions they ask, observe their behavior, and look at how they dress.

9. Your sensory learning preferences can be visual, auditory, or tactile. Adjusting your learning activities to match your preferences makes learning easier.

10. There are many other learning styles in addition to sequential and random. These include left-brain and right-brain learning, social and independent learning, and multiple intelligences.

CHAPTER ASSESSMENT

Terms Review

Match the following terms to their definitions.

L auditory learner

G balanced learner

J hemisphericity

K independent learner

H learning styles

C multiple intelligences

B random learner

E sensory learning preferences

I sequential learner

F social learner

D tactile learner

A visual learner

a. A learner who prefers to use his or her eyes to learn

b. A learner who prefers to learn in a less-structured manner

c. Intrapersonal, logical, and kinesthetic are examples

d. A learner who prefers to use his or her sense of touch to learn

e. Includes visual, auditory, and tactile learners

f. A learner who prefers to learn with others

g. A learner who possesses both sequential and random preferences

h. How you absorb and process information

i. A learner who prefers a more logical, step-by-step approach to solving problems and taking in information

j. Also known as the right-brain, left-brain theory

k. Someone who prefers to learn on his or her own

l. A learner who prefers to use his or her ears to learn

Review

Based on the information you learned in this chapter, answer the following questions using your own words and thoughts.

1. a. Is your preferred learning style sequential or random?

   _____

   b. What does this style mean about the way you learn?

   _____

   _____

2. If your learning style is random, how can you learn in sequential style (and vice versa)?

   _____

   _____

   _____

   _____

   _____

   _____

   _____

3. a. Which sensory learning preference do you lean toward—visual, auditory, or tactile/kinesthetic?

   _____

   _____

   b. What does this style mean about the way you learn?

   _____

   _____

   _____

   _____

4. List at least eight learning strategies that accommodate your sensory learning preference.

   _____

   _____

   _____

   _____

   _____

5. Based on your sensory learning preference, what do instructors do that help you learn?

   _____

   _____

   _____

   _____

6. How do you learn an instructor's preferred teaching style?

_____

_____

_____

_____

_____

7. Why do you think it's important to know an instructor's preferred teaching style?

_____

_____

_____

_____

8. What are some things you can do if an instructor's style does not match yours?

_____

_____

_____

_____

_____

9. a. Which of the multiple intelligences are your strongest?

_____

b. How might you gain strength in the weaker ones?

_____

_____

_____

_____

10. From what you learned about learning styles, how do you see this influencing the way you work with and for others?

_____

_____

_____

_____

11. After studying this chapter, what do you know about the way you learn? What can you do to make your learning more successful?

_____

_____

_____

_____

CASE STUDIES

for Creative and Critical Thinking

 ACADEMIC CASE—Connecting to History Lecture

Dr. Warner entered his U.S. Constitution History course sporting his usual attire: tweed jacket, tie, blue jeans, and sneakers. He casually jotted his lecture outline on the chalkboard as he greeting incoming students. His classroom featured highly organized bookshelves and displays of historical documents laid out chronologically on the walls. Dr. Warner always started his lecture cross-legged on top of his desk, taking sips of his bottled water as he discussed current events with his class, usually asking students to relate the discussion to the previous lecture material. He would continue by lecturing from his many PowerPoint slides, giving specific details his students knew they would be tested on while weaving in historical stories. His students often complained of suffering from "writer's cramp" by the end of his class, but they always appreciated his passion and attention to detail when lecturing.

1. Do you think Dr. Warner has the preferences of a sequential instructor, a random instructor, or a balanced instructor? Which of his qualities support your answer?

_____

_____

_____

_____

_____

2. Why is it important to know which style your instructor prefers to use?

_____

_____

_____

_____

3. Which of Dr. Warner's qualities would most benefit your learning style preferences?

_____

_____

_____

_____

4. When you think of what is required of teaching history, would you imagine someone like Dr. Warner? Why or why not?

_____

_____

_____

_____

WORKPLACE CASE—Connecting to Workplace Training

David and Carlos were taking a real estate course as part of their training to become sales agents. Carlos, who was an active participant in the discussions and even volunteered to role-play as a difficult client, enjoyed the course. David found it frustrating. Carlos was so involved in the activities he lost track of time. David, on the other hand, felt unprepared for the activities and pressed the instructor for the correct answers to the situations being discussed by the group. On his evaluation of the course, Carlos stated he liked the many viewpoints expressed. David's evaluation listed several suggested improvements, among which were more lecture and reading materials, detailed, accurate answers to questions, and clear, step-by-step instructions.

1. What learning style do you think David prefers? What might he do to develop his non-preferred learning style?

_____

_____

_____

_____

_____

2. What learning style do you think Carlos prefers? What might he do to develop his non-preferred learning style?

_____

_____

_____

_____

_____

3. In the real estate business where you need to deal with all kinds of people, which learning preference(s) would make for a more successful real estate agent?

_____

_____

_____

_____

_____

4. Can you predict who will be more successful in the real estate business? Why do you think so?

_____

_____

_____

_____

_____

3 Creating Concentration

Terms

- arm-swing rule
- concentration
- effective learning space
- ineffective learning space
- learning environment
- learning influences
- mental learning environment
- mind wandering
- physical learning space
- physiology

Chapter Goals

After studying and working with the information in this chapter, you should be able to:

- Identify the influences that affect your concentration and understand the effects of mind wandering.
- Identify the makeup of an effective physical and mental learning environment so you can make better choices for improving your concentration while learning.

Jerrold, who is taking a finance course on the Internet, has completed the curriculum and is now preparing for the final exam. Once he is ready, all he needs to do is to log in and take the exam sometime before the end of the week.

As a stock clerk at the local supermarket, he has little time during the day to study. His nights are not much better, as he volunteers at the fire department and spends time with his girlfriend.

If things are quiet at work during his 45-minute lunch, he pulls out his study materials. He also pulls out his cell phone and spends a few minutes to check in with his girlfriend, or a coworker stops by to chat. When it's time to get back to work, Jerrold is frustrated because he has spent most of his time talking and eating, but not studying. When he finds time to study at home, he usually begins after 9:00 p.m. when he's quite tired from the day.

His typical study place is in bed with the television on. If he is interested in the study material, he will roll over on his side and ignore the TV. Sometimes he sits in a recliner or on the couch with music playing. Occasionally, he gets telephone calls or his cat begs for attention by sitting on top of his study material.

Tomorrow is the last day he can take the exam and he doesn't feel ready at all. He wishes he had another week to study.

What do you suggest Jerrold do at work to be able to concentrate better during the short time he has for studying? What can he do at home?

Concentration is the art of being focused and the ability to pay attention. Without concentration, you have no memory of what you hear, see, and read. Concentration is a frame of mind that enables you to stay centered on the activity or work you are doing. You know when you're concentrating because time seems to go by quickly, distractions that normally take you off task don't bother you, and you have a lot of mental or physical energy for the task. Your mind and body are naturally "going with the flow." You have probably experienced intense concentration—a time when you were so focused on what you were doing that you didn't hear someone approach and jumped in surprise when he or she touched you or spoke. Maybe you played, or watched, a play-off game where the outcome came down to the final seconds. You were probably quite focused at that time!

Good concentration is a result of being active, mindful, and conscious. Knowing how to concentrate is directly related to your ability to learn. Many influences affect concentration—the amount of time and energy you spend in the learning process. The influences discussed in this chapter are those that specifically affect your concentration.

An **effective learning space** is one where concentration comes easily and more learning occurs. An **ineffective learning space** causes you to waste time and makes learning difficult. You can learn how to increase your concentration by being aware of and choosing the appropriate physical and mental learning environment.

In this chapter, you will learn about 1) becoming aware of the influences in your learning space, 2) understanding how these influences affect you, and 3) creating an effective learning space for improving your overall learning. You will also discover the available opportunities that make your learning easier and more enjoyable.

> What does good concentration feel like for you? When does it happen?

What helps you concentrate and focus like the person in this photo?

©Getty Images/PhotoDisc

The following self-evaluation will give you an idea of how familiar, or unfamiliar, you are with some of the topics and terms discussed in this chapter. After reading each statement, circle the letter Y, S, or N to indicate the answer that is most appropriate for you. Answer honestly. Rate yourself at the end; then complete the information on your Self-Check Progress Chart.

Y = yes; frequently   S = sometimes   N = no; never

1. I read and study in a quiet, distraction-free environment.   Y   S   **Ⓝ**

2. I read and study without a radio or television on.   Y   S   **Ⓝ**

3. I resist taking phone calls or checking e-mail while reading or studying.   **Ⓨ**   S   N

4. I work at an uncluttered desk or table with good lighting.   Y   **Ⓢ**   N

5. I am aware of the room temperature and can make myself comfortable.   **Ⓨ**   S   N

6. I am aware of, and try to reduce, mental distractions before learning.   **Ⓨ**   S   N

7. I am usually relaxed when I have a lot of studying to do.   Y   **Ⓢ**   N

8. I know several ways to increase my concentration while reading and studying.   Y   **Ⓢ**   N

9. I reserve most of my reading and studying for the time of day when I am most alert.   **Ⓨ**   S   N

10. I enjoy learning.   Y   **Ⓢ**   N

Rate Yourself:

Number of Ys _4_ × 100 = _400_

Number of Ss _4_ × 50 = _200_

Number of Ns _2_ × 0 = _0_   **Total** _600_

Your Learning Influences

A **learning influence** is something that affects how well you concentrate while trying to learn. Some are physical; others are mental. Some influences are helpful in keeping your concentration, while many others are distracting. The helpful ones are considered positive, while the distracting ones are considered negative.

ACTIVITY 1

Below is a list of common influences that can affect your concentration. Think about how each of the influences affects the way you concentrate; and decide whether it is positive/helpful (+), negative/ unhelpful (−), or sometimes helpful/sometimes unhelpful (=). For example, if you find yourself very focused when you are under time pressure, place a plus (+) in the blank. If you find you are continually distracted by time pressure with little ability to focus, place a minus (−) in the blank. However, if you find you are both focused and distracted equally, place an equal (=) in the blank. Add other influences that can affect your concentration.

Location

+ At your desk

+ At a table

− On a couch

− On a recliner

− In bed

___ Other:_____

State of Mind/Being

+ Interested

− Not interested

+ Alert

− Sleepy

= Relaxed

− Stressed

= Time-pressured

= Not time-pressured

− Preoccupied

− Tired

+ Well rested

− Hungry

___ Other:_____

External Environment

= Warm

= Cool

+ Well lit

− Dimly lit

= Noisy

= Quiet

___ Other:_____

Distractions

= Other people

− Telephone

− E-mail

= Television

= Music

___ Other:_____

Type of Written Material

= Familiar content

= Unfamiliar content

+ Wide columns

− Narrow columns

= Large print size

= Small print size

+ Good copy quality

− Poor copy quality

___ Other:_____

Delivery of Information

= Lecture

= Discussion

= Reading

= Writing

= On computer screen

= One-on-one instruction

= Group interaction

= Research

= Hands-on learning

= Visual demonstration

___ Other:_____

Purpose/Usability

− For a meeting

= For your boss or instructor

+ For a presentation

+ For a test

+ For pleasure

+ For background knowledge

___ Other:_____

Mind Wandering: The Enemy of Concentration

Your mind must focus before it can learn. When you focus, you concentrate on the learning material and content. **Mind wandering**, on the other hand, is the enemy of concentration. Also known as daydreaming, mind wandering is a momentary lack of mental concentration or focus. It can last a second, five seconds, thirty seconds, or longer. It is natural—and necessary for learning. All human beings daydream. Unfortunately, many students do it too much. They are great at mind wandering and often not so great at focusing.

When you read or study, some mind wandering may be helpful. If you are building a mental bridge of knowledge from the new information to the old, then mind wandering can be productive. For example, if you are learning about the installation of electrical sockets, your mind may wander to the time you got an electrical shock as a child when you stuck your finger in a socket—that thought is important for your learning.

However, if, while installing the sockets, your mind wanders to your plans for the coming weekend, that thought is not productive. Not only will it delay the completion of the project, but you will also have a higher chance of getting an electrical shock because you weren't focusing on the task at hand. Nonproductive thoughts break your concentration, slow down and interrupt your learning process, and ultimately affect your ability to understand the information you are trying to comprehend. It is important to be aware of the mental thoughts that cause your mind to wander and break your concentration.

NETBookmark

To feel concentration first-hand, go online to find out what others write about in the area of concentration. Go to your favorite search engine and type in "concentration" or "concentration and memory." (You will find listings about concentration camps but look for those sites that relate to learning.) Be aware of how focused you are while you are searching and reading. Think about what makes you so focused.

For links to additional information about concentration, go to:

http://sskills.swlearning.com

© Getty Images/PhotoDisc

Which photo more closely resembles your learning space?

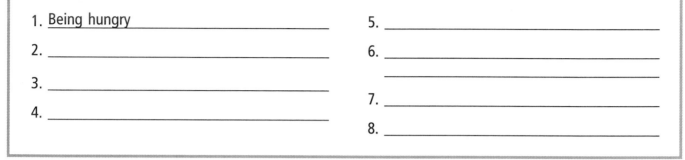

ACTIVITY 2

Think about the wandering thoughts that break your concentration when you read, work, or study. List below as many specific thoughts as you can.

1. Being hungry _____

2. _____

3. _____

4. _____

5. _____

6. _____
   _____

7. _____

8. _____

Once you have listed as many thoughts as possible in Activity 2, compare them with your classmates' answers. You may remind each other of items you forgot. Continue to add to your list as you remember thoughts that interfere with your concentration. This can help you get a realistic picture of just how many miscellaneous thoughts cross your mind when you believe you are concentrating.

From Activity 2, did you discover any mental distractions you would like to eliminate forever? Unfortunately, you may be able to avoid them only temporarily. For example, you can stop thinking about how hungry you are by eating a snack, but eventually you will be hungry again. Mind wandering can be reduced, but not totally eliminated. Now that you're aware of what breaks your concentration, you have a fighting chance of doing something about it!

EFFECTS ON LEARNING. So what happens when your other thoughts get your mind off track? If your mind wanders on your way home, you might miss your stop, drive past your exit, or even worse, get into an accident. When your mind wanders at work, you have a higher chance of making a mistake or doing something wrong. It's the same while reading or studying—you will spend more time than needed, make more mistakes, and understand less. Though some daydreaming is needed, students tend to do it too much. From the common-sense ideas presented in this chapter, see which of them you want to start doing that can immediately reduce your mind wandering.

Ways to Improve Concentration

Since mind wandering is a natural and human characteristic, you can never get rid of it forever. If you were asked to never daydream again while reading or studying, could you do it? The honest answer is no! Nonetheless, if you recognize the fact that you are daydreaming, you can at least learn how to reduce it. The very first step in reducing mind wandering is to catch yourself doing it. Then you can do something about it. By reducing mind wandering, you will be able to learn more in less time with better concentration.

Success tip

According to the research of Becky Patterson, Ph.D., Professor Emeritus of the University of Alaska and author of *Concentration: Strategies for Attaining Focus:*

- An average college student's concentration period while reading is only 16 minutes!
- Young children have concentration periods that last for just 20 seconds!

It is amazing that we ever learn anything with such small intervals of concentration. By understanding that our concentration naturally doesn't last very long, we have to work at keeping it.

Challenge yourself to focus more by:

- using many of the active reading and learning strategies in this book.
- setting up a place to work that enables you to focus for longer periods of time.
- reading and studying at your more alert times of day.

With a partner or on your own, consider what you can do to reduce mind wandering while learning. Keep track of your strategies below. As you continue to work through this book and learn more ways to develop good concentration, refer to this list and add more items. If you run out of room, use another piece of paper. Remember, mind wandering cannot be eliminated, only reduced.

1. Catch myself when I start daydreaming! _____
2. _____
3. _____
4. _____
5. _____
6. _____
7. _____
8. _____
9. _____
10. _____

Checkpoint

1 What is a learning influence?

_____

_____

2 What influences you positively when you learn?

_____

_____

3 What influences you negatively?

_____

_____

_____

Your Learning Environment

As human beings, we react to our environment. When it is warm, we get sleepy. When it is noisy, we become distracted. When we have a lot on our minds, we have a hard time concentrating. A **learning environment** is the combination of influences that are present while you are learning or working.

There are two learning environments: physical and mental. Your physical environment includes external surroundings, such as room type, lighting, and noise level. Your mental environment is your internal state, which includes your attitude, how you feel, and what you are thinking about.

Both the physical and mental environments directly affect how well you can concentrate when learning or working. In turn, how well you concentrate directly affects how much you learn and how much time you have to spend in the learning process.

What's Around You?

Your **physical learning space** is the place where you choose to read and study. It may be in your bedroom or kitchen, at the library, or at work. You could be seated in a reclining chair, on a couch, or at a desk or table. The room could be noisy or quiet. It could be filled with clutter or be neat and organized. All of these influences can affect your learning.

ACTIVITY 4

To understand physical influences that can affect learning, look at the sample floor plan below:

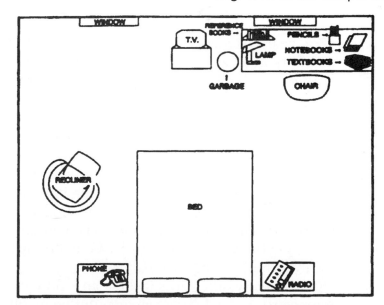

1. Highlight or circle the influences that might distract you while reading or studying.
2. Working in a group, discuss the influences that increase concentration and those that hinder it. For example, a desk might promote concentration, while a bed might cause sleepiness.

ACTIVITY 4 (continued)

3. Then, if you think an influence affects concentration negatively, brainstorm about things you can do to eliminate or change it. For example, clear the clutter off the desk and use the desk when studying to concentrate better and learn faster.

Now visualize the place (or places) in which you read, study, and learn. It could be some place at work or at home. Then using the sample diagram above as an example, sketch a simple floor plan of the space. Place an X or other marking that indicates where you are in the room. Be sure to include where the following items are as they pertain to your location. Identify what you can do to make your personal learning place more conducive to learning.

desks	television	other people	textbooks	pets
tables	radio	pens/pencils	lighting	clutter
chairs	dictionary	doorways/door	sources	telephone
bed	windows	computer	food/drink	

> *"The average person puts only 25% of his energy and ability into his work. The world takes off its hat to those who put in more than 50% of their capacity, and stands on its head for those few and far between souls who devote 100%."*
>
> **—Andrew Carnegie, Industrialist and millionaire**

✳ 15 Options for Achieving Concentration ✳ *Must Know!!*

You are ultimately in charge of how well you concentrate. As you read through the following strategies for increasing your focus while learning, checkmark the strategies you think are most useful so you can refer to them later.

✳ **1. CHOOSE YOUR WORKSPACE WISELY.** Consider the following equation:

$$\text{If a Bed} = \text{Sleep}$$
$$\text{and a Desk} = \text{Work,}$$
$$\text{then a Bed} \neq \text{Work.}$$

For years, students have chosen a bed, the floor, a couch, or a comfortable chair as places to study. Yet, the brain associates these locations with relaxing or sleeping. A desk or table, on the other hand, is a place that our brain associates with working. If you think about it, that's why schools and libraries are filled with tables and desks, not beds! If you try to study in a place where you usually relax, you will find learning to be more challenging and time-consuming.

By moving to a desk or table to do your reading and studying, you can concentrate better, thereby getting more work done in less time. A desk or table also has a convenient writing surface and plenty of space to spread out. At the other locations, you are often distracted, either because you want to move to a different body position or you need to balance the learning material.

Some ideal work spaces include an empty classroom, office, or conference room, or a quiet cafeteria during its off hours. An uncluttered desk in your room can work as long as you eliminate distractions like the television, loud music with lyrics, the telephone rings, and the e-mail dings. Some students study effectively in a library carrel but less successfully on a comfortable couch. Be aware of room temperature. Many libraries are overly warm, which can make you feel sluggish or sleepy.

✳2. MANAGE YOUR CLUTTER. Your desktop or tabletop should be clear of clutter, except for the materials you need for studying. You should have enough room for your elbows, reading material, a notebook, and any other necessary items. If your desk or table is cluttered, try the **arm-swing rule**; that is, gently sweep a semicircle of clear space in front of you using the length of space from your elbow to your fingertips. You may end up with a clutter fortress piled up around the semicircle, but nothing directly in front of you. When you have learning to do, clutter is a distraction.

✳3. ENSURE GOOD LIGHTING. Some people require a bright space, while others prefer a dimmer environment. It is easier to learn when the lighting is just right for your eyes. For example, if fluorescent lights bother you, place a lamp on your table, or sit by natural sunlight. If outside light bothers you, draw the curtains.

✳4. FEED YOUR BODY RIGHT. What you eat plays an important role in how well or how poorly you concentrate. Protein foods (such as cheese, meat, fish) and vegetables keep the mind alert, while carbohydrates (such as pasta, bread, and processed white sugars), make you sleepy. Caffeine (commonly found in coffee, tea, soft drinks, and chocolate) acts as a stimulant in low doses. In high doses, it can cause jitters, heart palpitations, diarrhea, and sleeplessness. So when you want to concentrate, eat more protein in relation to your carbohydrates, and limit your caffeine.

■ Focus on Ethics

You're taking an online course with people you don't know, and you've been assigned to work on a team project. You have been given the responsibility to write the final report, but your mother is sick and you have taken on a lot more responsibilities around the house. You are under a lot of pressure, but don't want to let your teammates down, so you don't say anything.

You keep putting off getting started and you tell your teammates you're working on it. On the day before the course ends, you send an e-mail to your teammates telling them that you're very sorry but you were not able to get the work done.

Where did you go wrong? What could you have done differently to avoid this situation? Would you have acted differently if it was a traditional face-to-face class rather than an online course?

✳5. AVOID FOOD. Food and serious learning don't mix well. Think about it. When you try to eat and study at the same time, which gets more of your attention? The food, of course! You will be more effective if you eat first, then study. If you want to study while you eat, review material or read background information that requires less concentration.

✳6. CREATE ROOM TEMPERATURE COMFORT. Room temperature is also important. An overly hot room makes you sleepy, while an overly cold one makes you think about getting warm. You end up focusing more on how warm or cold you are than on your learning. Getting comfortable in a fixed temperature environment may mean putting on a sweater or turning on a fan. By working in a room that's a comfortable temperature, you will improve your concentration, resulting in more effective and efficient learning.

7. LISTEN TO YOUR OWN THOUGHTS. Listening to anything but your own thoughts interferes with good concentration. Eliminating distractions such as vocal music, television, telephones, e-mail beeps, and other people can greatly increase the amount of learning you can accomplish.

8. LISTEN TO MOZART. Though you may disagree, listening to music with words *does* interfere with your ability to learn. You may think you are "tuning it out," but when you hear a song that you like, you may find yourself tapping your feet, humming along, or daydreaming. If you need music while studying, try classical music. Research shows that playing classical music softly in the background, especially Mozart, may boost your brain power while you are studying. Classical music helps you focus and concentrate better than music with words.

9. TURN OFF THE TELEVISION. Watching television also interferes with your concentration when studying. Instead of focusing on just learning, you are adding listening AND watching. In a half-hour period, if you do your work only at the commercial breaks, you might be lucky to accomplish five minutes of work. Even if you can hear a television in another room, you will be distracted. Your concentration should be on your learning, so it is a good idea to stay away from the television when trying to learn.

ACTIVITY 5

During your next learning session, work without music for ten minutes. Then turn your favorite music on at your usual volume, and work for another ten minutes. Then, listen to classical music for another ten minutes. In which ten-minute period did you get more done or learn more? Some say that silence is more distracting than music, but that too can be tuned out with a little practice. Write a few sentences to describe the more effective learning situation for you.

_____

_____

_____

_____

_____

_____

_____

*10. HOLD ALL CALLS AND IM'S. Receiving telephone calls or engaging in IM conversations during your study time is both distracting and time consuming. Thanks to other human beings and answering devices, you have the ability to hold your calls until you complete your work. If you choose to study between 7:00 and 8:30 in the evening, you can leave a message on your answering machine, or you can tell the person answering the phone for you to let your callers know that you will return their calls after 8:30. If you don't respond to your friends' text messages, they will think you are away from your computer, which you are, and they will get back to you later. Both ideas will provide uninterrupted time for studying.

*11. LET E-MAIL WAIT. Checking e-mail is just like answering the phone. If you choose to wait until you are finished with your work, your concentration will stay on track.

*12. MOVE TO A QUIETER PLACE. Reading or working when other people are around can make concentrating difficult. If you do your reading or working in a public place such as a library, it may be quiet, but other people will always be moving around. If you read or work at home, your family may interrupt you more often than necessary. If you read at work, your boss or coworkers will inevitably interrupt you. In all cases, you have the ability to prevent these distractions. At the library, find a quiet corner of the building where few people go. At home, explain to your family your need for uninterrupted time, and move to a place where you can close the door. At work, move to a place where no one will find you, such as an empty conference room or the cafeteria during off-hours. These options provide more uninterrupted work time and a better chance of increasing your concentration.

Focus on Technology

While reading from a computer screen can sometimes seem daunting and slow, there are certain features that can make the process better than reading paper documents. When you use eBook software like Microsoft® Reader you may find that having a search function, post-it note capabilities, and the ability to easily carry hundreds of thousands of pages of text with you is well worth the few drawbacks.

To get started reading eBooks go to Microsoft's web site (search online for "Microsoft Reader") and download Microsoft's Reader software. There are versions for desktop, laptop, tablet, and pocket PCs. Once you have downloaded the software you will have access to thousands of eBook titles—many of which are available free.

*13. DUMP YOUR TO-DO LIST. If while you are reading or working, you find yourself thinking of other things you need to be doing, try writing them on a piece of paper. At inappropriate times your mind will almost always wander to things you need to do. Keeping track of your thoughts on paper and referring to the paper from time to time can be very effective for clearing your mind and focusing on your work in front of you.

> To take on the task of learning means you realize and accept that you don't know everything. It essentially means you will make mistakes along the way in your quest for knowledge.

14. TAKE SHORT, FREQUENT BREAKS. Since people concentrate for about 20 minutes or less at a time, it would make sense to capitalize on your natural body rhythms and take a *short* break every 20 to 30 minutes. Generally, do some quick physical activity like getting a bottle of water or walking around the block. If you are fully concentrating and involved in a task, then work until a natural break occurs.

15. SET A TIME GOAL. If you know you have only 25 minutes to work on a project and you want to get through half of it, you will be more apt to finish if you stick to a time frame. Another example of this occurs when you naturally set goals by saying you will read until you reach the end of a chapter or an article. It may help motivate you to keep going and stay focused.

What's on Your Mind?

What your mind thinks about while you are learning is called your **mental learning environment**. As you have already discovered, you often have many things on your mind that are unrelated to the learning task. You also have natural breaks in your concentration. It is during the breaks that you sometimes talk to yourself.

You may say negative or non-productive statements such as, "I don't know how I'm going to finish all of this tonight," or "I'm going to fail the test tomorrow." You might say positive or productive statements, such as, "I really learned a lot today," or "I'm glad I've kept up with my work." The kind of self-talk you choose is based on your attitude and your physiology.

> There is every reason in the world to believe that you can achieve anything you want.

DEVELOPING POSITIVE SELF-TALK. To take on the task of learning means you realize and accept that you don't know everything. It essentially means you will make mistakes along the way in your quest for knowledge. *Accepting this reality will greatly improve your self-confidence and your ability to develop positive self-talk.* You will no longer dread mistakes, but welcome them.

A high level of confidence in your ability to try new things and think new thoughts will make your learning easier. In Chapter 1, you learned how important it is to develop a positive belief in yourself. You were also shown how to think positively. (You may want to take time now to go back and review Chapter 1.) Making the commitment to be a lifelong learner is a positive step toward a successful future. *There is every reason in the world to believe that you can achieve anything you want.*

Developing a positive attitude about your ability to learn makes the amount of time and energy you spend more enjoyable. Only you are in charge of your own attitude and learning!

BECOMING AWARE OF YOUR PHYSIOLOGY. Your **physiology**, simply defined as how your body feels, affects your thoughts and concentration while reading and studying. Here are a few things to consider when you want to learn.

Must Know

1. *Get Enough Sleep.* If you are feeling tired or ill, you will daydream and think more about getting sleep than about the work in front of you. You may try to continue to study, but you will waste a lot of time and find learning difficult. When you are really exhausted, you may wisely decide to put off the learning activity in favor of getting some sleep so that you don't waste your time. Your best option is to find a way to get enough sleep on a regular basis.

2. *Learn at Your Peak Time(s) of Day.* Your physiology changes throughout the day, with certain times of the day better for learning than others. Your ability to concentrate is easier when you feel fully awake and more difficult when you do not. Some individuals consider themselves morning people, while others consider themselves night owls. Planning your study time around your peak times of the day or when you feel best will make the time you spend more effective.

3. *Take Care of Human Needs.* If you are hungry, need to use the bathroom, or feel ill, your concentration will be interrupted with these basic human functions. Do what you can to take care of them so your comfort level will be maximized for good concentration.

> **"Learning is not attained by chance. It must be sought for with ardor and attended to with diligence."**
>
> **—Abigail Adams, Second First Lady of the United States**

Taking Control of Your Concentration

Blaming external or internal factors for your inability to concentrate is easy to do. However, you can take an active role in setting up a learning environment that maximizes your concentration needs.

ACTIVITY 6

Complete the blanks below to explain how each item affects your ability to learn.

If I am tired, I _____

If I am rested, I _____

If I am hungry, I _____

If I am not hungry, I _____

If I feel ill, I _____

If I feel well, I _____

Compare your responses with those of others in your class, and discuss the effects of each. Talk about what you might do to improve your concentration in all of the above situations.

_____

_____

In Activity 1, you created a list of learning influences and decided whether each influence was positive, negative, or both. Using the columns below and the information you learned in this chapter, rearrange your learning influence list into the two categories below. (Hint: The negative influences are usually on the mind-wandering side, and the positive influences are usually on the concentration side.) You are encouraged to add more influences to either side of your list as you think of them. Review your two lists. Do you now know what you need to eliminate or add to create an effective learning space? Remember to add to your list on page 64, Activity 3.

Mind Wandering Is a Result of ...

Being tired

Learning late at night

_____

_____

_____

_____

_____

_____

Concentration Is a Result of ...

Being well rested

Learning earlier in the day

_____

_____

_____

_____

_____

_____

Checkpoint

1 What elements of your physical environment distract you the most?

_____

_____

2 What elements of your mental environment distract you the most?

_____

_____

3 What can you do right now to ensure better concentration for reading, learning, and working?

_____

_____

_____

CHAPTER SUMMARY

1. Many influences affect the way you learn. Some are positive, and others are negative.

2. Concentration is vital to learning. Mind wandering is the enemy of concentration. Distractions are the primary cause of mind wandering.

3. You lose concentration and waste time when your mind wanders. Mind wandering can prevent you from understanding what you are trying to learn.

4. Mind wandering is effective only when it relates to the material you are learning.

5. Reducing mind wandering is the same as increasing concentration. There are many ways to improve your concentration while trying to learn. The first step in reducing mind wandering is to catch yourself doing it.

6. An effective physical learning environment consists of an appropriate place to learn without distractions.

7. An effective mental learning environment consists of a high level of learning self-confidence and an awareness of how you feel.

8. Taking control of your learning environment with specific strategies can help you concentrate better.

CHAPTER ASSESSMENT

Terms Review

Fill in the blanks with the appropriate key terms on the left.

arm-swing rule
concentration
effective learning space
ineffective learning space
learning environment
learning influences
mental learning environment
mind wandering
physical learning space
physiology

1. What your mind thinks about while you are learning is considered your _Mental learning_.

2. An uncluttered desk or table, good lighting, and no distractions are ingredients in a(n) _Physical/Effective Learning space_.

3. A(n) _effective/Physical_ enables you to learn more in less time.

4. A(n) _Ineffective learning space_ distracts and forces you to waste learning time.

5. _Concentration_ is the enemy of daydreaming.

6. Your _learning environment_ is the combination of influences that are present while you are learning or working.

7. _Mind wandering_ is also called daydreaming.

8. Sweeping away clutter in your work area is called _arm-swing rule_.

9. How your body feels is considered your _physiology_.

10. The combination of all your _learning influences_ affect how well you concentrate while trying to learn.

Review

TRUE or FALSE Review

_F_ 1. The average college student concentrates for an average of 46 minutes.

_F_ 2. Daydreaming happens when you fall asleep during the day.

_T_ 3. Though mind wandering takes you off task, it can be helpful when you are relating new information to old.

_F_ 4. Students can effectively study for exams while watching television.

_T_ 5. The recommended music to listen to while studying is classical music, especially Mozart.

_T_ 6. Reading in bed encourages mind wandering because it is a place the body has learned to relax.

_F_ 7. Taking phone calls while studying has been shown to increase test scores.

_T_ 8. If you believe you can, you can; if you believe you can't, you probably can't.

_T_ 9. Reading and studying at your peak times of day will help you learn more in less time.

_T_ 10. Eating a big pasta meal before studying will make you sleepier than if you had chicken and salad.

Answer the following questions based on the information you learned in this chapter.

1. What are learning influences? Which ones influence your learning the most?

_____

_____

_____

_____

_____

2. What is the relationship between mind wandering and concentration?

_____

_____

_____

_____

3. What are some typical causes of mind wandering for you?

_____

_____

_____

_____

_____

WORKPLACE CASE—Connecting to the Home Office Environment

Will worked as a mortgage broker in a large office in downtown Los Angeles. He hated the traffic and wanted to find a way to work more from home. He approached his boss who was supportive of the idea. Learning to work at home was new for Will, but he really wanted to make it succeed.

The problem is that Will is a good neighbor and a great car mechanic on the weekends. Whenever someone has car trouble, he stops what is doing to help. Now that he is home more often during the week, his neighbors have started calling and coming to his door more frequently with "just a little problem." And, as usual, Will drops everything to help. After a few months, Will's boss complains about his work. "You're way behind in your customer calls, and when I try to call you, you're never there," said his boss. "What ARE you doing?!"

1. What would you advise Will to do to improve his ability to concentrate on his work without alienating his friends and neighbors?

_____

_____

_____

_____

2. What office work habits can Will bring into his new home office that would improve his effectiveness?

_____

_____

_____

_____

_____

3. At what point do you think Will should go back to the downtown office?

_____

_____

_____

_____

_____

4. What other concentration challenges do you think Will faces working from home? What might he do about them?

_____

_____

_____

_____

4 Learning Time Management

Terms

- academic calendar
- daily activity log
- goal
- learning goal
- long-term goal
- monthly calendar
- palmtop calendar
- procrastination
- productive time
- rewards
- short-term goal
- syllabus
- unproductive time
- weekly activity log
- weekly project planner

Chapter Goals

After studying and working with the information in this chapter, you should be able to:

- Identify several short-term and long-term goals so you can make smarter choices about where you spend your time.
- Use daily and weekly time logs to analyze how you spend your time.
- Understand how much time is needed for learning.
- Use a weekly project planner to track assignments and daily responsibilities, and use a calendar to schedule school deadlines, appointments, and social events.
- Define procrastination, identify several ways to overcome it, and use effective strategies to master your time.

It is Friday morning, and Juanita isn't thinking about the weekend. She is thinking about Monday, the day of her job interview at Wicks and Sticks, a wholesale candle and gift company she would really like to work for. Though Juanita has been on job interviews before, she feels this one is really important. She *loves* making her own candles and even has a few designs of her own. "What better way to make money than to do something I love!" she thinks.

She has put a lot of mental energy into wishing she had the job. She realizes that the more she knows about the company, the better her chances are for being hired. Though this interview has been scheduled for two weeks, she has been so busy with schoolwork, committee meetings, and work at the sandwich shop that she hasn't found the time to do any background research on the company.

To make matters even worse, she's in her cousin's wedding this weekend. Tonight is the rehearsal dinner, and tomorrow is the wedding.

On Sunday, she's expected to spend time with family and out-of-town guests. If she's lucky and not too exhausted, she may have a few hours Sunday evening to surf the Web for more information about the company. Unfortunately, she doesn't have enough time now to call the company and request the annual report or any other background information.

What could Juanita have done to be better prepared for this important interview?

How many hours are there in a day? The answer for most people is "not enough." No matter how hard you try, you simply cannot get more than 24 hours out of a day, or 168 hours in a week.

Between school, family, and work responsibilities, each day seems to be filled with things to do. Yet you may not have set aside time for yourself or for learning. If you are a student involved in athletics, you must schedule practice and workout time *in addition to* class and study time. If you have a job, you must juggle your job and family responsibilities with learning and study time.

Many people who wish for more time don't realize that they are the *only* ones who can control where they spend it. If you take a good look at how you currently spend each 24 hours, you will probably find ways to make better use of your time.

On the following pages, you will take a specific look at how you spend your time. For now, think about how many hours per night you sleep. If you get an average of eight hours a night, that leaves just sixteen hours of awake time to prepare meals, get washed up and dressed, commute, attend school, go to work, watch TV, talk to friends, do the shopping, and so on. It is amazing how many things occupy our waking hours.

"Work smarter, not harder" is one of the important ideas expressed throughout this book. This chapter will help you discover how you currently spend your time and learn what choices you have for spending your time more wisely. Being smart about how you use your time is probably the most important step you can take toward making your learning, and life in general, easier.

We all know how to waste time, but not many of us know how to make the most of the time we have. As you begin this chapter, think about what you might already do that helps you *not* waste your time, or more specifically, spend your time wisely.

In this chapter, you will 1) identify how your time is spent, 2) recognize how much time you really need, 3) identify your goals so you can spend your time wisely, 4) learn helpful tips and suggestions for planning your time, and 5) learn strategies for overcoming procrastination and mastering your time.

©Getty Images/PhotoDisc

It doesn't matter how you keep track of your time; it's what you DO in that time that matters!

"*It takes time to save time.*"

**—Alec McKenzie,
Popular time
management specialist**

Do you know where YOUR time goes?

The following self-evaluation will give you an idea of how familiar, or unfamiliar, you are with some of the topics and terms discussed in this chapter. After reading each statement, circle the letter Y, S, or N to indicate the answer that is most appropriate for you. Answer honestly. Rate yourself at the end; then complete the information on your Self-Check Progress Chart.

Y = yes; frequently   S = sometimes   N = no; never

1. I know what is important to me.   **Ⓨ**   S   N

2. I make time for those things I feel are most important.   Y   **Ⓢ**   N

3. I know how I spend my time.   Y   S   **Ⓝ**

4. I know that learning requires time and repetition.   **Ⓨ**   S   N

5. I keep and follow a monthly calendar.   Y   S   **Ⓝ**

6. I keep and follow a weekly planner.   Y   **Ⓢ**   N

7. I plan ahead for project due dates and future events (writing projects, tests, presentations).   Y   S   **Ⓝ**

8. I set goals for myself.   Y   **Ⓢ**   ~~N~~

9. I reward myself when I reach a goal.   **Ⓨ**   S   N

10. I know what procrastination is and how it affects my ability to manage my time.   Y   **Ⓢ**   N

Rate Yourself:

Number of Ys ___3___ × 100 = _300_

Number of Ss ___4___ × 50 = _200_

Number of Ns ___3___ × 0 = _0_   Total _500_

What Is Most Important to You?

"*Begin with the end in mind.*"

—**Stephen Covey, Author of *The 7 Habits of Highly Effective People***

If you know what is important to you today, tomorrow, or five years from now, you can budget your time wisely in order to meet your goals. Right now you probably make time for the most important activities and for the ones over which you have little or no control, such as a boss' request to meet a deadline. Being more active, conscious, and mindful about how you use your time will enable you to do those things that are truly most important to you.

So what *is* important to you? What are your goals? Do you desire academic success? Do you wish to be a good mother or father or daughter or son? Do you want to be active in your community? Do you aspire to be a first-rate nurse, electrician, or landscaper?

Setting Personal Goals

A **goal** is something you want to have, want to do, or hope to be. Goals may be short-term or long-term. A **short-term goal** is usually considered something you want to achieve within the next six months to a year. Examples include buying a car, choosing a major course of study, learning a new computer program, and planning a surprise party.

A **long-term goal** is usually something that takes longer than six months to a year to achieve. Examples include getting a college degree, becoming a medical assistant, and planning a wedding. Research shows that people who think about their goals tend to reach more of them than people who don't think about their goals. And individuals who take the time to write them down and look at them on a regular basis almost always reach their goals. Some people put their most important goals on a small card that they carry in their wallet. Some post them in their workspace or next to their computer where they will see them and be reminded of them on a regular basis. Let's test this theory and get you to start writing your goals. (After all, you do want success, right?)

We spend our days in many ways. When each day is over, have you made time for the activities that are most important to you?

©Getty Images/PhotoDisc

On the first three blank lines below, list some of your short-term goals being as specific as possible. On the next three lines, list some of your long-term goals. Be as specific and realistic as possible. For example, if you say that one of your short-term goals is to earn a million dollars, you will find this goal somewhat unrealistic or difficult to achieve. If you find it difficult to come up with five goals, write at least one. You are being limited to five goals because working toward even one goal takes a lot of time and energy.

Identifying Short-Term Goals   Example: I want to plan my spring break trip.

1. _I want to plan my Christmas vacation to Florida_

2. _I want to pass all of my classes_

3. _I want to get my license_

Identifying Long-Term Goals   Example: I want to get a college degree.

1. _I want to become a Interior Designer and work alongside my dad_

2. _I want to move to Florida and attend_

3. _I want to graduate with my Associates degree_

Making Your Goal SMART

The goals you have written in Activity 1 are a great start toward achieving something important to you. Now let's make them a little smarter. A smart goal is one that answers most of these questions:

—What specifically is it? (**S**pecific)

—How much/many is it? (**M**easurement)

—How can you do it? (**A**ctions)

—Can you reach it? (**R**ealistic)

—When will you do it? (**T**ime)

Using the short-term goal example in Activity 1, the questions could be answered like this: What specifically is it? *A spring break trip to Daytona Beach.* How much/many is it? *Seven days.* How can you do it? *If I get two friends to share expenses.* Can you reach it? *Yes; by traveling on a plane and staying at a hotel on the beach.* When will you do it? *I will make reservations by February 15.*

The smarter goal then would be: *I'd like to make plane and beachfront hotel reservations for a seven-day, spring break trip to Daytona Beach by February 15, with two friends who can share expenses.* Now go back to your goals in Activity 1 and make them smarter!

You have identified your goals, which is the first step toward managing your time. The second step requires planning and taking action in order to achieve your goals. For each of your goals listed in Activity 1, write the actions you believe you need to take in order to achieve them. Be as specific as possible. Use the following examples as a model. Notice the detailed actions. Writing specific actions will help you reach your goals sooner.

Sample Short-Term Goals Action List

Example: To plan my spring vacation, I need to:

1. Know who's coming with me.

2. Decide where we want to go.

3. Decide how much money is needed.

4. Look on the Internet for travel deals.

5. Check my wardrobe.

6. Schedule my work projects and family events around my time away.

Sample Long-Term Goals Action List

Example: To get a college degree, I need to:

1. Research colleges with programs I am interested in.

2. Choose and apply to several colleges.

3. Secure loan(s).

4. Find and work with an academic advisor.

5. Do well in my classes.

6. Manage my time well.

Short-Term Goals Action List

My Goal: _I want to plan my Christmas vacation to Florida_

1. ~~I am going alone~~ earn $ to buy plane tickets and extra spending $ _aka! Get a Job!_

2. ~~Talk~~ Talk to my mom about going down

3. Buy Plane tickets # according to scheduale

4. Pack my bags

5. Set alarm for plane to get there on time

6. Make sure to bring entertainment for plane ride

Long-Term Goals Action List

My Goal: _I want to graduate w/ my Associates degree_

1. I must complete ~~my~~ all of my homework on time for every class

2. Pass all of my classes w/ a B- or above

3. Work w/ Tutors when I need help.

4. Manage my time w/ schedual

5. ~~Get~~ Get a job and start paying off loans.

6. _____

Becoming aware of
what you do and
how it relates to your
goals is a valuable
step toward reaching
your goals and
getting what you
want out of life.

Choices for Spending Time

Knowing what is important to you helps you plan your time according to *your* needs, not someone else's. Becoming aware of how you currently spend your time is the next step to planning how best to spend your time in the future. There are basically two ways to spend time: productively and unproductively. Spending **productive time** involves engaging in some activity that gets you closer to your goal(s). If learning a new computer program is one of your goals, then spending time at your computer trying out the program is a productive use of your time. If you intend to keep a clean house, then doing dishes and vacuuming is a good use of your time.

On the other hand, spending **unproductive time** is when you are *not* engaged in an activity that carries you toward your goal(s). Spending time at your computer aimlessly surfing the Web will not help you learn the new program and is an unproductive use of your time. (But surfing the Web for a project or for the answer to a question is a productive use of your time.) If you decide to watch TV or read the paper instead of cleaning the house, you are using your time unproductively. (However, if your intent is to relax, then those activities are a good use of your time.) In the end, what is considered productive depends entirely upon your goals and intentions.

Achieving a balance between the time you spend on productive versus unproductive activities is a daily challenge. We all know how easy it would be to ignore an alarm clock, get up when we want, and do only what we please all day. But reality dictates that we go to work or school and take care of our families and ourselves. Becoming aware of how what you do relates to your goals is a productive step in reaching your goals and getting what you want out of life.

Checkpoint

1 What is a goal?

_____

_____

2 What are some of your goals?

_____

_____

3 What makes your goals smarter?

_____

_____

Where Does Your Time Go?

Where *does* your time go? Actually, it doesn't go anywhere. Just like money, you spend it. You have 24 hours to spend each day, and each day you spend it in different ways.

Keeping a **daily activity log**, a list of the activities you do from the time you get up until you go to sleep (Figure 4-1), is a simple way to really see how you spend your time. It is also a good way to plan a daily schedule.

FIGURE 4-1

Sample Daily Activity Log

DAILY ACTIVITY LOG

Time	Activity	Time	Activity
6:00 a.m.	Get up and shower	4:00	"
6:30	Eat breakfast	4:30	Commute home
7:00	Commute to work	5:00	Watch TV
7:30	"	5:30	Make dinner
8:00	Work	6:00	Eat dinner
8:30	"	6:30	Clean up
9:00	"	7:00	Phone calls
9:30	"	7:30	Fix window
10:00	"	8:00	Check e-mail
10:30	"	8:30	Read newspaper
11:00	"	9:00	Study
11:30	"	9:30	"
12:00 p.m.	Lunch / Go to class	10:00	Read in bed/Get snack
12:30	English class	10:30	"
1:00	"	11:00	Watch TV
1:30	"	11:30	Go to sleep
2:00	Talk with friends	12:00 a.m.	"
2:30	Science lab	12:30	"
3:00	"	1:00	"
3:30	Spanish class	1:30	"

ACTIVITY 3

To get an accurate account of how *you* spend your time, complete this Daily Activity Log. Record every activity you do during the day. Be specific about your activities and the amount of time required for each. Use the log in Figure 4-1 as an example.

Daily Activity Log

6:00 a.m.	Sleep	4:30	Going home
6:30	Get up	5:00	arrive home
7:00	Getting ready	5:30	Chores
7:30	Dressed and on way to school	6:00	↓
8:00	Study time	6:30	Dinner
8:30		7:00	↓
9:00	↓	7:30	
9:30	Class	8:00	Prepare for next day of school ⁱ⁵ min
10:00		8:30	TV Time
10:45	↓	9:00	Prepare grandmother for bed
11:00	Active learning	9:30	Shower
11:30		10:00	Talk w/ Boyfriend
12:05 p.m.	↓	10:30	↓
12:30	Lunch Break	11:00	
1:00		11:30	Sleep till 7:30 am
1:30	↓	12:00 a.m.	
2:00		2:30	
2:30	Study time	12:30	
3:00	↓	1:00	
3:45		1:30	↓
4:00	Class B+N		

A **Weekly Activity Log** is similar to a Daily Activity Log, except that it shows your activities for a full week.

FIGURE 4-2

Sample Weekly Activity Log

Time	Monday	Tuesday	Wednesday	Thursday	Friday	Saturday	Sunday
6:00 a.m.	Get up and shower	→			→		
6:30	Eat breakfast	→			→		
7	Commute to work	→			→		
7:30	"	→			→		
8	Work	→			→		
8:30	"	→			→		
9	"	→			→	Get up Read paper	Get up Read paper
9:30	"	→			→	"	"
10	"	→			→	Mow lawn	Check e-mail
10:30	"	→			→	"	Bake cookies
11	"	→			→	Shower	"
11:30	"	→			→	Shop	Brunch with Bob
12:00 p.m.	Lunch Go to class	Lunch	Lunch Go to class	Lunch	Lunch Go to class	"	"
12:30	Class	Work	Class	Work	Class	Unload groceries	"
1	"	"	"	"	"	Laundry	"
1:30	"	"	"	"	"	"	Study
2	"	"	"	"	"	Check e-mail	"
2:30	Get snack	"	Get snack	"	Get snack	Surf Web	"
3	Class	Work	Class	Work	Class	Surf Web	Study

Figure 4-2: Sample Weekly Activity Log—*continued*

Time	Monday	Tuesday	Wednesday	Thursday	Friday	Saturday	Sunday
3:30	"	"	"	"	"	Nap	"
4	"	Go to gym	"	Go to gym	"	Study	"
4:30	Commute home	Workout and shower	Library research	Workout and shower	Meet Becca for dinner	"	"
5	Watch TV	"	"	"	"	"	Workout and shower
5:30	Make dinner	Commute home	Commute home	Commute home	"	"	"
6	Eat dinner	Watch TV	Make dinner	Volleyball	"	Phone calls	Watch TV
6:30	Clean up	Make dinner	Dinner	"	Go to movies	Meet Julia for dinner	"
7	Phone calls	Dinner	Clean up Phone calls	Go home Dinner	"	"	Get pizza
7:30	Fix window	Clean up	Phone calls	"	"	"	Dinner
8	Check e-mail	Phone calls	Study	Phone calls	"	John's party	Phone calls
8:30	Read newspaper	"	"	Watch TV	"	"	"
9	Study	Read newspaper	"	"	"	"	Study
9:30	"	Study	"	"	"	"	"
10	Read in bed Get snack	Watch TV	"	Study	Out for ice cream	"	Watch TV
10:30	"	"	Take bath	"	"	"	"
11	Watch TV	"	Watch TV	"	Go home Watch TV	"	"
11:30	Go to sleep	Go to sleep	Go to sleep	Go to sleep	Go to sleep	"	Go to sleep
12:00 a.m.						"	
12:30						Go to sleep	
1							
1:30							

To get an accurate account of how *you* spend your time, complete this Weekly Activity Log. Record every activity you do during the next seven days. Be specific about your activities and the amount of time required for each. Use the log in Figure 4-2 as an example.

Weekly Activity Log for the Week of _____

Time	Monday	Tuesday	Wednesday	Thursday	Friday	Saturday	Sunday
6:00 a.m.							
6:30							
7							
7:30							
8							
8:30							
9							
9:30							
10							
10:30							
11							
11:30							
12:00 p.m.							
12:30							
1							
1:30							
2							
2:30							
3							

ACTIVITY 4 (continued)

Time	Monday	Tuesday	Wednesday	Thursday	Friday	Saturday	Sunday
3:30							
4							
4:30							
5							
5:30							
6							
6:30							
7							
7:30							
8							
8:30							
9							
9:30							
10							
10:30							
11							
11:30							
12:00 a.m.							
12:30							
1:00							

Once you complete the Weekly Activity Log in Activity 4, answer the following questions. Use a calculator, if needed.

How much time did you spend in the following ways?	Weekly Total		Average Number of Hours per Day			
Sleeping				5		
Eating and Grooming				4.5		
Commuting				~~3~~		
Studying, Reading, or Learning	Class	28	Class 2.5	Study 2	Reading 2	
Writing E-mail +text—Outside of Work	7			1	~~2~~ ~~1~~	
Surfing the Web—Outside of Work	14			2		
Exercising, Sports, or Leisure Activities	7			1		
Socializing with Friends				4		
Watching TV	14			2		
Not Accounted for—Unknown						
Other Ways You Spent Your Time						

So, how well are you spending your time? Are you generally productive in your nonschool and work hours? Or do you waste time with nonproductive activities? Your Weekly Activity Log and your goals list are useful tools for identifying how you spend your time. You can use this knowledge to make better use of the time you have.

Checkpoint

1 What is a weekly activity log?

_____

_____

2 What did you learn from yours, and how might you spend your time differently?

_____

_____

"*Start by doing what's necessary; then do what's possible; and suddenly you are doing the impossible.***"**

—St. Francis of Assisi

How Much Time Do You Need?

How much time do you need? Probably more than you currently have. For just a moment, imagine you are given an extra hour a day to spend in any way you want. Chances are the first thing that comes to mind isn't school work! So, let this section help you make the time you need to do your school work so you can have that extra hour, or more, to do what you want to do. For the purpose of this section, you will concentrate on how much time you spend in class and how that relates to studying and doing school-related projects.

As a general rule, the amount of study time a student needs for studying or doing school work is based on the number of hours he or she attends class each week. For every hour you spend in a classroom, you should set aside in your weekly schedule *at least* an equal number of hours for doing homework, reviewing, practicing, or studying. For example, if you are in class for six hours a week, then you should allocate at least six hours of study time sometime during that week. If you require more time to learn—perhaps because you are not using effective or efficient learning strategies—you may need two hours of study time for each class hour. If you have a light amount of homework or are efficient at getting it done, you will find yourself with unexpected free time.

Individuals taking training for work can adapt this information to meet their training schedule. For example, you may be taking a two-day computer-training course, not a semester-long program. If so, you will need at least two more days of study time, which is usually broken up over several weeks for you to review, practice, and study the new concepts.

Taking the total number of hours per week you are in class (see Activity 6), look at your Weekly Activity Log and see if you scheduled *at least* an equal number of hours for homework and study time. If you did, good for you! If not, start looking for ways to make room in your schedule for more homework and study time. If you find you don't need the extra study time, you'll have more free time. Just remember that any new learning requires additional time outside the classroom. Repeated exposure to and experience with the subject matter will solidify your knowledge.

Adding up the hours you spend in class and comparing them to learning hours you spend outside of class will help you think smarter about planning your study time.

How many hours are you in class per week? You can use your Weekly Activity Log and the following equation to figure it out. An example has been completed based on a computer course that meets one and a half hours a day, three times a week.

Subject Class Hours per Day	× Meetings per Week	= Hours per Week
Computer Science $1\frac{1}{2}$	× _____ 3 _____	= _____ $4\frac{1}{2}$ _____
_____	× _____	= _____
_____	× _____	= _____
_____	× _____	= _____
_____	× _____	= _____
_____	× _____	= _____
_____	× _____	= _____
_____	× _____	= _____

Total Classroom Hours per Week = _____

Now look at your Weekly Activity Log and see how much time you spend in learning activities (including reading, studying, researching, etc.) outside of class. Do the total number of classroom hours match your study hours on your log, or is one more than other? Remember, the idea is to schedule *at least* one hour of study time to every hour of classroom time.

Checkpoint

1 Why is scheduling enough time important for learning?

_____

_____

2 What did you discover about how much time you need for learning?

_____

_____

3 What can you do to ensure sufficient learning time?

_____

_____

"Plan your work for today and every day, then work your plan."

—**Dr. Norman Vincent Peale, Author of** *The Power of Positive Thinking*

Planning Your Time

Incorporating school into your life means that you will spend time going to class and doing homework. But it also means that you will have to study for exams, do research, create projects, and write essays and papers.

The best way to plan everything you have to do and want to do is to use a combination of time management systems: a monthly calendar, a weekly project planner, and/or a daily project planner. Calendars are meant for the big picture, non-routine events such as appointments, meetings, sporting events, social events, birthdays, and deadlines. They are *not* meant for small project details and to-do's. A weekly or daily project planner is more appropriate for these activities.

Most people keep one of three common monthly calendar systems: an academic calendar (used primarily by students), a monthly calendar (used by many individuals including businesspeople and families), and a palmtop calendar (used mostly by businesspeople). Many people also use a weekly or daily project planner in addition to their monthly calendar to keep track of more detailed to-do's. This section discusses these different time management options. Decide which one or ones work best for you.

■ Focus on Ethics

You're a key member of your school's football team, which has gone undefeated all season and is about to enter the playoffs. You've worked hard in the classroom all year, but now you've fallen behind in one class that has a major paper due the week before the playoffs. The teacher is a real stickler for work being turned in on time, but you know there is no way you are going to be able to finish the paper and make all the football practices the coach has planned. The coach has told the team that anyone not showing up for practices will not be allowed to play in the game.

One of the other players tells you about an online service that, for a fee, will prepare papers written to your specifications. You realize that this may be cheating, but you're planning your college and your future around playing football. Is this your best option? What other choices can you make?

Using an Academic Calendar

An **academic calendar** is made up of 12 monthly calendars, typically from September to August. It is meant to be used by individuals going to school or taking training courses. Whether your school runs on a quarterly, trimester, semester, or yearly schedule, an academic calendar is flexible enough to accommodate everyone.

An academic calendar is where you keep track of large assignments, papers, projects, and other requirements due on a certain date. It acts as an engagement book for important school and personal activities for a school term or year. Alternately, you can use individual monthly calendars for the number of months in your term.

To set up an academic calendar, it helps to have a **syllabus** (plural: syllabi), or schedule of assignments, from the instructor of each class you take. These are usually handed out the first week of class. If the instructor does not have a syllabus, you can still complete an academic calendar using what you already know and making changes or additions as time goes on.

Once you have your syllabus, follow the steps in Activity 7 to complete an academic calendar. You may use Figure 4-3 as an example. Use a dark pencil or erasable pen so you can make changes. If assignments or dates change, you can easily make changes.

FIGURE 4-3

Sample Academic Calendar

Time	Monday	Tuesday	Wednesday	Thursday	Friday	Saturday	Sunday
Sept. 7 - 13	Labor Day	Classes begin					
Sept. 14 - 20							
Sept. 21 - 27			Trigo-nometry quiz			Julie & Jack's wedding	Family dinner
Sept. 28 - Oct. 4					Electronics quiz		
Oct. 5 - 11							
Oct. 12 - 18	Columbus Day - no classes					Coldplay concert	
Oct. 19 - 25			Trigo-nometry mid-term		Electronics mid-term		
Oct. 26 - Nov. 1	Blueprint reading quiz						
Nov. 2 - 8				Motor control demo			
Nov. 9 - 15	Veteran's Day		Trigo-nometry quiz				
Nov. 16 - 22		Nursing project due			To Phila-delphia	Phila-delphia	Phila-delphia
Nov. 23 - 29			Last day of classes	Thanks-giving break	Thanks-giving break	Thanks-giving break	Thanks-giving break
Nov. 30 - Dec. 6	Electronics final		Trigo-nometry final		School ends		

Complete your school calendar for the current term by following the instructions given in the steps below. You may opt to use individual monthly calendars instead of the format shown here.

Step 1: Identify the beginning and end of the term. Label the "Week" column in either of two ways. You may list the number of the term week (for example, 1, 2, 3) or the dates of the week (for example, Sept. 7–13).

Week column of term calendar

Week	Week
1	Sept. 7–13
2	Sept. 14–20
3	Sept. 21–27

Step 2: Fill in all school holidays and important school events.

Step 3: From the information provided on your syllabus, fill in important dates for tests, quizzes, research papers, and projects. (Daily assignments should not be written on this form; they will be included on the Weekly Project Planner explained in the next section.)

Step 4: Write the dates of any important social events you already know about, such as family get-togethers, parties, and concerts.

The best way to plan everything you have to do and want to do is to use a calendar. Choose the calendar system that's right for you!

©Getty Images/PhotoDisc

ACTIVITY 7 (continued)

Date/Week	Monday	Tuesday	Wednesday	Thursday	Friday	Saturday	Sunday

You can use your academic calendar to make out a schedule for completing papers and projects. Typically, you need a lot of time to complete papers and projects. For example, if today is Tuesday and you have a paper due six weeks from today, you can plan each of the steps you must do to complete the assignment.

Week 1:	By Friday	Decide on a topic
Week 2:	Tuesday	Start research
Week 3:	Tuesday	Continue research
	Thursday	Continue research
Week 4:	Tuesday	Write outline of paper
Week 5:	Tuesday	Write first draft
Week 6:	Sunday	Revise draft
	Tuesday	Hand in paper

Now that you have a calendar for keeping track of school-related dates and social events, you still need a way to keep track of daily assignments and responsibilities.

Using a Weekly Project Planner

A **weekly project planner** is like a detailed assignment pad. It contains a to-do list specific to one day. It looks like a calendar but is divided into 5 one-day periods with plenty of space to write. It is an effective way to keep track of assignments and plan study time according to the school calendar.

When you were in grade school, you might have carried a small notepad to write your assignments in. Or you might have written them inside your notebooks or textbooks. Now that you are older, you should have one place to keep track of *all* your study demands.

One blank weekly project planner is shown in Activity 8. Since this page represents one week in a term, you will need to make enough copies of this form to equal the number of weeks in your term. For example, if your term consists of 12 weeks of classes, you will need 12 copies.

Many other people also use a weekly project planner, though it may look a little different. It, too, will consist of individual days with space to write notes.

If Ms. Gregory is running an important meeting on Monday, October 15, she might write a reminder in her weekly project planner on Wednesday, October 10, to begin her

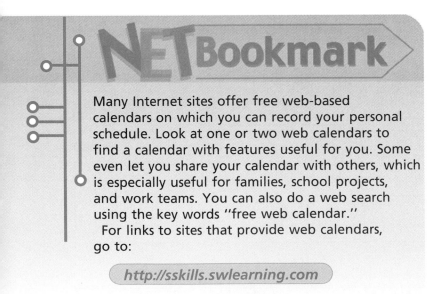

Many Internet sites offer free web-based calendars on which you can record your personal schedule. Look at one or two web calendars to find a calendar with features useful for you. Some even let you share your calendar with others, which is especially useful for families, school projects, and work teams. You can also do a web search using the key words "free web calendar."

For links to sites that provide web calendars, go to:

http://sskills.swlearning.com

preparation. If you are responsible for bringing a class snack on Tuesday, January 22, you might write a note in your weekly project planner on Sunday, January 20, to remind you to go shopping or to plan time for baking. See Figure 4-4 as an example. Use Activity 8 to complete your personal weekly project planner.

FIGURE 4-4

Sample Weekly Project Planner

Project Planner for Week No. __5__

Subject → (List hardest to easiest)	Physics	Mechanical Drawing	Computer Programming	English Composition	Spanish
MON. Oct. 5	p. 62—Evans problems 1-4 Write complete solutions	Work on machine spec	No class	For Wed. — Write a one-page essay on my career goals	Review verbs
TUES. Oct. 6	p. 71—Evans problems 6-12 Write complete solutions	Make corrections to spec	Read Chap. 3 "How to Read Error Messages" Do ques. @ end of chapter	Work on essay due tomorrow	Review verbs Complete handout
WED. Oct. 7 Lisa's b'day	No class	Finalize spec to hand in tomorrow	Go to lab and test program Keep journal of error msgs.	p. 36-40 Read Warriner's p. 41-42 Do exer. A, B, & D	Review verbs
THURS. Oct. 8	Review for quiz tomorrow	Begin wire drawing due Wed. next week	Go to lab and revise steps 6-24	No class	Quiz on verbs
FRI. Oct. 9 2 p.m. Dr. appt.	p. 76—Evans problems 1-3 Write complete solutions	No class- Continue wire drawing	Read Chap. 4 "If/When commands" Do 20 ques. @ end of chapter	No homework	No class

Develop a Weekly Project Planner for yourself by following the steps below and completing the blank planner on page 101. Refer to the previous discussion as needed.

Step 1: Before you can use your Weekly Project Planner, you need to set up all of the daily and weekly information for the term. This is done once, at the beginning of the term. At the top left of the schedule, where it says "Weekly Project Planner for _____", you can fill in the blank in two ways—either by using the week number (for example, Week 1 through 12, if 12 is the number of weeks in your term) or by writing in the actual dates (for example, Sept. 7–13 or Sept. 14–20).

Step 2: In the boxes labeled MON _____, TUES. _____, and so on, fill in the weekly dates (such as MON. Sept. 7, TUES. Sept. 8, and so on). This schedule runs Monday through Friday, but you can adapt it if you are taking weekend courses.

Step 3: List the subjects you are taking, from the hardest, or most challenging, to the easiest, or least challenging, going across the top line of the planner. This is done so that you will pay attention to your hardest subject first. The subject order may change week-to-week, as some classes may be harder for you while others might become easier.

   When doing homework, most students put off doing the hardest subject for last, when they are either too tired or just not willing to spend the time with it. However, if you do your hardest subject first, you will have a much better chance of succeeding in that class. If you are only taking one or two classes, you can create a modified version of the planner by covering up or eliminating several of the vertical lines so the boxes can be enlarged.

Step 4: Using your school calendar to assist you, bring forward to the Weekly Project Planner all important information, such as tests, paper and project deadlines, and school holidays. As the semester progresses, you can make changes to the planner. How you note the due dates of your assignments is up to you.

Step 5: Carry both the Weekly Project Planner and the Academic Calendar with you at all times, either in a folder with pockets or in a three-ring binder. When you are given a new assignment or if a date or an assignment changes, you can easily make changes to your planners. Most important of all, make the planner work for YOU.

©Brand X Pictures

Tablet PCs offer special features, such as handwriting recognition, speech recognition capabilities, and a rotating screen.

ACTIVITY 8 (continued)

Weekly Project Planner for _____

Subject → (List hardest to easiest)					
MON. _____					
TUES. _____					
WED. _____					
THURS. _____					
FRI. _____					

Using a Monthly Calendar

In today's hectic world of doing more and doing it faster, people are turning to **monthly calendars** to help keep them on track. (Office supply stores have a variety of shapes and sizes from which to choose.) Working people use a monthly calendar to make and keep appointments. Some also use them to plan for long-term work projects. Parents and guardians track their children's appointments, lessons, and sports and social events, as well as their own activities. If you are a student, you could combine the concepts of either the academic calendar or the monthly calendar with a weekly project planner. If you plan to use just a monthly calendar, keep in mind that it is not meant to serve as a to-do list.

Using a Palmtop Calendar

A **palmtop calendar** is one of the most popular electronic handheld organizers available. It contains a daily calendar, an appointment scheduler, a location for a to-do list and memos, and an address book. Many business professionals like palmtop calendars, and software companies have made them even more powerful by adding telephone capabilities and wireless Internet access for doing e-mail and surfing the Web.

With a palmtop calendar, you see only one day's scheduled activities at a time. This is similar to using a Daily Activity Log (see "Where Does Your Time Go?") as your time planner. Palmtop calendars are great for planning day-to-day details, but they do not provide the user with a full view of a month or a week. Some people prefer just the daily view, while others prefer to have the benefit of the bigger picture to better plan their time. Try out different calendar systems to determine which one works best for you.

Checkpoint

1 Which calendar system is best for you? Why?

_____

_____

2 For what purpose might you use a Weekly Project Planner?

_____

_____

3 For what purpose might you use a Daily Log?

_____

_____

Finding Time

What you have been doing up to this point is figuring out how you actually spend your time and then discovering ways to keep track of it by using an Academic Calendar, Weekly Project Planner, Monthly Calendar, or Palmtop Calendar. What you haven't done yet is learn how to plan your schedule so you can do everything you need to do and still have time left for things you want to do.

There are three ways to make sure you have more time in a day. *The first and most important way to gain more time is to plan it!* It's like getting in a car and going somewhere. You need to know where you are going and have a plan to get there. Without a plan, you will waste your time and take longer to get to your destination—if you get there at all!

A *second way to gain more time in a day is to do more in less time.* You are discovering in this book how to learn more efficiently, which includes how to study effectively in less time. Using active learning strategies will help you gain more time. This can be as simple as doubling up on activities. For example, if you have three errands, you might try to combine them instead of doing one at time, making one round-trip instead of three. If you commute on a bus or train or carpool, you can study during your ride. At lunch, you can review notes. Use your imagination, and think of how you can get more done in less time.

Yet a third way to gain more time is to use short periods of otherwise wasted time. Activities such as commuting or taking an overly-long lunch can be time wasters, but they can be used for dual purposes. For example, businesspeople often combine meetings with meals. You can use your waiting time productively by always carrying around some of your reading material or studying with you.

On your Daily or Weekly Activity Logs, see if you can locate any wasted, unproductive time that could be turned into productive time. Do you have a free half-hour between classes during which you can either socialize with friends or study? If your education is important to you, you might choose to spend that time studying instead of socializing.

Do you watch a lot of television, spend an excessive amount of time in aimless computer play, or talk frequently on the phone? Often,

> ## 3 Ways to Get More Time in Your Day:
> 1. Plan it!
> 2. Do more in less time.
> 3. Use short periods of otherwise wasted time.

■ Focus on Technology

Benefits of a Tablet PC: If you are thinking of buying a laptop or notebook PC, perhaps you should know the potential added benefits of a Tablet PC. Tablet PC's typically have the full functionality of a notebook, as well as some added features including: handwriting recognition (you can take notes directly on the screen with a special stylus, and the Tablet PC software will convert your handwriting to "typed" material), speech recognition capabilities, and a rotating screen. For students, this means that you can take your tablet to class with you, take notes (including diagrams and charts) directly on the screen and save them into a folder created for each class. And, when you get tired of writing, you can type!

Tablet PC software is being developed rapidly. If you want to check out what is available for the Tablet PC (including software for PDA's, Smart Phones, and mobile devices) search the Web for sites such as Microsoft, HP, Gateway, and Handango.

these times might be better spent by reducing your television and computer time and limiting your phone time. It is amazing to learn just how much time in our day these activities absorb.

If you decide to limit your phone conversations to 15 minutes instead of 30 minutes, in one week you will have an extra hour and forty-five minutes. And if you decide to cut out just 30 minutes of television per day, in one week you would have an extra three and half hours! See where you can limit unproductive activities and replace them with productive ones.

ACTIVITY 9

What can you do to do more in less time or use time that is otherwise wasted? Write your thoughts below.

_____

_____

_____

_____

_____

_____

Time management expert, Alan Lakein suggests, when faced with several things you want to do, ask yourself, "What's the BEST use of my time, RIGHT NOW?!"

Sometimes even the best-planned schedules must change because of unplanned events. When this happens and you must make a choice regarding what to do, ask yourself, *"What is the best use of my time, right now?"* Your honest answer will make sense based on the things that are truly important to you. Consider this scenario:

It's 12:00 p.m. and you have a one-hour break between classes. You have in mind to grab a sandwich and go to the quiet corner of the library to get some assigned reading done. You have no other time today to do it because you go to work right after school. Three friends see you and beg you to sit with them to plan one of your friend's birthday parties. What do you do?

This is a tough situation but ask yourself, "Is this the best use of my time, right now?" And if you honestly say no, then be aware that you have options. You can let them know you are interested in helping but can't right now. See if they would e-mail or call you with what they talked about so you can get caught up for the next meeting.

If you honestly responded "yes" to the question, then know that it was your conscious choice and you will have to find another time for the reading. Remember, you are *always* in charge of where you spend your time. It's up to you to make the smart decisions.

Working with a partner, discuss the following scenarios. What would you do in each of the following situations?

Situation No. 1

It's 6:30 p.m. on a Monday night. You have a test on Wednesday that you want to study for tonight between 6:30 and 7:15 p.m.
 After that, you are planning to go to a community meeting that will not be over until at least 10:00 p.m. Your friend calls you on the phone to chat—nothing very important, just a casual conversation. What do you do?

_____

_____

_____

_____

_____

_____

Situation No. 2

It's 8:00 p.m. on a Sunday night. You have an oral presentation due on Tuesday. You have already done your research, but you still need several hours to prepare for the presentation. Because of work and other family commitments, you have no other time before Tuesday to complete this assignment. Your mother needs your immediate help moving furniture in the basement and can't do it without you. What do you do?

_____

_____

_____

_____

_____

_____

Procrastination and Other Time Wasters

Procrastination means putting off doing something unpleasant or burdensome until a future time. Most of us, unfortunately, are excellent procrastinators. We put work off until the last minute and cram to get it done, hoping not to do a slipshod job. The reality is that only a few people can cram well and do a good job. The others just think they can. (See Chapter 5 for more about cramming for exams.)

With a partner or on your own, list some reasons why you put things off until a future time. Then discuss what happens as a result of this procrastinating.

_____

_____

_____

_____

_____

_____

_____

_____

_____

_____

Success tip

Did you know that just by being aware of the top reasons why people procrastinate, you might not procrastinate as much?! They are:

1. An assignment or project is too big or overwhelming.
2. The assignment is unpleasant.
3. Fear about doing the assignment, such as having to get up in front of people to make a presentation.

So now that you know, you just might procrastinate less!

Need to Know!

REDUCING PROCRASTINATION. So how can you reduce procrastination? Since procrastination means doing nothing, simply doing something is the way to overcome it. Here are some actions to consider:

1. *Start small.* If you take your big assignment and break it down into smaller pieces, you will be able to break through your procrastination. It's like trying to eat a pizza whole; you can't do it. But you can eat it one bite at a time. For example, when studying for an exam, study a little each day instead of all at once. When you have to write an essay, break the project into manageable parts by first outlining your ideas, then writing a first draft, then editing the copy, and finally completing the final draft. Each step can be done at different times, making the job much more tolerable. You have also made time for writing a quality paper instead of one you crammed together the night before it is due. Your stress will be reduced and your brain will thank you for it.

2. *Realize how miserable you'll feel until the work is done.* If you don't want that annoying feeling hanging over you, remind yourself how good it will feel to be finished with the assignment. Then get started!

3. *Tell yourself you are wasting time.* You are wasting time if you are not working on your project. If time is valuable to you, why waste it?

4. *Be accountable to someone else.* If you set a deadline with someone, you will be less likely to break it. For example, tell your friends you can't meet them until after you finish your research. Then, get to work.

5. *Add variety.* If you do not enjoy working on a certain subject, try creative learning methods such as using flash cards or studying with a friend. Or, alternate the unpleasant work with more pleasant work.

6. *Remember how good it feels when you are done.* Remember that great feeling you get when you finally complete a task that has weighed heavily on your mind.

7. *Promise yourself a reward.* When you finish doing your work, give yourself a reward.

※ *Need to Know!*

Study Goals and Rewards

Doing activities according to the top priority sometimes means that you can't do what you want at the moment. Studying may be the last thing you want to do. Perhaps you would rather watch television, IM your friends, or go shopping. But if you want to do well in your classes, you must find time to study.

How often do you feel like studying? If you wait until you feel like it, you might never open a book! So how do you motivate yourself to study when you are tired? Or when you have other commitments?

If you set a learning goal and reward yourself for reaching the goal, learning will become easier. You will also have a higher level of concentration because you are determined to complete the work on time.

A **learning goal** means completing your projects and assignments in a reasonable time frame. A **reward** is something you give yourself in return for your effort. For example, suppose you are a nursing student who has to read a chapter in the nursing handbook and then write a patient report. You also need to review your medicine interactions for a quiz the following day. In your estimation, these tasks should take you no more than an hour and a half. If you begin doing your work at 6:30 p.m., your learning goal should be to complete the work by 8:00 p.m.

At 8:00 p.m., when the work is completed, you can reward yourself with a non-work-related activity, such as watching television, having a favorite snack, or reading a favorite magazine. You can plan to go out with friends or rent a new movie. You decide what will motivate you best.

By deciding on your reward ahead of time, you will be motivated to finish your work as quickly as possible, leaving you with more time to do whatever you want. This is one of the best ways to work smarter, not harder.

The next time you sit down to study, think about setting a learning goal and then rewarding yourself upon its completion. This way you will be less tempted to interrupt your learning time, thereby getting your work done efficiently.

Different people enjoy different rewards. How would you reward yourself for reaching a learning goal? Make a list.

_____   _____

_____   _____

_____   _____

_____   _____

_____   _____

_____   _____

_____   _____

Success tip

According to R. Alec MacKenzie—a time management guru—for every minute you plan, you save two minutes in execution. For example, if you take 15 minutes at the end of each day to plan the following day, you would then save 30 minutes that next day because of the forethought and planning. How might this affect your life?

⟨← Additional Ways to Master Your Time →⟩

What follows is a list of more ways you can use to master your time. See if any of them are useful to you.

1. *Prepare for the morning the evening before.* Put out your clothes, make lunches, pack your books.

2. *Get up 15 minutes earlier in the morning.* Use the time to plan your day, review your assignments, or catch up on the news.

3. *Don't rely on your memory.* Write your assignments, appointments, and due dates on a calendar.

4. *Schedule a realistic day.* Avoid planning for every minute. Leave extra time in your day for getting to appointments and studying.

5. *Leave room in your day for the unexpected.* This will allow you to do what you need to do, regardless of what happens. If the unexpected never happens, you will have more free time.

6. *Do one thing at a time.* If you try to do two things at once, you become inefficient. Concentrate on the here and now.

7. *Let things slide from time to time.* The world will not come to an end if you do your laundry on Sunday instead of Saturday.

8. *Learn to say "No!"* Say no to social activities or invitations when you don't have the time or energy.

9. *Get enough sleep.* When you are well rested, you are more capable of handling anything that comes your way.

10. *Learn to relax.* Take deep breaths, stretch, or exercise to relieve tension and stress.

What special methods are helpful when you need to control your time? List five ways you master time.

1. _____

_____

2. _____

_____

3. _____

_____

4. _____

_____

5. _____

_____

Checkpoint

1 What is procrastination?

_____

_____

_____

2 What is a learning goal?

_____

_____

_____

3 Why is it important to reward yourself for reaching a learning goal?

_____

_____

_____

_____

CHAPTER SUMMARY

1. Every day has 24 hours, no more, no less. To spend your time productively means you must work toward a goal. To spend your time unproductively means you are engaged in an activity that is not working toward a goal.

2. Knowing what is important to you and having short-term and long-term goals will help you make wise choices about how you spend your time.

3. Students should plan at least one hour of study time per week for every hour in class.

4. There are three common calendar systems: Academic, Monthly, and Palmtop. An Academic Calendar helps you keep track of school and assignment-related dates and social events. A Monthly Calendar helps you track appointments, family activities, meetings, and birthdays. A Palmtop Calendar is best for planning the details of one day at a time.

5. A Weekly Project Planner will help you keep track of your daily responsibilities and assignments.

6. There are three things you can do to have more time in a day: plan the day, do more in less time, and use short periods of otherwise wasted time.

7. Procrastination means putting off doing something unpleasant or burdensome until a future time. Ways of overcoming procrastination include starting with small actions, adding variety to the task, and promising yourself a reward upon completing the task.

8. Setting a learning goal means planning to do a certain amount of work in a given time. When you have achieved your goal, give yourself a reward in return for your effort. Setting learning goals and planning for rewards can help you save time and make learning rewarding.

CHAPTER ASSESSMENT

Terms Review

Fill in the blanks with the appropriate key terms on the left.

academic calendar

daily activity log

learning goal

long-term goal

monthly calendar

palmtop calendar

procrastinating

productive time

reward

short-term goal

syllabus

unproductive time

weekly activity log

weekly project planner

1. A schedule of assignments is called a _syllabus_.

2. A _Palmtop Calendar_ is used by many business people to manage their time.

3. A(n) _Academic calendar_ consists of 12 monthly calendars, typically from September to August and used by those taking classes.

4. A _Long-term goal_ is something you want to have, do, or be within the next 3 to 5 years.

5. The desire to complete a project or assignment within a specific time is considered a(n) _learning goal_.

6. A _Short-term goal_ is something you want to have, do, or be within the next 6 months to a year.

7. To see how you spend a day, you can use a(n) _daily activity log_.

8. You can keep track of appointments best on a(n) _Monthly calendar_.

9. When you put off doing something burdensome or overwhelming, you are _Procrastinating_ .

10. A(n) _weekly Project Planner_ is like an assignment pad in that you track assignments and can plan your study time with it.

11. You are spending _Productive time_ in activities that lead to achieving goals.

12. A _reward_ is something you give yourself in return for your effort.

13. You are spending _unproductive time_ in activities that do *not* lead to achieving a goal.

14. To see how you spend 7 days in a row, you can use a(n) _weekly activity log_ .

Review

Based on the information you learned in this chapter, answer the following questions using your own words and thoughts.

1. Why is learning how to manage your time important?

_____

_____

_____

_____

2. Why is it important to know your goals?

_____

_____

_____

_____

3. For what purpose can a Daily Activity Log be used?

_____

_____

_____

_____

4. For what purpose can a Weekly Activity Log be used?

_____

_____

_____

_____

5. Describe the three calendar systems.

_____

_____

_____

_____

_____

_____

_____

6. Describe a Weekly Project Planner.

_____

_____

_____

7. What is procrastination, and what can you do to reduce it?

_____ pg 106 Know 7 tips _____

_____

_____

_____

8. Describe how setting learning goals and then rewarding yourself for reaching them can help make studying easier.

_____

_____

_____

_____

9. Which of the time management formats explained in this chapter do you find most useful and why?

_____

_____

10. If you studied Chapter 2, do you think sequential or random-preferenced learners naturally manage their time better? Why do you think so?

_____

_____

_____

11. As a result of working through this chapter, what are you going to do to manage your time better?

_____

_____

_____

_____

S tudying and taking tests are necessary parts of the student experience. You have been doing both for years. They are among the most important activities that students face while in school and are important for getting into college.

Increasingly, test taking is becoming common for some working people, too. Many certified professionals (such as teachers, nurses, insurance agents, financial planners, lawyers, and accountants) are required to obtain a certain number of continuing education units (**CEUs**) per year in order to keep their certifications. Some CEUs are obtained by attending classes, while others can be fulfilled by taking proficiency tests.

People must pass tests in many careers in order to advance in their professions. Firefighters and police officers take tests to be promoted. Insurance agents may take tests on policies before being allowed to sell them. Computer specialists sometimes take tests on hardware and software products so they can be certified in selling or servicing them. As long as a person's knowledge is evaluated through traditional tests, studying and test taking will remain necessary activities for anyone who wants to be successful in school or in a career.

In order to guarantee consistent testing success, a student needs to be both an effective learner *and* an effective test taker. An effective learner studies smart, not hard.

In this chapter, you will take a closer look at your own study habits and strategies. (Chapter 10 will look more specifically at test-taking strategies.) You will read about some strategies you may already practice and others you may want to start. Your goal for this chapter is to find at least *three* ways you can increase your testing success through your studying. Once you find the strategies most useful for you, you can be successful each time you prepare for a test.

> To guarantee success at test taking, a student needs to be both an effective learner *and* an effective test taker. What factors do you think make a student an effective learner?

Test taking is a necessary part of most academic programs. How well or poorly you do is a direct result of how smart *you study.*

The following self-evaluation will give you an idea of how familiar, or unfamiliar, you are with some of the topics and terms discussed in this chapter. After reading each statement, circle the letter Y, S, or N to indicate the answer that is most appropriate for you. Answer honestly. Rate yourself at the end; then complete the information on your Self-Check Progress Chart.

Y = yes; frequently   S = sometimes   N = no; never

1. Before the day of a test, I know what material will be covered.   Y (S) N

2. Before the day of a test, I know what type of test will be given (multiple choice, essay, and so on).   (Y) S N

3. I try to eat healthy foods, get enough sleep, and exercise regularly.   Y S (N)

4. I know the difference between memorizing and learning.   (Y) S N

5. I avoid cramming for tests.   Y (S) N

6. I do my most difficult and challenging work first.   (Y) S N

7. I study for a test a little each day for several days or weeks before the testing date.   Y (S) N

8. I am good at predicting test questions from my notes and reading material.   Y S (N)

9. When learning new information, I use memory devices.   Y (S) N

10. I learn from my testing mistakes and take action to prevent them in the future.   (Y) S N

Rate Yourself:

Number of Ys __4__ × 100 = __400__

Number of Ss __4__ × 50 = __200__

Number of Ns __2__ × 0 = __0__   **Total __600__**

What Is a Testing Success Factor?

A **testing success factor** is something that contributes to a successful test result. Since you want the end product of your studying efforts to be learning as well as success on a test, you need to be aware of the key testing success factors. Over the years, you have probably learned some of the testing success factors, but others may be new to you. The key is to become aware of them and continue to use the strategies that work for you and abandon those that don't.

As you work through the rest of this chapter, note how many factors are familiar to you and how many are new to you. Keep in mind that being familiar with an idea doesn't mean you use it. So look for both new ideas and familiar ideas that you would like to start incorporating into your existing study habits.

Focus on Technology

If you want to read faster, and finish your reading tests on time or early, you are going to have to practice. There is just no way around it. However, there is software available that can help you with the practice: AceReader. Not only can AceReader software help you read faster, it is an incredibly useful tool for assessing your reading level and speed, using flashcards as a memory device, and learning a language.

You can download a free trial version of the software from the Ace Reader web site. Conduct a search on the Internet or access the Ace Reader link from the *Success Skills* web site (http://sskills.swlearning.com).

ACTIVITY 1

Think about all of the tests you have taken in the past. Create a list of factors that helped you perform well. Here are a few examples: "I studied with a friend," "I got a good night's sleep," and "I studied ahead of time." Work individually at first. Then, with two or three classmates, try to identify the most important factors.

_____

_____

_____

_____

_____

_____

_____

_____

_____

_____

Being Prepared

If you think about it, every day of your life is a test. Just like an academic test, how well or how poorly your day goes depends on how well or how poorly you prepared for it. Each student needs to prepare for a test in his or her own way; however, there are several common factors that can ensure testing success.

Read the following situation. Then write your responses to the questions that follow. You may work alone or in a group.

Scott wakes up one morning, climbs into the shower, and turns on the water. He then realizes he's out of soap. He steps out of the warm shower into the chilly air, dripping water across the floor while he gets a bar of soap from the cabinet. When he finishes the shower, he realizes that he forgot to bring a towel into the bathroom. He trails water in the hallway as he rummages through the closet for a towel. After his shower, Scott looks for his lucky sweater, and then remembers it is in the laundry. Though he is disappointed, he eventually finds something else to wear and gets dressed. He decides to eat a bowl of cereal before leaving for the day, but finds he is out of milk. Then he spends 10 minutes searching for his bus pass. Finally, he gets to the bus stop—just in time to see the 8:00 bus driving away.

1. Were any of the events in this situation successful? If so, what were they?

   _____

   _____

2. Which events were not very successful?

   _____

   _____

3. What does "being successful" mean to you?

   _____

   _____

4. What are the factors necessary for Scott's success in the future?

   _____

   _____

   _____

   _____

This situation is a simple, yet powerful, example of how lack of preparation leads to inefficiency and poor results. It also illustrates how preparation can ensure efficiency and good results.

Being prepared is an important success factor for performing well, especially for taking tests. List what you think a student has to have or do in order to be prepared to take a test. Think about what has worked for you. You can add these ideas to the list of testing success factors you created in Activity 1.

_____

_____

_____

_____

_____

_____

_____

_____

_____

Do Your Assignments on Time

Why do you think completing assignments when they are due is important for effective learning? What can happen if you do not complete an assignment on time?

Most instructors base their assignments on what they will be discussing in class on a given day. So, if you read the pages you are assigned for the day they are due, you will better understand the day's lecture. If you don't complete an assignment when it is due, not only will you be at a disadvantage in the class, but also you will have twice as much work to do for the following class. Some students get so far behind that they never complete all of their assignments. What can you do to make sure you complete your assignments *on time*?

If you are a student taking classes, then you have a set schedule for reading or studying. It can be found on your syllabus. By plugging the information from the syllabus (test dates, reading assignments, papers, etc.) into your monthly calendar or weekly assignment planner, you will know what work is due when.

If you are a working person and studying independently for an exam, you typically have no predetermined schedule. Without a schedule, you may try to do all the studying close to your exam date, which is not an effective way to learn. Again, the key is to write down your assignments in your calendar or planner so you can plan ahead.

Consider setting your own deadlines. This will encourage you to break the material up into smaller pieces, helping to make the learning permanent. You will have enough time to get help in problem areas, and you will lower your stress level.

Successful students read and take some notes on their text assignments before the assignments are discussed in class. What advantage do you think this gives them?

Take Good Notes

Chapter 6 contains all the information you need about effective notetaking. If you have already studied Chapter 6, try to answer these questions based on what you learned. Otherwise, quickly browse through that information now and answer the following questions.

1. Why is taking good notes a success factor for tests?

   Prepares you for the test

   _____

2. What should your notes include for effective studying?

   _____

   _____

Know What Material to Study

This may sound simple, but all too often students do not ask what material they should study, and they find out too late that they studied the wrong information. The easiest and most accurate way to learn what will be covered on a test is to ask your instructor. (If you are studying independently, read the testing guidelines of your study material.) Even if your syllabus tells you that Chapters 6 through 10 will be covered, your instructor may decide to test you only on Chapters 6 through 9 or may decide to include Chapter 11. If this happens and you are not aware of the change, you will be studying more or less than is needed. Though studying more is better than less, neither is an effective use of your time.

Know What Kind of Test Will Be Given

Before renting a movie from a video store, don't you want to know what the movie is about? Before going to a concert, don't you want to know what kind of music you will hear? Before taking a test, wouldn't you like to know what kind of test will be given? Because knowledge can be tested many different ways, you should know how you will be responsible for the information you study. Here are some of the most common types of tests. Most can be taken on paper or on a computer screen. (For specific information about test taking on a computer, see Chapter 10.)

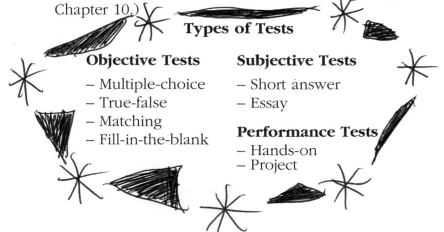

Types of Tests

Objective Tests
- Multiple-choice
- True-false
- Matching
- Fill-in-the-blank

Subjective Tests
- Short answer
- Essay

Performance Tests
- Hands-on
- Project

"Concentrate on the essentials ... you will then be accomplishing the greatest results with the effort expended."

—R. Alec MacKenzie, Time management specialist

How you study should depend on the type of test you will take. One type of test is an **objective test**. Objective tests require correct answers and include multiple-choice, matching, true-false, and fill-in-the-blank questions. A lot of tests are objective tests because they are simple for instructors to create and easier to grade; the response is either correct or incorrect.

Another type of test is the **subjective test**; it includes short-answer and essay questions. These tests are set up to demonstrate not only whether you know the correct answer, but also what your opinion is and how you communicate your ideas in writing. You will take subjective tests more often when an instructor wants to know if you can explain a concept clearly or wants to know your thoughts about a topic. Responses are strong or weak as opposed to correct or incorrect. One way to create a stronger subjective test response is to include the vocabulary of your class in your responses. This tells the instructor you truly understand the content.

The last type of test is a **performance test**. Performance tests measure how well you can execute, or perform, a certain task or activity. Certain subjects lend themselves nicely to this evaluation, especially anything to do with using one's hands, such as medical courses and trades like electricians, plumbers, carpenters, and culinary arts.

When studying for a multiple-choice, true-false, or matching test, you need to become familiar with the specific information from your class or textbook reading. Your task is to identify the correct answer, not to explain the answer yourself.

When you prepare for a fill-in-the-blank test, you need to learn and effectively recall small pieces of information as they appear in context. This means you must know small details.

For short-answer and essay tests, you need to learn and remember specific information, have a complete understanding of the material, and be able to explain the ideas clearly. A good working knowledge of the content-area vocabulary is necessary as well. These tests require the most amount of studying because they ask for the greatest amount of knowledge.

Application of knowledge, which is the point of a performance test, is the true test of understanding. In a computer class, for example, you may be asked to word process and format a business letter correctly, and then print two copies. In order to perform this activity, you must learn how to create, format, and print the letter and then practice doing these tasks. You are not asked specific questions; rather you are tested on your ability to apply the knowledge.

Frequently instructors give tests that include several types of questions, so you may need to prepare for more than one. For example, to get your driver's license, you need to take an objective test (usually multiple choice) and a performance test (actually driving the car under an instructor's supervision).

©Getty Images/ PhotoDisc

Many of the tests you take are objective tests where you just have to identify the correct answer. They are easier to study for than subjective or performance tests where you have to come up with the answers on your own.

With the information you just read about the different types of tests and how you are responsible for them, how would you prepare and study for each of the tests listed below? Be specific.

Multiple-choice _____

_____

True-false _____

_____

Matching _____

_____

Fill-in-the-blank _____

_____

_____

Short answer _____

_____

_____

Essay _____

_____

_____

_____

_____

_____

_____

Hands-on _____

_____

_____

_____

_____

_____

_____

_____

Optimize Your Health

Being prepared physically for a test is just as important as being prepared mentally. Optimizing your health means paying attention to your eating, sleeping, and exercise habits and taking good care of yourself. After all, if you are not well nourished, well rested, and in good shape, your brain isn't either.

Opinions vary about the makeup of a healthy diet. Basically, a diet low in refined sugar products (cookies, cakes, candy) and carbohydrates (white bread, pasta) and high in protein (chicken, fish, yogurt) and fruits and vegetables is a good base for most people. To keep your brain alert for studying, it is a good idea to eat protein foods and vegetables and to avoid heavy carbohydrates and sugars.

Regarding sleep requirements, research suggests that the average person needs seven to nine hours of sleep per night. Are you aware of how much sleep your body needs? A consistent deficit of sleep can cause memory loss, forgetfulness, and lack of focus. Higher incidents of car accidents have also been attributed to lack of sleep.

Regular exercise helps keep your body and your brain tuned up. Just three times a week, 30 or more minutes at a time, of walking, running, rollerblading, etc. will help you reduce stress, sleep better and learn more easily.

In addition to your eating, sleeping, and exercise habits, remember to visit your doctor regularly for check-ups and, if needed, for any persistent physical discomforts. You also might consider getting an eye exam or a hearing test. Since your eyes and ears are valuable learning tools, it is wise to keep them both tuned up.

> The way you move and breathe affects the way you think and feel. Are you getting enough movement and exercise in your life?

Checkpoint

1 What does "being prepared" mean for a student?

_____

_____

2 Name and describe the three types of tests.

_____

_____

3 Think about your eating, sleeping, and exercise habits. What might you want to do differently to optimize your health?

_____

_____

_____

Avoiding Cramming

Cramming refers to trying to memorize a lot of information in a very short period of time. Millions of students cram for their exams every term, but that doesn't make it right!

Cramming is usually the result of a time management problem. Students who always cram don't make plans for how they are going to handle all their homework assignments and reading along with their family and social life and possibly the hours involved in working a job. It always seems that the test creeps up on them unexpectedly, causing them to cram the night before. Many times, other assignments are left undone because studying for the test tomorrow now takes priority.

Cramming is a stressful and ineffective way to study. When you are stressed, you don't think as well or as clearly or retain information as easily. In addition, most facts memorized during a cramming session disappear quickly, which defeats the purpose of studying. By waiting until the night before, you are gambling that 1) you are going to feel good enough to get the studying done and 2) you have done all the assignments and have all the information you need to review and study. Gambling is dangerous, and this is not a sure bet.

If you think about it, you wouldn't (nor could you!) cram a whole pizza in your mouth at once; instead you would eat one bite at a time. So, it makes sense that you don't want to cram all the study material into your brain in one night when you could easily do it a little bit at a time, giving it time to digest.

ACTIVITY 5

Respond to the following questions, basing your answers on your personal experience. (This is assuming you have crammed for a test sometime in your school career!) You may work alone or with another person.

1. What are some reasons for cramming? _____

_____

_____

2. What typically happens when you cram? _____

_____

_____

3. Why might cramming not be an effective means for learning? _____

_____

_____

_____

Memorizing Versus Learning

When you say you are planning to study, do you distinguish between *memorizing* a list of vocabulary and *learning* a list of vocabulary? Do you know that there is a difference between memorizing and learning?

Memorizing means trying to commit information to memory by rote or mechanical repetition. Memorizing is the result of trying to remember a lot of information in a short period of time. For tests, you memorize lists, vocabulary terms, people's names, events, formulas, dates, facts, and other information. Sometimes you might try to memorize the names of new acquaintances that you meet at a party or the detailed directions to the party location.

Contrary to what you might think, memorizing is *not* learning. It is using information for a short period of time, for example, identifying correct answers on multiple-choice, true-false, or matching tests. If you try to memorize information for a fill-in-the-blank, short-answer, or essay test, you will have a difficult time responding accurately to the questions. Since these tests require you to recall information and to understand and communicate that information, they are not suited for memorization. Many students get by, but rarely do very well, memorizing for tests. Those names you tried to memorize fade quickly, unless you wrote them down. If you went back to that same place where the party was held a few weeks later, you would need a refresher on how to get there.

Memorizing is an inefficient way to learn; if you want to use information sometime in the future, you will have to study it again. Has this ever happened to you? You memorized information for a test at the beginning of the term and found at the end of the term that you had to study most of it all over again.

Learning is much more than memorizing. It is acquiring knowledge through systematic, methodical study (or in simpler terms, by frequent review). In order to learn, you must remember the information over a long period of time. The information you study becomes part of your valuable **background knowledge**, which is what you already know based on your previous experiences and learning. If the object of getting an education is to understand and learn for use in the future, then what's the point in memorizing?

To learn new information, two factors are needed: time and repetition. Figure 5-1 describes the levels of short-term memory and long-term memory. Levels 1 and 2 are a part of your short-term memory, while levels 3 and 4 are a part of your long-term memory.

Level 1

Level 1 is your shortest short-term memory. It is good for only approximately five to eight seconds. This is where you process information, such as writing a new phone number or reading an unfamiliar address on an envelope. Later in the same day, if someone asks you for the phone number or address, you are unable to recall it without looking at the piece of paper. The expression "in one ear and out the other" has been traced to this behavior.

> Memorizing is the result of trying to remember a lot of information in a short period of time. Learning is acquiring knowledge through systematic, methodical study, or frequent review. Which do you think your brain prefers?

FIGURE 5-1

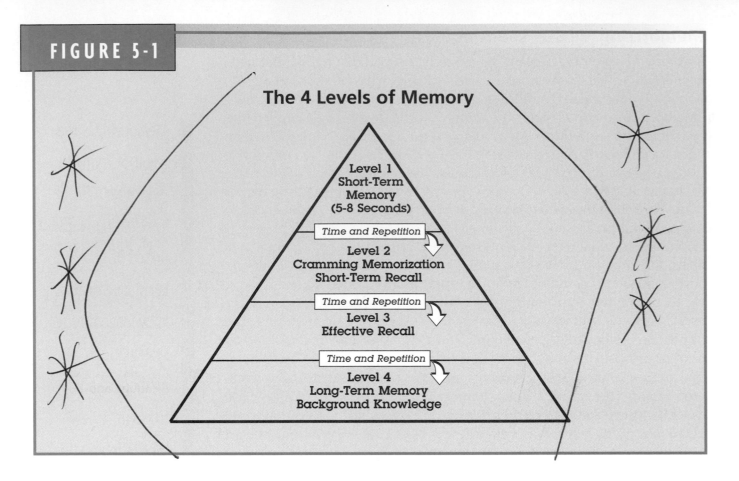

The 4 Levels of Memory

Level 1
Short-Term
Memory
(5-8 Seconds)

Time and Repetition

Level 2
Cramming Memorization
Short-Term Recall

Time and Repetition

Level 3
Effective Recall

Time and Repetition

Level 4
Long-Term Memory
Background Knowledge

> Frequent review over a period of time helps you learn, not just memorize. Are you a memorizer or a learner?

Level 2

Level 2 is your cramming, or memorization, level. This is where you try to cram a great deal of information into your head by mechanical repetition for slightly longer retention. (Refer to the section on cramming in this chapter.)

Since time and repetition are the two key factors in going from short-term to long-term memory, this repetition is an active process, but not the most effective way of achieving long-term memory. When learning anything new, you will pass through all the levels, including this one. The idea, however, is to keep going, not stop here.

Level 3

Level 3 is your **effective recall level**. This is where you can recall, or remember, studied information in a variety of ways. Effective recall demands that you have a solid understanding of the information and that you can apply it in the area you are studying. At this level, you can identify the information and talk or write intelligently on the subject.

To be able to recall information effectively, 1) you need to be *active* in your learning (see Chapter 1) and 2) review *frequently*.

For example, while in class, if you listen and hear what the instructor says, take good notes, and ask and answer questions, you will begin to understand the information. If while reading, you read actively and take notes, you will begin to understand the material instead of just memorizing it. Reviewing any material you have read will reinforce what you already know. In summary, if you are active in your learning and review your information frequently, you will easily cross the time-and-repetition boundary from short-term memory to long-term memory.

Level 4

Level 4 is your long-term memory where learning is permanently stored. This is also called your **background knowledge**. To get from effective recall to this learned level, you must continue to learn actively and to review frequently. Cramming is out of the question!

So what does this look like in real life? If you are reading about a place in Africa, then you could re-read the information several times and then test yourself on any new vocabulary. But you can make it more interesting by creating related repetitions like searching out websites that might have photos or talking with a friend who has been to Africa. Maybe you can take out a documentary film on Africa from your local library archives to give your mind another kind of memory. The more repetition of information you provide your brain over a period of time, the longer it will stay in your memory.

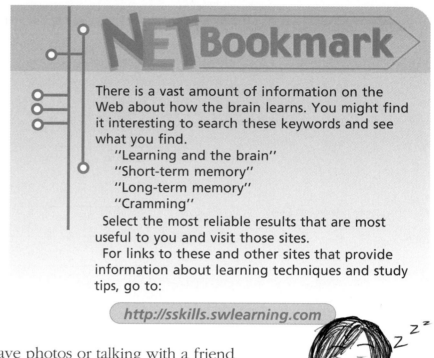

There is a vast amount of information on the Web about how the brain learns. You might find it interesting to search these keywords and see what you find.
"Learning and the brain"
"Short-term memory"
"Long-term memory"
"Cramming"
Select the most reliable results that are most useful to you and visit those sites.
For links to these and other sites that provide information about learning techniques and study tips, go to:

http://sskills.swlearning.com

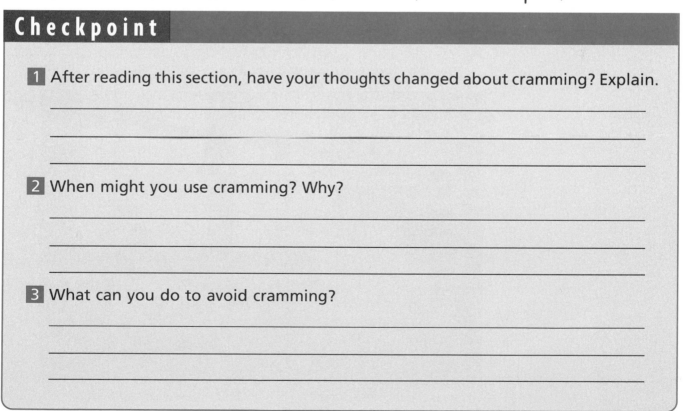

Checkpoint

1 After reading this section, have your thoughts changed about cramming? Explain.

_____

_____

_____

2 When might you use cramming? Why?

_____

_____

_____

3 What can you do to avoid cramming?

_____

_____

_____

Learning Actively

You have already learned, and hopefully begun to use, some active learning strategies. Read through the following strategies, looking for more ways to "learn by doing."

Create an Effective Learning Environment

Do you remember Chapter 3? The entire chapter was devoted to creating an effective learning environment. Without looking back, complete the following statements:

1. An effective learning environment includes

   _____

   _____

   _____

   _____

   _____

2. An effective learning environment is important because

   _____

   _____

3. I can create an effective learning environment by

   _____

   _____

   _____

If you have difficulty completing these statements, review Chapter 3.

Your brain likes to study where it learns. Consider studying in an empty classroom, preferably the one in which you will be taking the test!

Find a Study Buddy

When you are learning, either in a classroom situation or on your own, it is common to doubt yourself: "Did I write what I needed?" "What is meant by that?" "Am I studying the right things for this test?" By working with another person on the same material, you can gauge your level of understanding, compare notes and ideas, and possibly teach the other person something as you learn from that person, too.

It's best to find a study buddy whom you like and whose work habits are similar to yours. Begin working together early in the learning process. If you wait until test time, you might find the person is not as helpful as you originally thought, which wastes your preparation time.

Though socializing is a benefit of working with others, it can also be a hindrance to getting serious work done. Together with your study buddy, come up with a few working guidelines.

- Reserve the first 10–15 minutes of each work session for socializing; then begin to work seriously.

- If you really enjoy socializing with your study buddy, make separate plans to do something social like meet at a coffee shop to talk or go out to eat. This way, you are more ready to work than socialize during planned study times.

- Decide how often to take breaks and how long they will be. Be firm with your decided time frames.

- If the workload is to be split, agree to responsibilities and deadlines.

Without guidelines, you might socialize more than study!

The acronym TEAM stands for Together Everyone Achieves More. By working effectively with others, everyone can win.

Have a Study Order

Active learning is easier when you have a step-by-step approach for learning. The order is determined by importance and difficulty first, then by your level of fatigue.

Though the guidelines for study order given below are somewhat flexible, use your common sense in applying them to your personal study style.

1. *Work on Hardest Material First.* If you save the hardest studying for last, you may become tired and stressed. You're looking forward to being finished, and studying will become more difficult.

2. *Do Reading Before Writing.* Reading takes more mental concentration than writing, so it is wise to read early in your day or work session. If the assignment is long, break the material into small sections, and read some in between other work.

3. *Study First and Last.* Since repetition and time are the keys to long-term memory, studying before you get into new material and again after you finish new material will help you learn better and faster. Doing so also breaks up a big chunk of information into smaller pieces.

> "*A single conversation across a table with a wise man is worth a month's study of books.*"
> —**Chinese proverb'**

Suggest an effective study order for the assignments below. Pretend that math is your hardest subject. Then, state your reasons for picking the order you did. Notice that five blanks are provided in the Order of Study column, and only four assignments are shown in the Assignment column. One of the assignments needs to be repeated.

Assignment

A. Write a one-page essay on ways to build background knowledge.

B. Read Chapter 12 in *Psychology.*

C. Study for electrical design test in three days.

D. Do ten math problems on pages 54–57.

Order of Study

1. _____

2. _____

3. _____

4. _____

5. _____

Reasons for the order I chose:

_____

_____

_____

_____

_____

_____

Plan Your Study Time and Breaks

All of the information you have learned in this chapter will be wasted if you don't plan enough study time before a test. Chapter 4 presented a great deal of information on managing and planning your time. Now is a good time to review that information if you do not remember how to manage your time or if you have not begun using a time planner.

Planning study breaks helps you to learn. Research shows that you remember the first and last pieces of information you study better than the information in the middle. For this reason, you should take frequent breaks in between multiple short study sessions. A short study session could be 15 minutes or half an hour. Choosing 15-minute study sessions doesn't mean you only study 15 minutes every hour. It means you have three to four sessions per hour with a few minutes' break between each session.

If you choose 30-minute sessions, you should study for 30 minutes, take a break of about 5 minutes, and begin another 30-minute study session. The only time you should not stop for a break is when you are totally involved and concentrating on what you are doing. Here, taking a break would negatively affect your learning.

Since short study sessions are recommended, using the free time you may have found between daily activities or classes will allow you to get some of your work done earlier in the day. The later you plan your study sessions, the harder it is to concentrate and learn because you are naturally more tired at the end of a day than at the beginning.

When you have finished your studying for the day, reward yourself. It could be a call to a friend, a hot bath, an ice cream cone, or a little extra sleep. After all, you have just worked hard and deserve to be rewarded!

ACTIVITY 7

One problem you may encounter when taking short breaks is that they can become much longer than you had expected. It is very easy to become distracted and sidetracked.

1. Brainstorm to generate a list of things you can do in a two-minute break, a five-minute break, and a ten-minute break. Use your imagination.

Two-Minute Break: _____

_____

_____

Five-Minute Break: _____

_____

_____

Ten-Minute Break: _____

_____

_____

2. What are some things that you should avoid doing because they will distract you for *longer* than ten minutes?

_____

_____

_____

_____

_____

_____

_____

_____

Remember to Use Memory Devices

Tests measure your working memory and knowledge base. To help yourself remember, you can use several **memory devices**, techniques to help you recall the information you need to study.

TRY A POSITIVE ATTITUDE. In order to remember anything, you first have to want to remember! While remembering everything may not be realistic, as a learner who takes tests, you need to remember a great deal of information. By approaching your learning in a positive way, you will find studying easier.

TRY RECITATION USING YOUR OWN WORDS. You will learn more when you reinforce your learning in as many ways as possible. You can reinforce your learning through hearing, writing, reading, reviewing, and reciting.

By the time you study for a test, you may have already heard the instructor present the information, written your notes, read the assignments, and reviewed your notes. The last reinforcement is recitation, or repeating aloud from memory the information you are studying.

Many people try to memorize exactly what an instructor or a dictionary says without giving any thought to what it means. A better use of your learning time is to first understand what you are studying, put the concepts into your own words, and then recite them.

Read the following textbook glossary definition of the marketing term *elastic demand.*

Focus on Ethics

You have a part-time job at the school you are attending. Part of the job calls for you to make photocopies. One day you are given a stack of papers to copy. As you go through the papers, you notice that they include the midterm exam for a class your best friend is taking right now. You know he is struggling in this class and really needs help if he is going to pass.

Would it be ethical for you to keep a photocopy of the exam for your friend? Would it be ethical for you to read the exam as you copy it and try to memorize the information on it? Why or why not? Would your answers change if *you* were the one taking the class?

Glossary Definition

Elastic demand—Demand for a product that increases or decreases dramatically when the price changes.

The definition itself is not easy to understand, let alone remember. Using your imagination and your own words, you can come up with an easier-to-remember definition of elastic demand.

Your Own Words

Elastic demand—Changing demand due to price changes.

The words *elastic* and *demand* may also hold some other meanings for you, helping to anchor the information in your mind. Now that the information is in your own words, ask yourself a question: "What is elastic demand?" Without looking at your notes, repeat the definition aloud from memory. If you have trouble remembering it, review again until the answer comes easily for you or until you find an even easier way to remember the definition!

Put the following information in your own words. The first two are defined terms; the last two are informational paragraphs.

1. Fluorescent lights: Tubelike bulbs that are used for general illumination purposes. The major advantage is moderate price.

_____

_____

2. Bank cards: Third-party credit cards, such as VISA™ and MasterCard™. Individual banks issue cards to consumers who, when they use the credit cards for purchases, owe the amount charged to the bank.

_____

_____

_____

3. Electronic retailing: Has arrived in many forms, affects all retailers. Electronic retailing provides consumers with the convenience of at-home shopping through web sites and TV shopping channels, which are constantly updating their merchandise. Consumers can examine product information and make purchases from their homes.

_____

_____

_____

_____

_____

4. What is marketing? Marketing means identifying the need for goods or services, developing products or services to meet the needs, communicating the benefits to people or organizations needing the goods or services, and distributing the goods or services to the proper markets. The American Marketing Association provides us with a more formal definition. Marketing is the process of planning and executing the conception, pricing, promotion, and distribution of ideas, goods, and services to create exchanges that satisfy personal and organizational objectives. To a businessperson, marketing means having the right product at the right place at the right time at the right price and at a profit.

_____

_____

_____

_____

_____

_____

Try Acronyms

Acronyms are words or names formed from the first letters or groups of letters in a phrase. Acronyms help you remember because they organize information according to the way you need or want to learn it. When you study for a test, be creative and make up your own acronyms. Read the list of acronyms shown in Figure 5-2 on the next page. Some may be familiar to you; others may not.

Try Mnemonic Sentences, Rhymes, or Jingles

Mnemonic sentences are similar to acronyms. They help you organize your ideas, but instead of creating a word, you make up a sentence. Creating a rhyme or song jingle can make the information even easier to remember. The more creative, even sillier, the sentence, the easier it is to remember. Take, for example, the nine planets listed in order according to their distance from the sun:

M̲ercury V̲enus E̲arth M̲ars J̲upiter S̲aturn U̲ranus N̲eptune P̲luto
The first letters of these words are: M V E M J S U N P.

The acronym would be difficult to remember but if you create a sentence using the letters in order, you will remember the sequence more easily. For example:

M̲y V̲ery E̲ducated M̲other J̲ust S̲erved U̲s N̲ine P̲izzas

When learning to read music, you use a popular mnemonic sentence that represents the lines of the music staff: EGBDF (from the bottom).

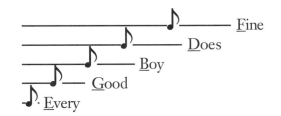

Try Linking Ideas

Your memory will work better if you associate, or link, related ideas. Also, remembering information in a meaningful order is easier than remembering information in a random order. Isn't ABCDEFG easier to remember than FBAGDEC?

For instance, in science class you might need to learn the parts of a flower. The parts of a flower are:

stigma, anther, pistil, sepal, stamen, petal

You could rearrange the parts in alphabetical order for easier remembering:

anther, petal, pistil, sepal, stamen, stigma

You could create an acronym:

appsss

FIGURE 5-2

Sample Acronyms

Word or Term	Acronym
RAdio Detecting And Ranging	RADAR
TeleVision	TV
Portable Document Format	PDF
Motion Picture Experts Group	MPEG
Motion Picture Experts Group Audio Layer 3	MP3
Digital Versatile Disc	DVD
Internet Pod	iPod
The colors of the rainbow:	
Red, Orange, Yellow, Green, Blue, Indigo, Violet	ROY G. BIV
American Telephone & Telegraph	AT&T
Collect On Delivery	COD
Light Amplification by Simulated Emission of Radiation	LASER
Accounting term refers to warehouse inventory:	
Last In, First Out	LIFO
First In, First Out	FIFO
Financial documents being signed by two people:	
Joint Tenancy With Rights Of Survivorship	JTWROS

You could create a mnemonic sentence with order of the acronym:

A purple pansy shared sunflower's sunshine.

You could create a mnemonic sentence in its original order:

Susan and Pam sent Sam presents.

Try Visualization

Visualization refers to creating or recalling mental pictures related to what you are learning. Have you ever tried to remember something while taking a test and visualized the page the information was on? This is your visual memory at work.

Using the parts of the flower example, you can draw your own picture of the flower and work on remembering the picture and its parts. When you take a test, your visual memory will help you to recall the information.

Success tip

Approximately 90 percent of your memory is stored visually in pictures, so trying to visualize what you want to remember is a powerful study tool.

Now it's your turn to be creative. Below is a list of miscellaneous facts and information. Using the memory devices discussed in this chapter, how would you go about remembering the information? You can work individually or in a group.

1. The Great Lakes (listed in no special order):
   Ontario, Michigan, Huron, Erie, Superior
   HOMES
   _____

   _____

2. The six parts of soil:
   air, humus, mineral salts, water, bacteria, rock particles

   _____

   _____

   _____

3. Three ways to reduce rabies:

   a. Immunize more dogs and cats

   b. Enforce leash laws

   c. Educate the public about the dangers of rabies

   _____

   _____

   _____

4. Ways to improve listening:

   a. Listen for the speaker's main ideas   c. Watch for nonverbal signals

   b. Listen for specific details   d. Take notes

   _____

   _____

   _____

5. Where retail consumers make purchases:

   a. Department stores   d. Web sites   g. Supermarkets

   b. TV shopping channels   e. Superstores   h. Warehouse clubs

   c. Specialty stores   f. Discount department stores   i. Catalog sales

   _____

   _____

   _____

Anticipate Test Questions

As a student who learns by doing, you will get better at discovering what your instructors think is important. Paying close attention to their personalities, verbal signals, and what they write on the board or PowerPoints will give you clues. (See Chapter 6 for ways to identify more clues.) If you can become a champion of what your instructors are most interested in and can impress them with your knowledge of the subject, then you will have prepared well. Learning to predict test questions based on the highlighting and marginal comments in your notes from classes and reading assignments will enhance testing success. (Refer to Chapters 6 and 7 for more information about predicting test questions.)

ACTIVITY 10

Look at your notes from a recent class. Using your experience as a student with this instructor, come up with three possible test questions. (Make sure you have the answers.)

1. _____
   _____

2. _____
   _____

3. _____
   _____

Checkpoint

1 Which memory device(s) do you like and want to use more often? Why?

_____
_____

2 Why is it important to plan your study time and breaks?

_____
_____

3 How can you predict test questions from your notes?

_____
_____

"The greatest accomplishment is not in never falling, but in rising again after you fall."

—Vince Lombardi, Former professional football coach and Hall of Famer

Learning from Your Mistakes

In Chapter 1, you were introduced to the value of making mistakes. They are an expected and natural part of the learning process. Understanding how many tests you take throughout your school years shows you that one or two poor results need to be taken in perspective. There are many tests to do better on in your future. Let's look at approximately how many tests a college student takes in order to earn a two-year degree, and adapt the information to your own situation. Sixteen courses must be completed for a two-year degree. For each course, a minimum of two tests per class (a mid-term and a final) are usually given. This equals a minimum of 32 tests in two years.

16 courses × 2 tests per course = 32 tests

For a four-year degree, expect twice as many tests, or 64.

If you a take a test each week or at the end of every chapter or section you study, you obviously have even more tests.

Since test taking is so important to your overall success in earning a degree, how can you ensure greater success on each one?

Review Returned Tests

Some instructors do not return tests, but others do. If you don't get your test back, ask your instructor for an appointment to review it. If the test is returned, examine it carefully. Look first at where you did well and think about what you did to achieve that success. Then look at the areas where you need to improve and commit yourself to doing better the next time. Did you read the directions carefully? Did you study the important handouts? Were your notes helpful in studying? Did you read all of the assignments you were tested on? Whatever you did, or did not do, find a way to improve the next time you take a test.

Figure Out What Worked... and What Didn't

Once you figure out what worked and what didn't on each test, then you can more intelligently decide on the improvements you need to make. Know that it is still a trial-and-error process in getting it right more times than not. You will try different strategies—some of which may work, and others may not. By even improving in just one area—like reading all the right assignments or reading directions more carefully—you will see positive results. If at first you don't succeed, use a different approach and try again. It's worth the effort!

Be Honest with Yourself

Say you spent three hours at the library studying for a test. In that three-hour time frame, a friend dropped by to chat, and you took a 30-minute snack break. You also decided that while you were at the library you would check out the music collection. Of the three hours you were at the library, how much of it was quality study time—a little less than two hours at most? Being honest with yourself means saying you spent two hours studying, not three. An hour of quality study time can make a difference in your results.

One way to discover areas to improve upon is to use the Success Factors Checklist on page 140. For every test, use this checklist as a reminder of what you must do to produce a successful testing result and as a means of tracking your study activities.

Ask for Help

You are not meant to know it all. If you did, you wouldn't be in school in the first place! Being successful as a student sometimes means getting help from others.

When you are having trouble with the subject matter, ask your instructor or another qualified person for help. In order to get help from your instructors, be advised that they will have little patience with you if you wait until the day before or even the day of the test. Requests for help should be arranged long before the day of the test.

Fellow classmates are a good resource for help, especially if they can be relied upon as effective study partners. You can establish a review group that gets together several times before a test to swap notes and to test each other on the content. One of the best ways of reinforcing learning is to teach it to others. Use your fellow classmates as a sounding board for this powerful learning experience.

If you would like help with your writing skills or extra help with a certain class, look into your school's learning skills center, counseling center, tutoring center, or related campus location. Help may also be found online. By doing an effective search, you might find handouts or even a virtual tutor who can help you.

> Successful students recognize they need help and actively seek it out. Have you ever needed help with one of your subjects? If so, were you willing to ask for that help? Whom did you go to, and what did that help do for you?

Checkpoint

1 Describe the four ways you can learn from your mistakes.

_____

_____

_____

2 To whom or where do you go when you need help?

_____

_____

_____

3 Which success factors are you strongest and weakest in?

_____

_____

_____

Success Factors Checklist

For every test, use the following checklist as a reminder of what you must do to produce a successful testing result. The checklist can also be used as a means of tracking your study activities. If you find areas you have not checked or would like to improve for your next test, place an asterisk (*) next to the items, and make your own plan of improvement.

Course Name_____ Date of Test_____

Being Prepared

I prepared for this test by:

- ❏ doing my assignments on time.
- ❏ taking good notes.
- ❏ knowing what material to study. (List what you need to study.)

_____

- ❏ knowing what kind of test it will be. (Write it below.)

_____

- ❏ optimizing my health.
- ❏ other ways: _____

Avoiding Cramming

I avoided cramming for my test by:

- ❏ reviewing a little each day before a test.
- ❏ other ways: _____

Learning Actively

I actively learned the information for this test by:

- ❏ creating an effective learning environment.
- ❏ finding a study buddy.
- ❏ having an effective study order.
- ❏ planning my study time and breaks.
- ❏ remembering to use memory devices.
- ❏ other ways: _____

Anticipating Test Questions

I anticipated test questions by:

- ❏ paying attention to my instructor's personality and verbal clues (if applicable).
- ❏ using effective highlighting and margin notes from my reading assignments.
- ❏ other ways: _____

Learning from Mistakes

I learn from mistakes by:

- ❏ reviewing returned tests.
- ❏ figuring out what worked and what didn't.
- ❏ being honest with myself.
- ❏ asking for help.
- ❏ other ways: _____

CHAPTER SUMMARY

1. The five success factors for studying for any test are being prepared, avoiding cramming, learning actively, anticipating test questions, and learning from mistakes.

2. Being prepared is one of the most important qualities of a test taker. Being prepared means doing assignments on time, taking good notes, knowing what material to study, knowing what kind of test will be given, and optimizing your health.

3. Memorizing is *not* learning. Memorizing is trying to commit information to memory by mindless repetition. Learning means acquiring knowledge through systematic, methodical study.

4. Being an active learner makes studying easier and ensures better results. This includes creating an effective learning environment, finding a study buddy, having a study order, planning study time and breaks, and remembering to use memory devices.

5. In order to remember, you can try six memory devices: wanting to remember, reciting using your own words, using acronyms, using mnemonic sentences, linking ideas, and visualizing.

6. Making mistakes is the best way to learn, provided you learn from your mistakes.

CHAPTER ASSESSMENT

Terms Review

Fill in the blanks with the appropriate key terms on the left.

acronyms

background knowledge

CEUs

cramming

effective recall

learning

memorizing

memory devices

mnemonic sentence

objective tests

performance tests

subjective tests

testing success factor

1. A sentence formed from the first letter of the information you want to remember is a _mnemonic s_.

2. Examples of _objective_ include multiple-choice, true-false, and fill-in-the-blank questions.

3. _CEUs_ are required by many professions.

4. _cramming_ refers to trying to memorize a lot of information in a short period of time.

5. Effective recall and long-term memory are _Learning_ levels of memory.

6. Short-term memory and short-term recall are _____ levels of memory.

7. _____ is where learning is permanently stored.

8. Words or names formed from the first letter of groups of letters in a phrase are called _acronyms_.

9. When you can remember studied information in a variety of ways, this is called _effective recall_.

10. _Subjective_ include short answer and essay questions.

11. A _testing suc_ is something you have control over that results in a positive testing result.

12. _perform_ measure how well you can execute a certain task or activity.

13. Maintaining a positive attitude and reciting information in your own words are examples of _mem devices_.

Review

Based on the information you learned in this chapter, answer the following questions using your own words and thoughts.

1. What do you think "studying smart" means?

_____

_____

_____

_____

_____

_____

2. Being prepared for a test means many things. What does it mean for you? (Think about the classes that you are taking now or plan to take in the future.)

_____

_____

_____

_____

_____

3. What is the difference between memorizing and learning?

_____

_____

_____

_____

_____

4. How can you learn instead of memorize?

_____

_____

_____

_____

_____

5. Learning actively means many things. What does it mean for you?

_____

_____

_____

_____

6. a. Of the memory devices discussed in this chapter, which ones were you already familiar with?

_____

_____

_____

_____

b. Which memory devices are you going to try during your next study session?

_____

_____

_____

_____

c. Which memory devices don't you like and why?

_____

_____

_____

_____

7. Learning from your mistakes is the best way to learn. Write about a mistake you made as a student and what you did or should have done to learn from it.

_____

_____

_____

_____

_____

8. Of the three types of tests discussed in this chapter, which are easier for you? More difficult? Why?

_____

_____

_____

_____

9. If you were taking a self-study course where you were responsible for all your learning, which success factors would work best? Which wouldn't apply?

_____

_____

_____

_____

10. Now that you have learned about the testing success factors, review the list you created in Activity 1 and compare it to what you now know. What are the most important things you learned?

_____

_____

_____

_____

_____

CASE STUDIES

for Creative and Critical Thinking

 ACADEMIC CASE—Connecting to Studying with Peers

Jennifer asked Leah to meet with her in the study room of their residence hall the night before their sociology exam to review and exchange notes. Leah reluctantly agreed and waited patiently as Jennifer was running late. Jennifer had missed the last four lectures, which included two videos and a guest speaker. She had arranged this meeting to catch up on the subject material with Leah, who was one of the best students in the class.

"Thanks so much for meeting me tonight," Jennifer said as she sat down. "I've really fallen behind." Leah smiled and took out her notebook. "Can I copy your notes from this week's lectures?" Jennifer asked. "Okay," Leah replied as she handed over her notes. Jennifer took them to the copy machine where she spent the next fifteen minutes copying notes. While she was away, Leah looked through some of the practice questions she had composed throughout the week from her class notes and reading assignments. Their professor had recommended using this strategy in preparing for his exams.

When Jennifer returned, Leah suggested that they swap practice questions. "I haven't had time to do that," Jennifer explained, "but can I copy yours?" Leah sighed and handed them over, thinking that she was unlikely to get much out of this study session.

1. Will Jennifer do well on tomorrow's exam? Why or why not?

_____

_____

_____

_____

2. What success factors did Leah implement in preparing for her exam?

_____

_____

_____

_____

3. What can Jennifer do to become a better test taker?

_____

_____

_____

_____

4. Should Leah have given the notes so willingly to Jennifer? Why or why not?

_____

_____

_____

_____

Steve applied to work at the local swimming pool as a summer lifeguard. To become certified, he had to attend classes over several weeks, pass a written test, and demonstrate his ability to perform certain rescue maneuvers in the water. Steve wanted to be prepared for any emergency, so he studied the safety material seriously. He read through his assignments before each class, asked the instructors questions, wrote their responses, and reviewed the comments he received from the instructors on the weekly quizzes. Despite his hard work, the night before the written test, Steve was nervous about doing well.

1. Steve used some effective study techniques. What were they?

_____

_____

_____

_____

_____

_____

2. Are there any other strategies you think Steve might benefit from doing?

_____

_____

_____

_____

_____

_____

3. What would you recommend Steve do the night before the written test? What would help him be prepared to do his best on the test?

_____

_____

_____

_____

_____

4. Seeing as Steve is pretty well prepared for this test, there is always a possibility he might not do as well as he thinks. If this happens, what do you think might have contributed to his performance?

_____

_____

_____

_____

_____

6 Taking Notes in Class

Terms

- body (of summary paper)
- cause
- chronological order
- classification
- compare
- contrast
- effect
- Mind Mapping
- recall column
- summary paper

Chapter Goals

After studying and working with the information in this chapter, you should be able to:

- Identify THE reason for taking notes.
- Summarize effective note-taking habits.
- Identify and list the personality and verbal clues that instructors give.
- Explain how to take notes and learn, using the Cornell Method of Note Taking and with Mind Mapping®.

Like many students, Jessica works during the day and takes classes in the evening. Her long-term goal is to become a social worker or psychologist, so she signs up to take Psychology 101 at her local community college.

The class meets one evening a week for three hours in a lecture hall that holds 100 students. Jessica brings one pen and several pieces of notebook paper in a folder labeled "Psych 101" to the first class. She also brings a digital recorder because her cousin suggested she listen to the lecture after class to make sure she understood all the information. She sits down in one of the back rows of the hall, sets up the recorder, and gets ready to listen.

The professor starts by reviewing the syllabus and distributing handouts about the night's lecture. The notes are organized well in outline form and seem to include most of what is being discussed. Jessica decides to just sit back and listen. She has had a long, tiring day at work and is almost too tired to concentrate. She is glad she has brought the recorder so she does not have to take notes. She figures she already has most of the notes on the handout, and the digital recorder will capture the rest.

When Jessica returns home, she loads the recording onto her MP3 player, so she can listen to it during her commute to work the next day. On the morning train ride to work, she presses start, but to her dismay, she can hardly hear the professor! The recording is very mumbled and unclear. Unfortunately, she doesn't have any notes of her own to refer back to.

Even if Jessica is able to get a better recording from someone else in the class, what do you see happening to Jessica's learning if she continues to use this system?

How many times have you written a list of things to do? Or a shopping list for the grocery store? Or a telephone message for someone? Believe it or not, these common activities are note-taking activities. Writing notes on paper is a simple and effective means of remembering important information.

Taking *good* notes is extremely important to your success as a learner and a worker. For students, the content of classroom lectures often becomes the content of exams. For all learners, taking notes from reading material is an important strategy for building knowledge. (See Chapter 7 for information about taking notes from reading material.) Workers need to take notes about meetings, projects, and other work activities.

Taking good notes is like making a photo of what happens on a particular day. Without notes, you lose the picture of the class or meeting, and studying becomes more difficult. With notes, you have something visual and concrete to refer to whenever necessary.

Throughout this chapter, remember that no two learners take notes in exactly the same way. Your notes—however you choose to take them—must be useful and complete enough for *you* to learn easily. The key is to adapt the information provided in this chapter to your own style of learning and note taking.

What methods do you use to capture the key concepts from instructors or meeting leaders?

©Digital Vision

Good note takers are more successful learners than poor note takers and non-note takers. Which are you?

Self-Check ✔

The following self-evaluation will give you an idea of how familiar, or unfamiliar, you are with some of the topics and terms discussed in this chapter. After reading each statement, circle the letter Y, S, or N to indicate the answer that is most appropriate for you. Answer honestly. Rate yourself at the end; then complete the information on your Self-Check Progress Chart.

Y = yes; frequently   S = sometimes   N = no; never

1. I come prepared to meetings and classes with the tools for note taking.   Y   S   N

2. I can pick out the important information from a lecture or meeting to take notes on.   Y   S   N

3. I take notes from others using key words, not full sentences.   Y   S   N

4. I abbreviate often when I take notes.   Y   S   N

5. I frequently use my own words when taking notes.   Y   S   N

6. At work and at home, I am good at taking detailed messages.   Y   S   N

7. I know at least four effective note-taking habits.   Y   S   N

8. I am aware of personality clues of speakers.   Y   S   N

9. I am aware of verbal clues of speakers.   Y   S   N

10. My class or meeting notes are easy to study and learn from.   Y   S   N

Rate Yourself:

Number of Ys _____ × 100 = _____

Number of Ss _____ × 50 = _____

Number of Ns _____ × 0 = _____   **Total_____**

Why Take Notes?

Taking notes in your classes or meetings is a proven way to organize and remember what is discussed. Your notes will also provide you with good information to study from for tests. Taking notes—either by hand or on the computer—is like taking a snapshot photo of the session. Your visual memory is triggered by looking at the notes, which helps you remember the information. You might even remember what was going on in your life on that day. That is how strong your visual memory is!

Think about it. If you aren't focused on taking notes in your class or meeting, where does your focus drift to more often than not? It will probably go right out the window. *THE most important reason to take notes in any situation is to improve your concentration.* Any lack of concentration is a learning handicap that can be improved by actively taking notes. If you are a student in a classroom or a business professional in a presentation or a meeting room, the more you concentrate, the more successful you will be at understanding, remembering, and using the information you hear.

Increased concentration and better learning can be a result of using a variety of methods to reinforce the information you are trying to learn. Your learning circumstances dictate which of the following strategies will be most helpful for reinforcing your learning. Whether you are taking notes from a speaker, from written material, for a test, or for a meeting, you will decide on the proper strategies. The more strategies you use, the better your chances of success!

1. Hear the information.
2. Write it down.
3. See it either on paper or in your "mind's eye."
4. Draw a picture of it.
5. Outline it.
6. Summarize it.
7. Discuss it with others.
8. Review it.
9. Teach it.

During a lecture or discussion, writing down your version of what you see, hear, or read will keep your brain focused on the task at hand and reduce the tendency to think non-related thoughts.

Later, having notes *to review and study* from will save you review time, help you learn more, and improve your test scores. Notes will also help you *organize the information and establish main ideas.* They will help you *retain the information longer* and will serve as a visual reminder of what was said. They will also *aid in discussions* and possibly *remind you of something unusual* or specific that happened on a certain day.

You might think of taking notes as a handwriting activity, which for many students it is. But more and more, students and professionals are using their computers and other technologies for taking notes. Use whatever method works for you—or a combination of both methods.

Throughout the rest of this chapter, note taking refers to good, useful note-taking strategies. The first step is to be prepared to take notes.

Success tip

William Glasser, an educational reformist, suggests that **we remember:**

- **10%** of what we **read.**
- **20%** of what we **hear.**
- **30%** of what we **see.**
- **50%** of what we **see and hear.**
- **70%** of what we **discuss** with others.
- **80%** of what we personally **experience.**
- **95%** of what we **teach** each other.

So, it would make smart sense to reinforce your learning by reviewing with others, finding ways to get personally involved, and/or practicing teaching the information to others—even a stuffed animal will suffice!

Think about the times you took notes in a class or meeting and the times you didn't. Discuss the pros and cons of each strategy with a partner or small group. Write your thoughts in the columns below.

PROS	CONS
Better recollection, Know the topic, something to study from, remember what was said in class, shows you're engaged or paying attention	Forget key material when studing, looks like you're not engaged in class

Imagine you are in a class or a meeting without a pen or notepaper. All you are able to do is listen. Will you concentrate on what is being said, or will your mind wander? Why do you think that is so? Now imagine you have a pen and notepaper in front of you and are taking notes. Why might you concentrate more this way?

_____

_____

_____

_____

Checkpoint

1 Without looking back, list at least five ways you can reinforce your learning.

_____

_____

_____

2 What is THE most important reason for taking notes?

_____

_____

3 What are some other reasons for taking notes?

_____

_____

_____

Preparing to Take Good Notes

You have been taking notes for years in your own way. Your way may be very effective, or it may be comfortable but ineffective. As you read the next sections, try to identify your note-taking habits. More importantly, look for new ways to make your note taking more effective.

The Tools for Note Taking

In order to do a good job at anything, you need to have the right tools for the job. Before you can take good notes, you need to be prepared with the appropriate note-taking tools.

THREE-RING BINDER. A useful tool for note taking in class is a three-ring binder notebook. In contrast to a spiral notebook, the three-ring binder:

- Allows you to remove or insert additional pages or handouts while maintaining the order of your notes.

- Allows you to lend some pages of your notes to another student without lending the whole notebook.

- Provides protection with its plastic cover, especially during wet weather.

- May be used more than once.

- Helps keep your notes organized.

8½″ × 11″ LINED PAPER WITH THREE-HOLE PUNCH. Smaller paper may be okay for taking notes in business meetings, but generally, you need larger paper to hold more information. If you buy the paper already three-hole punched, you can just slip your notes into the notebook. Otherwise, you can buy a three-hole puncher and do it yourself. The puncher also comes in handy for making three holes in any handouts and articles you want to put in your notebook.

■ Focus on Ethics

You have a job with an advertising agency and you've been asked to do some research on consumer buying habits to help the agency prepare a proposal to attract a new client. In the course of your research you come across a number of relevant articles and statistics. Most of the information supports the position that consumers like a certain product, but there is some data that would seem to suggest they do not.

Rather than seeming like you might be backing down from your position, you decide that the few articles that go against your consumer theory are not worth mentioning, so you prepare your report citing only the information that supports your position. What could happen if you did this?

SUMMARY PAPER. **Summary paper** is used for the Cornell Method of Note Taking discussed on page 160. It is not the same as regular notebook paper. Instead of having a 1-inch margin on the left, summary paper has a 3-inch left margin. Figure 6-1 is an illustration of summary paper. You can make this paper yourself by taking lined notebook paper and using a pen to mark off a 3-inch margin.

You can also purchase summary paper through most school bookstores or special order it from office supply stores. (Summary paper is also called 3-inch Law Margin Rule.)

FIGURE 6-1

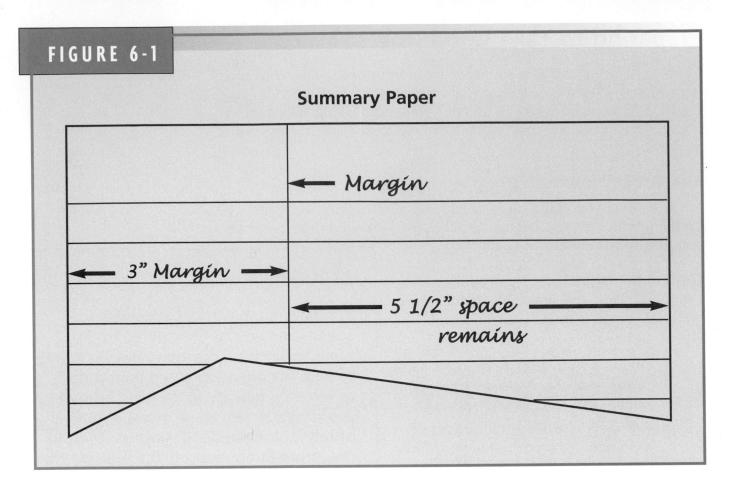

Summary Paper

> **"The beautiful thing about learning is that no one can take it away from you."**
>
> —B.B. King, American blues guitarist/ songwriter

PLAIN WHITE PAPER. For the Mind Mapping note-taking method discussed on page 165, you will use unlined white paper, preferably three-hole punched.

ERASABLE PEN OR DARK PENCIL. For correcting mistakes and making changes or additions, you will want to use an erasable pen or dark pencil. These provide flexibility to your note taking.

AN AUDIO RECORDER. When used appropriately, an audio recorder—such as a tape deck, MP3 player, or digital recorder—can support your note-taking efforts, but *not* replace them. If you use an audio recorder in a class or meeting and *don't* take notes, you will be forced to listen to the entire session afterward to review the information. If the recording is of poor quality (which is often the case because the speaker moves away from the recorder), or the batteries run out, or your recorder is full and can't record more, you won't have anything to review. Recording a lecture also causes you to listen passively instead of actively.

If you want to use a recorder effectively, take good notes, pretending the recorder isn't there. To save time, use the recording as a review while driving in your car or exercising. Always ask the speaker's permission before recording.

Before moving on to the next section of this chapter, create a few pieces of summary paper (3-inch left margin rule). Have an erasable pen or pencil handy.

Effective Note-Taking Habits

There are many effective note-taking habits that are easy to use. Some are specific for classroom learning while others are for self-learning or business use. As you read each description, decide which strategies might work best for your situation:

- **Pre-view related readings before a class or meeting.** If, according to your syllabus or your instructor's comments, you know that Chapter 4 will be discussed in your next computer class, it makes sense to familiarize yourself with the material by taking a few minutes to pre-view or skim over the chapter (see Chapter 8) *before* class. If your boss says the focus of an upcoming meeting is the new procedures manual, then looking it over ahead of time will give you some background knowledge that will help you take good notes as well as actively participate in the discussion. You will also understand the information better.

- **Start each day with a fresh piece of paper.** Every page of your notes is like a photo of what happens on a given day. By starting each day with a fresh piece of paper, you will keep your "photos" separate and leave room to add information.

- **Write on only one side of the paper.** Writing on just the right side of an open notebook gives you open space on the left side to add drawings, formulas, or other related notes from readings. It is better than using the backside of the paper as it avoids flipping back and forth.

- **Always date and title every page.** If you write the date and title of the topics being covered at the top of each page, you will have an easy reference to turn to later. If you take more than one page of notes, be sure to number the pages in order on the top right-hand side as pg. 1, pg. 2, pg. 3, etc.

- **Write in the shortest form possible.** When taking notes from an instructor or in a meeting, you do not have a lot of time to write everything that is said, nor should you. Since the brain doesn't love words (it prefers pictures), it is a waste of time to try to write in full sentences. Instead, use abbreviations and the most important key words. Think short, sweet, and to the point.

- **Use abbreviations.** Using abbreviations, or shortened words or phrases, makes note taking easier. They are easy to use, and you create them. Only you have to understand them.

- **Use key words.** Key words are the larger, more important words in a sentence. They are typically three letters in length or longer and carry the most meaning of a sentence. By writing key words, you save time, concentrate on the main ideas and end up with fewer words. A good example of writing in key words is a newspaper headline. There are only a few key words that give the essence of the article. Try writing some yourself.

Success tip

Some simple ways to create your own abbreviations in your notes are to shorten the words, use symbols, or omit the vowels. For example, if you are learning about different forms of communication, and the word *communication* is repeated frequently, you can shorten the word to "comm."

Likewise, if you are discussing a topic related to money or finances, you can use the symbol "$" in your notes. If you are discussing management issues, you can omit the vowels and use, "mngmnt," or an even shorter term, "mgmt."

"*Learning is what most adults will do for a living in the 21st century.*"

—S.J. Perelman, American humorist and essayist

■ **Use your own words.** When you take notes, it isn't necessary to write word-for-word what a person says. If you are instructed to write something exactly as it is stated, do so; but if you are writing notes on your own, learn to use your own words. *Writing your own words forces you to understand what is said before you write.*

©Getty Images/PhotoDisc

A variety of effective note-taking strategies can be used to enhance your concentration and learning.

Checkpoint

1 Name some tools for note taking.

_____

_____

2 How is summary paper different from other notepaper?

_____

_____

3 Without looking back, list as many effective note-taking habits as you can remember.

_____

_____

_____

Taking Notes from Instructors

Though this section focuses on taking notes from instructors, you can learn a great deal about how to take notes from anyone in any situation, such as meetings or phone conversations. One of the biggest problems listeners have is daydreaming. Consider this: A person talks at a rate of approximately 150 words per minute and thinks at a rate of at least 350 words per minute. As a result, there are 200 words per minute that are not being processed in the brain. So, to reduce this daydreaming, the speaker needs to keep the listener's attention with more than words, or the listener needs to focus and take notes. If you watch *and* listen carefully to speakers, their actions and words will help you quickly identify the important information.

As a classroom student, taking good notes from an instructor can only improve your chances of doing well; however, many students face the problem of not knowing what information is worth writing in note form. Some try to write everything. This is not practical—or even possible.

Being an effective note taker means being an active and skilled observer and listener. Finding and writing the appropriate information is easy, once you learn how to watch and listen effectively. There is no right or wrong information, only too much or too little.

Six Instructor Personality Clues

Everything an instructor says is important. Your job is to figure out what is *most* important since you can't write everything. Review this list of common personality clues to help you decide what is best to write down. These are also known as "action clues."

1. **They tell you it's important.** Instructors may say, "This will be on the test," or "You need to know this." Write it down! Unfortunately, they don't always make it this obvious.

2. **They repeat information.** If you listen carefully, you may hear your instructors repeat information. This is their way of telling you that the information is important enough to write down. An instructor will use repetition when discussing a new vocabulary term, an important name or date, or a difficult concept.

3. **They write the information on the board or flipchart.** Do you think you will take good notes by only including what an instructor writes on the board? Many students believe these are the only notes they need. Typically, though, what instructors write is information that supports their lectures. It does not usually represent *all* of the important information. As a result, learn to use the notes on the board as supplemental information. Use any PowerPoint presentation as a guideline for what you need to focus on.

4. **They change their voice and facial expressions.** Because your instructors are human, their voices and facial expressions

change when they describe something exciting or of interest to them. Think about your instructors and what they do when they are enthusiastic about a subject. Do their voices get louder or softer? Do they speak faster or slower? Do their faces and eyes "light up"? Do their eyes stare with more intensity than usual? Do their faces become flushed with color? Some instructors actually get so excited about their topic that they perspire and breathe heavily!

If any of these changes occur, pay close attention to what the instructor is saying and take notes. If your instructor is excited about something or finds an idea interesting, chances are you will see it again, most likely on a test.

 5. **They pause.** When an instructor stops speaking for a few moments, it is to give you time to write what he or she just said. Pay attention so you can use this pause in the lecture to capture the material in your notes. If you are not listening or you're daydreaming, then the quiet in the room will capture your attention. Other students will be furiously writing, while you will be wondering what you just missed. If this happens, use the active learning technique of asking your instructor to repeat what he or she just said.

6. **They use handouts.** Many instructors provide handouts related to the topic being discussed in class. These handouts are important, so you should make a note to review them while you are studying. A simple note will suffice: "Review handout of mgmt. styles—9/16 class," for example.

ACTIVITY 2

In one of your next classes or meetings, try to identify the speaker's action clues. What does the speaker do to tell you something is important? Write your thoughts in the space below.

_____

_____

_____

_____

_____

_____

_____

Six Instructor Verbal Clues

Not only is *how* instructors say things important but also *what* they say. These verbal clues literally "clue" you in to what you might need to take notes on. What follows are descriptions of common verbal clues that tell you the information is important and to take notes. You will probably encounter this same information on a test. How an instructor or other speaker delivers information and what he or she says provide you with clues.

"*The more we learn, the more unique we become.*"

—Renata Caine, Professor of Education

DEFINITIONS. When an instructor teaches a new topic, chances are that terms go with the topic. For example, let's say the topic is automation. Automation is defined by your instructor as "mechanical tools that do a job with less human effort." Your instructor gives you an example of a computer.

Your notes could look similar to this:

> ***Automation = mechanical tools that do job w/less human effort (e.g., a computer)***

The pattern is *new word, definition, example* or *concept.*

DESCRIPTION. Continuing with the automation topic, the instructor might describe in more detail what is meant by automation:

> "Automation makes work more efficient. When an assistant makes a mistake on a typewritten letter, the whole letter had to be retyped. With word-processing software on a computer, the assistant only has to make necessary changes on the screen and reprint the document. This saves time and increases the amount of work that can be done in a day."

Your notes could resemble these:

> ***computer > efficient than typewriter, saves time & amt. of work in day.***

The pattern is *description of the term* and *list of its qualities.*

COMPARE AND CONTRAST. Comparing is used to look at things that are similar; **contrasting** is used to look at things that are different. Continuing with the technology example, suppose your instructor says:

> "There are obvious similarities between a typewriter and a computer. They both have keys that produce typed information, they both are found in offices, and they both are used by office workers. But this is where the similarities end. Computers produce information much faster than typewriters. Their 'brains,' called memory, are programmed to do many more functions than a typewriter and to save the information for future use."

Your notes should reflect these similarities and differences because they are fair game for a test. You could expect this instructor to ask,

Good notes include:

- Definitions

- Descriptions

- Comparisons and Contrasts

- Chronological Order

- Classification

- Cause and Effect

Which are easiest for you to identify? Which are more challenging?

"What are some similarities and differences between a typewriter and a computer?" or "Compare and contrast the typewriter and the computer." You could write your notes many ways, but they should answer the question, "How are the two items alike, and how are they different?" One good example is as follows:

Typewriter vs. Computer Similarities
- _keys produce typed info_
- _found in offices_
- _used by office workers_

Differences
- _Comp's faster_
- _Comp's have a memory for programming_
- _Comp's save info for future_

These notes are written in an informal outline that is explained in more detail in the next section of this chapter.

CHRONOLOGICAL ORDER. Chronological order is the same as time order or step-by-step order. In class discussion on automation, the instructor may tell you the date the typewriter was invented and then continue giving dates that coincide with the development of automation and computers. Your notes should accurately document the dates and what happened.

> _1867 = 1st manual typewriter_
>
> _1956 = 1st electronic typewriter_
>
> _1964 = 1st word-processing computer_

Your instructor could tell you step-by-step how to turn on a computer. Your notes should include all the steps of the process.

> **_How to turn on a computer:_**
>
> _Step No. 1—Turn on hard drive. Wait 5 seconds_
>
> _Step No. 2—Turn on monitor_
>
> _Step No. 3—Turn on printer_

Some courses lend themselves perfectly to chronological order notes, such as history (dates and timelines), science (step-by-step experiments), and literature (timelines of events in stories). Can you think of any others?

CLASSIFICATION. Classification means what class, group, or category a subject falls into. For example, a college student in the first year of study is in the freshman class. Computers belong in the category of automation. Almost every concept you learn belongs to a class, group, or category of information. Your notes should answer the question "To which class, group, or category does this information belong?"

CAUSE AND EFFECT. When something happens (the **cause**) a result occurs (the **effect**). If you don't turn the lights off when you leave a room (the cause), your electric bill will increase (the effect). If you don't put gas in your car (the cause), eventually it will stop running (the effect). If you try to mix water with oil (the cause), they will separate (the effect).

ACTIVITY 3

In your next few classes or meetings, listen carefully for all types of verbal clues. Write them down. Use the space below to classify the clues according to those described in the previous section.

_____

_____

_____

_____

Predicting Test Questions

If you listen attentively, observe the instructor's behavior, and take notes based on the instructor's actions and verbal clues, you have useful information for an upcoming test. By paying attention to what the instructor thinks is important, you will be able to predict test questions and know which areas to focus on during your review time. In the next section, you will learn how to use summary paper for predicting test questions and studying for tests.

Checkpoint

1 What are the six action clues to observe when taking notes from an instructor?

_____

_____

_____

2 What are the six verbal clues to identify?

_____

_____

3 How can you become good at predicting test questions?

_____

_____

How to Take Notes

Up to this point, you have not been instructed in any specific note-taking method. Rather, you have learned what good note takers do. Now you will be given more information on the choices you have when taking your notes. Remember that you are to use and adapt the information to your own style of learning and note taking.

Before writing down anything, it is helpful to know if the speaker's lecture style is sequential or random. If the speaker is sequential, he or she may follow an outline, which means that taking organized and logical notes will be fairly easy. If the speaker is random, keeping organized, logical notes will be more of a challenge. (For more information on identifying teaching styles, refer to Chapter 2.)

Sequential learners and random learners need to be able to take good notes from both styles of speakers. Two recommended methods are described below. The first method, the Cornell Method of Note Taking, will probably be favored by a sequential learner, while the second method, Mind Mapping, will probably be favored by the random learner. Both types of learners can benefit from knowing both methods and using the one best suited to the style of the speaker.

The Cornell Method of Note Taking

The Cornell Method is a unique note-taking format that has proven to be highly effective for college students for over 50 years. Many businesspeople also use this method for taking notes in meetings and for general business use.

The Cornell Method was developed by Walter Pauk, a professor at Cornell University in the early 1950s. He noted that many students were not performing well on their exams, even though they were attending classes and completing their assignments. He was concerned about an entire freshman class who were admitted to the University using the same high standards as always but had significantly higher failure rates. Professor Pauk found that students were lacking good notes to study from because they did not use an effective method for taking notes. Even though they were doing everything else right, their exam performance was weakened by their lack of note-taking skills. He developed a system to assist note takers with organizing their information.

Look at Figure 6-2. Notice the labels that have been added to indicate the parts of the summary paper: "**body**" on the right side of the margin and "**recall column**" on the left. Each of these two columns is used in a specific way.

THE BODY. The body, or the right-hand side of the margin, is where you write the bulk of your notes. These notes are best written in an informal outline that organizes your thoughts on the page. Outlines are easy to study and quickly let you know which ideas are more important than others. An informal outline is shown in Figure 6-3.

FIGURE 6-2

Labeling the Parts of the Summary Paper

RECALL COLUMN	BODY	pg. 1
	Note taking in class 2/2/06	

FIGURE 6-3

An Informal Outline

Informal Outline	= Organizes thoughts
They look like	Themes, Topics, or Main Idea
	-supporting idea or info.
	-detail
	-example
OR numbered →	Theme, Topic, or Main Idea
	1. Supporting idea or info.
	a. detail
	example
	b. detail
	example
	2. Supporting idea or info.
	a. detail
	example

Learning to take notes in informal outlines becomes easier with practice. Notice that:

- The most important ideas are closest to the margin.

- The supporting ideas and details are indented and farther away.

- Indenting *too* much will cause you to run out of space.

- You can indicate new details by using numbers and letters or symbols, such as dashes, bullets, or asterisks.

- Keeping similar items lined up makes your notes easy to read. (If all of your notes were lined up next to the margin, you would have difficulty deciding which ideas were more important than others.)

- Skipping lines between main ideas gives you the flexibility to add to or change your notes.

- Writing legibly, though not required for writing outlines, will help you when reviewing your notes.

THE RECALL COLUMN. The recall column is the most important part of the Cornell Method. This left-hand column is used for information you want to recall, or remember, and is based on the notes you took on the right side. Information in the recall column can be a simple word (a vocabulary word), a name, or a date. The information can also be a mathematical formula or the number of details you want to remember. *One of the best uses of the recall column is to make up questions about your notes from the right side of the page to help you predict what may be on a test.* When you finish studying from Cornell notes, you should be able to look at the recall column and accurately describe what you need to know from the right side, or body, of the notes.

Look at the notes in Figure 6-4. Imagine you are the student who took these notes and you have an upcoming test on them. Look specifically at the recall column and the notes in the body directly across from it. These notes demonstrate four examples of how the recall column can be used.

1. **Vocabulary Terms.** The first example begins with the word "Lectures." This is a vocabulary term to know for your test, so it is set apart in the recall column.

2. **Question Format.** A question, created to reflect the information in the body of your notes, is a good tool for knowing what to study for a test. Based on the notes you took, it would be fair for the instructor to ask on a test, "What are five things you can do in class to take good notes?" If you can answer this question while you are studying, then you will be able to answer it on a test.

3. **Restatement.** Restating means rephrasing what is in the body of your notes, such as "three reasons for taking good notes."

FIGURE 6-4

Notes Using the Recall Column

	NOTE TAKING IN CLASS 2/2/06
(vocabulary term)	
Lectures	=ideas & concepts presented by an instructor
	—will forget unless written
(Question format)	
What are the 5	What to do:
things to do in	1) Concentrate on lecture
class? ✳	2) Develop good note-taking system
✳	—informal outline
✳	3) Pick out important pts.
	—list 4 key terms
	4) Learn to write in short forms
	5) Review notes ASAP to fill in & refresh memory.
(Restatement)	
3 Reasons for	<u>Reasons for taking good notes</u>
taking good notes	—help U pay attention
	—help U remember
	—help U organize ideas
(Title)	Ways to Prevent Mind Wandering
Prevent Mind	—Choose seat <u>in front</u> of room.
Wandering	—Avoid friends
(5)	—Keep thoughts on what tchr. saying
	—be an active listener
	—take notes

If you can remember all three reasons while you study, then answering them on a test will be easy.

4. **Creating a Title.** You base a title on the notes in the body and write it in the recall column. The circled number "5" under this title indicates that you have five things to remember about preventing mind wandering, according to your instructor's lecture.

The recall column is usually filled in *after class,* preferably the day of the class or, at the latest, the day after. This is so you don't forget what happened in class. It is quite challenging to fill in the recall column while you are in class because taking notes in the body requires most of your time and concentration.

You can, however, learn to use the recall column for information such as a name, date, event, or topic. If you are taking notes on anything that needs to be defined, you can immediately place the word on the left side and define it on the right. You can put topics that are being described on the left and their descriptions on the right. You can write topics that are being compared and contrasted on the left and identify how they are alike or different on the right. You can write a math formula on the left and the actual calculation on the right. And, instead of writing topics and other main ideas in the body of your notes, you can use the recall column (so you don't have to take time later).

Before completing your recall column, add missing information and cross out the unimportant information in the body of your notes. Then look at your notes and decide what word, question, restatement, or title you need to put in your recall column that will help you summarize what is important on the page.

Using the recall column makes studying easy. It is an active way of reviewing your notes and making studying more effective. Practice this by covering up the body of your notes with a blank piece of paper. Begin testing yourself based on the information you wrote in the recall column. You can recite the information aloud or write it on the blank paper to compare to your actual notes. Another way to ensure that you understand the notes is to place a blank paper over your recall column and test yourself on the information written in the body. Think of the recall column as a flash card, giving you an active way to review your notes. The goal is to recall all of the information accurately. Keep working at this skill until you master the information.

Using the recall column means you should never have to rewrite your notes again. Rewriting is usually a passive process that just takes a lot of time. Many students who re-write their notes admit that they do it in front of the television, which is not too effective for learning. Even if your notes are messy, you can neaten them by using the recall column to organize and clarify.

■ Focus on Technology

If you think it is difficult to create and then remember abbreviations when taking notes, consider using abbreviations many students are already familiar with: three-letter acronyms (TLAs).

If you IM, e-mail, visit chat rooms, or blogs, chances are you have seen and/or used some of the following acronyms (they aren't ALL TLAs, some might even be FLAs!):

BRB	be right back	FYI	for your information
BTW	by the way	DV8	deviate
LOL	laugh out loud	ATM	at the moment
AKA	also known as	MTF	more to follow
GIGO	garbage in, garbage out	TBD	to be determined
TMI	too much information	IMO	in my opinion
XLNT	excellent	NE1	anyone
PPL	people	SOL	sooner or later

It just might be worth using these abbreviations that you already know (background knowledge) to help you with what you are trying to learn. What other abbreviations do you use?

Locate some notes you recently took in a class, in a meeting, or from reading material. Tape them on top of the body section (right side) of a piece of summary paper. You should now have a blank 3-inch margin on the left and your notes out to the right. Fill in the recall column as best you can using the ideas presented above and your own creativity. Remember, you don't want to rewrite your notes; only include as much as you need to "recall" the information. What other information might you put in a recall column?

_____

_____

_____

_____

_____

_____

_____

_____

_____

Mind Mapping

Mind Mapping is a creative way to take notes that organizes ideas through visual patterns and pictures. For some people, worrying about an outline while taking notes interferes with their ability to focus on the information from the speaker. Mind Mapping allows flexibility for jotting down the information you need.

When you first look at a Mind Map, the information doesn't seem to be organized at all. Looking closer, you will see that it is very organized with a natural association of ideas in clusters or groups. Each cluster of ideas creates a visual picture, which helps you remember the ideas better.

To create a Mind Map, start in the center of a piece of *unlined* paper with the main idea or topic, and branch the supporting ideas and details in various directions, as shown in Figure 6-5.

If you are a sequential learner in a random instructor's class, Mind Mapping will help you get the instructor's ideas down on paper without worrying about the proper order. Because there is little order in the random instructor's lecture anyway, it is best not to try to put order into the lecture during class. Try jotting your thoughts down in Mind Map form, and then make an outline from the mapped notes as a later review. Using summary paper makes it easy to add the outline.

FIGURE 6-5

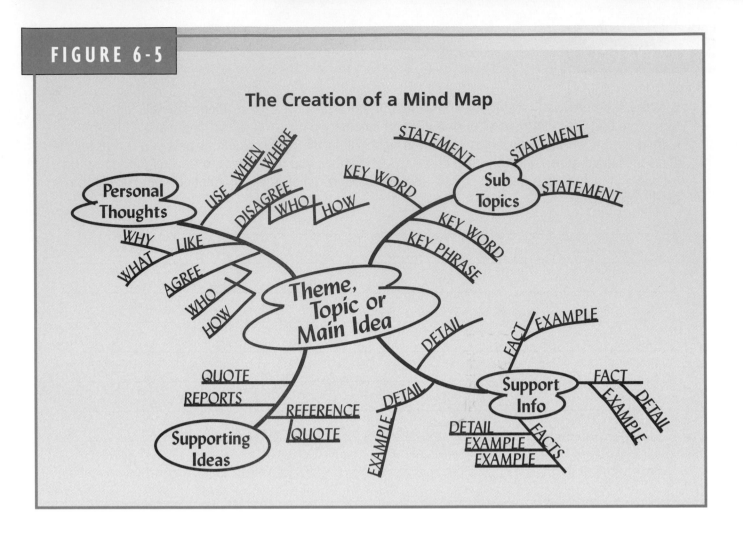

The Creation of a Mind Map

The extra step of restructuring your notes into a more sequential order is a good review, essential for learning success. By taking notes in Mind Map form, you will also be better able to see the "big picture," the connections, and the relationships—all tested later by the random instructor.

If you are a sequential learner, the very idea of taking notes in this way might make you feel uncomfortable. Remember the concept of flexing to other learning styles (Chapter 2)? This will be a good challenge to see if you can truly flex to the more random style. If you can do this, you will better understand, and have patience with, those who are more random learners.

If you are a random learner in a sequential instructor's class, Mind Mapping will ensure that you get all the details and facts into your notes during a lecture. When you, as a random learner, review your notes, you can add more details to the map, highlight the main ideas, and number items in terms of importance. You can outline the information if you wish.

Look at Figures 6-6 and 6-7. These particular Mind Maps contain all the key ideas that were discussed in Chapter 2 about identifying teaching styles. Figure 6-6 is a sequential approach to Mind Mapping, while Figure 6-7 is a more random approach. Though the styles look different, they are both Mind Maps.

FIGURE 6-6

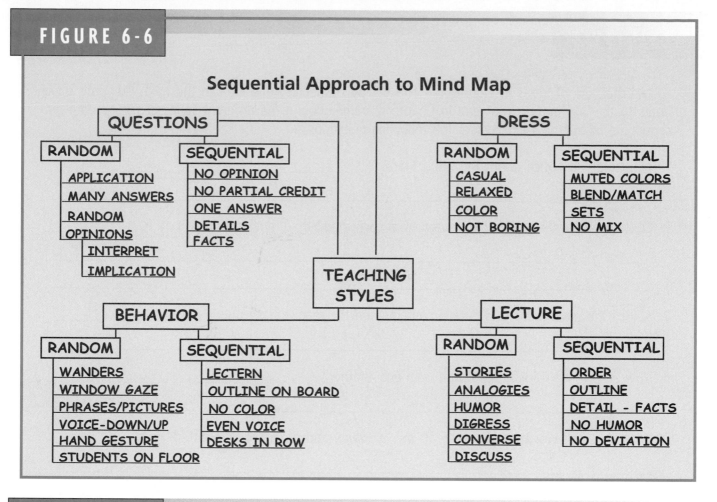

Sequential Approach to Mind Map

TEACHING STYLES

QUESTIONS

RANDOM	SEQUENTIAL
APPLICATION	NO OPINION
MANY ANSWERS	NO PARTIAL CREDIT
RANDOM	ONE ANSWER
OPINIONS	DETAILS
INTERPRET	FACTS
IMPLICATION	

DRESS

RANDOM	SEQUENTIAL
CASUAL	MUTED COLORS
RELAXED	BLEND/MATCH
COLOR	SETS
NOT BORING	NO MIX

BEHAVIOR

RANDOM	SEQUENTIAL
WANDERS	LECTERN
WINDOW GAZE	OUTLINE ON BOARD
PHRASES/PICTURES	NO COLOR
VOICE-DOWN/UP	EVEN VOICE
HAND GESTURE	DESKS IN ROW
STUDENTS ON FLOOR	

LECTURE

RANDOM	SEQUENTIAL
STORIES	ORDER
ANALOGIES	OUTLINE
HUMOR	DETAIL - FACTS
DIGRESS	NO HUMOR
CONVERSE	NO DEVIATION
DISCUSS	

FIGURE 6-7

Random Approach to Mind Map

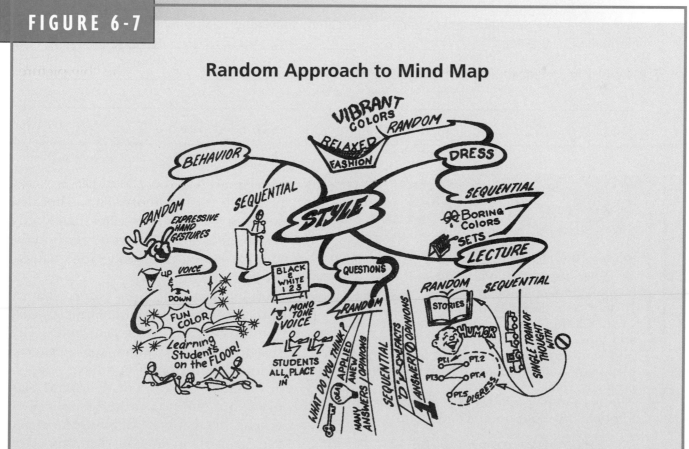

Follow the flow of ideas in Figures 6-6 and 6-7 by connecting one idea to the next. Compare these notes to the information you read in Chapter 2, remembering the different styles of the random and sequential instructor. Then answer the following questions.

1. What did you notice about the Mind Map? _____

    _____

2. Could an informal outline be created from each map? If so, how would you do it? _____

    _____

    _____

3. Are all the main ideas and details contained on the map? _____

    _____

4. How are the main ideas separated from one another? _____

    _____

5. Why are small words (such as *of, at, the, a, when*) and other words omitted? _____

    _____

    _____

6. Why is it easy to determine relationships, connections, similarities, and differences about the information in the map? _____

7. Why is it important to leave white space around the map? _____

    _____

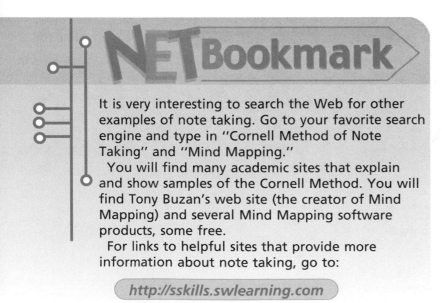

NET Bookmark

It is very interesting to search the Web for other examples of note taking. Go to your favorite search engine and type in "Cornell Method of Note Taking" and "Mind Mapping."
   You will find many academic sites that explain and show samples of the Cornell Method. You will find Tony Buzan's web site (the creator of Mind Mapping) and several Mind Mapping software products, some free.
   For links to helpful sites that provide more information about note taking, go to:

http://sskills.swlearning.com

In Figure 6-7, the added pictures will also help your memory. This is because we remember pictures better than words. If you enjoy doodling, you may find the Mind Map method an outlet for what you do naturally.

Adding different print sizes, shapes, and colors to your Mind Map is an easy and fun way to review your notes. This personalization will improve later recall of the information. If you have notes in an outline, you can create a Mind Map from your outline as a study tool. When you finish creating your Mind Maps, you can hang them in your learning area, as you would a picture. The more you look at something, the more you learn.

By choosing and working effectively with a note-taking method that fits your learning style, you will possess a valuable tool for your learning success. Using the other methods will also help you succeed with instructors whose styles are different from yours. The most important thing to remember about note taking is to use whatever method works best for you.

Checkpoint

1 Describe the Cornell Method of Note Taking.

_____

_____

2 Describe Mind Mapping.

_____

_____

3 Which method of note taking would a sequential learner prefer? Which method of note taking would a random learner prefer? Why?

_____

_____

©Getty Images/PhotoDisc

To gather and organize many ideas, you can use Mind Mapping to gather ideas and the Cornell Method to organize them!

CHAPTER SUMMARY

1. Of the many reasons to take notes, the most important is to improve your concentration.

2. Getting prepared to take notes includes having the appropriate tools for the job. Without the proper tools, the job cannot be done well.

3. Effective note-taking habits lead to good notes. This includes using abbreviations, key words, and your own words.

4. Watching a speaker for action clues and listening for verbal clues will provide information about what is important enough to take notes on and what may be on a test.

5. The Cornell Method of Note Taking is an effective method for taking sequential notes. Learning to use the recall column helps in organizing your thoughts and gives you a tool to study from.

6. Mind Mapping is an effective method for taking random notes. It is a creative way to organize ideas through visual patterns and pictures.

CHAPTER ASSESSMENT

Terms Review

Fill in the blanks with the appropriate key terms on the left. You can use a term more than once.

body (of summary paper)

cause

chronological order

classification

compare

contrast

effect

Mind Mapping

recall column

summary paper

1. When taking notes in a science class, you will most likely be writing down a _cause_, or what happened, and its _effect_, or the end result.

2. When discussing characters in literature, you will look at how they _compare_, or are similar, and how they, _contrast_ or are different.

3. When taking notes using the Cornell Method, the place you put the bulk of your notes is called the _body_, and it is located on the right side of the page.

4. The 3" margin on _summary paper_ is where the _recall column_ is.

5. You can use the _recall column_ to test yourself using your notes in the body.

6. If you are in a random instructor's class, it is best to use _mind Mapping_ to follow the instructor's ideas.

7. In a history class, the instructor will discuss events in a timeline, or _Chronological order_.

8. When taking notes, it is smart to think about the _classification_ of the information, or what class, group or category the information belongs in.

Review

Based on the information you learned in this chapter, answer the following questions using your own words and thoughts.

1. In your view, what are the most important reasons for you to take notes in your classes?

   _____

   _____

   _____

   _____

2. What tools do you need to take good Cornell notes? Mind Maps?

   _____

   _____

   _____

   _____

3. What are some effective note-taking habits? Write as many as you can remember.

   _____

   _____

   _____

   _____

   _____

4. What are some personality clues that your instructors use in class? What do you think they mean?

   _____

   _____

   _____

   _____

   _____

   _____

5. What are some verbal clues that your instructors use? What do you think they mean?

   _____

   _____

   _____

   _____

   _____

6. Of the two note-taking methods recommended in this chapter, is there one that you think will work better for you? Why or why not?

   _____

   _____

   _____

   _____

7. If you are a sequential learner in a random instructor's class, what would you suggest in order to take good notes?

_____

_____

_____

_____

8. If you are a random learner in a sequential instructor's class, what would you suggest in order to take good notes?

_____

_____

_____

_____

9. In a business meeting, which note-taking method might you use? Why?

_____

_____

_____

_____

10. From everything you read about and learned in this chapter, what pieces of information are the most valuable to you and why?

_____

_____

_____

_____

_____

11. In a small group, look at other students' notebooks and the notes they take. Compare them to yours and discuss the following:

a. What do you like about their notes?

b. What do you dislike about their notes?

c. Are they useful for studying for a test?

d. What do you suggest that would make the notes more useful?

e. On the lines below, write your observations and report on what your group discussed.

_____

_____

_____

_____

_____

CASE STUDIES
for Creative and Critical Thinking

ACADEMIC CASE—Connecting to a Lecture-Based Course

Dylan sat down in the lecture hall for the first sociology lecture of the winter semester. Dr. Clark presented important class information in the semi-darkened room using PowerPoint, as the graduate assistants distributed the lecture outlines for the course. Dylan thumbed through the outlines thinking, "This is great. I don't have to take any notes, and if I miss a class, I'll be all set." He put his notebook and pen away and followed the outlined notes as Dr. Clark began her lecture. A short film was presented about the people of Africa, which Dylan enjoyed but didn't write anything about. About midway through the class, Dylan started daydreaming about basketball practice as his eyes wandered toward the windows to watch the beautiful falling snow. He regained his concentration just in time to hear Dr. Clark say, "...and that will be the subject of an essay question on the first exam." Students then began packing up their things as the class had come to an end. Dylan walked out of the lecture hall feeling that it had been a good class.

1. Though Dylan thought it was a good class, what do you foresee happening to Dylan as the term progresses?

_____

_____

_____

_____

_____

2. Why do you think Dylan lost his concentration during the lecture?

_____

_____

_____

_____

_____

3. Do you think it is wise for Dylan to use the lecture outlines instead of attending a class? Why?

_____

_____

_____

_____

_____

4. What advice would you give to Dylan concerning note taking?

_____

_____

_____

_____

_____

Bob and Rochelle went to their local library to hear a well-known speaker whose topic was highly interesting to both of them, "Careers in the 21st Century." Both had just graduated high school and were looking for the perfect job. Each planned to take notes; Bob had a notebook, and Rochelle brought a 3" x 5" assignment pad. During the event, Bob wrote many of notes and when it was over, was enthusiastic, mentioning several key points the speaker had made. In contrast, Rochelle felt she had learned little from the lecture. She had only written down a few things and didn't have much of value to take away. "How did you understand so much of what she said?" Rochelle asked Bob with frustration. "I paid attention to the speaker's clues and followed her outline," replied Bob. "It seemed pretty obvious to me."

1. What specific clues from the speaker do you think Bob watched and listened for to identify important information?

   _____

   _____

   _____

   _____

   _____

2. Later, Bob told Rochelle that he used a recall column during the lecture. How, specifically, might Bob have used a recall column?

   _____

   _____

   _____

   _____

   _____

3. Do you think Rochelle wasted her time? What could she have done to make the time she spent more valuable?

   _____

   _____

   _____

   _____

   _____

4. In your opinion, what is the value of writing notes?

   _____

   _____

   _____

   _____

   _____

Taking Notes from Reading Material

7

Chapter Goals

After studying and working with the information in this chapter, you should be able to:

- Discuss the importance of reading actively and using note-taking strategies.
- Define *highlighting* and explain the most effective way to use it.
- Distinguish between the types of margin notes and explain how to use them to enhance your reading.
- Describe *full notes* and discuss when to use them.
- Use effective note-taking skills to take notes from fiction reading.

Terms

- effective highlighting
- full notes
- just reading
- margin notes
- reading actively
- summary
- symbolism

Ashley and Jordan are study partners in their Marketing class. However, when it comes to reading assignments, they are very different. Ashley finds the reading tedious, especially the 60-page chapters the instructor assigns each week. The night before a reading assignment is due, she settles into her cozy couch with her highlighter and book and starts to read. She highlights everything she thinks is important, which ends up being at least half of every page. She constantly fights off sleepiness and finally finishes four hours later. The next day in class during a class discussion, she doesn't remember much of what she read. She is constantly going back into the book to find the information being discussed by others. She also has to plan extra review time before the exam to re-read the chapters.

Jordan, on the other hand, previews the chapters and breaks them down into manageable sections. He reads one section a night and takes notes at his kitchen table. Sometimes he highlights key words; but, mostly, he uses summary paper to document the important information. He keeps a running list of new vocabulary terms and their definitions in the back of his notebook. During class discussions, he uses his notes and successfully backs up his points with details from the reading. When it comes time for a test, he reviews his notes and rarely has to re-read the text.

What makes Jordan's note taking and study habits effective and efficient? Why are Ashley's habits ineffective and inefficient?

Did you know that taking notes from your reading material is incredibly effective for keeping your concentration? It does take some time to create good notes, but the notes, if taken appropriately, will save you a great deal of time in learning, understanding, and reviewing the material.

So, when is it best to spend time taking notes? If you are unfamiliar with the material and you will need it for a class discussion or exam, then taking notes is a wise use of your time. Likewise, for work purposes, if you need the information for a business meeting or presentation, then taking notes is also a good use of your time. Writing useful notes is a good skill to have when you need to remind yourself about something, like an upcoming event, a new due date for a paper, or to take your insurance forms to the doctor's office. Of course, these notes are shorter than class notes but certainly as important.

Though it is recommended that you take some form of notes from any reading material you have to learn from, be aware that there are times when it is unnecessary. If you have a lot of background knowledge or won't need the material for a class discussion or exam, then taking notes will likely waste your time. When your purpose for reading is purely pleasure, then taking notes may also misuse your time. Some people, out of habit, use a highlighter on everything they read, but a highlighter used without thought will also waste your time.

Start by reading information about the Active Learning Staircase on page 179. In this chapter, you will learn about note-taking options that will enhance your reading, concentration, and note-taking abilities.

What methods do you use to capture the key concepts and information from your reading?

©Getty Images/PhotoDisc

Taking notes from reading materials is an effective way to learn about a subject.

The following self-evaluation will give you an idea of how familiar, or unfamiliar, you are with some of the topics and terms discussed in this chapter. After reading each statement, circle the letter Y, S, or N to indicate the answer that is most appropriate for you. Answer honestly. Rate yourself at the end; then complete the information on your Self-Check Progress Chart.

Y = yes; frequently   S = sometimes   N = no; never

1. The notes I take from my reading are easy to study and learn from.   Y   S   N

2. When reading material that I need to learn or refer to later, I usually take some form of notes.   Y   S   N

3. I know how to study without a lot of re-reading.   Y   S   N

4. I take notes from reading using key words, not full sentences.   Y   S   N

5. I mark areas I don't understand in my text so I can ask questions about them.   Y   S   N

6. I know how to use a highlighter effectively.   Y   S   N

7. I know how to create margin notes.   Y   S   N

8. I can locate the important information in reading material and take effective notes from it.   Y   S   N

9. I use note taking as an active way to concentrate and learn when I read.   Y   S   N

10. I learn more when I take effective notes.   Y   S   N

Rate Yourself:

Number of Ys _____ × 100 = _____

Number of Ss _____ × 50 = _____

Number of Ns _____ × 0 = _____   **Total_____**

"Just Reading" Versus Active Reading

On The Active Learning Staircase in Figure 7-1 on the next page, "**just reading**" is the most passive learning method. This is when you read from the beginning to the end of the material without pre-viewing the material (see Chapter 8 for more details on pre-viewing) or taking notes. Reading in this way encourages your mind to wander frequently, and you lose your concentration easily. It is ineffective because, if you are lucky, you will only comprehend and retain about 10 percent of what you read over a three-day period. The loss continues over time without repeated exposure to the material.

NETBookmark

Other ideas and examples for note taking are just a few clicks away on your computer. Go to your favorite search engine and key "note taking from reading" and see what sites are included in your search results. (Note: Choose your search terms carefully. If you put in "highlighting," you are sure to get a lot of information on highlighting hair!)

For links to some sites that provide helpful information about note taking from reading, go to:

http://sskills.swlearning.com

Reading actively is much more than "just reading." Active reading occurs when you use some or all of the following reading strategies, which are discussed in greater detail in Chapters 8 and 9.

1. Pre-viewing the chapter—to gain background knowledge.

2. Reading key words—to read faster and concentrate more.

3. Reading phrases—to read faster and concentrate more.

4. Reading with a pacer—to read faster and concentrate more.

5. Adjusting your reading speed—to reduce wasted time.

©Getty Images/PhotoDisc

By reading actively, you can reduce mind wandering, read faster, concentrate more, and improve comprehension.

By reading actively, you reduce mind wandering while learning at the same time. This active reading method results in *50 percent (or more)* comprehension and retention that lasts over a three-day period.

When you add other active note-taking strategies (such as highlighting, writing margin notes, and taking full notes), you climb even higher on the staircase. Reading actively with an effective note-taking strategy is a powerful learning combination!

FIGURE 7-1

Active Learning Staircase for Note Taking

A C T I V E

| | | Full Notes |
| Margin Notes |
| Effective Highlighting |
| Reading Actively |
| Just Reading |

P A S S I V E

Checkpoint

1 What does "just reading" mean?

_____

_____

2 What does "reading actively" mean?

_____

_____

_____

3 Why do you think you have better comprehension and retention when you read actively?

_____

_____

_____

Professor Claude Olney, the author of the study skills program, *Where There's a Will, There's an A*, said, "Ineffective highlighting postpones learning." What do you think he meant by this?

Effective Highlighting

Highlighting means using a colored marker to underline or write over the important information in reading material. Highlighting helps you become a more engaged and active learner because you focus on locating the most important information. It leaves less time and energy for mind wandering.

Passive learners often highlight also, but their method is ineffective. They highlight too much information, often wasting their time highlighting whole paragraphs and pages. When it comes time to study for a test or review for a meeting, they lose more time because they have to re-read everything they highlighted. Some learners use their highlighters for a glorified coloring activity. They highlight a few lines; then, instead of moving on, they color in the white spaces they see between the lines, and then color a neat box around the lines. Others just use a fancy color-coding system that requires them to remember what color they used for what purpose.

When a passive learner highlights a paragraph, he or she is saying, "This is important information, but I am too lazy to learn it now. I'll come back to it and read it again at another time." Active learners highlight less and try to understand as much as possible *while they are reading*. This avoids re-reading later, which wastes time.

Effective highlighting means:

1. *Reading a complete paragraph or section before highlighting anything.* This keeps you from highlighting too much. When you read material for the first time, everything may seem important because the information is new and unfamiliar. However, if you are patient and finish reading the paragraph or section *before* using your highlighter, you will have a better understanding of how the ideas are related and what ideas are most important to highlight.

2. *Rarely highlighting more than a few words or a phrase at a time.* Within an important paragraph, you will find key words and phrases, vocabulary terms, statistics, a name, an event, a dollar amount, a date, or other information that should be highlighted. Learning to highlight *less* can lead to *more* learning.

3. *Deciding what is most important.* Keep in mind that what is important to one reader may not be important to another. If you are worried that you did not highlight the "right" information, remember that there is no right or wrong information to highlight—only too much or too little.

Effective highlighting, coupled with reading actively, again results in 50 percent or more comprehension and retention lasting over a three-day period. How much more information you understand and remember depends upon how effective your highlighting methods are. Compare the highlighting in Figures 7-2 and 7-3. Which example is more effective? Which version would you rather use for studying?

FIGURE 7-2

Brian's Highlighting Example

CHARACTERISTICS OF E-COMMERCE CUSTOMERS

The Internet is still an innovative technology. While the number of people using the Internet grows each day, only a small percentage of businesses and final consumers use the Internet for shopping. Abundant research, much of which is available on the Internet, has been completed in the attempt to understand who is using the Internet.

INTERNET CONSUMERS

The typical U.S. Internet user is young, Caucasian, employed, well educated, and a suburban dweller with above-average income. Almost as many females as males use the Internet. African-American and Hispanic usage rates are lower than average. However, they are increasing at a faster rate than that of Caucasian users. The lowest participation rates are found in the youngest (under 13) and oldest (over 65) age groups.

People who purchase online are characterized as innovators and risk-takers. They are interested in new products, services, and ideas. They want to be viewed by others as trendsetters and opinion leaders. People who are less likely to purchase products online have greater needs for safety and security. They take longer to complete the decision-making process. They want to be viewed as making good economic decisions.

The average online consumer makes a relatively small number of purchases, spends less than $100 online per year, and is most likely to purchase familiar, low-cost products. People with annual incomes exceeding $100,000 purchase more than five times as much online per year, and usually buy more expensive items.

FIGURE 7-3

Carol's Highlighting Example

CHARACTERISTICS OF E-COMMERCE CUSTOMERS

The Internet is still an innovative technology. While the number of people using the Internet grows each day, only a small percentage of businesses and final consumers use the Internet for shopping. Abundant research, much of which is available on the Internet, has been completed in the attempt to understand who is using the Internet.

INTERNET CONSUMERS

The typical U.S. Internet user is young, Caucasian, employed, well educated, and a suburban dweller with above-average income. Almost as many females as males use the Internet. African-American and Hispanic usage rates are lower than average. However, they are increasing at a faster rate than that of Caucasian users. The lowest participation rates are found in the youngest (under 13) and oldest (over 65) age groups.

People who purchase online are characterized as innovators and risk-takers. They are interested in new products, services, and ideas. They want to be viewed by others as trendsetters and opinion leaders. People who are less likely to purchase products online have greater needs for safety and security. They take longer to complete the decision-making process. They want to be viewed as making good economic decisions.

The average online consumer makes a relatively small number of purchases, spends less than $100 online per year, and is most likely to purchase familiar, low-cost products. People with annual incomes exceeding $100,000 purchase more than five times as much online per year, and usually buy more expensive items.

Source: Kleindl and Burrow. *E-Commerce Marketing.* © 2005 Thomson/South-Western.

Look over Figure 7-2 and Figure 7-3, the examples of Brian's and Carol's use of a highlighter. Who will spend more time learning? Who will spend less time? Why?

_____

_____

_____

_____

With a highlighter pen, highlight what you think is the most important information in the following paragraph. *Read the entire paragraph before deciding what to highlight.* Pretend that you will have to study from it for an upcoming test. Compare your highlights with your classmates.

A job application is a form provided by an employer that asks you to list your qualifications, work history, and work-related personal experience. Because application forms are uniform, reviewers find them easy to use when comparing applicants for certain positions. Some employers require only a job application, while others may require one in addition to a resume. Overall, interviewers are interested in how accurate you are in sharing your experience. They don't want candidates who exaggerate their abilities, as they will not be able to do the job effectively, and could also get hurt if the job involves handling dangerous equipment or machinery.

Checkpoint

1 What is the passive way to use a highlighter?

_____

_____

2 What is the active way to use a highlighter?

_____

_____

3 How can effective highlighting save you learning time?

_____

_____

_____

Creating Margin Notes

Margin notes are yet another step up the Active Learning Staircase. **Margin notes** are either summary notes, questions, or personal comments you create in the margin of your material. The notes are used just like the recall column in the Cornell Method of Note Taking (see Chapter 6).

Creating margin notes is an active form of note taking because you are forced to locate—or concentrate on finding—the important information. Once you locate it, you then condense it down to some key words, a heading, a question, or other summary you personally write in the margin. When it comes time to review, you will spend most of your time reviewing from your margin notes. As a result, you will have less information to re-read as well as an effective, time-saving method for review.

Margin notes are most effective if you:

1. *Read a complete paragraph or section before writing anything.* Everything you read seems important when the material is new or unfamiliar. If you are patient and finish reading a paragraph or section, you will have a better understanding of how ideas are related and what material is most important to summarize.

2. *Decide what is most important.* In some paragraphs, you may think everything is important. In others, none of the information may seem important. Remember, there is no right or wrong information for margin notes—only too much or too little.

3. *Use your own words, key words, and abbreviations.* Margin space is limited, so writing less is more effective. Creating and writing a title in the margin for a paragraph or section helps you identify the main idea you want to capture. Other markings that can be added to margin notes include:

   - Placing a question mark (?) in the margin next to information you don't understand (so you can remind yourself to find the answer).

   - Placing an asterisk (*) next to very important information.

   - Placing an exclamation point (!) next to something that surprised you.

Can you think of any others?

Writing margin notes, as with other methods of active reading, takes time but adds to your ability to comprehend and retain 50 percent or more of the material for over three days. How much more depends upon the effectiveness of your methods.

Look at Figure 7-4, Maya's Summary-in-the-Margin Notes, and Figure 7-5, Kaitlin's Question-in-the-Margin Notes. These are two sample ways to use the margin for notes.

> Creating margin notes forces you to understand and concentrate on the important information. It also saves time when it comes time to review.

Summary-in-the-Margin Notes

A **summary** is a brief statement or restatement of main points. It is a shortened version of what you consider important in the text you are reading. For the paragraphs of Maya's text, you will see several separate summaries in the margin.

The information in each one could possibly show up on a test. The first summary in the second paragraph indicates a description to remember. A bracket surrounds the description in case Maya needs to review it quickly. *Using a bracket is a simple and time-saving form of highlighting.* Notice that the numbering indicates each of the ideas she wants to recall. This type of numbering is effective when you need to remember a series of related ideas.

The next summaries indicate important ideas and are written in Maya's own abbreviated language. Maya does not think the notes are equally important, but she expects to possibly be tested on each of them.

FIGURE 7-4

Maya's Summary-in-the-Margin Notes

CHARACTERISTICS OF E-COMMERCE CUSTOMERS

Internet = Innovative Tech.

Few buy online

The Internet is still an innovative technology. While the number of people using the Internet grows each day, only a small percentage of businesses and final consumers use the Internet for shopping. Abundant research, much of which is available on the Internet, has been completed in the attempt to understand who is using the Internet.

INTERNET CONSUMERS

Typical user: 6 qualities

Females = Males African-Amer. & Hisp. < avg. Smallest groups: under 13/over 65

⑤The typical U.S. Internet user is young①, Caucasian②, employed③, well educated④, and a suburban dweller with above⑥-average income. Almost as many females as males use the Internet. African-American and Hispanic usage rates are lower than average. However, they are increasing at a faster rate than that of Caucasian users. The lowest participation rates are found in the youngest (under 13) and oldest (over 65) age groups.

Purchasers are innovators and risk-takers

Non-purchasers need safety and security

People who purchase online are characterized as innovators and risk-takers. They are interested in new products, services, and ideas. They want to be viewed by others as trendsetters and opinion leaders. People who are less likely to purchase products online have greater needs for safety and security. They take longer to complete the decision-making process. They want to be viewed as making good economic decisions.

Avg. consumer spends < $100

↑ 100K income = buy 5x more & expensive items

The average online consumer makes a relatively small number of purchases, spends less than $100 online per year, and is most likely to purchase familiar, low-cost products. People with annual incomes exceeding $100,000 purchase more than five times as much online per year, and usually buy more expensive items.

Source: Kleindl and Burrow. *E-Commerce Marketing.* © 2005 Thomson/South-Western.

Question-in-the-Margin Notes

In the margin of Kaitlin's text, you will find questions. She prefers to summarize important ideas as questions, similar to what she might find on a test. The answer to each question is easily found by re-reading the text next to the question. Notice that she uses her own form of abbreviation. She indicates exactly how many things she needs to recall when a question can be answered in more than one way. ("What are the qualities of U.S. users?" 6.) When you create questions, keep in mind the types of questions you think your instructor might ask on a test. Pretend as if you are creating the test from the material. When you study using your questions, you can cover up the material, just like when you use the recall column of the Cornell Method, and test yourself using your own questions.

FIGURE 7-5

Kaitlin's Questions-in-the-Margin Notes

CHARACTERISTICS OF E-COMMERCE CUSTOMERS

What kind of technology is the Internet?

Do a lot of people buy online?

The Internet is still an innovative technology. While the number of people using the Internet grows each day, only a small percentage of businesses and final consumers use the Internet for shopping. Abundant research, much of which is available on the Internet, has been completed in the attempt to understand who is using the Internet.

INTERNET CONSUMERS

What are the qualities of U.S. users? (6)

What groups participate? Who uses it the least?

The typical U.S. Internet user is young, Caucasian, employed, well educated, and a suburban dweller with above-average income. Almost as many females as males use the Internet. African-American and Hispanic usage rates are lower than average. However, they are increasing at a faster rate than that of Caucasian users. The lowest participation rates are found in the youngest (under 13) and oldest (over 65) age groups.

What are online purchasers like?

What do non-purchasers need?

People who purchase online are characterized as innovators and risk-takers. They are interested in new products, services, and ideas. They want to be viewed by others as trendsetters and opinion leaders. People who are less likely to purchase products online have greater needs for safety and security. They take longer to complete the decision-making process. They want to be viewed as making good economic decisions.

How much $ does the avg. online consumer spend?

Who buys 5x as much?

The average online consumer makes a relatively small number of purchases, spends less than $100 online per year, and is most likely to purchase familiar, low-cost products. People with annual incomes exceeding $100,000 purchase more than five times as much online per year, and usually buy more expensive items.

Source: Kleindl and Burrow. *E-Commerce Marketing.* © 2005 Thomson/South-Western.

"The only place where success comes before work is in the dictionary."

—Vidal Sassoon, Influential hair stylist and creator of hair care products

Combining Margin Notes and Effective Highlighting

You might think that using both margin notes and effective highlighting is like wearing a belt *and* suspenders, but in some cases (not all the time) using both can be very effective. By combining effective highlighting and margin notes, you can quickly identify important ideas and reinforce others. Several highlighted words or phrases, in addition to margin notes, provide good review material. Don't waste time becoming preoccupied with the mechanics of combining the two methods.

Studying with Margin Notes

Margin notes, either in summary form or as questions, force you to:

- Concentrate on what you are reading.
- Focus on what is really important.
- Reduce your study time when you review.

Imagine it is now time to review the reading in Figure 7-4 or Figure 7-5 in preparation for a test. Cover the text with a blank piece of paper while you review the summaries or questions. Test yourself to see how much you know and what information you need to review. You can write your responses on the paper covering the text, or you can say the answers aloud.

When you finish reviewing, remove the paper, and check yourself. If you are having trouble recalling a certain piece of information, place your own reference mark next to it and review the material again.

Checkpoint

1 What are margin notes?

_____

_____

2 What are two suggested ways to create margin notes?

_____

_____

3 How can you best learn with margin notes?

_____

_____

_____

_____

Taking Full Notes

Full notes are the top step on the Active Learning Staircase. They also take the most time, at first, but save a lot of time when reviewing. Taking full notes is used mostly for when you need to learn technical or difficult material. Using a combination of effective highlighting and margin notes will be sufficient for most of your non-fiction reading.

Full notes means reducing the text back into the author's outline using summary paper. You write the outline in the recall column on the left-side margin and fill in the important details in the body of notes on the right-side margin. (For more information on how to find the author's outline, see pre-viewing in Chapter 8.) Full notes can also be taken in the form of a Mind Map using unlined paper.

Taking full notes along with reading actively results in 75 percent or more (!) comprehension and retention lasting over three days. How much more depends upon the effectiveness of your methods.

Look at the text in Figure 7-6. Each paragraph contains many important facts and pieces of useful information. Understanding and thoroughly learning the information is important for doing well on a test. Though effective highlighting and margin notes may be enough in some situations, full notes become a more effective study tool for difficult material like this.

If you would like to learn how to take full notes, begin by using reading material required for school or work. This will be the best use of your time and active learning energy. An example of full notes appears in Figure 7-7.

■ Focus on Ethics

You're enrolled in a social studies class where students are encouraged to share openly about their beliefs and their lives. One of the ground rules of the class is, "What's said here, stays here."

One of the other students in the class is your best friend's boyfriend, who one day lets it slip that he's been seeing another girl. You know that your friend is not aware of this. You want to abide by the rules of the class, but you also want to protect your friend and feel that she should know her boyfriend has been cheating on her.

What do you do? How do you balance privacy with friendship? What do you think is the purpose of a "What's said here, stays here" policy in a classroom environment?

©Getty Images/PhotoDisc

Full notes require 100% focus to get 75% comprehension and retention—a good investment of your time and learning energy!

FIGURE 7-6

Text Sample for Using Full Notes

WHAT CIVIL LITIGATION IS

Civil litigation is the process of resolving private disputes through the court system. Unless the parties are able to resolve their dispute, the litigation process usually results in a trial, or hearing, where the parties present their evidence to a judge or jury. The judge or jury then decides the dispute. Before this happens, however, a great deal of investigation, research, and preparation takes place. Although most of this occurs outside of the courtroom, it is an important part of the litigation process. Litigation attorneys and their assistants often spend considerable time gathering and analyzing the facts as well as researching the law. Formal legal documents must be prepared and filed with the court, witnesses must be interviewed, and other evidence must be identified and located.

Civil Law v. Criminal Law

Not all disputes that end in litigation are civil in nature, for our court system handles both civil and criminal cases. However, the litigation procedures for civil cases vary considerably from the litigation procedures employed in a criminal case. Being able to distinguish a civil case from a criminal one is therefore very important.

The rules of civil litigation, sometimes referred to as **civil procedure**, apply only if a civil law is involved. **Civil laws** are those that deal with private disputes between parties. If a lawsuit results, it is between the disputing parties. The parties may be individuals, organizations, or governmental entities. Civil law includes such areas as contracts, real estate, commercial and business transactions, and torts (civil wrongs or injuries not stemming from a contract). A typical civil case is illustrated by the following situation. While shopping at Dave's Department Store, Kirkland trips on torn carpeting, seriously injuring himself. The carpeting had been torn for several weeks, but the store had ignored the condition. Kirkland requests that the department store pay for his injuries, but the store refuses. Kirkland could sue the department store, asking the court to force the store to pay for his medical bills, for his lost wages, and for any pain and suffering he may have experienced. The basis for such a lawsuit is found in the law of torts, in particular, negligence. The procedures and rules that would govern that lawsuit are known as the rules of civil procedure or civil litigation.

Criminal law, on the other hand, deals with acts that are offenses against society as a whole, and includes such acts as murder, robbery, and drunk driving. If a criminal action results, it is usually between the government and the accused. The procedures and rules that apply when an individual is accused of committing a crime are known as the rules of **criminal procedure**. To a large extent, the Bill of Rights found in the U.S. Constitution governs the rules of criminal procedure. In a criminal case the defendant enjoys various rights, such as the right not to testify against himself. The defendant also has the right to a court-appointed counsel if he or she is indigent, and is entitled to speedy trial, all rights found in the Constitution. None of these rights exist in civil cases.

Source: Kerley, Peggy, et al. *Civil Litigation for the Paralegal.* © 2000 Delmar Publishers Inc.

FIGURE 7-7

Tyler's Samples Using Full Notes

pp 3-22	What Civil litigation is 4/6/08
Civil Litigation	= resolving private disputes thru court system
trial or hearing	= parties present evidence to judge or jury
litigation attys	
& assts.	= gather & analyze facts/research law
	- legal doc's prep'd & filed
	- witnesses interviewed
	- other evidence identified & located
Civil law vs. Criminal law	
Civil Procedure	= rules of civil Litigation
Civil Laws	= laws dealing w/prin disputes btw parties
⑤	- contracts
	- real estate
	- com'l & bus. transactions
torts	- torts (= civil wrongs)
	- negligence
Criminal law	= offense against society
④	- murder
	- robbery
	- drunk driving
	- disputes btw gov't & accused
criminal procedure	= rules that apply when someone is accused of a crime
Bill of Rights	= governs criminal procedures
defendant's rights	= 1) to not testify against himself
③	2) has right to court appointed counsel
	3) entitled to speedy trial

Read the notes in Figure 7-7, Tyler's notes using summary paper. Think about or discuss with your classmates the following questions. Write your answers below.

1. What is your first impression of Tyler's notes? _____

2. What do you notice about them? _____

3. Do you think Tyler learned better by creating full notes? _____

   Explain your answer. _____

4. Would he have learned as much using another method of note taking? _____

   Explain. _____

   _____

5. Do you think his time was well spent? Why or why not? _____

   _____

   _____

6. When it comes time to study for your test, which would you rather have: the full text or the notes? Why? _____

   _____

Checkpoint

1 What is meant by writing full notes?

_____

_____

2 Why is summary paper ideal for writing full notes?

_____

_____

_____

3 Though full notes are the most time-consuming note-taking method, how does this method ultimately save you time?

_____

_____

_____

About Fiction Note Taking

Taking notes from fiction material, such as a novel or another piece of literature, requires a few special considerations. Effective highlighting and making notes in the margin are useful. However, since there is no author outline as with a textbook or other nonfiction material, taking full notes from fiction isn't as predictable.

While there is no single best way to take notes from fiction, here are some good ideas:

- Keep track of the characters, as this is the most challenging part of any story. You can designate a piece of paper or a large index card for each character. As he or she is introduced in the story, write the name at the top. Write descriptions about the characters, including their relationship to others, examples of what they say, examples of what they do, examples of what other characters say about them, and examples of what the author says about them.

- Be aware of **symbolism**, or something that represents and stands for something else. For example, when the beautiful red rose dies, it could symbolize death somewhere else in the story. Or, when a character waves a starched white handkerchief, it could symbolize his or her surrendering to a person or situation.

- Look for quotable quotes. Instructors love to include quotes from stories on tests to see if you remember who said them and what was meant in the context of the story. Highlight them or make note of them in your notes.

- Identify and take notes about the basic elements of fiction. These are the elements you can expect to find in every short story, novel, or play:

  Title – a clue pointing you towards the theme of the story

  Setting – a time and place

Focus on Technology

Using technology to help you take and organize notes when researching can save you a lot of time and frustration. Much of the information you might be required to study and learn is of a compare and contrast nature, such as comparative literature or comparative religion. Sociology, psychology, and anthropology would all contain elements that can be compared, as would history, biology, and economics. A useful strategy for organizing compared information is to use a grid or table.

- Create a blank grid, or multi-column or table format, in your word processing program. Print several copies out and keep them with your study materials.

- Any time you are reading information that can be organized using a grid, simply fill in the information in the appropriate columns and rows.

- Alternatively, you can create a grid template in your word processing program and type your information directly into your computer.

- If you are researching online you can cut and paste your target information; just remember to be vigilant about plagiarism laws and giving credit to your sources. It can be quite simple then to change and rearrange large amounts of information.

- Another bonus is that you don't necessarily have to print it out; you can always study directly from your computer.

Taking notes from fiction material, such as a novel, requires special considerations.

Point of View – spoken either in the first person (a character serves as the narrator) or third person (a narrator outside the story)

Conflict (part of the plot) – problems that change the belief system or lives of characters involved

Climax and Resolution (part of the plot) – the moment in the story when the character makes a decision that leads to the ultimate resolution of the conflict

Checkpoint

1 **Why is it a good idea to take notes from fiction?**

_____

_____

2 **What might your fiction notes include?**

_____

_____

_____

3 **How might you study with your fiction notes?**

_____

_____

_____

CHAPTER SUMMARY

1. Learning how to take effective notes from reading material will increase your concentration while reading, save review time, and make your learning more active.

2. "Just reading" is the most passive and ineffective way to read and learn. Reading actively focuses you and results in better comprehension and retention.

3. Highlighting only key words and phrases is more effective than highlighting whole paragraphs and pages.

4. Creating either summary-in-the margin or question-in-the-margin notes increases your concentration while reading, saves you time when reviewing, and forces you to predict test questions at the same time.

5. Taking full notes is reserved for technical or difficult material that is new to you and/or which you need to learn in detail.

6. You can take notes from fiction by tracking the characters, looking for symbolism and quotable quotes, and paying attention to the basic elements of fiction.

CHAPTER ASSESSMENT

Terms Review

Fill in the blanks with the appropriate key terms on the left. You can use a term more than once.

effective highlighting

full notes

just reading

margin notes

reading actively

summary

symbolism

1. Reading using key words and phrases is an example of
   _____.

2. When the there is a thunderstorm in the story, it could be an example of
   _____.

3. Writing your notes as a title, statement, or question is best done as
   _____.

4. Ideally, _____ immediately points out the most important information without all the small, unimportant words included.

5. If you read without a strategy or taking notes, this is considered
   _____.

6. A _____ is a shortened version of what you consider important in the text you are reading.

7. Recreating the author's outline using summary paper is called
   _____.

8. Write the 5 steps of the Active Learning Staircase in order from the most passive to the most active.
   _____, _____, _____,
   _____, _____.

Review

Based on the information you learned in this chapter, answer the following questions using your own words and thoughts.

1. Describe the Active Learning Staircase as it relates to learning from reading materials.

_____

_____

_____

_____

_____

2. When should notes be taken from reading materials?

_____

_____

3. When should you **NOT** take notes from reading materials?

_____

_____

4. How do you decide which note-taking method to use?

_____

_____

_____

5. What is the difference between passive reading and reading actively?

_____

_____

_____

6. What is the most effective way to use a highlighter?

_____

_____

_____

7. What are the most effective ways to create margin notes?

_____

_____

_____

8. When is taking full notes a good idea? How can full notes help your reading?

_____

_____

_____

_____

9. In your view, what are the most important reasons to take notes from reading materials? Why?

_____

_____

_____

_____

Review Exercise

Practice taking notes on the paragraphs below about the Internet's beginning. First use effective highlighting; then add margin notes. Then, on a piece of summary paper, write full notes. Though you wouldn't ever need to use all three strategies on your reading, it is good to practice all three here. Remember, there is really no right or wrong—just too much or not enough information.

The origins of the Internet started in the U.S. Defense Department in the early 1970's with a group called ARPA—the Advance Research Projects Agency. The military needed to keep defense computers interconnected in case the country was attacked by nuclear weapons. They developed a system in which information was sent in packets along a complex network of electronic paths. If any one path or computer was destroyed, information could still continue to travel along alternate paths. Since many universities were conducting research for the Defense Department at that time, they began to use this system for transferring information and messages.

Next came the idea for a system that would allow users to post information on a computer that others could visit—the first Internet sites. Instead of just transferring information along the network, users could now visit specific sites in order to retrieve the information they needed. In just a few years, the amazing potential of this system of interconnected networks was realized in the World Wide Web, transforming the ways we communicate and share information. The Internet now includes over 50 million users worldwide, and is growing. It contains hundreds of thousands of web sites, from major corporations and media outlets to second-grade classrooms and skateboarder's conventions.

Despite the amazing benefits to online research, there are risks for online users to avoid. The Web may house thousands of valuable research and sales sites, but it is also home to a plethora of inaccurate information. Many people think that because something is posted on the Web, it must be true. This is farthest from the truth. The Web is a great place to post rumors and false and misleading information. Users are advised to evaluate the sites they visit by asking themselves the following four questions:

- What is the purpose of the site?
- Whose interests does it serve?
- Who is its intended audience?
- What is the source of the information?

Source: _Media Matters: Critical Thinking in the Information Age._ © 2000 South-Western Educational Publishing.

CASE STUDIES

for Creative and Critical Thinking

 ACADEMIC CASE—Connecting to Economics and Study Habits

Holden needed some help. He had a three-course load during the fall semester, and he was getting mixed results. He was an A student in his American History and Chemistry courses, but was struggling to maintain a C- average in Economics. Holden approached preparing for exams in all of his courses in the same way: he pre-viewed the chapters, read each section carefully before highlighting key phrases and definitions, and wrote short notes in the margins for quick review. Despite spending the same amount of time on each subject and doing well on the History and Chemistry exams, he continued to have trouble with Economics. There was a lot more vocabulary to learn and concepts to understand. The tests consisted of many short essays on economic policies and social opinion. He needs to learn his economics material better.

1. What is Holden doing that is effective?

_____

_____

_____

_____

_____

2. What can he do to help himself learn the vocabulary?

_____

_____

_____

_____

_____

3. Why does spending the same amount of time studying each subject not guarantee the same results?

_____

_____

_____

_____

4. What else might Holden do to improve his grade in Economics?

_____

_____

_____

_____

Ever since Connor was young, he was fascinated with electricity. So, it made logical sense that he attended a career-technical school to learn how to be an electrician. After the first few weeks, however, his test results were less than stellar. He read the highly technical course materials diligently and attended the electric labs. His friend Brenda had done well on the most recent test, and Connor asked her what she had done to improve. "I found that highlighting the text wasn't enough for difficult material like this," Brenda told him. Brenda said she was using additional note-taking techniques including full notes and Mind Mapping. She found the Mind Mapping especially effective because she could color code her ideas and not have to keep them in strict order. Since Connor's future career depended on him getting a good grade, he was anxious to try anything to do well on his next test.

1. Up to this point, what has Connor done that shows he has potential to be an excellent electrician?

_____

_____

_____

_____

_____

2. Why might Connor want to use full notes instead of just highlighting or even margin notes?

_____

_____

_____

_____

_____

3. Describe for Connor's benefit the basic structure of full notes. Explain how he might organize his notes so that they are easy to review for his next test.

_____

_____

_____

_____

_____

4. Think about what work electricians perform and brainstorm at least two ways Connor might use Mind Mapping to learn.

_____

_____

_____

_____

_____

8 Improving Reading Comprehension

Chapter Goals

After studying and working with the information in this chapter, you should be able to:

- Identify what active readers know and do, including distinguishing between nonfiction and fiction reading, and finding your reading purpose and responsibility before you begin.
- Describe the procedure for pre-viewing a nonfiction book, chapter, or article.
- Understand the role background knowledge plays in reading and learning, and identify and describe five approaches to dealing with unfamiliar words.

Bryce is taking a course in American history and is assigned several textbook chapters of reading per week. He also has some reading to do for his three other classes, making it challenging to read it all, let alone remember what he reads.

When Bryce finally sits down to do his reading assignments, he opens the book to the first page and reads word for word until the end. His mind frequently wanders to his other assignments, happenings of the day, and upcoming social events with his friends. Because he's so distracted, he frequently stops reading to IM a friend, make a phone call, or watch a TV show.

When he gets back to the assignment, he finds he has to reread quite a bit of material to even remember where he left off. When he finally finishes the assignment, he dutifully checks it off his homework assignment sheet. But he doesn't feel great about it because he has only the slightest idea of what he just read and hopes he won't have to answer any detailed questions in class or on a test. When it's time to review for a test, he finds he has to reread most of the chapters because he doesn't remember what they were about. Sometimes, mostly because of time or energy limitations, he doesn't get to review all the material. "What's the point," he thinks. "I don't really understand it anyway."

Bryce spends a lot of time reading but not understanding. No wonder he doesn't like to read.

What do you think is the problem with Bryce's way of reading?

Reading and understanding factual nonfiction material, like textbooks, may be one of the most challenging learning tasks you experience—for several reasons. The first and most important is that you are working with inadequate and antiquated reading skills learned way back in elementary school. Second, there is a vast amount of reading material to choose from that is available both on paper and online, for school, work, and pleasure. Third, finding time to read in today's busy world is challenging, and, lastly, knowledge and one's ability to gain it have become necessities in the working world.

Reading is a necessary lifelong skill for personal and professional success. Your workload can include reading both on paper and on screen. You read in school to participate in classroom discussions and to complete homework assignments, quizzes, and tests. You read at work to gain knowledge, learn a new skill, understand information, participate in discussions, and grow in a career. Anyone with a computer reads all the time: e-mail correspondence, web pages, instant messages, and so on. You may also read for pleasure, or to become a healthier person or a better parent, friend, or spouse.

This chapter will focus on 1) a reading skill called pre-viewing that can be used with all of your nonfiction reading, 2) methods to build vocabulary, and 3) ways to use your background knowledge to learn new words easily.

> What is your reading workload like? How do you manage it?

With all the nonfiction material available to read both on paper and online, how can you best understand it all? All it takes is using a strategy or two.

Self-Check ✔

The following self-evaluation will give you an idea of how familiar, or unfamiliar, you are with some of the topics and terms discussed in this chapter. After reading each statement, circle the letter Y, S, or N to indicate the answer that is most appropriate for you. Answer honestly. Rate yourself at the end; then complete the information on your Self-Check Progress Chart.

Y = yes; frequently   S = sometimes   N = no; never

1. I understand what active readers know and do.   Y   S   N

2. I know the difference between nonfiction and fiction material.   Y   S   N

3. I am aware of my purpose and responsibility before I read.   Y   S   N

4. I know how to pre-view a nonfiction book or magazine.   Y   S   N

5. I know how to pre-view a nonfiction chapter or article.   Y   S   N

6. When I come across a word I don't know, I use context clues to understand its meaning.   Y   S   N

7. When I come across a word I don't know, I use prefixes, roots, and suffixes to identify its meaning.   Y   S   N

8. When I come across a word I don't know, I use a dictionary effectively.   Y   S   N

9. I have a system for tracking new words.   Y   S   N

10. I can manage my reading workload.   Y   S   N

Rate Yourself:

Number of Ys _____ × 100 = _____

Number of Ss _____ × 50 = _____

Number of Ns _____ × 0 = _____   **Total** _____

What Active Readers Know and Do

Many differences exist between passive and active readers. **Passive readers** like Bryce were probably never taught how to use comprehension strategies in their reading or learning. They typically read from the beginning to end of their assignments, daydreaming often, and not understanding much. In effect, they go through the motions of doing the reading but don't end up with the comprehension they need to do a good job on their assignments or tests.

Some readers have figured out, on their own, what they have to do to get good comprehension. They naturally use strategies that reduce their daydreaming and build comprehension. The majority of readers, however, haven't been so fortunate—they instead just need to be taught a few useful strategies. **Active readers** use pre-reading strategies (here called **pre-viewing**), continually build a strong vocabulary, and use their **background knowledge** (what they already know based on previous experiences) to create understanding.

ACTIVITY 1

Here is a list of qualities of passive and active readers. Notice that the traits in the two columns are opposites. Before starting this activity, read down each column and mentally think which one might list more of your qualities. Then, comparing the quality listed on the left with the one directly across on the right, place a check mark next to the quality that best describes you. If you believe you are in between the qualities (meaning you possess some of both), place a check mark in the middle column.

Passive Reader Qualities	In Between	Active Reader Qualities
☐ Unaware of purpose and responsibility before reading	☐	☐ Aware of purpose and responsibility before reading
☐ Cannot identify where the main ideas are located	☐	☐ Knows where the main ideas are located
☐ Understands poorly	☐	☐ Understands well
☐ Mind wanders frequently	☐	☐ Mind wanders occasionally
☐ Reads slowly most of the time	☐	☐ Reads rapidly, especially with familiar material
☐ Does not vary reading speed	☐	☐ Uses different reading speeds for different purposes
☐ Has a limited vocabulary	☐	☐ Has a wide vocabulary
☐ Reads the same types of material repeatedly	☐	☐ Reads diverse materials
☐ Cannot identify the writer's outline (nonfiction)	☐	☐ Can identify the writer's outline (nonfiction)
☐ Does not evaluate what is read	☐	☐ Evaluates what is read
☐ Rarely takes notes	☐	☐ Takes good notes when the situation calls for it
☐ Has a limited background of general knowledge and experience	☐	☐ Has a broad background of general knowledge and experience
☐ Reads seldom and dislikes it	☐	☐ Reads often and enjoys it

After you have worked with this chapter and Chapter 9, "Revving Up Your Reading," you will be asked to return to this list and reevaluate your reading qualities. Hopefully, you will see a positive difference. In this chapter and in Chapter 9, you will learn how to become an active reader. Some of the first steps toward this goal are to be able to identify nonfiction and fiction reading material and to know your purpose and responsibility for reading.

The Difference Between Nonfiction and Fiction

Nonfiction reading material is factual in nature. Textbooks, how-to books, encyclopedias, and most magazine articles are examples of factual material. Nonfiction contains information on many topics and is the most challenging to comprehend. The information in this chapter will concentrate on reading nonfiction, since most school- and work-related learning requires reading factual material.

Fiction reading is imaginative in nature and is composed of invented ideas. Novels, short stories, and some magazine articles are examples of fiction. The challenge of fiction reading is following the story line and being able to interpret its meaning. (Refer to Chapter 7 for ideas on how to take notes from fiction material.) Figure 8-1 lists several examples of nonfiction and fiction.

FIGURE 8-1

Examples of Nonfiction and Fiction Reading

Nonfiction

Textbooks
- *Your Career: How to Make It Happen*
—Julie Griffin Levitt
- *E-Commerce Marketing*
—Brad Alan Kleindl and James L. Burrow

Magazines
- *Newsweek*
- *Sports Illustrated*
- *National Geographic*

Newspapers
- *The New York Times*
- *The Wall Street Journal*
- *Chicago Tribune*

Fiction

Novels
- *To Kill a Mockingbird*
—Harper Lee
- *One Hundred Years of Solitude*
—Gabriel Garcia Marquez

Short Story Collections
- *The Lottery: And Other Stories*
—Shirley Jackson
- *The Golden Apples of the Sun*
—Ray Bradbury

Poetry Collections
- *The Waste Land*
—T. S. Eliot
- *And Still I Rise*
—Maya Angelou

Drama
- *Hamlet*
—William Shakespeare

Think about the books, magazines, and other materials you are currently reading. Which are nonfiction and which are fiction? What do you find challenging about each?

_____

_____

_____

_____

_____

Finding Your Purpose and Reading Responsibility

In Chapter 1, knowing your purpose and responsibility for learning was presented as a way to become actively involved with all learning tasks. In this chapter, it is specific to reading.

Your **reading purpose** is the reason why you are reading. It might also be considered your intent for reading. The purpose can be as simple as "because I want to read for my own information" or as challenging as "it was assigned, and I am responsible for understanding it."

Your **reading responsibility** refers to the ways you are accountable for the information. Reading responsibilities include (1) becoming familiar with the information for a class discussion or for a meeting, (2) being able to perform well on a quiz or test, (3) answering another person's questions, or (4) adding the information into your background knowledge for future use.

Each responsibility requires a different amount of reading and study time. For example, if your reading task is to prepare for a class discussion, you do not need to spend a lot of time studying the information in depth—you need only to be familiar with it. If your task is to write a report based on what you read, then you need to read more closely, take notes, and think about how the material relates to your report.

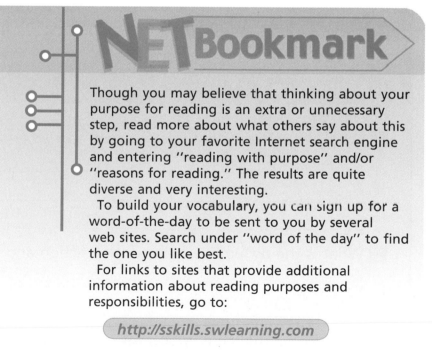

Though you may believe that thinking about your purpose for reading is an extra or unnecessary step, read more about what others say about this by going to your favorite Internet search engine and entering "reading with purpose" and/or "reasons for reading." The results are quite diverse and very interesting.

To build your vocabulary, you can sign up for a word-of-the-day to be sent to you by several web sites. Search under "word of the day" to find the one you like best.

For links to sites that provide additional information about reading purposes and responsibilities, go to:

http://sskills.swlearning.com

Without knowing your purpose or your reading responsibility, you are a passive reader who wastes time and has no direction. By knowing your purpose and reading responsibility, you become an active reader who is efficient with time and gets the information needed without wasting valuable time.

ACTIVITY 3

Think about several reading tasks you have to do or have recently completed. Write a description for each one.

a. Identify your reading purpose (the reason why you are reading).

b. Identify your reading responsibility (what you need to do as a result of your reading).

c. Identify other purposes and responsibilities.

Example: Reading Task: *Read a section of the software manual.*

a. Learn how to use the new software.

b. Use the software to do work tasks.

c. Advance my career.

Reading Task: _____

a. _____

b. _____

c. _____

Reading Task: _____

a. _____

b. _____

c. _____

Checkpoint

1 What are some differences between passive and active readers?

_____

_____

_____

2 What is the difference between nonfiction and fiction material?

_____

_____

3 Why do you think it is important to have a reading purpose and responsibility?

_____

_____

_____

_____

Pre-Viewing

Consider possible answers to the following questions relating to preparation:

- Why do football players watch films of their opponents' games *before* facing them?

- Why do drivers and other travelers ask for directions or look at road maps *before* traveling? How else can people find directions to their destinations?

- Why do people read film reviews in the newspaper *before* going to movies? How else can they get information about films they are planning to see?

The first question responds to the need for *preparing a plan of attack*. Football teams must create a strategy of attack against their opponents, which they can do more easily if they know the strategies their opponents have used in previous games. This gives them a competitive edge on the playing field.

The second question speaks to the need for *mapping out a direction*. Without directions, people get lost, frustrated, and detoured from their destinations. On the other hand, with directions, people are able to get where they want to go and can reach their destinations in a reasonable amount of time.

The third question responds to the need for *using time effectively*. If you blindly select a movie, not knowing whether it is a horror movie, a comedy, an action-adventure, or another type of film, you may end up wasting your time and money by watching something you don't like. A little preparation can make the time you spend at the movies worthwhile and enjoyable.

How does this relate to reading? When approaching reading, most people are passive, like Bryce. They don't establish a plan of attack or map a direction, so they waste time by reading from the first word to the last. Active readers, on the other hand, prepare a plan of attack, map out a direction, and create a course of action for using their time wisely.

Pre-viewing is one of the best strategies for becoming an active reader. **Pre-viewing** means examining nonfiction material to discover the writer's outline *before* reading in detail. The outline provides structure and clues to the content.

By pre-viewing, you learn how the material is organized, what and where the main ideas are, and what content will be covered. Pre-viewing is an important tool for understanding ALL nonfiction reading tasks.

The only small drawback to pre-viewing, commonly mentioned by beginning pre-viewers, is that it initially takes more time than just reading from beginning to end. At first, pre-viewing may take ten minutes for a ten-page chapter or article. However, once you know what to look for and are skilled at finding the information quickly, it

> **"There are those who travel and those who are going somewhere. They are different and yet they are the same. The most successful is the one who knows where he is going."**
>
> **—Mark Caine, Contemporary author**

Would you willingly volunteer to spend a few hours with someone you *never* met or knew *anything* about? Most people feel more comfortable with a little background information before entering such a situation.

The same is true for reading. Most people feel more comfortable knowing a little about the material before jumping in and spending time. So the next time you are reading nonfiction and you find yourself "lost," not knowing why you are reading, or what you are reading about, STOP and take the time to pre-view it. The little time you spend will save you a lot of time and ensure better comprehension.

should take less than five minutes. The benefits of taking time to pre-view *before* reading are as follows:

1. It builds background knowledge for easier learning.
2. It helps to transfer new information into long-term memory because you will have seen the material more than once.
3. It helps you to be active in your reading by having a plan of attack and a mapped direction.

It takes time to save time, and the time you spend pre-viewing is well spent toward learning.

Pre-Viewing a Nonfiction Book

Pre-viewing a nonfiction book, such as a computer manual, school textbook, or how-to book, is easy once you know what to look for. This pre-view process needs to be done just once—the first time you pick up a new book, before you start reading—to familiarize yourself with the material. Think of it as shaking hands with a new friend.

Pre-viewing a nonfiction book is accomplished by briefly focusing on each of the following elements.

THE TITLE AND SUBTITLE. The title of a nonfiction book tells you the topic, or the main idea. For example, a text entitled *Automotive Electronics* tells you that the book contains information about the electronic workings of a car. However, the text may not provide information about changing a car's oil or tires. A subtitle gives you more information. For instance, *Automotive Electronics: An Advanced Course* suggests that the basics will not be discussed and that more difficult topics will be emphasized.

THE AUTHOR. Chances are that you will have never heard of a book's author. So why even look at the name? Because the qualifications of the author or authors are important. Is he or she a specialist on the topic? Does the person have any college degrees or related work experience on the topic? Has the author published any other works on the subject?

This information can be found on a book's title page (for example, Dr. John Jones, Ph.D., Professor of Auto Mechanics at Abernathy College), on a page entitled "About the Author," or sometimes at the end of the book. (See page iii of this book for information about the author of this book.)

THE COPYRIGHT DATE. A text's copyright date is found on the left-hand page, immediately before or immediately after the title page, and is usually located next to the symbol ©. The copyright date, sometimes referred to as the publishing date, tells you how recent or how old the information is. For example, if you are taking a computer course and the book you are assigned is three years old, you know that developments in the field over the last three years will not be covered. A book with more than one copyright date has been revised or updated or is popular enough to have been reprinted. If a significant portion of a book has been revised, reworded, or rewritten, the title will indicate this by identifying the edition number (2d edition, 3d edition, and so on).

THE PREFACE. The preface of a textbook is usually found immediately before or after the table of contents. The preface may also be referred to as the foreword or the introduction. Many readers skip the preface thinking there is no important information there. However, many times it tells you why the author wrote the book and what you need to know about how the book is organized.

THE TABLE OF CONTENTS. Nonfiction books are written in *outline* form. The table of contents is essentially the outline of the text. By reviewing the table of contents, you can better understand the strategy the author used in writing the book, learn what will be covered, and discover what direction the author intends for communicating the information to the reader. Some textbook outlines are divided into *units* or *parts*, which show the general topics; then they are divided again into *chapters*, which indicate more specific areas of discussion.

THE APPENDIX, INDEX, GLOSSARY, AND BIBLIOGRAPHY. The *appendix, index, glossary,* and *bibliography,* usually found at the back of a book, provide additional information. By pre-viewing them, you will know what resources are available to you. Too many readers do not realize that these valuable learning tools are right in their own hands.

An appendix contains supplementary information that further explains a subject in the text. It might also contain an answer key to chapter questions or tests.

An index is an alphabetical listing of names, places, topics, and the numbers of the pages on which they are mentioned or discussed. The index is helpful when searching for specific information, especially when researching a specific topic.

A glossary is a list of terms with accompanying definitions. In a book entitled *Computer Basics,* the glossary would list the jargon, or specialized vocabulary terms, relating to computers. Though a regular dictionary may contain the same vocabulary terms, the textbook glossary will give practical definitions for use in your course.

A bibliography describes what resources the author used in writing the book. You can use the bibliography to do further research on a specific topic or to read additional perspectives on a topic.

Figure 8-2 is a quick-reference worksheet you can copy and use for pre-viewing a nonfiction book. It is meant to remind you of what to look for in a book. After locating the information in several different books, you will probably be able to pre-view a book without using the worksheet.

Place a check mark in the blank before each item once you have pre-viewed it in a book. After each item, write any related information you believe is appropriate or important. As you become used to pre-viewing nonfiction books, keep this list as a reminder tool.

> *"Almost all men are intelligent; it's the method they lack."*
>
> **—F. W. Nichol, Business educator**

Locate a nonfiction textbook, preferably one you have not seen before. Answer the following questions.

1. What is the title of the textbook? What does the title suggest about the content? _____

_____

2. What is the subtitle of the text, if any? What additional information does it provide about the book's content? _____

_____

3. What can you learn about the author(s) of your text? _____

_____

_____

4. What is the copyright date of the text? What does it tell you about the book? _____

_____

_____

5. What is the edition of the text? What do you think this means? _____

_____

_____

6. Read the preface of the text. What information does it give you? _____

_____

_____

7. Review the table of contents. How is the author's outline presented to you? Does it give the structure of your book? _____

_____

_____

8. Does the text have an appendix, an index, a glossary, and/or a bibliography? _____

_____

_____

9. How would this information be helpful to your learning? _____

_____

_____

_____

FIGURE 8-2

A Quick-Reference Worksheet

_____Title: _____

_____

_____Author(s): _____

_____

_____Copyright Date: _____

_____Preface or Introduction: _____

_____Table of Contents: _____

_____Units or Sections: _____

_____Chapters: _____

_____

_____Appendix: _____

_____Index: _____

_____Glossary: _____

_____Bibliography: _____

_____Other Comments: _____

_____

_____

_____

Pre-Viewing a Nonfiction Chapter or Article

Once you have pre-viewed a complete nonfiction book or magazine article, you are ready to pre-view a single chapter or section. This will provide you with the detailed information you need to prepare a plan of attack, map out your direction, and create a course of action for using your time wisely.

Pre-viewing a single chapter or an article is accomplished by briefly focusing on each of the following elements.

THE TITLE. The title of a chapter or an article tells you the topic or main idea. A title alone may not describe the specifics, but it will give you a general idea of the subject matter.

HEADINGS AND SUBHEADINGS. Headings and subheadings provide you with more specific information about the chapter as well as an outline of the information. Publishers usually indicate headings and subheadings by printing them on separate lines or in slightly larger print than the rest of the text. Figure 8-3 illustrates headings and subheadings in more detail.

FIGURE 8-3

Headings and Subheadings

This is a → **KNOW THE CORE ELEMENTS OF SUCCESSFUL**
heading   **INTERVIEWING**

You are screened into an interview because you appear qualified on paper. The employer uses the interview to learn whether you have the personal qualities needed to fit into the organization and to further confirm your work performance qualifications.

This is a → **The First 30 Seconds Count**
subheading

People often form opinions about others within 30 seconds of first meeting them! For this reason, the first 30 seconds can make or break an interview. Interviewers say they form strong opinions about an applicant in the time it takes the applicant to walk across the room, say "Hello," and sit down.

This is a → **Image and Appearance**
subheading

Have you ever looked at a display of CDs or books and been drawn to one with an appealing cover? The same concept applies in interviews. Remember: By the time you have walked into the room and sat down, the interviewer has decided whether you will be considered for the position. Your image and appearance help determine the first impression you make and may count for as much as 25 percent of the employer's positive or negative hiring decision.

This is a → **Know how the outer package helps the sale**
subheading
to the above   Cosmetic firms are well aware of the impact of the package; some people spend six times as much for the package
subheading   as they do for the product inside! Products that are packaged attractively far outsell those that are not.

Source: Levitt, Julie Griffin. *Your Career: How to Make It Happen.* © 2006 Thomson South-Western.

THE LENGTH OF READING. The length of a chapter or an article is important because it suggests how much time you can expect to spend reading. If the material is long, you may want to break the reading into smaller, more manageable sections. This helps you take more control over your reading time.

INTRODUCTORY PARAGRAPHS. Introductory paragraphs are the first several paragraphs of the material. They are, in effect, the start of your reading journey. These paragraphs give you an overview of what is ahead. Some chapters include an outline on the first page. If your chapter has one, look it over because it will tell you what material will be discussed.

TOPIC SENTENCES. Topic sentences in nonfiction material are almost always found in the first sentence of every paragraph. A **topic sentence** provides you with the main idea of a paragraph. Though there may be more than one topic sentence in a paragraph, you need to pre-view only the first sentence. By looking at the topic sentences *before* beginning to read, you will know specifically what information will be presented and in what order.

When pre-viewing topic sentences, be careful not to read every sentence in the paragraph. Until you become accustomed to pre-viewing, you will tend to read passively from the first word to the last. Here, you are asked to read actively, looking only for topic sentences, and following the author's train of thought instead of your wandering mind.

SUMMARY PARAGRAPHS. Summary, or concluding, paragraphs are found at the end of the chapter or article. They tell you, in effect, where your journey will end and summarize where you have been. Some books make this easy for you by including a subheading called "summary" or "conclusion" at the end of a chapter.

ACTIVITY 5

Locate a nonfiction chapter or article, preferably one you have not seen before. Find the information requested below, and respond to the questions. Use a separate piece of paper if more room is needed.

1. List the title, headings, and subheadings, in order, of your chapter or article.

   _____

   _____

2. Count and note the number of pages. Then estimate how long it will take you to read the chapter or article. What did you find?

   _____

   _____

3. Pre-view the introductory paragraphs of your chapter or article. What material do you expect to read about?

   _____

   _____

4. Pre-view the topic sentences of every paragraph. If the chapter or article is long, work with one section (or approximately ten pages). What kinds of specific information do the topic sentences tell you to expect to read about?

   _____

   _____

5. Pre-view the summary or concluding paragraphs of your chapter. What other information do they suggest?

   _____

   _____

In addition to the outline of the chapter—the way the writer has sequenced his or her thoughts—there are other writing clues to observe.

BOLDFACE AND ITALICIZED PRINT. **Boldface** and *italicized print* are other ways that publishers indicate something is important, such as a

This is a margin note. It is printed in the margin to point out something important from this page. Often, it is a direct quote from the text or some comment about the content that deserves your extra attention.

new vocabulary term, a person's name, a date, or an event. **Boldface** words, **dark print like this**, usually indicate a new vocabulary term, while *italicized* words, *slanted printing like this*, usually mean something important or reference the source of a quote.

If your material has many boldface or italicized words or includes a list of key terms you will responsible for, it helps to create a way to become familiar with them *before* you read. Some readers keep a running vocabulary list with definitions, while others make flash cards.

MARGIN NOTES AND FOOTNOTES. Margin notes are located in the blank space outside the printed text on a page. They usually point out an important idea the author wants you to understand. They may also contain additional information related to the subject.

Footnotes are indicated with superscript numbers like this.[1] They are found either at the bottom of the page, at the end of a chapter, or at the end of a book. They provide explanatory comments or reference notes that relate to a specific piece of information on a page. For example, if the author wants to provide more information about osmosis[12], you would look for footnote number 12. Review footnotes before you begin reading to learn whether you need the information to better understand the text.

ILLUSTRATIONS AND CAPTIONS. The saying "a picture is worth a thousand words" is a good reason to pre-view illustrations and captions. Illustrations include any photos, figures, graphs, tables, or cartoons. **Captions** provide information above, below, or alongside the illustration to explain its content or purpose. Publishers provide illustrations and captions to help the reader better understand the material being presented.

END-OF-CHAPTER QUESTIONS. The questions at the end of the chapter of a textbook are useful for students. Though some students feel they are cheating when they look ahead, these questions are vital for establishing your purpose in learning the material and in fulfilling your reading responsibility. They tell you what the author wants you to learn from the chapter and offer a way to check your understanding of the material. By pre-viewing them, you will know what you need to spend your time on while you are reading, and you will be better prepared to answer the questions quickly and effectively. These questions are also fair game on a test.

Many different types of questions and information requests are used in an end-of-chapter review. A vocabulary or key term list provides new vocabulary for the chapter. A review or discussion section asks questions about the information presented.

You may be asked to discuss your answers either on paper or with another classmate. By answering all the questions, you will have a clearer understanding of the material. Activities or projects are a way to learn first-hand about the information discussed in the chapter. They are useful and active ways to apply new information to the real world.

Pre-viewing a chapter before reading is like looking at a road map before taking a car trip. Once you have an idea of where you are going, the trip goes more smoothly, comfortably, and efficiently.

©Getty Images/PhotoDisc

ACTIVITY 6

Using the same chapter or article from Activity 5, find the information requested below, and respond to the questions. Use a separate piece of paper if needed.

1. Look for boldface and italicized words. Make a list of any that you don't know; then find the meaning of each one.

   _____

   _____

2. Look for margin notes and footnotes. Read any important information provided in the margins, and observe where the footnotes are located. What do you see?

   _____

   _____

3. Look at the illustrations and captions. What do they say about what you will be reading?

   _____

   _____

4. Review the questions at the end of your chapter (for textbooks only). How many different types of questions are asked? Which type seems the easiest? Most difficult? Which are most time consuming to answer?

   _____

   _____

   _____

   _____

At this point, you have spent time becoming familiar with your reading and have gained valuable background knowledge that will make the reading easier. Are you able to read familiar material faster with better comprehension than unfamiliar material?

Figure 8-4 is a quick-reference worksheet you can copy and use for pre-viewing a chapter or an article. It is meant to remind you of what to look for to enhance your understanding of the material. After locating the information several times, you will probably be able to pre-view without using the worksheet.

Place a check mark in the blank before each item once you have pre-viewed it in a chapter or an article. After each item, fill in the information requested with any related information you believe is appropriate or important. Once you feel comfortable with pre-viewing, keep this list as a reminder tool.

FIGURE 8-4

A Quick-Reference Worksheet

Pre-Viewing a Chapter or an Article

The Reading: _____

_____ Purpose: _____

_____ Reading Responsibility: _____

_____ Chapter Title: _____

_____ Headings and Subheadings: _____

_____

_____

_____ Length of Material: _____

_____ Expected Reading Time: _____

_____ Introductory Paragraphs: _____

_____

_____

_____ Topic Sentences: _____

_____

_____ Summary or Concluding Paragraphs: _____

_____

_____

_____ Boldface and Italicized Print: _____

_____ Margin Notes and Footnotes: _____

_____ Illustrations and Captions: _____

_____ End-of-Chapter Questions: _____

_____

You should now be able to pre-view effectively because you know how to prepare a plan of attack, map out a direction, and create a course of action for using your time wisely. It works with entire books or individual chapters. Since all nonfiction material is similar in structure, you can now approach any reading with confidence and assurance.

A NOTE ABOUT PRE-VIEWING AND GOOD WRITING. Since your job as a nonfiction reader is to find the writer's main ideas, you have a responsibility to make those ideas easy to find when you write. This job will be easier if 1) you create an outline before you write and 2) you pre-view your writing after you write by focusing on the first sentences of paragraphs.

If you recently wrote an essay or paper, do this now: Read your introduction, the first sentence only of each paragraph, and then the conclusion. Is your outline easy to follow? If not, use this easy review strategy to make your writing more organized and understandable for your readers!

Focus on Technology

Refresh Your Eyes! If you find your eyes getting dry and itchy after working at your computer, try this refreshing tip:

While sitting at the computer, rub your hands together rapidly for 10 seconds, gently close your eyes and criss-cross your hands over your eyes while resting your elbows on a table. Visualize yourself in a very relaxing place. Picture the scene with as much detail as possible, following the movements of people, noticing colors, smells, tastes, and sounds. Do this for 3-5 minutes. Take a few deep breaths. It will relax you mentally and help refresh your dry eyes. Experts recommend taking a break from the computer screen every 45-60 minutes.

Checkpoint

1 In your own words, what does pre-viewing mean?

_____

_____

_____

2 What are some benefits of pre-viewing?

_____

_____

_____

3 What are the drawbacks, if any, to pre-viewing?

_____

_____

_____

"*When you have a wide vocabulary, NOTHING surprises you!*"

—Alan Weiss, Business speaker and author of 23 books

Building Vocabulary

The easiest way to ensure understanding of what you read is to develop a broad vocabulary. No matter what your reading strategy is, the more words you know and understand, the easier comprehension will be. Which of the following statements is (are) true?

1. Words have specific meanings.
2. Words are given meaning depending upon the way they are used.

If you believe both statements are true, you are right. Every word has a specific meaning, and words change their meaning depending upon how they are used. So, how can you ever learn all of the meanings of words? The best two things you can do are 1) recognize your word choices and 2) realize that many words have more than one meaning.

The most commonly used ways to build vocabulary include 1) looking for context clues, 2) using word structures, 3) skipping words (only at certain times), 4) using a dictionary, and 5) asking someone. Though each way of building vocabulary will be discussed, the ones introduced first are those that encourage you to use the dictionary you already have—your brain. *If you can figure out word meanings on your own, you will build your vocabulary more quickly and easily.*

Using Background Knowledge

Learning new vocabulary is easiest when you start with your own **background knowledge**. Background knowledge is what you already know based on your previous experiences and learning.

Since you already know many words, you can use them to increase the size of your vocabulary. If, for example, you know how to change the oil in your car, you have some background knowledge in the way a car functions. If you were taking a course in automotive repair, this information would be useful in learning more about a car's workings. Without knowing how to change a car's oil or anything about the engine, your job of learning would be more challenging. The following strategies use your background knowledge to build vocabulary.

LOOKING FOR CONTEXT CLUES. Gaining a good understanding of what you are reading without wasting time can be accomplished by using context clues. **Context clues** are the words surrounding the unknown word. They give hints to the meaning of the vocabulary word. Many times, you will be able to predict or guess the meaning of the word by using these clues. Since getting an exact dictionary definition isn't always necessary and sometimes is not possible, you can develop a working definition that is good enough to help you understand the passage you are reading.

Though always helpful, context clues may not be enough to help you guess the meaning of the unknown word. For example, *mononucleosis* is commonly found among young people who work hard and do not eat well or get enough sleep.

In the following sentences, use context clues to predict the meaning of each word in italics.

1. Though the weather was not in their favor, the research team members were *optimistic* that their mission would be successful.

   _____

   _____

   _____

2. In the concert hall, the enthusiastic fans *congregated* around the band like bees around honey.

   _____

   _____

   _____

3. The telephone company helped the assistant save space on her desk by *consolidating* the four telephone lines into one.

   _____

   _____

   _____

4. After listening to the *interminable* speeches, the graduates were tired and anxious to leave the heat of the auditorium.

   _____

   _____

   _____

   _____

In a sentence that uses a complex word like *mononucleosis*, figuring out the definition through context is not possible using word structures. The option described below for learning vocabulary will be more helpful.

USING WORD STRUCTURES. Word structures are the parts of words called prefixes, roots, and suffixes. A **root word** is the basic part of a word that conveys the word's foundation or origin. The other two parts are added to a root, and each of them changes the word meaning. A **prefix** is the portion of the word added to the beginning, and a **suffix** is the portion of the word added at the end. Each of these parts is a link to a chain of meaning. If you learn to identify the meaning of one or more parts of a word, you will be able to closely predict the meaning of a word.

The word *mononucleosis*, in the previous example, is made up of a prefix, a root, and a suffix. With this information, you could determine that the meaning of *mononucleosis* is "the condition of one cell." (See Figure 8-5.)

A single word part can be found in many words. A list of other words that contain the word *mono* follows. Notice how the meaning of *mono*—one—is present in all the definitions in Figure 8-6.

FIGURE 8-5

Word Structures

Type of Word Structure	Word	Meaning of Word Structure
prefix	mono	one
root	nucle(us)	cell
suffix	osis	condition of

FIGURE 8-6

Word Structures Example

Example	Definition
monorail	**one** rail
monograph	a writing about **one** thing
monochromatic	consisting of **one** color
monomania	excessive concentration on **one** idea or thought
monopoly	**one** seller of a product or service
monocular	involving **one** eye
monogamy	having **one** mate at a time
monologue	a talk by **one** speaker
monomial	a mathematical expression consisting of **one** term
monoplane	an airplane with **one** set of wings
monosyllabic	describing a word with **one** syllable
monotony	doing **one** thing over and over again
monolith	**one** massive stone, usually in the form of an obelisk or column
monolingual	using only **one** language

Using the prefixes, root words, suffixes and their meanings and examples provided below, create new words that use the same word structures. Also, provide the meanings of the words you create. You can work individually or with a partner to complete this activity.

Prefix	Meaning	New Word and Its Meaning
bi-	two	binocular = involving **two** eyes
		bicycle
in-	not	inseparable = **not** able to be pulled apart
		inconclusive
re-	again, back	reconstruct = to build **again**
		rework, redo,

Root Word	Meaning	New Word and Its Meaning
bio	life	microbiology = study of small **living** things
		biography
dem	people	epidemic = affecting a lot of **people** (such as a disease)
		democrat
graph	writing	monograph = a **writing** about one thing
		geography,
nov	new	renovate = to make **new** again
		novel,
thermo	heat	thermostat = a device that measures **heat**
		thermosphere

Suffix	Meaning	New Word and Its Meaning
-able	capable of	portable = **capable of** being carried
		stable,
-ation	the act of	collation = **the act of** putting things together
		rotation, notation
-ous	full of	religious = **full of** belief in religion
		volprous

These are just a few of the common prefixes, roots, and suffixes you can learn. Remember, every word part you recognize and understand is another valuable addition to your background knowledge.

SKIPPING WORDS. Skipping an unfamiliar word is not the best way to build your vocabulary. However, it is an effective way to avoid wasting time while still understanding most of what you've read. The trick is to make sure you understand enough.

Read the following two paragraphs. Of the two, which contains an italicized word that you think could be skipped, and which one contains a word that needs to be defined?

Paragraph One:

A scanned photograph can be *cropped* using desktop publishing software, which makes *cropping* electronically a relatively simple procedure. If you must *crop* a photograph by hand, never draw *crop* marks directly on the photograph.

Paragraph Two:

Illness has always been a part of the human condition. Care has been given according to the *folkways* and beliefs of society. Care also depends on the knowledge and kinds of treatments available.

In the first paragraph, the word *crop* appears several times and describes a concept that would be lost if you did not know what the word *crop* meant. *Cropping* means trimming a photograph to make it smaller or focus on part of the image.

In the second paragraph, the word *folkways* serves as a descriptive word that doesn't carry a lot of importance to the meaning of the sentence. *Folkways* are the traditional patterns of life common to people. In this case, you might not take the time to figure out the word in paragraph two, but you would want to determine the meaning of the word in paragraph one.

You may decide that skipping a word would not greatly affect your understanding. If that is the case, then don't spend time trying to determine the meaning of the word. But if you don't understand what you are reading because you don't know a word, you should try to figure out its meaning.

USING A DICTIONARY. Using a dictionary is a common way to find out the meaning of an unfamiliar word if you cannot determine its meaning otherwise. Keep a dictionary nearby during your study sessions so it is handy to use.

Using a dictionary can be a time-consuming process. If you can figure out the word by using your brain as a dictionary instead (using context clues or word structures), you will be able to continue your reading quickly. If you cannot figure out the word on your own, you'll have to use the dictionary—a process that will take longer.

> "*If you want to make good use of your time, you've got to know what's most important and then give it all you've got.*"
> —Lee Iacocca, Former CEO of Chrysler

When you use a dictionary, you have to stop reading, find a dictionary, go back to your reading, and find the unfamiliar word again, determine how it is spelled, and then look it up in the dictionary by flipping pages until you locate the word. If the word has more than one meaning, you will look at each meaning and decide which one best fits the context of your reading. Once you identify the correct meaning of the word, you will close the dictionary, locate the place where you stopped reading, and reread a few lines to remember what the material was about. This process takes *much* longer than using context clues and word structures.

The other problem with using a dictionary is that you may not remember the word a week or a month later without looking it up again. You don't always remember new things the first time you come across them. This is why relying on the dictionary as the only way to find the meaning of unfamiliar words is not as effective as using your background knowledge.

Remembering words through the use of repetition or frequent review is helpful. Smart dictionary users write an unfamiliar word on a piece of paper (Figure 8-7) or an index card (Figure 8-8). The word is on one side; the meaning on the other. This allows you to review the words repeatedly without wasting time looking them up more than once. They then become part of your background knowledge for use in the future.

> Relying on a dictionary as the only way of finding the meaning of unfamiliar words is not as effective as using your background knowledge.

FIGURE 8-7

Using Notebook Paper for Learning New Vocabulary

	Chapter 7 pp. 91-97	Wind and the Landscape
○		
	Erosion=	A wearing away of land due to wind or waves—it happens over time
	Dunes=	Sand deposited by wind in the form of hills or ridges
	Transverse dunes=	Long, wavelike ridges—found on beaches
	Parabolic dunes=	Contain a blowout in the center with high-ridge sides
	Barchan dunes=	Crescent-shaped dunes
	Waves=	Formed by wind blowing over water
	Wave period=	Time required for a wave to go
○		the distance of one wave length
	Tsunamis=	Waves created by earthquakes; very large and destructive length

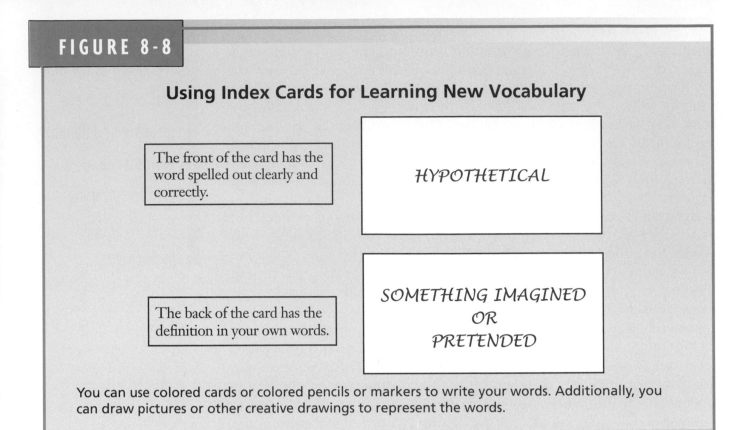

FIGURE 8-8

Using Index Cards for Learning New Vocabulary

The front of the card has the word spelled out clearly and correctly.

HYPOTHETICAL

The back of the card has the definition in your own words.

SOMETHING IMAGINED OR PRETENDED

You can use colored cards or colored pencils or markers to write your words. Additionally, you can draw pictures or other creative drawings to represent the words.

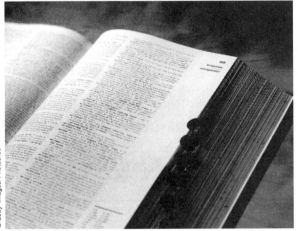

All dictionaries provide definitions, but if you want the shorter version, try the abridged first.

©Getty Images/PhotoDisc

TYPES OF DICTIONARIES. There are several types of dictionaries. An **unabridged dictionary** is the most complete because it includes all words and definitions. An **abridged dictionary** is a shorter version of an unabridged dictionary. It is smaller in size because words are omitted. However, an abridged dictionary is useful for finding the meaning of most vocabulary words. Abridged dictionaries are popular because they are easy to carry and store. Many dictionary publishers also sell a pocket or vest dictionary that is convenient for school or work.

A **thesaurus** is a type of dictionary that contains only synonyms and antonyms. **Synonyms** are words that are similar in meaning; **antonyms** are words that are opposite in meaning. A thesaurus is useful for expanding your background knowledge and for writing essays and reports. Figure 8-9 shows sample entries from a *thesaurus*.

Another type of dictionary is a "walking dictionary." This is not a book but a person (such as a relative, an instructor, a coworker, or a friend) you ask to help you figure out a word you don't understand. *Before asking a walking dictionary the meaning of a word, you should try to figure the meaning out on your own.* The person you ask can save you time, but he or she cannot help you remember the word when you come across it again, which is another good reason to write down new words on notebook paper or index cards.

FIGURE 8-9

Thesaurus Example

Word	Meaning	Synonym	Antonym
danger	the state of being exposed to injury, pain, or loss risk	hazard, jeopardy, peril	security
silence	absence of sound or noise	noiselessness, quiet, quietness, stillness soundlessness	din, uproar, noise

Vocabulary of Your Trade

Every career has unique vocabulary. Your job is to master and use this vocabulary while speaking and writing. You find the terms in an instructor's lecture, nonfiction books, related projects, and work experiences. In nonfiction books, the terms are often printed in italics or boldface. There may also be a vocabulary list at the beginning or end of a chapter. A glossary—a specialized dictionary—may be in the back of the book to help you find word meanings.

CREATE YOUR OWN GLOSSARY. If the words in a chapter are unfamiliar to you, you will find learning them easier if you write the words and their definitions on notepaper or on index cards before you read. This gives you a self-made study system and valuable background knowledge that helps you understand the information you read.

USE WORD STRUCTURES. Using what you know about prefixes, roots, and suffixes is very useful in learning specialized terms. For example, if you were taking a medical course or a science course, the following word structures would be used often. Note how the meaning of the word part relates to the meaning of the word.

anti- = against

    anticoagulant = prevents the formation of blood clots

    antiseptic = prevents growth of germs

cardio(a)- = heart

    cardiology = the study of the heart

    tachy**cardia** = a rapid heartbeat

■ Focus on Ethics

You work part-time answering the phone in a pharmacy. One day, a customer calls with a question regarding the proper dosage of a medication—something you've never heard of with a long, complex name. You don't want to appear ignorant, so you don't ask the customer for the correct spelling. Instead, you write a message for the pharmacist, taking a guess at the name of the medication. Unknowingly, you write the name of another medication with a very similar name. Why might this be a serious problem? How could it have been prevented?

-ectomy = to take out; to remove

    hyster**ectomy** = to remove the uterus

    tonsill**ectomy** = to take out the tonsils

-itis = inflammation of; swelling

    tendon**itis** = inflammation of the tendons

    bronch**itis** = inflammation of the windpipe

If you were taking paralegal studies or a government course, the following word structures would be common. Note how the meaning of the word part relates to the meaning of the word.

appel- = to appeal to; to ask for help

    appellant = a person bringing an appeal

    appellee = a person who is against an appeal

jur- = to judge; having to do with justice; to swear

    jurisdiction = the power of a court to judge a particular case

    jury = a group of people who judge a court case

Every subject has a unique vocabulary. Learning new terms is easier when you apply the strategies in this chapter.

Checkpoint

1 Why is knowing a large number of words important?

_____

_____

_____

_____

2 What are the easiest ways to learn new words?

_____

_____

_____

3 Why is it important to develop a broad vocabulary?

_____

_____

_____

CHAPTER SUMMARY

1. Becoming an active learner means becoming an active reader. Active readers develop a plan of attack, map out a direction, and create a course of action for using their time wisely. Having a reading purpose and responsibility is an active beginning for any reading assignment.

2. Nonfiction material is factual in nature, while fiction is made up, or imaginative. Academic textbooks are nonfiction.

3. Pre-viewing is examining material before reading it to discover clues to its contents.

4. You should pre-view a nonfiction book before you begin reading the book for the first time to familiarize yourself with the material.

5. Pre-viewing a nonfiction chapter or article allows you to determine the author's outline and other important information related to the topic. Pre-viewing also provides background knowledge about what you will be learning.

6. Your background knowledge is what you already know based on your previous experiences and learning. The more background knowledge you have, the easier it is to discover word definitions using the dictionary you were born with—your brain.

7. Looking for context clues and using word structures are two ways to build vocabulary using background knowledge.

8. Skipping unfamiliar words is not the best way to build your vocabulary. You can, however, skip an unfamiliar word when you believe your understanding won't be greatly affected.

9. Use a dictionary to learn the meanings of unfamiliar words. The best time to use a dictionary is when you cannot figure out a word's meaning using your background knowledge.

10. There are four types of dictionaries: unabridged, abridged, thesaurus, and "walking."

11. Keeping track of your vocabulary by writing any new word and its definition on notebook paper or index cards is useful.

12. Learning career vocabulary is easier if you create your own glossary and use word structures.

CHAPTER ASSESSMENT

Terms Review

Match the following terms to their definitions.

B	abridged dictionary	a.	The most complete dictionary
P	active reader	b.	A shorter dictionary that is useful for defining most words
H	antonyms	c.	The portion of a word that is added to the beginning
Q	background knowledge	d.	The main part of a word that conveys the meaning
R	caption	e.	The portion of a word that is added to the end
N	context clues	f.	A reference noted by a superscript number next to a word
M	fiction	g.	Words that have similar meanings
F	footnote	h.	Words that have opposite meanings
S	margin note	i.	The ways you are accountable for the information you read

_L_ nonfiction

_O_ passive reader

_C_ prefix

_K_ pre-viewing

_U_ reading purpose

_I_ reading responsibility

_D_ root word

_E_ suffix

_G_ synonyms

_T_ thesaurus

_J_ topic sentence

_A_ unabridged dictionary

j. Sentence that gives the reader the main idea of the paragraph

k. Examining nonfiction material to discover the writer's outline *before* reading in detail

l. Reading material that is factual in nature

m. Reading material that is invented and imaginative in nature

n. Words surrounding an unknown word that can give hints to its meaning

o. A reader who reads everything from the beginning to the end without mapping the direction or having a plan of attack

p. A reader who uses pre-reading strategies to enhance vocabulary and understanding

q. What a reader already knows based on previous experiences

r. Information that explains the content or purpose of an illustration

s. A direct quote from the text or some comment about the content that deserves extra attention in the margin

t. A kind of dictionary that only has synonyms and antonyms, not definitions

u. Your reason for reading

Review

Based on the information you learned in this chapter, answer the following questions using your own words and thoughts.

1. What is pre-viewing? Why is pre-viewing important?

_____

_____

_____

_____

2. When you pre-view a nonfiction book, what do you look for?

_____

_____

_____

_____

3. When you pre-view a nonfiction chapter or article, what do you look for?

_____

_____

_____

_____

_____

_____

4. What do you think the differences in learning are between someone who pre-views and someone who doesn't?

_____

_____

_____

_____

5. What is background knowledge? How does it influence your ability to learn new vocabulary?

_____

_____

_____

_____

6. What does background knowledge have to do with learning in general?

_____

_____

_____

_____

7. What is the relationship between pre-viewing and background knowledge?

_____

_____

_____

_____

8. What are some ways to figure out the meaning of an unknown word? Describe at least three.

_____

_____

_____

_____

9. What would you recommend another learner do to build his or her vocabulary?

_____

_____

_____

_____

10. What are the most important things you learned from this chapter?

_____

_____

_____

_____

CASE STUDIES

for Creative and Critical Thinking

 ACADEMIC CASE—Connecting to Biology and the Sciences

Julia had three days to prepare for a cell biology exam, and she hadn't even cracked the book. She didn't know where to start, so she just read the chapters from start to finish. After all, that's what was assigned. Julia came across many sentences she didn't understand because the vocabulary was unfamiliar. She always has trouble with new words. One sentence in particular baffled her, which read "Bacterial mRNAs are often *polycistronic*, while eukaryotic cells generally encode only a single protein." She didn't understand the term *polycistronic*, so she decided to look it up in the dictionary. It wasn't there. She tried the glossary in the back of her book. As bad luck would have it, it wasn't defined there either. She knows she needs the term for her exam, and she is at a loss for what to do.

1. What other strategy(ies) can Julia use to find the meaning of her unknown word?

_____

_____

_____

_____

_____

2. Using your background knowledge and parts of the unknown word *polycistronic*, what other words come to mind?

_____

_____

_____

_____

3. What are some of the best ways to learn vocabulary? Will Julia do well with just three days to go?

_____

_____

_____

_____

_____

4. Knowing what you know about how to read and learn vocabulary, what suggestions would you give Julia?

_____

_____

_____

_____

_____

When Eva's work group asked her to run the next meeting, she knew she needed to know general meeting guidelines called "Robert's Rules of Order" to make it an effective session. At her local library, she located six books on how to conduct meetings with Robert's Rules of Order and took them all to a reading table. She felt overwhelmed when she looked at the stack of books in front of her. "Which one or two of the books would be most useful?" she wondered. "Do I have to read them all?!" She nervously looked at her watch thinking about all the other things she needed to do, knowing she didn't have time to read all six books.

1. Based on her time constraints, what "plan of attack" would you suggest to Eva to help her organize how she will examine the six books?

_____

_____

_____

_____

_____

_____

2. What information would be most important for Eva to look at in each book so she can choose the one or two books that will be most useful to her?

_____

_____

_____

_____

_____

3. Once she picks the two books, how can she find the information quickly without reading it all?

_____

_____

_____

_____

_____

_____

4. Where else can Eva look for the information she needs?

_____

_____

_____

_____

_____

_____

9 Revving Up Your Reading

Terms

- alphabetical
- category
- chronological
- column width
- eye span
- flexible reader
- key words
- pacer
- peripheral vision
- phrases
- scanning
- skimming
- textual

Chapter Goals

After studying and working with the information in this chapter, you should be able to:

- Identify the reading gears and qualities of a flexible reader.
- Explain the unlearning to relearn concept and identify the main reason to read faster.
- Describe THE tools for reading faster.
- Describe the similarities and differences between skimming and scanning.
- Identify the three factors for determining your reading speed and begin using the recommended tools on your own daily reading.

Kim, a customer service representative for an insurance company was mumbling quietly to himself, "Oh, no. I'm running out of time again. I can't believe I let this happen."

"What's the matter now?" asked Aaliyah, a coworker who was sitting beside him.

"I'm so backed up on my reading, it's ridiculous!" exclaimed Kim. "Between all the meetings, people dropping by my office, the e-mail that beeps constantly, and the phone that keeps ringing, I can't get any work done. Our department's policies are being revamped, and I'm supposed to read the proposed changes before every meeting. Sometimes there are 30 to 60 pages in each report, and we have weekly meetings! I really hate being unprepared for these meetings, but I just can't manage to read all the policy changes in time. And it's not very interesting stuff—it reminds me of the reading I had in my finance class last semester."

"Are you still taking night classes?" asked Aaliyah.

"Yes, an English Lit course. You should see the pile of reading I have for that course, too! My professor thinks all I have to do in my life is read. Even if all I did was read, I STILL don't think I'd finish it all. How am I *ever* going to get through all of this reading?"

Do you have any suggestions that might help Kim manage his reading workload?

Speed reading courses, which became popular in the early 1950s, are needed now more than ever. First, people want to do more in less time. Reading has typically been a time-consuming task that seems to take forever—especially for those who want to learn from printed material.

Second, there is an information explosion causing information overload. Information is produced and processed faster today than ever before due to computers and other high-tech advances. When someone comes up with a new idea or way of doing something, it often ends up being published on the Internet or in magazines, newspapers, or books. According to the American Booksellers Association of America, there were more than 180,000 new titles added to *Books in Print* in 2004 alone! This figure is up sharply from 104,000 in 1993. This does not include magazines, newspapers, junk mail, and other forms of printed and electronic information! Because the Internet is so easy to use, a massive amount of information is added every day.

Third, reading faster with good comprehension enables students and professionals to keep current in their fields and to advance in their careers. Reading is an important tool for those who want to be successful.

Finally, people need better and faster reading skills to help them concentrate and focus. Slower readers daydream much more than faster readers. Faster readers, provided they are using the effective strategies introduced in this book, concentrate better and ultimately understand more in less time.

In Chapter 8, you learned how to pre-view both a nonfiction book and a nonfiction chapter. Pre-viewing helps you read faster because you become familiar with the material first. In this chapter, you will learn other tools to help you read faster and better. You will also learn to read efficiently, which is as important as reading quickly.

> Information is produced and processed faster today than ever before due to computers and other high-tech advances. Are you prepared with effective reading skills to manage it all?

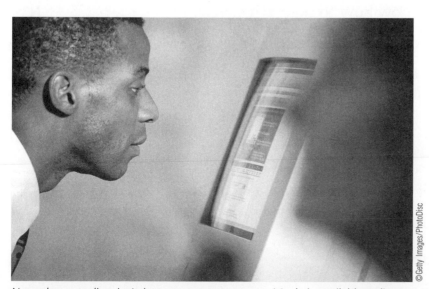

Nowadays, reading isn't just on paper anymore. Much is available online as well. The better your skills are on paper, the better they will be on-screen!

The following self-evaluation will give you an idea of how familiar, or unfamiliar, you are with some of the topics and terms discussed in this chapter. After reading each statement, circle the letter Y, S, or N to indicate the answer that is most appropriate for you. Answer honestly. Rate yourself at the end; then complete the information on your Self-Check Progress Chart.

Y = yes; frequently   S = sometimes   N = no; never

1. I can handle my reading workload with ease.   Y   S   N

2. I know how to effectively increase my reading speed.   Y   S   N

3. I know how to locate and read key words.   Y   S   N

4. I know how to locate and read in phrases.   Y   S   N

5. I know how to use my hands or a white card to help me increase my reading speed.   Y   S   N

6. I know how to adjust my reading speed according to my purpose and background knowledge.   Y   S   N

7. I know the difference between skimming and scanning.   Y   S   N

8. I know how to skim effectively.   Y   S   N

9. I can scan accurately.   Y   S   N

10. I know that reading everything all the time is not an efficient use of my time.   Y   S   N

Rate Yourself:

Number of Ys _____ × 100 = _____

Number of Ss _____ × 50 = _____

Number of Ns _____ × 0 = _____   **Total**_____

The Reading Gears

Unskilled, passive readers are like one-speed vehicles. They read their favorite magazine and an academic textbook at the same speed. Skilled, active readers are like multi-speed vehicles. They change speeds according to the type of material, their reading purpose, and their background knowledge. They know when to speed up and when to slow down.

There are basically *three reading gears,* or speeds, that a reader typically uses. (See Figure 9-1.) *Low gear* ranges from about 100 words per minute (wpm) to 300 wpm and is used for word-for-word reading, as in studying, proofreading, or committing information to memory. First gear is also used for material that is difficult or about which you have little or no background knowledge. In low gear, you look for a high level of comprehension—about 80 to 90 percent.

If you read everything in *low gear,* you are definitely a passive reader. Chances are you talk while you are reading—either physically moving your lips or hearing your voice reading every word. Talking to yourself while reading slows you down, tires your eyes, and hinders comprehension. It causes your eyes to stop on every word instead of allowing you to focus on the more important words or thought units. Reading key words or phrases and using pacers, described next in this chapter, will help you avoid reading everything in low gear.

"Speed readers" don't read everything fast. They possess the ability to read faster and choose when to speed up and when to slow down. Are you in control of *your* reading speed?

FIGURE 9-1

The Reading Gears

Reading Gear	Type of Reading	Reading Speed in Words-per-Minute	Percent of Comprehension
LOW	Difficult material Studying Note taking Unfamiliar material	100–300	High (80%+)
MIDDLE	Everyday reading Magazines Newspapers Somewhat familiar material	300–600	Average (70%)
HIGH	All kinds of material Skimming Scanning Familiar material	600–1000	Lower (50%+)

"The first lesson reading teaches you is . . . how to be alone."

—Jonathan Franzen, Best-selling author

Middle gear ranges from 300 wpm to 600 wpm. Reading in the middle gear is appropriate for everyday reading, such as newspapers and magazines, and for somewhat familiar material. There is every reason to believe you can read literature and other fiction at this rate or faster. Most stories don't require you to have a lot of background knowledge; rather, the stories paint the pictures you need to understand the material.

Having some background knowledge helps, too. In middle gear, you aim for a comprehension ranging from 70 to 90 percent. You can also cover more material in less time.

High gear is almost twice as fast as middle gear, or from about 600 wpm to 1,000 wpm. Reading in high gear is appropriate for skimming and pre-viewing, where you don't read everything but still get the gist of the material. In high gear, your level of comprehension may be lower or higher than in middle gear, depending on your background knowledge.

Scanning is also done at high-gear speed, but because you look only for a piece of specific information, the speed can go even higher than 1,000 wpm. With scanning, accurately finding what you are seeking means 100 percent comprehension. Both skimming and scanning are described in more detail later in this chapter.

Shifting gears happens often when you read and works best if you do it intentionally. Speed shifts, either up or down, naturally occur because the material changes from familiar to unfamiliar or because your internal concentration level changes. This is another reason why setting up an effective reading environment is helpful for efficient reading. Pre-viewing helps you to gauge where you might be able to speed up and where you might need to slow down.

Just as a car has the ability to shift from slow to fast, readers also can shift gears— once they have the tools and knowledge to understand when to do it.

Identify which gear might be appropriate for the following reading. Is one gear enough, or could more than one gear be used?

Type of Reading	Purpose	Background Knowledge	Gear
Newspaper	To be knowledgeable about current events	Varies	*Middle to High*
Magazine	To build my background knowledge	Varies	
Textbook	To read an assigned chapter	Some	
Web site	To research Albert Einstein	None	
Instructions	To replace an oil filter	Some	
Manual	To locate a specific topic	Little	
Instructions	To download music from a web site	None	
Fiction book	To relax and enjoy	None	

Checkpoint

1 What specifically are the reading gears?

_____

_____

2 What helps you decide what speed you might use when you read?

_____

_____

3 What do you think could naturally happen to comprehension when you first increase your reading speed?

_____

_____

"*There are two ways of meeting difficulties. You alter the difficulties or you alter yourself to meet them.*"

—Phyllis Bottome, Novelist and lecturer

Learning to Read More in Less Time

Learning to read faster is a skill that is developed over a period of time. Since most people learn to read in the first grade—around age six—you can subtract six years from your current age; the result is the number of years you have been developing your reading habits. Whenever you try to change anything, including reading habits, you will feel a little uncomfortable at first because you are taking a new approach. But, by practicing the new habits, you will become comfortable with them and gain better reading skills. *This is called unlearning to relearn.*

Unlearning to Relearn

Unlearning to relearn can happen only *after* you have already learned how to do something. In this case, you have already learned to read. In order to improve your reading, you first need to unlearn the ways you have been reading; then relearn reading skills.

Let's take the example of a car with an automatic shift versus a car with a manual shift. Suppose you become an excellent driver using an automatic car. You are both comfortable and capable behind the wheel. However, the first time you try to drive a stick shift, you have trouble working the clutch, stall out in the middle of intersections, and grind the gears. You don't feel comfortable or capable. This is what unlearning can feel like.

At this point in driving, you might want to give up, thinking that you are no good at driving a stick shift. On the other hand, if driving a stick shift is necessary or important enough, continued practice will help you learn how to drive the car. Relearning the skill takes a little time and energy. Relearning means finding what works for you while making some mistakes along the way. With a little practice and desire, you can master the stick shift and once again become an excellent driver.

ACTIVITY 2

Discuss with a partner or group what other skills might require unlearning to relearn. Write your thoughts below.

_____

_____

_____

_____

_____

_____

While you are reading this chapter, have fun playing with some of the suggested tools for increasing your reading speed. Keep in mind that feeling uncomfortable is a positive sign that you are breaking an old habit and working toward creating a new one. The key is to keep experimenting with the new tools until they work for you. Not all of the tools work equally well for everyone, but by giving them a try, you will find the ones that work best for you.

THE Reason to Read Faster

You have already learned some of the reasons why reading faster is important. However, *the* main reason—concentration—has not been discussed yet. What do you think the relationship is between reading faster and your ability to concentrate? To read faster, you have to concentrate!

Speeding up forces you to focus. Compare reading faster to walking down a street. When you walk down a street, you can window shop, chew gum, talk with a friend, daydream, kick a rock, and so on. Now if you were to run down the same street, which of these activities could you still do well?

This example shows that you cannot do as many things as well when you run as opposed to when you walk. The same is true for reading. When you speed up, you are forced to focus and concentrate, which reduces your ability to daydream. By concentrating on the reading, you understand better what you are reading, learn more from everything you read, and finish your reading in a shorter amount of time. Does this sound like something you'd like to do? Read on!

Checkpoint

1 How might reading faster help you learn better?

_____

_____

2 What is meant by "unlearning to relearn"?

_____

_____

3 How does the speed of reading affect concentration?

_____

_____

_____

How to Increase Your Reading Speed

Remember that just reading, or beginning with the first word and stopping with the last, is the most passive way to read. When you add pre-viewing to your reading habits (Chapter 8), you begin to become more active.

The next three powerful strategies for reading actively include (1) reading key words and phrases, (2) using a pacer, and (3) adjusting your speed. These strategies will help you read more efficiently.

The ability to read faster depends on a natural human visual ability called peripheral vision. Your **peripheral vision** is the distance you are able to see on your left and right while staring straight ahead.

When you look at a page, you cannot see a wide distance. What you do see is your eye span. Your **eye span** is how much information you see at a time when you look down at a page. Reading faster can be accomplished by working with your peripheral vision to increase your eye span. There are three simple tools you can use to increase your eye span to read faster: reading key words, reading phrases, and using pacers.

ACTIVITY 3

Stare straight ahead at a point on a wall or at an object. Extend both arms in front of you with your fingertips pointing up. Without moving your head, and still staring at the point, slowly spread your arms out and back to each side while still seeing your hands. When your hands disappear from sight, bring them back in a little. Once you have found the farthest point your hands can spread without disappearing, look at how far apart they are. This is the range of your peripheral vision. If your vision, for whatever reason, is mostly from one eye, you probably will still have peripheral vision ability from that eye. How wide is your peripheral vision?

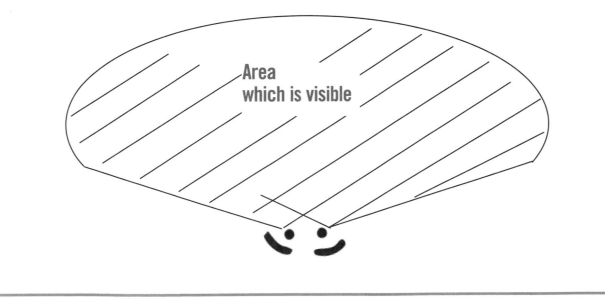

Area which is visible

Reading Key Words

Key words are the bigger, more important words in text. They are *usually* more than three letters long and carry the most meaning in a sentence. For example, most people read the following 13-word sentence word for word:

When you pick up a book, the world is literally at your fingertips.

However, by looking for and stopping your eyes only on the more important words, you can still understand the text while saving time. Read only the words in bold below:

When you **pick** up a **book,** the **world** is **literally** at your **fingertips.**

Now look at the words that are *not* in bold. Are you familiar with them? Haven't you seen them thousands of times? Are they as important as the words in bold? When reading only key words, understand that you are *not skipping* the other words. You are simply spreading your peripheral vision to increase your eye span to see both the key words and the non-key words at the same time.

Now is the time to remember the unlearn-to-relearn idea. Learning to read key words is probably very different for you. If you feel uncomfortable, that's good! This is the first step toward relearning. With a little practice, you will feel more comfortable and find that you are reading quicker than before with the same or better understanding.

The paragraph in Activity 4 contains 117 words; 67 were identified as the key words. Think about it: If you can learn to read and understand a 117-word paragraph by reading only 67 key words, what will that do to your reading time? What will it naturally do to the word-for-word talking in your head?

ACTIVITY 4

Read **only** the key words indicated in boldface in the following paragraph. Try to spread your peripheral vision to see *both* the non-boldface and boldface words. Can you understand the text without reading every word?

One of the **characteristics** of the **modern world** is the **ease** and **degree** of **travel. Historically, people** have **always traveled,** but **much** of that **travel** was **not** for **pleasure. While** the **terms "travel"** and **"tourism"** are **often used interchangeably** and the **terms** may **appear synonymous,** in the **past, travel** was generally **undertaken** for **financial, military,** or **business reasons, while tourism** was **travel** for the sake of **recreation** and for the **enjoyment** of **new** and **different places** and **people. While people** have **always traveled** to **some extent** for the **thrill** of **travel** or **curiosity about other places, mass tourism** is a **modern phenomenon. Until** the **last few decades,** only a **select few** were **able** to **travel** for **tourism.**

Use the following paragraphs to practice finding key words. Don't read each sentence first to figure out which words are more important to the meaning of the sentence; this will waste your time. Instead, as you read, *quickly* underline the bigger words. They will generally be three letters or more, so your eyes will naturally stop on them. After you are finished, reread the key words to see if the paragraph makes sense. Change your underlines as needed. The first sentences are completed for you. There are no right or wrong key words as long as they make sense to you. (If you want more practice underlining key words, you can use newspapers, magazines, and nonfiction books. Try reading key words on a few pages in this book. Keep in mind that reading key words is only one tool for increasing your reading speed.)

Paragraph 1

<u>Once</u> in a <u>while</u>, you may <u>think</u> that a <u>store</u> or <u>company</u> you are <u>dealing</u> <u>with</u> has <u>made</u> a <u>mistake</u>. The store or company could also give you some other reason to make a complaint. Maybe you bought something and were told you would receive it in a few weeks. After months go by and you still do not have the item, you receive damaged goods that you want to take back. Getting big businesses to take care of complaints is sometimes hard. Have faith; there are ways to register a complaint so that it will be handled.

Paragraph 2

<u>There</u> is <u>strong</u> <u>evidence</u> to <u>suggest</u> that the <u>use</u> of <u>standardized</u> <u>tests</u>, which <u>assess</u> <u>abilities</u>, <u>personalities</u>, and <u>integrity</u>, is a <u>valuable</u> <u>screening</u> <u>tool</u> in the <u>pre-employment</u> <u>process</u>. While initially, companies and selection experts were hesitant about the use of these tools, many hospitality organizations now use testing as a regular component in the selection process. We predict that testing will become both more sophisticated and more widely used in our industry.

Note: Once you have begun to master the key word idea, *don't use your pen to underline because it will slow you down.* Your eyes and brain need to do it on their own.

Reading Phrases

Most passive and unskilled readers read one word at a time, which is inefficient and time-consuming. As you learned in the last section, not all words are equally important. Reading key words allows you to get the information you need without reading word for word.

Some people find the key word idea challenging, so here's another one to try called *phrasing*. Read the following paragraph, and notice that each phrase, or thought, is indicated between slash marks.

Doctors have found/ that many people/ spend many hours/ in sleep/ for which/ there is/ no physical need./ When these habits/ are changed/ and these people/ try to do with less,/ they often find no difference/ in health/ or efficiency./ You might experiment/ with reducing your sleep time/ by half an hour./

Give yourself/ a few days/ to get adjusted/ to the new pattern./ If you are as effective/ as you were before,/ you will gain/ the equivalent/ of a week of Sundays/ in the course/ of a year./

Reading phrases is a way to make reading more effective. A **phrase** is a group of words that expresses a thought. A thought can be short or long. If you can think of a sentence as a group of thoughts, then phrasing will be very comfortable. If you can learn to read in thoughts instead of word for word, you will better understand what is written and read faster.

The term **column width** pertains to how wide or narrow the printed text is on a page. Newspapers and magazines are typically printed with narrow columns. Educational material is printed with both wide and narrow columns as illustrated in Figure 9-2. Reading in key words works very well with all kinds of columns, but reading phrases works best when reading wide-column material. Because with phrasing you want to put words together, narrow columns can be frustrating and choppy to read.

ACTIVITY 6

Look for phrases, or groups of words that form a thought, in the paragraphs below. Don't read each sentence first to figure out the phrases; this will waste your time. Instead, *quickly* place a slash mark as you read where you believe one thought ends and another begins. Then, reread the paragraph to see if your phrases make sense. Change the slash marks as needed. The first sentences are completed for you. There is no right or wrong length to a phrase, as long as it makes sense to you. (If you want more practice with phrasing, you can use newspapers, magazines, and nonfiction books.)

Paragraph 1

Once in a while,/ you may think/ that a store or company/ you are dealing with/ has made a mistake./ The store or company could also give you some other reason to make a complaint. Maybe you bought something and were told you would receive it in a few weeks. After months go by and you still do not have the item, you receive damaged goods that you want to take back. Getting big businesses to take care of complaints is sometimes hard. Have faith; there are ways to register a complaint so that it will be handled.

Paragraph 2

There is strong evidence/ to suggest/ that the use of standardized tests,/ which assess abilities,/ personalities,/ and integrity,/ is a valuable screening tool/ in the pre-employment process./ While initially companies and selection experts were hesitant about the use of these tools, many hospitality organizations now use testing as a regular component in the selection process. We predict that testing will become both more sophisticated and more widely used in our industry.

Note: Once you have begun to master the phrasing idea, *don't use your pen to make slash marks because it will slow you down.* Your eyes and brain need to do it on their own.

FIGURE 9-2

Multiple Column Widths on the Same Page

The marketing mix and budget are also affected by the way the company has spent money in the past. If the company was responsible for the transportation of its products, it may have invested in trucks or other equipment needed to move products from the business to customers. Warehouses or distribution centers may have been built to handle the inventory. If the company has already made those investments, it will typically try to use marketing mixes that take advantage of those resources. If a company has relied on other businesses to store and transport products in the past, it may be very expensive for the company to change and instead provide those marketing activities itself.

FIGURE 20-8
Most of the revenue a business receives is the result of sales of its primary products and services. There are also secondary sources that contribute to income.

Revenue Sources from Marketing Activities

world *view*

The World Bank

Following World War II, the governments of 45 countries gathered in Bretton Woods, New Hampshire, to form an international bank. The purpose of the bank was to help in the rebuilding of Europe following the war. Five hundred million dollars were loaned to European countries to aid them in recovering from war damage. By 1980, the World Bank had made loans of more than $10 billion.

The focus of the World Bank has broadened in its 60-year history. It continues to make low-interest loans to countries for reconstruction and relief following wars and internal conflicts. However, its primary focus is now on fighting poverty and improving the standard of living in developing countries. Not only does it loan money for those efforts, but it also offers consulting and technical support for education and health services.

A recent project helped build shelters offering food, clothing, and education to street children in Turkey. The Bank helped establish the African Virtual University (AVU), an interactive, instructional telecommunications network serving 17 African countries. It established community programs in Burkina Faso, Africa, to fight the HIV/Aids problem. It provided resources for low-cost home loans in Jordan to move citizens out of public housing.

The World Bank demonstrates that combining financial resources with people committed to addressing global issues can make a difference in the lives of individuals. It is clearly an organization concerned about more than the bottom line.

Think Critically

(1) Why would a bank want to provide more than loans as a part of its services?

(2) What is the value of having a World Bank rather than relying on the bank system in each country?

Marketing activities are completed in order to generate revenue. Most of the revenue for a business results from the sale of products and services. The marketing plan identifies the markets that the company plans to serve. Marketing activities are developed to meet the needs of customers in the market so that they will purchase the products or services offered by the company. There are several parts of the marketing mix that can affect the amount of revenue. Sources of revenue affected by mix elements are shown in Figure 20-8.

Source: James L. Burrow. Marketing. Thomson South-Western, 2006.

Using Pacers

Do you ever use your hands when you read? You naturally use your fingers or hands to look up a name in the phone book because it helps you keep your place and focuses your attention. The key to using your hands effectively when reading is knowing the right way(s) to do it.

Pacers can be either your hands or a white card that helps you keep your place while reading. They force you to focus and move your eyes down the page faster. Learning how to use pacers correctly is important because these tools, when used incorrectly, will slow you down.

PACER AS A PLACE KEEPER. Many readers have a hard time tracking their eyes from the end of one line to the beginning of the next. If you miss the next line, you have trouble understanding the author's ideas. You also waste your time because you have to go back to find your place. Reading wide-column material is especially challenging because the return distance from the end of one line to the beginning of the next is long. If you can use your hands or a white card to keep your place, you will be able to understand your reading material better; the ideas will flow more smoothly. You will also save time because you won't lose your place.

PACER AS AN EYE MOVER. Pacers are also used to force the eyes to move forward faster, especially when you are tired or bored. If you are reading facing a window or an aisle and a person walks by, your eyes naturally follow the person for a moment. This is because *the eyes naturally follow movement.* If you can create movement on your page, your eyes will follow, helping you move faster down the page.

PACER RULES. To use a pacer correctly, try following these two important rules:

1. Keep the pacer moving downward, not across the page.
2. Don't stop the pacer or go back to re-read.

While using pacers may be challenging at first, these two guidelines will help you learn how to use pacing tools well.

THE PACERS. The following activity describes five different pacers to experiment with. You may not like all of them, but you should be able to find at least one you will be comfortable using.

> "*If you have knowledge, let others light their candles in it.*"
> —**Margaret Fuller, 19th century writer and political activist**

◼ Focus on Technology

Take a Break. Technology can be great—really great—but take a break from it regularly, or it will rule your life. When you schedule time to read or study (and you *should* schedule time to read or study), turn off your cell phone, leave an away message on your online "space" (wherever it is you hang out), turn off your e-mail notification, and do whatever else you need to do to stop technology from invading your thinking time. You may be surprised by how much you can achieve *without technology.*

Read each pacer description and study the accompanying figure. Then, reading either this book or some other material, try using the pacer on several paragraphs. Keep the pacer rules in mind.

1. **The Center Pull Method**
   The Center Pull Method is done by placing the index finger of either your right or left hand under the first line of the text in the center of the column. While your eyes read from left to right, your finger pulls your eyes down the page. (This works best with narrow columns.)

2. **The Left Pull Method**

The Left Pull Method is similar to the Center Pull Method. Place your index finger of either hand on the left margin or the beginning of the line. Your finger pulls your eyes down the page while keeping your place. This works well with all material.

3. **The Two-Finger Pull Method**
   The Two-Finger Pull Method uses the index fingers of both hands. Place your left index finger on the left margin or the beginning of the line, and place your right index finger at the end of the same line. While your eyes move from left to right, your hands should move down with your eyes. Your fingertips should be on the same line as your eyes most of the time. (This works well with all material, especially wide columns.)

4. **The Thumb or Pen Push Method**

The Thumb or Pen Push Method works from the top down. Place your thumb or a closed pen above the words you want to read. Start your thumb or pen moving down, and try to read fast enough to keep your thumb or pen moving. This works well with narrow columns.

ACTIVITY 7 (continued)

5. The White Card Method

For the White Card Method, use a blank white card or piece of paper. *The card should be equal in length to the size of the column you are reading.* A blank 3″ × 5″ index card can be used for both narrow and wide columns depending on which edge of the card you use. You can tape two cards together for very wide columns.

While you can place a card above or below the line of text, the most effective method is above the line. If you place the card below the line, it is easy to regress, or to go back over material you just read. The card also covers the text you are about to read. This is like placing a wall between you and the upcoming words. On the other hand, placing the card *above* the line covers what you have already read, which avoids regression. It also leaves exposed the words you are about to read. So, to use the card effectively, place it ON TOP of the words you have read, and leave exposed the words you are going to read. Start moving the card down the page.

Combining Your Reading Tools

You now have three new tools to help you read faster. They are (1) keys words, (2) phrases, and (3) pacers. When you read faster, you increase your concentration. More concentration means more comprehension, and more comprehension means better retention.

As you practice your reading tools, you may find that combining them is very powerful. For example, reading key words with a pacer, reading phrases with a pacer, or reading a combination of key words and phrases are extremely helpful strategies for increasing your reading speed. The key is to use the tool or tools that help you read actively, not passively.

Checkpoint

1 Describe the three tools for increasing reading speed.

_____

_____

2 When might you use them?

_____

_____

3 What are the benefits of using them?

_____

_____

"The true art of memory is the art of attention."

—Samuel Johnson, 18th century author

Skimming and Scanning

Skimming and scanning are two very different strategies for reading faster. They are each used for different purposes, and they are not meant to be used all the time. They are at the fast end of the speed range, while studying is at the slow end. You may already use skimming when you do research or read a newspaper. You already do scanning when you look for something specific like a name in a phone directory.

People who know how to skim and scan are **flexible readers**. They read according to their purpose and get the information they need quickly without wasting time. They do not read everything, which is what increases their reading speed. Their skill lies in knowing what specific information to read and which technique will best meet their needs.

What Is Skimming?

Skimming is one of the tools you can use to read more in less time. **Skimming** refers to looking only for the general or main ideas. With skimming, your overall understanding is reduced because you don't read everything. You read only what is important to your purpose. Fortunately, you have some background knowledge in skimming, though you may not realize it. In Chapter 8, you learned about a form of skimming called pre-viewing.

There are a few differences between skimming and pre-viewing. Pre-viewing occurs before the actual reading process and requires you to search only for the main ideas in the writer's outline. Skimming, on the other hand, takes place while reading and allows you to look for details in addition to the main ideas.

HOW TO SKIM. To skim, you read at a fast speed, but you don't read everything. *What you read is more important than what you leave out.* So, what material do you read and what material do you leave out?

Let's say you are researching a long chapter or a web site. By reading the first few paragraphs in detail, you will get a good idea of what information will be discussed. Once you know where the reading is headed, you can begin to read only the first sentence of each paragraph. Also called *topic sentences,* they give you the main idea of the paragraph. If you do not get the main idea in the topic sentence, or if the paragraph greatly interests you, then you may want to skim more.

At the end of each topic sentence, your eyes should drop down through the rest of the paragraph, looking for important pieces of information, such as names, dates, or events. Continue to read only topic sentences, dropping down through the rest of the paragraphs, until you are near the end. Since the last few paragraphs may contain a conclusion or summary, you should stop skimming there and read in detail. Remember that your overall comprehension will be lower than if you read in detail. If while skimming, you feel you are grasping the main ideas, then you are skimming correctly.

Figure 9-3 provides an example for you to use for practice. While skimming the material, your eyes should move quickly down the page. Quickly skim Figure 9-3 by being very aware of where your eyes are going and how they are moving and feeling.

FIGURE 9-3

Passage for Skimming Practice

When you apply for a job, you may simply be asked to complete the job application. However, you may be asked to submit a resume, especially if you apply for a job by mail.

If you are asked to mail in (or e-mail in) your resume, you should also include a letter of application, or a cover letter. A resume cover letter should contain the following:

- Position for which you are applying
- Reasons why you are qualified
- Your particular skills suited for the job
- A request for an interview.

Your resume should include your educational history and job experience. When you write a resume, you should emphasize the experience that relates to the job for which you are applying. If you are applying for a job as an administrative assistant, you should mention any past experience in this area, even if it was volunteer work. If the job you are applying for is your first, you might mention high school classes and any special honors related to the job. As you gain work experience, you should update your resume.

The appearance of your resume and cover letter is important. If they are sloppy and contain misspelled words and errors in typing, it is a poor reflection on you. Your resume and cover letter should be printed on good quality white paper. If you are not sure of yourself, have someone check your work for misspelled words and typographical errors. Arrange the contents of your resume so that the categories are clear and the general appearance is neat. You don't want your resume to appear cluttered. The person hiring should be able to get an idea of your educational and professional background at a glance. Most resumes are limited to one page.

There are two types of resumes: chronological and functional. A **chronological resume** is the most common where you list your employment history in order, with the most recent job first. If you don't have work experience, you can list work you have done at school, at home, in the community, or as a volunteer.

Another type of resume is the **functional resume**. In such a resume, you list a brief summary of your experience and then specifically list your skills and abilities. This is followed by a list of employers and then your education.

You may want to create your resume using a word processing template. You can find a variety of such templates online. Also, print shops such as Kinko's, and state employment offices offer resume services. By using a word processor, you can quickly and easily make updates and customize your resume to fit the job description of the job for which you are applying.

Source: Donnelly, Mary Queen. *Skills for Consumer Success.* © 2005 Thomson South-Western.

WHEN TO SKIM. Because skimming is done at a fast speed with less-than-normal comprehension, you shouldn't skim all the time. There are many times, however, when skimming is very useful.

Suppose you are taking a presentation skills class and have to deliver an oral report in a few days about the first automobiles ever made. You locate six books and four newspaper articles about this topic. (Chapter 12 will provide information on how to do this.) Because you must be ready soon, you do not have time to read each word, but you need a large quantity of solid information.

Skimming will help you locate the information quickly while making sure you use your time wisely. It will also increase the amount of usable material you obtain for your research.

Suppose you have an exam in a few days. You need to review the material you learned, but you don't want to reread everything. By skimming, you can quickly locate the information you haven't mastered yet and study only that material.

Most people skim when they read a magazine or newspaper, looking for information that interests them enough to spend their time on it. They get the gist of the articles, which is enough to decide whether to continue reading or move on to something more interesting.

While reading, ask yourself the following questions to help you decide whether or not to skim. If you answer yes to any of these, then skimming is a useful tool.

- Do I have a lot to read and only a small amount of time?
- Is a pre-view or re-view enough?
- Do I already know something about this?
- Can any of the material be skipped?

If you have sufficient background knowledge or believe you don't need the information, then skip it! That's right—don't read it at all!

Believe it or not, skipping material may sometimes be the best use of your time. Just because someone wrote something doesn't mean you have to read it. *If you pick and choose carefully what you skim and skip, you will be pleasantly surprised at the large amount of information you can get through in a short period of time.*

You can experiment with all your new reading strategies in the Chapter 9 Reading Exercises provided by your instructor. You will time yourself and answer questions while gaining needed practice in skimming, scanning, and adjusting your reading speed. Also, newspapers and your favorite magazines and web sites provide great practice material because you read things you have some familiarity with.

NETBookmark

Skimming and scanning are two very useful activities to learn for faster reading on paper as well as on screen. Go to your favorite search engine and enter the terms "skimming and scanning" to find more information and some fun, challenging exercises.

For additional information about skimming and scanning, go to:

http://sskills.swlearning.com

Respond to the following questions about how skimming might be helpful to you.

1. How can skimming help your reading speed? _____
_____

2. How can it satisfy your reading purpose? _____
_____

3. How can it help with your educational reading material? _____
_____

4. How can it help with your career? _____
_____

5. How can it help with research? _____
_____

6. How can it help when you read newspapers or magazines? _____
_____

7. In what other ways do you think skimming might be helpful to you? _____
_____

What Is Scanning?

Scanning is another useful tool for reading in high gear. Unlike skimming, when **scanning**, you look *only* for a specific fact or piece of information without reading everything. You scan when you look for your favorite show listed in the cable guide, for your friend's phone number in a telephone book, and for the sports scores in the newspaper. For scanning to be successful, you need to understand how your material is structured as well as comprehend what you read so you can locate the specific information you need. Scanning also allows you to find details and other information in a hurry.

HOW TO SCAN. Because you already scan many different types of material in your daily life, learning more details about scanning will be easy. Establishing your purpose, locating the appropriate material, and knowing how the information is structured before you start scanning is essential.

If you need to find the meaning of a word, using a dictionary is the most appropriate tool to accomplish this purpose. To look up the word *loquacious*, you should immediately look for it under the L section. Starting from A at the beginning of the dictionary would be a huge waste of time. (*Loquacious* means "very talkative," by the way!)

In daily life, you have many reasons to look for specific information. What specific information do you currently need or expect to need in the future? What sources will you use to find it? Identify where you would find the information listed below. In the first column, add a few more types of information you might need.

Information I Need	Where to Look for It
The meaning of an unknown word	*dictionary*
What courses to take	*school catalog*
The time a television show is aired	
Information on Gandhi	
The ZIP code for Cary, SC	
The day of the week for July 4th this year	
How to print labels on the computer	
The population of South Africa	
How to program a cell phone	

The material you scan is typically arranged in the following ways: alphabetically, chronologically, non-alphabetically, by category, or textually. **Alphabetical** information is arranged in order from A to Z, while **chronological** information is arranged in time or numerical order.

Information can be also be arranged in non-alphabetical order, such as a television listing, or by **category**, listings of like items such as an auto parts catalog. Sometimes information is located within the written paragraphs of text, also known as a **textual** sense, as in an encyclopedia entry.

Look at the types of reading material listed on the left. How do you think text is arranged in each? Write the words Alphabetical, Chronological, Non-alphabetical, by Category, or Textual on the right to identify the arrangement of each type of material.

Type of Material	Arrangement of Material
Dictionary	_Alphabetical_
Television listing	_Non-alphabetical_
Encyclopedia entry	_Textual_
Book index	
History reading passage	
ZIP code directory	
Magazine article	
Sports page of the newspaper	
Reference listing in a book	
Newspaper article	
Computer manual	

Learning to use your hands while scanning is very helpful in locating specific information. Do you do anything with your hands to locate a word in a dictionary? To find a meeting time on your calendar? To read a train or bus schedule? Using a pacer is extremely helpful in focusing your attention and keeping your place while scanning a column of material.

Your peripheral vision can also help you scan effectively. When your hand moves down a list of names, you see not only the name your finger is pointing to, but also the names above and below. Let your eyes work for you when searching for information.

Keep the concept of key words in mind while scanning. Your purpose will determine the key words. Suppose you are looking for the time a train leaves from New York City for Washington, D.C. The key words to keep in mind are "from New York City" and "to Washington, D.C." If you are looking for the cost of a computer printer with the code number PX-710, the key word to locate in a list of many printers is "PX-710."

WHEN TO SCAN. You scan when your aim is to find specific pieces of information. If you were doing the research for a presentation, you could scan the index of books, web sites, and reference materials. You would discover whether they contain any information you want and the pages where the information can be found.

In the past, you probably scanned without knowing you were doing it. Now with the information provided in this section, you can use scanning more frequently. The more you practice, the more effective your scanning will become. Finally, the most important benefit of scanning is its ability to help you become a more flexible reader. Scanning adds another high gear to your reading.

ACTIVITY 11

Scanning is a reading survival skill. Finding specific information quickly and accurately can make your life easier. Respond to the following questions about how scanning might be used in your daily life.

1. How can scanning be used to increase your reading speed?

   _____

   _____

2. How can it be used to satisfy your reading purpose?

   _____

   _____

3. How can it be used to help with your class work and other educational reading?

   _____

   _____

4. How can it be used for doing research?

   _____

   _____

5. How can it be used for reading newspapers and magazines?

   _____

   _____

6. How can scanning be helpful to you in other ways?

   _____

   _____

PERMISSION NOT TO READ EVERYTHING. Because you may be accustomed to reading every word and may be uncomfortable leaving some words out, you need to give yourself permission to overlook some words by skimming, scanning, and skipping material according to your reading purpose. Your permission slip from the author follows.

Permission Slip

I, _____, am hereby granted permission not to read everything. I am also not required to remember everything I read. By doing so, I am not cheating. I understand that skimming, scanning, or skipping material may be the best way to accomplish my reading purpose. I understand that just because material has been written, I do not have to read it all. By exercising this right, I will be able to read actively, read more in less time, and still get the information I need without reading it all.

My signature of approval of these methods gives me permission to be a flexible reader now and forever more!

Your signature _____

The author's signature _Abby Marks Beale_

Checkpoint

1 What is skimming?

_____

_____

2 What is scanning?

_____

_____

3 When might you skim?

_____

_____

_____

4 When might you scan?

_____

_____

_____

Learning to adjust your reading speed is like adding stick-shift gears to an automatic car. Gears allow you to read at different speeds for different purposes.

Adjusting Your Reading Speed

When driving a car, you should not drive fast all the time. On an open highway, you can certainly go faster than on city streets because on city streets, you need to slow down for pedestrians, stoplights, and other cars. Your driving speed needs to change according to the conditions of the road.

Similarly, you shouldn't read fast all the time. If you always read fast, you may miss important information. If you read slowly all the time, you will daydream more and waste your time. So how fast should you read?

Three Factors for Determining Reading Speed

Most readers think they only have two reading speeds: fast and/or slow. In reality, there are degrees of fast and degrees of slow. Your reading speed depends mainly on the following three factors: your *purpose for reading,* the *difficulty of the material,* and your *familiarity with the subject matter or background knowledge.*

Reading speed depends first on your *reading purpose*—why you are reading what you are reading. (In Chapter 8, you were introduced to reading purpose.) Let's say your reading purpose is to get only the main ideas of a nonfiction chapter. In this case, you read fairly quickly, looking for the main ideas while avoiding the details. If your reading purpose is to learn step-by-step how to put a faucet on a sink, you would read more slowly.

Your reading speed also can depend on how *difficult the reading material is.* If you are reading material that contains complex vocabulary or technical information, you need to read more slowly than when the vocabulary is easy and the information is not as technical.

Finally, your *background knowledge*—or what you already know—greatly affects your ability to increase your reading speed. The more you already know about a topic or material, the faster you can read. The less familiar you are with it, the slower you will read. By previewing a chapter, you will be able to increase your reading speed because you are familiar with the chapter content before you begin reading more thoroughly.

When to Speed Up and When to Slow Down

Since reading one way all the time—either fast or slow—is not efficient, learning when to speed up and when to slow down is a useful skill.

While reading an article or a chapter, your reading speed naturally goes up and down depending on how much you daydream, how familiar the material is, and other factors. If you learn to change your reading speed *on purpose,* instead of accidentally, you will complete your reading in an efficient amount of time and with better understanding.

Success *tip*

Reading on a computer screen can reduce your reading speed by 25 to 30 percent compared to reading on paper. This may be why people have a tendency to print out longer documents on paper to read them. Since so much is available to you to read on screen, challenge yourself to use your new reading skills to read better and faster on screen and print less. You will save time AND save trees!

Factors that help you speed up your reading are shown in the first column, and factors that cause you to slow down your reading are shown in the second column. Working with a partner or small group, list several conditions or influences that help you read faster. Then, list in the second column the factors that cause you to slow down. (Important clue: There is usually an opposite relationship between one side and the other!)

Things That Help Me Speed Up

Reading for main ideas (purpose)

Easy vocabulary

Some background knowledge

Preparation for class discussion

_____

_____

_____

_____

_____

Things That Cause Me to Slow Down

Reading for details (purpose)

Difficult vocabulary

Little background knowledge

Preparation for quiz or test

_____

_____

_____

_____

_____

Since all readers are different, you may not always agree on the factors for reading faster or slower. What is essential is that you know what affects *your* ability to speed up or slow down. This is an important quality of an active, efficient reader!

Flexibility Is the Key

Being an active reader means being a flexible reader. Flexible readers adjust their reading strategies according to their reading purpose, the difficulty of material, and their background knowledge. In this chapter, you discovered why it is important to adjust your reading speed. You also became aware of the factors that affect reading and speed, and you learned new tools to apply to your reading to increase your speed. This combination of awareness and skill will make you a flexible reader.

■ Focus on Ethics

The final exam in your class is going to be an open book test, and you are also allowed to bring your laptop computer with you so you can access information from the Internet. On the day of the exam, rather than using your computer to research answers to the questions, you use it to IM your friend who has already taken the course and received an "A". You tell him the questions and he sends back the answers. Since it is an open book test and the teacher is letting you use your computer to help find the answers, you're surprised when the teacher walks by, sees what you are doing, and tells you that you are cheating. You will get a failing grade in the course as a result. You felt you were simply using your time and your computer creatively. Besides, in the business world, you know that people regularly ask their colleagues for answers to questions. What was wrong with your thoughts and actions?

ACTIVITY 13

Now that you have read about and experienced some active reading tools, go back to Chapter 8 and reevaluate your reading abilities in Activity 1—Qualities of Passive and Active Readers. Summarize your abilities on the lines below. Have any of your qualities changed? Explain your thoughts below.

_____

_____

_____

_____

_____

_____

With all you have learned about increasing your reading speed and effectiveness, it's a good time to check in on your reading attitude. Perhaps you started this chapter with a positive reading attitude. But, chances are you have felt challenged by your academic reading and therefore, have a more negative attitude. The important question to ask yourself is: "Do I feel more positive about my abilities as a reader now that I have some strategies to use?" You may never love reading academic material, but you can certainly learn to manage it better with these easy-to-apply concepts. So, if you haven't made a commitment to any one of these methods, you might want to go back and find one now.

Checkpoint

1 Why should you adjust your reading speed?

_____

_____

_____

2 What helps you read faster?

_____

_____

3 What slows you down?

_____

_____

CHAPTER SUMMARY

1. The three basic reading gears are low, middle, and high.
2. Unlearning is uncomfortable but important for improving a skill or habit.
3. Learning to read faster increases your concentration.
4. Reading faster can be accomplished by using your peripheral vision to increase your eye span.
5. The three strategies for increasing eye span are
   - Reading key words.
   - Reading phrases.
   - Using pacers.
6. The strategies you use to enhance reading speed can depend on the width of the text column.
7. The three factors for determining reading speed are
   - Reading purpose.
   - Difficulty of the material.
   - Background knowledge.
8. Skimming means looking for the general or main ideas. It is similar to pre-viewing and should be used when your purpose is to get an overview of the material. Skimming can help you obtain information quickly without wasting time.
9. Scanning means looking for a piece of specific information, like a topic in an index. Using a pacer and your peripheral vision can help you quickly find what you need.
10. Flexible readers shift their reading gears depending on their purpose and background knowledge.
11. The most important thing about learning to read actively is to figure out what works best for you.

CHAPTER ASSESSMENT

Terms Review

Fill in the blanks with the appropriate key terms on the left. Use each term only once.

alphabetical

category

chronological

column width

eye span

flexible reader

key words

pacers

peripheral vision

phrases

scanning

skimming

textual

1. Your _____ and your _____ enable you to see more words at a glance when reading.

2. When scanning information, you will come across material that is presented by _____ or in groups, that is _____ or in time order, _____ or within the paragraphs, or _____ by letter order from A to Z.

3. When reading, looking for the bigger, more important words that are usually three letters in length or longer is called reading _____.

4. _____ help keep your place and focus while reading.

5. Reading groups of words that form a thought, or _____, is easier if the _____ is wide.

6. When you are _____, you are looking for general, or main ideas. When you are _____, you are looking for something specific.

7. Being able to read intentionally using different reading speeds enables you to be a _____.

Review

Based on the information you learned in this chapter, answer the following questions using your own words and thoughts.

1. Why is learning how to read faster important? Give at least three reasons.

_____

_____

_____

_____

2. Why is changing your reading habits difficult? How can you improve your skills?

_____

_____

_____

_____

3. How does your peripheral vision affect the way you read?

_____

_____

_____

_____

4. What can you do to expand your peripheral vision while reading?

_____

_____

_____

_____

5. Why is it helpful to know about the reading gears?

_____

_____

_____

_____

6. What are the similarities and differences between skimming and scanning?

_____

_____

_____

_____

7. What would you tell another reader about how to skim?

_____

_____

_____

_____

8. What would you tell another reader about how to scan?

_____

_____

_____

_____

9. Which of the reading tools do you find most useful?

_____

_____

_____

_____

10. Which of the reading tools do you find least useful?

_____

_____

_____

_____

11. Going back to Kim on the first page of this chapter, do you have any new suggestions to help him manage his reading load?

_____

_____

_____

_____

12. Why should you learn to adjust your reading speed?

_____

_____

_____

_____

13. What can you do to adjust your reading speed?

_____

_____

_____

_____

CASE STUDIES

for Creative and Critical Thinking

 ACADEMIC CASE—Connecting to Preparing for Term Papers

Tyrell is a Sports Medicine major with a big task on his hands. He has two term papers due, and because of other projects he has had to complete, he now has only two weeks to complete them both. The first paper is for his *Athletic Injuries* class, a paper about runner's injuries. His other assignment is for his *Health and Wellness* course, a nutrition paper on vitamins and supplements and their effect on an athlete's performance. In preparation for writing his papers, Tyrell went to the school library, located and printed ten research articles on each subject, and took out a few books. Later that evening, he began to worry as he looked at the stack of reading. He knew he wasn't a fast reader, and he needed to come up with a strategy to read them as quickly as possible.

1. What techniques do you recommend Tyrell use to get through his research material?

_____

_____

_____

_____

_____

_____

2. Tyrell likes both courses but has a lot more background knowledge in his *Athletic Injuries* course. How will this help or hurt his ability to write these papers?

_____

_____

_____

_____

3. How will faster reading strategies help Tyrell for this assignment? For future assignments?

_____

_____

_____

_____

4. Though you can get a lot of information from reading, where else might Tyrell go to gather information that doesn't involve just reading?

_____

_____

_____

_____

_____

_____

Sameera is a paralegal. She understands that law offices get a lot of material to read and review to keep up with the changing laws. That's part of the job. But, when she looked at the stack of journals, newspapers, and case law books that had come in the mail during the last three weeks, she heaved a big sigh. She had been so busy that she had only looked at a few of them. They were piling up and creating clutter. She can't throw any of it away because she needs to go through it all to decide what is worth keeping and what she can guiltlessly throw away. Besides, she enjoys reading them when she has the time. Sameera is frustrated.

1. Sameera's responsibility for reading is to find useful material for herself and the lawyers in her office. What reading techniques would you recommend to Sameera to accomplish this responsibility?

_____

_____

_____

_____

2. What factors do you think Sameera should consider in deciding when to speed up and when to slow down as she reads the various articles? What conditions or influences would help her speed up or cause her to slow down?

_____

_____

_____

_____

_____

_____

3. If Sameera consistently comes across material that is not valuable to her or the lawyers, what do you suggest she do so she doesn't have to see it in her pile every month?

_____

_____

_____

4. What do you think Sameera needs to do to find more time for this reading project? And, once she finds the time, how can she protect it from interruptions?

_____

_____

_____

_____

_____

_____

10 Mastering Tests

Terms
- bad stress
- educated guess
- good stress
- multiple guess
- panic pushers
- perspective
- stress

Chapter Goals

After studying and working with the information in this chapter, you should be able to:

- Identify your reactions to test taking and determine how your reactions to test taking affect your ability to be successful.
- State the "rules" of the test-taking game.
- Identify and explain winning strategies for different types of tests, and use this information to improve your testing success.

For four years, Yoshi has worked as an information technology consultant at a large pharmaceutical company. He is good at his job, continues to learn new skills, and has made some close friends.

One day Sima, his supervisor, informs him that he will need to take a certification exam to meet a new company requirement. She tells him when and where the test will be held. She also gives him a 40-page study guide and asks him to read it ahead of time, which he dutifully does. "This is just like a test in school," he groaned, while thinking to himself, "I'm terrible at tests."

When Yoshi arrives at the testing site, he realizes that although he read the study guide, he doesn't know what the test format will be or how much time he will have. He is tired from staying up late the night before and hungry from skipping breakfast. He is starting to feel nervous, and he only worries more when he talks to the other test takers about how difficult the test is going to be. He grabs a seat in the back row of the crowded room, and strains to hear the administrator's instructions.

Yoshi begins by briefly scanning the directions and jumping right to the first test question. He answers the questions in order and loses a lot of time on a couple of difficult questions. When the test administrator announces that time is up, Yoshi has several questions that he has not yet answered. He is dismayed when he sees that they are on subjects he knows very well.

If Yoshi does not pass this test, he will have to take it again. What should he do differently next time?

Tests are evaluations to discover what you know and what you still need to learn. Today's students are faced with a wide variety of classroom and standardized tests that include formal tests to evaluate how much they have learned from classroom or web-based learning. Today's workers take tests for certification or to demonstrate job performance or share their knowledge with coworkers. Effective test-taking strategies are more important than ever.

For purposes of this chapter, the term "test" is generalized to include those formal learning evaluations given for classroom or web-based learning, and professional or career-type tests taken for on-the-job training, certifications, and continuing education credits. While reading the chapter, look for similarities and differences between formal and informal tests. Keep in mind that informal tests, like those of the workers, are subjectively evaluated (from one's own viewpoint) and are usually performance based.

Tests and grades do not come to an end when you finish school. In the workplace, many companies ask their employees to assess themselves using "360-degree feedback." Considered an informal test, it is THE workplace evaluation in which you evaluate yourself on a set of criteria, your manager evaluates you, and your peers and direct reports evaluate you too. Many times, your career path and salary depend on your results.

Throughout this chapter, tests are sometimes referred to as games. This is because taking a formal test is just like playing a game. The object is to get as many points as possible in the time you are given to play. The reality is that tests are games, and your testing success begins when you look at them this way. How well you do on any test, or game, depends on a combination of your knowledge, preparation, and test-taking ability. In this chapter, you will learn how to put that preparation into play and how to test effectively.

If you think of a test like a game, then test taking can be a fun challenge instead of a dreaded one.

> Taking a formal test is just like playing a game. The object is to get as many points as possible in the time you are given to play.

The following self-evaluation will give you an idea of how familiar, or unfamiliar, you are with some of the topics and terms discussed in this chapter. After reading each statement, circle the letter Y, S, or N to indicate the answer that is most appropriate for you. Answer honestly. Rate yourself at the end; then complete the information on your Self-Check Progress Chart.

Y = yes; frequently   S = sometimes   N = no; never

1. I know that a low test grade does not make me a failure.   Y   S   N

2. I realize that it is okay not to know everything on a test.   Y   S   N

3. I follow both written and oral test directions carefully.   Y   S   N

4. Before I begin a test, I pre-view it by looking for the point values.   Y   S   N

5. When pre-viewing my tests, I look for answers to other questions.   Y   S   N

6. I budget my time effectively when I take a test.   Y   S   N

7. On paper tests, I do the easiest questions first and come back later to the harder ones.   Y   S   N

8. I am aware of the differences between computer-based and paper tests.   Y   S   N

9. I review returned tests for topics I need to understand better.   Y   S   N

10. I learn from my testing mistakes.   Y   S   N

Rate Yourself:

Number of Ys _____ × 100 = _____

Number of Ss _____ × 50 = _____

Number of Ns _____ × 0 = _____   **Total_____**

Stress, Tests, and You

Tests and stress seem to go together naturally. Many people feel stress before a formal test, an oral presentation, or another important event where they have to prove what they know or can do. For some people, stress appears as fear and anxiety. For others, it takes the form of excitement and anticipation.

How does test taking affect you? Are you calm and relaxed or tense and uptight? Are you patient or impatient? How does your body react? Do your muscles tighten? Does your appetite disappear, or do you overeat? Do your sleeping habits change? Is your breathing irregular or steady?

Stress is not something that happens; rather, it is your body's reaction to something that happened or is about to happen. It can be good or bad.

Good stress helps you become motivated and energizes your body. It helps you perform better, even when you feel anxious or scared. It gets your adrenaline flowing, which tells your body and mind to become alert.

Bad stress makes performing well or achieving your goals challenging because of fear and worry. It undermines you and zaps your energy. Many medical researchers link an excess of bad stress to increased health problems such as depression, heart disease, and cancer. When you hear someone refer to being stressed, he or she is usually referring to bad stress.

Stress is a part of daily life for everyone, though some argue that students experience more bad stress than good. Do you experience any of these symptoms before or during a test?

What is your typical stress reaction before tests? If you react with good stress, good for you! If you react with bad stress, work on changing your mental perspective.

- Rebellious feelings and actions (cutting classes, refusing to participate in activities, or writing the wrong answer on a test on purpose)

- Feelings of fear or hopelessness

- Loss of appetite or constant hunger and snacking

- A short temper or a general feeling of impatience

- Difficulty sleeping or intentionally pulling "all nighters"

- Headaches, asthma attacks, upset stomach, or high blood pressure

When you feel these kinds of stresses, your body produces a chemical, called cortisol, that affects your ability to learn and remember. If you can get a handle on your stress with the suggestions in this chapter, you will better manage the stress that naturally comes with test taking.

When you think about playing softball, volleyball, or a board game, do you experience the same reactions as you do for an academic test? Probably not. Learning how to react to tests as if they were games can reduce your test-taking stress.

"Do not let what you cannot do interfere with what you can do."

—John Wooden, Former college basketball coach for UCLA

On own

This exercise will help you become aware of your reactions to test taking. Common stress reactions to test taking are described below. Place a check mark on the line next to reactions you experience; then check *when* the reaction happens to you. Add one or two other reactions you experience in testing situations.

Stress Reactions to Tests	Before	During	After
_____ I feel nervous.	_____	_____	_____
_____ I feel excited.	_____	_____	_____
_____ I feel relieved.	_____	_____	_____
_____ I feel optimistic and make positive comments.	_____	_____	_____
_____ I feel pessimistic and make negative comments.	_____	_____	_____
_____ I usually get a headache.	_____	_____	_____
_____ My neck, back, or shoulders ache.	_____	_____	_____
_____ I usually feel pretty good.	_____	_____	_____
_____ My breathing is rapid and shallow.	_____	_____	_____
_____ My breathing is relaxed and deep.	_____	_____	_____
_____ My heart pounds and my palms sweat.	_____	_____	_____
_____ I lose my appetite.	_____	_____	_____
_____ I panic.	_____	_____	_____
_____ I have trouble sleeping.	_____	_____	_____
_____ My mind goes blank.	_____	_____	_____
_____ I'm afraid I won't have enough time to finish.	_____	_____	_____
_____ I worry others may finish before me.	_____	_____	_____
_____ I worry that I've studied the wrong things.	_____	_____	_____
_____ I worry that I will do poorly.	_____	_____	_____
_____ I am confident in my ability to do well.	_____	_____	_____
_____ I am afraid I don't know everything.	_____	_____	_____
_____ I feel stupid.	_____	_____	_____
_____ _____	_____	_____	_____
_____ _____	_____	_____	_____

Now, think about, or discuss in a group, which of the above reactions are helpful. Which are hurtful? Why?

Test Results and Self-Worth

Do you think an athlete's self-worth depends on how well he or she plays a game on a specific day? If a baseball player hits the ball one out of three tries, he has a batting average of .333, or 33 percent, and is considered *very* successful. If he strikes out one day, does that lessen his overall ability? In some states, students who aspire to be lawyers can re-take the bar exam multiple times before striking out.

Unfortunately, many students allow one good or poor test grade to influence their self-worth. C or D grades may make them feel less valuable, while a grade of A or B may increase their self-worth.

Tests are *not* a judge of your self-worth. They are indicators of what you have learned, how well you communicate your knowledge, and what remains to be learned. Doing poorly one day should not affect your overall worth. It means you want to pay close attention to what you are doing or not doing and take action to improve for the next test.

Meeting Expectations

One of the reasons amateur athletes turn professional is because they (and their coaches and fans) have high expectations. When athletes don't perform well in one game, the coaches and fans don't abandon them. They look forward to the next game and hope for improvement.

People in your life also hope you do well, but they fully expect you might have some setbacks. There is no reason to think others will abandon you because of a few unsuccessful attempts.

Let your own expectations motivate you to improve. *You* are the only one who is responsible for meeting your *own* expectations. Though others may have expectations of you, what you expect from yourself is more important.

Success tip

If even the thought of taking a test makes your palms sweat and your heart pound, then consider learning some self-relaxation techniques like meditation or using affirmations. Meditation teaches you how to breathe in a conscious way and to be comfortable with your thoughts. Affirmations, or verbal positive intentions, are one-sentence statements you say several times a day like, "I am relaxed and calm for my test" or "I am a smart test taker."

Also, consider taking up the practice of yoga, as it can help relax the mind and the body to prepare you for a less stressful testing experience.

ACTIVITY 2

You have expectations of yourself as a learner. Perhaps you aspire to prepare to enter a certain career or to earn a promotion or raise in your current job. What are your expectations? Discuss them with a partner and summarize them in a short paragraph.

_____

_____

_____

_____

_____

_____

_____

It's All in Your Perspective

How would you describe a glass of water filled halfway? Would you say it is half-full or half-empty? Your response gives you some idea about your perspective on things.

Perspective is how you personally view things, based on your background and expectations. For the purposes of this chapter, perspective refers to how you view test results and learning. Suppose you are taking a basic electrical wiring course and on your first test you don't do well, even though you studied for the test. "Not doing well" could mean getting a B or a D, depending on your perspective. Perhaps you received a 68 on a test. You can think you did poorly, but you can also use a different perspective and think "Wow! I got 68 correct! Now I just have to work on getting the remaining 32."

It is important to remember that *one test does not make or break your academic career.* It doesn't mean that you are destined to do poorly on all your tests. And, it doesn't mean you are a failure. It does mean, however, that you have to look at and recognize what you can do to do better next time.

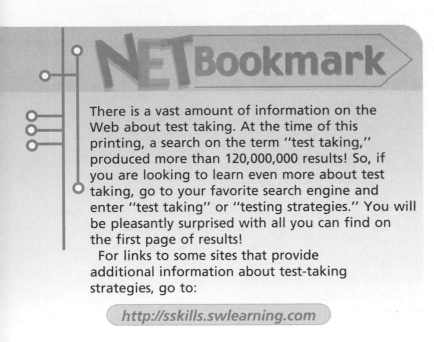

NETBookmark

There is a vast amount of information on the Web about test taking. At the time of this printing, a search on the term "test taking," produced more than 120,000,000 results! So, if you are looking to learn even more about test taking, go to your favorite search engine and enter "test taking" or "testing strategies." You will be pleasantly surprised with all you can find on the first page of results!

For links to some sites that provide additional information about test-taking strategies, go to:

http://sskills.swlearning.com

ACTIVITY 3

Respond to the following questions about perspective in testing situations. Try to be specific for each type of learning.

1. On four separate tests, you received the following grades: A-, C+, 83, and 62. How would you react?

_____

_____

2. At your job, you received a less than perfect year-end evaluation. How do you react? What role does your perspective play in your reaction?

_____

_____

3. What can you do to change your perspective to reduce stressful reactions to tests?

_____

_____

You Won't Know Everything

If you get everything right on tests all the time, then you should wonder why you are in school. You aren't supposed to know everything; you are in school to learn new things you don't yet know.

Many learners get a sinking feeling of disappointment when they are presented with a question they just can't answer. It could be on a test, or asked by a teacher, boss, or some other person in authority. You may go so far as to believe you are a total failure because you didn't know the answer. Of course, the more answers you know and can document accurately, the better your test result. But, it is unrealistic to think you will know all of the answers all of the time. Therefore, *you should focus on what you do know, not on what you don't know.* Accept that you will not know everything.

"I don't think of myself as a poor, deprived ghetto girl who made good. I think of myself as somebody who from an early age knew I was responsible for myself, and I had to make good."

—Oprah Winfrey

Take Responsibility and Learn from Past Mistakes

Some learners consistently blame their poor test results on the instructors. It is because of "them" that they didn't do well. Others assume responsibility for their own performance and don't blame anyone or anything else. Instead, they analyze past tests, habits, and results, to see where they can improve. They are more actively involved in their own learning and take responsibility for their own results when dealing with a challenging instructor. Which do you do?

ACTIVITY 4

Think about how you take responsibility for your learning success and testing outcomes. What do you say or do that shows your responsibility? What do you say or do that shows your lack of responsibility? List these below.

How I Take Responsibility

1. _____
2. _____
3. _____
4. _____
5. _____
6. _____
7. _____
8. _____
9. _____
10. _____

How I Do Not Take Responsibility

1. _____
2. _____
3. _____
4. _____
5. _____
6. _____
7. _____
8. _____
9. _____
10. _____

"Don't compromise yourself. You are all you've got."

—Janis Joplin, Musician

Take Care of Your Body

Another important way to reduce your stress is to take care of your body. It constantly gives you signals about its needs. For example, the average person needs minimally seven to nine hours of sleep per night to function at his or her best. Teenagers need even more. Without it, your brain doesn't remember things as well or as quickly and your ability to make sense of simple things is much more challenging. You also can't deal with bad stress effectively when you are not rested. Think about how you can get the sleep you need.

If you regularly skip meals or consume a lot of sugary snacks or simple carbohydrates (like white pasta and white bread), your body and mind will feel sluggish. Your blood sugar is constantly on a roller coaster, tiring you out instead of staying more even and providing stable energy. Try eating whole grain breads and pastas and adding more protein (like meat and dairy products) and fruits and vegetables to your diet. You will feel better within a few days.

With all the coffee shops around, you'd think caffeine is a good thing. Actually, too much caffeine is toxic and can cause dizziness, heart palpitations, nausea, diarrhea, and insomnia. Limit your caffeine to one or two doses a day, or consider switching to decaf.

Those who get regular exercise can honestly tell you that they have more energy than their friends who don't. If you take a brisk walk for just 20 minutes, you will have more energy in your day than someone who doesn't exercise. Consider adding more physical activity to your routine.

Ultimately, if you limit caffeine and other drugs and feed your body with enough sleep, healthy foods, and physical exercise, it will reward you with the resources and energy you need to learn.

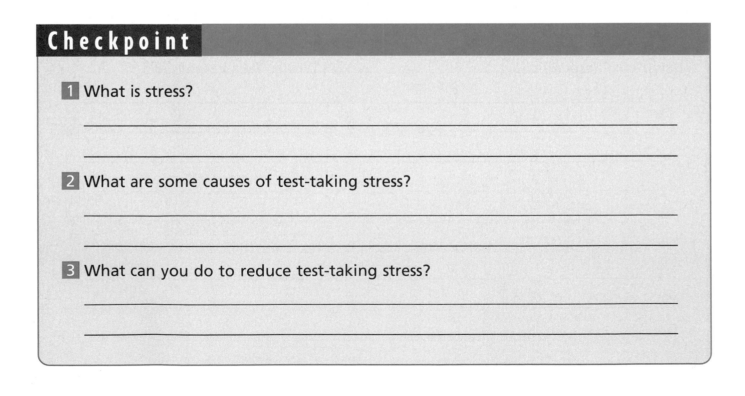

Checkpoint

1 What is stress?

_____

_____

2 What are some causes of test-taking stress?

_____

_____

3 What can you do to reduce test-taking stress?

_____

_____

The Ten Rules of the Test-Taking Game

The object of a formal test or game is to get as many points as possible in the time allowed. In each case, it benefits you to have a thorough understanding of the rules of the "game." While reading the following rules for test taking, place an asterisk (*) next to those you want to remember or review later.

Rule 1   Act as if You Will Succeed

Your thoughts are powerful. When you think negative thoughts, your stress level rises. Your confidence level drops, which often leads to feelings of failure.

The next time you are thinking negative thoughts about a test, try thinking positively instead. Smile and take at least six or seven deep, slow breaths. Close your eyes and imagine feeling confident and relaxed while taking the test. Picture in your mind getting the test back with a good grade written at the top. Try doing this now by thinking about an upcoming test. Do you feel different? (If this short exercise was powerful for you, you may be interested in learning more about the power of visualization. Consult your library or the Internet for more information.)

Rule 2   Arrive Ahead of Time

Use your time management skills to make sure you are on time or even early for a test. It sets your mind at ease. You will have a better chance of getting your favorite seat, mentally and physically relaxing, and preparing yourself for the game ahead.

Rule 3   Bring the Essential Testing Tools

Remember to bring the necessary testing tools along with you, including extra pens, sharpened pencils, erasers, a calculator, a watch, a dictionary, and other items you may need. You won't need your notes or a textbook unless it is an open-book test. Just a brief outline or flashcards of what you know well will be enough. Your instructor will have no sympathy for you if you forget any of the test-taking tools. You are 100% responsible for being prepared with the tools and supplies you will need.

Rule 4   Ignore Panic Pushers

If you do come early to the test, know that this isn't a time to cram in things you don't know. It is a time to review the things you do know. Some students, however, become nervous before a test and frantically ask you questions about the material studied in fear they don't know the answers. These are **panic pushers** because if you don't know the answers, you may panic and lose your confidence. Instead of talking with a panic pusher before a test, spend your time away from others concentrating on what you know, not on what you don't know.

Must Know!!

Study This!

Rule 5 Pre-View the Playing Field

Before you play any game, it is smart to pre-view the field. The information you find during your pre-view will help you determine your game-playing strategies. In baseball, players inspect the field looking for wet and slippery spots, and they judge the height of the fence to hit a home run over. Once you have received your test, you should do several things before you begin:

- **Write your name on your paper first.** This may seem obvious, but many students are so eager to get started they forget. If you forget, how will your instructor know that the excellent work is yours?!

- **Listen to instructions and read directions carefully.** Have you ever lost points on a test for not following directions? You may have known the answers to the questions, but you failed to follow the rules of the game. For example, if you see a column of vocabulary words on the left side of a test sheet and definitions on the right side, you might assume that you should match the two columns. However, if the directions said to look for opposite definitions, you would lose points for not following directions. Avoid careless errors by always reading directions *carefully* and asking your instructor to explain any directions that are unclear.

- **Determine the point spread.** Look at the total number of questions and the point value of each. Decide how much time you can spend on each question and still finish the test on time. Let's say your test is made up of 30 multiple-choice questions and two essays. Each of the multiple-choice questions is worth 2 points for a total of 60 points, and each essay is worth 20 points for a total of 40 points.

$$
\begin{array}{lll}
30 \text{ multiple-choice} \times 2 \text{ points} & = & 60 \text{ points} \\
2 \text{ essay} \hspace{1.6cm} \times 20 \text{ points} & = & +40 \text{ points} \\
\hline
& & 100 \text{ points}
\end{array}
$$

The points should add up to 100; if they don't, ask your instructor if you understand the breakdown correctly. Once you figure out the point values, you can budget your time accordingly.

- **Budget your time.** If you budget your time and stick to your time limits, you will always complete the test in the amount of time given. If you had 60 minutes to complete the test in the example above, approximately how much time should you spend on each of the multiple-choice questions? How much time, approximately, should you spend on each essay?

   Don't worry if others finish before you. Those who leave early don't always get the highest grades.

- **Look for answers within the test.** Be on the lookout for questions that answer other questions. Frequently, instructors will test you on a concept in more than one way. You may see a concept or word in a multiple-choice question and you can use it in a short-answer. Sometimes you can use the terminology from the objective questions for your essays. And, if you are lucky, your instructor will reword questions and list answer choices that include the answers to other questions. Look at the whole exam's content, not just one question at a time.

Rule 6   Write in the Margin

Before you begin the test, dump out of your brain any key terms, formulas, names, dates, and other information in the margin so you won't forget them. Then your brain can focus on just the questions. (Chapter 13, on writing essays and papers, discusses how to create a map in the margin so you can communicate your ideas in an organized fashion.)

Rule 7   Complete the Easy Questions First

Answering easy questions first helps build your confidence and comfort level. If you come across a tough question, mark it so you can come back to it later. Avoid spending so much time on a challenging question that you run out of time to answer the questions you do know.

Rule 8   Know if There Is a Guessing Penalty

Guessing penalties are found more often on standardized tests than on instructor-made tests. But, before assuming you don't have one, it's wise to ask. If your testing time is about to run out and there is no penalty, take a wild guess on questions you don't know. On the other hand, if your test carries a penalty for guessing, choose your answers wisely, and leave blank the answers you do not know.

Rule 9   Avoid Changing Your Answers

Have you ever chosen an answer, changed it, and learned later that your first choice was correct? Research indicates that three out of four times your first choice is usually correct; therefore, you should go with your first impression. If you have extra time at the end of a test, use it to review your work for careless errors, but avoid changing an answer unless you are *absolutely* sure it is wrong.

Rule 10   Write Clearly and Neatly

Imagine your instructor reading your writing. Is it easy to read and presentable, with the answers in the right places and no words crossed out, or does it look messy? The easier your test is for the instructor to read, the better your chances of getting a higher grade. Remember to use an erasable pen or pencil to keep your paper neat and to proofread for spelling and grammar errors. See Figure 10-1 for a visual review of the ten rules of test taking.

Success tip

Math and problem-solving tests require a few additional strategies:

- Write down all the key formulas you will need in the margin, so you can refer to them during the test.
- Show your work. Even if your answer is incorrect, you may receive partial credit for using the correct steps and formulas.
- Use estimates to check your work. If you are asked to multiply 29×11, you can expect an answer around 300. If your answer is closer to 3,000, you know you made a mistake in your calculation.
- Check your work for careless errors, such as transposing numbers, putting decimal points in the wrong place, and illegible handwriting.

FIGURE 10-1

Mind Map Review

The information on this map is a general review of the concepts discussed in Chapters 5 and 10. Read the map by following the thoughts and pictures on each of the branches. This will reinforce what you have already read and learned while preparing you for the next section on test-taking strategies.

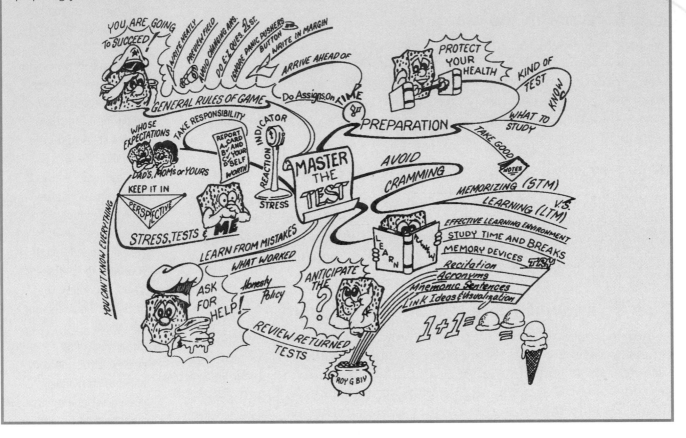

What You Need to Know about Computer-Based Tests

Sometime in your life, you will probably experience a computer-based test, if you have not already done so. Stockbrokers, teachers, architects, financial planners, and other professionals are required to take licensing and certification tests on the computer. Students can take certain pre-college tests, such as the GREs and GMATs, on a computer, too. Tutorials about how to use the computer are usually provided, so you can take these tests even if you have little or no computer experience.

Most computer-based tests are multiple-choice, and you can use the strategies discussed in this chapter to help you. Be aware that the multiple-choice questions are presented in either an *adaptive* or *linear* manner. An adaptive test selects the difficulty of the next question based on your previous answer. This means different test takers answer different questions. Linear questions are preset and given in numerical order. Most tests these days are adaptive.

Some of the strategies you learned about taking tests on paper may not apply when tests are taken on the computer. For example, on adaptive tests, you must answer the question the first time you see it. You can't go back and change your answer. You also can't mark it and come back to it later. Linear tests allow you to return to the question.

You can't pre-view the whole test, as you are only allowed to see one question at a time, and you can't go back looking for answers to other questions in those you have answered.

Reading a test on a computer screen is different from reading on paper. Some of the faster reading strategies (from Chapter 9) such as key words and phrasing can be used as well as the strategies presented in Chapter 12 about reading on-screen.

On both types of tests, your score depends on how well you answer the questions and on the number of questions you answer. So, managing your time is key. Makers of these tests suggest you familiarize yourself with the test format by completing the tutorials and sample questions before attempting the tests.

With most computer-based tests, results are provided immediately. However, before you finish, you are given a chance to cancel the test without seeing your score. If you cancel it, you will need to schedule another testing date and pay again. If you ask to see your score, you cannot cancel the test. You must accept the result of your performance.

For more information about computer-based tests, check out the web sites of some of the test makers by going to your favorite search engine and typing in Educational Testing Service and/or Prometric Testing.

Success tip

Online tests may intimidate you if you are unfamiliar with the computer, but keep in mind that most of these tests require only minimal computer knowledge.

- Be sure to take advantage of any tutorials offered before the test to get acquainted with the software and format.
- If you have a "save" option, during the test, be sure to save your answers periodically, to reduce the risk that answers will be lost.
- Be careful not to click on "Submit," "Finish," or "See my score," until you are sure you have completed all questions and you are satisfied with your answers.
- Be sure you know how to contact an instructor or administrator in case of a technical problem.

Checkpoint

1 What are the ten general rules for taking any test?

_____

_____

_____

2 Which rules do you already know and follow?

_____

_____

3 Which specific rules do you want to remember and use?

_____

_____

Winning Game Strategies

Now that you have read the rules of test taking, it's time to apply winning game strategies to objective tests, subjective tests, and performance tests. Chances are you already know many of the strategies and use them successfully. Your job is to look for the ones that you don't know or use and make them work for you. Some of the strategies will be useful all of the time, while other strategies will be useful only some of the time. By becoming aware of the strategies and putting them into practice, you will quickly find the ones that work best for you.

Multiple-Choice Questions

Multiple-choice questions are sometimes called **multiple guess**. When you don't know an answer, you actually have to take a wild guess. Taking a wild guess is a popular strategy, but it should be used only when all else fails. On the other hand, learning how to make educated guesses adds to your success. An **educated guess** is a result of using testing strategies to come up with your answer. See Figures 10-2 and 10-3 for examples.

FIGURE 10-2

Sample Multiple-Choice Questions

Many strategies can be used to answer multiple-choice questions correctly. Five multiple-choice questions are shown here. Strategies for answering these questions are shown in Figure 10-3. Read each question, circle which answer you think is best, and then review the strategies you can use to lead you to the correct answer.

1. Bears can be found wandering
   a. in the woods.
   b. in parks.
   c. in fields.
   d. in the mountains.
   e. all of the above.

2. Students frequently succeed in test taking because
   a. all tests are easy.
   b. they are usually prepared.
   c. they always do their assignments on time.
   d. they always try hard.

3. Migraine headaches are most commonly caused by
   a. allergic reactions to foods.
   b. lack of sleep.
   c. allergic reactions to medicine.
   d. heredity.

4. The reasons most students give for failing tests include
   a. studying the wrong information.
   b. cramming and being unprepared.
   c. not having enough time to study.
   d. being given unfair tests.

5. All of the following are ingredients of student success except
   a. taking good notes.
   b. studying ahead of time.
   c. learning from mistakes.
   d. cramming for exams.

FIGURE 10-3

Possible Strategies for Answering Multiple-Choice Questions

♦ **Question 1 – Look at all possible answers before choosing.**

Question 1 asks you to choose where bears are found wandering. To get to the correct response, mentally complete the question with each answer one-at-a-time and ask yourself if each statement is correct or not.

a. Bears can be found wandering <u>in the woods</u>. *Correct*

b. Bears can be found wandering <u>in parks</u>. *Correct*

c. Bears can be found wandering <u>in fields</u>. *Correct*

d. Bears can be found wandering <u>in the mountains</u>. *Correct*

e. Bears can be found wandering in <u>woods, parks, fields, and mountains</u>. *Correct*

    All answers to these questions are correct, but "e" is the best answer because it includes a, b, c, and d. If you answered this question without looking at all the choices, you might have chosen incorrectly.

♦ **Question 2 – Look for key words.**

Can you identify the key word in question 2? The key word is *frequently*. Now look at the answers. Which answer best reflects the same key word? "b" is correct because of the word *usually*. All the other answers give definite answers, such as *all* and *always*. The only answer that is not definite—*usually*—answers the question best. Other keywords to look for include words such as *except, not, rarely, often, every, must, only, never,* and *none*.

♦ **Question 3 – Look for similar answers.**

Many times in multiple-choice questions, you are asked to make a choice between two similar answers. Answers a and c are similar in question 3, which indicates that the answer may be one of them. If you had no idea of the answer to this question, looking for similar answers would help you narrow your wild-guess possibilities from a, b, c, and d to a and c. Now you can take an educated guess. The correct response to this question is "a". In this example, the strategy worked, but it may not work all the time.

♦ **Question 4 – Know what the question is asking.**

Does the test ask you to write the best answer or the worst answer? Are you looking for similarities or opposites? Is the question asking for a singular or plural answer? In question 4, you are asked to supply *more than* one reason, as indicated by the word *reasons*. The only answer that gives more than one reason is "b". Though some of the other responses may be a reason, the best answer to the question is "b".

♦ **Question 5 – Answer negatives positively first.**

Many students become confused when a question asks for an exception instead of the best answer. In question 5, if you look first for the answers that are important to student success, only the exception remains a choice.

a. Is taking good notes an ingredient to student success? Yes

b. Is studying ahead of time an ingredient to student success? Yes

c. Is learning from mistakes an ingredient to student success? Yes

d. Is cramming for exams an ingredient to student success? No

  A few more multiple-choice strategies exist, but instead of reading about them, you will discover them yourself in Activity 5. Make an educated guess at the questions that follow, and confirm your understanding of the strategies by reviewing the answers and explanations that appear on page 294.

Below is a series of multiple-choice questions. For many of the questions, you will make an educated guess. Use your background knowledge, common sense, and multiple-choice testing strategies. Questions 5 through 11 contain fictitious, or made up, words. Even so, each question has a correct answer. Circle your answer; then explain why you chose it. When you have completed all of the questions, turn to page 294 for the answers and explanations.

1. Dickens' *A Tale of Two Cities* takes place in what two cities?

    a. Glasgow and London   c. Paris and London

    b. New York and Paris   d. Dublin and Edinburgh

    I chose this answer because

    _____

2. Italy has been handicapped by all of the following *except*

    a. limited natural resources.   c. a lack of adequate ports.

    b. a shortage of fertile soil.   d. overpopulated farmlands.

    I chose this answer because

    _____

3. Which of the following is closest in value to 1/3?

    a. 1/4   b. 3/8   c. 3/16   d. 5/16   e. 7/16

    I chose this answer because

    _____

4. An example of a mismatched relationship is

    a. Chicago and Illinois.   c. Kansas City and Missouri.

    b. Birmingham and Florida.   d. Phoenix and Arizona.

    I chose this answer because

    _____

5. The purpose of the cluss in furmaling is to remove

    a. cluss-prags.   b. tremalis.   c. cloughs.   d. plumots.

    I chose this answer because

    _____

6. Trassig is true when

    a. lusp crosses the vom.   c. the belgo frulls.

    b. the viskal flans, if the viskal is donwil or zortil.   d. dissles lisk easily.

    I chose this answer because

    _____

ACTIVITY 5 (continued)

7. The sigla frequently overfesks the trelsum because
   a. all siglas are melious.
   c. the trelsum is usually tarious.
   b. siglas are always votial.
   d. no tresla are feskable.
   I chose this answer because

   _____

8. The fribbled breg minters best with an
   a. derst.   b. morst.   c. sortar.   d. ignu.
   I chose this answer because

   _____

9. Among the conditions for tristal doss are
   a. the spas fropt and the foths tinzed.
   c. few rakobs accept in sluth.
   b. the kredges trott with the orots.
   d. most of the polats are thenced.
   I chose this answer because

   _____

10. Which of the following (is, are) always present when trossels are being gruven?
    a. rint and yost   b. yost   c. shum and yost   d. yost and plume
    I chose this answer because

    _____

11. The mintering function of the ignu is most effectively carried out in
    a. a razma tool.
    c. the fribbled breg.
    b. the gorshing stanti.
    d. a frally sush.
    I chose this answer because

    _____

12. If a test contained a question that you didn't understand or know the answer to, which letter would you pick?
    a.   b.   c.   d.
    I chose this answer because

    _____

True-False Questions

True-false questions are probably the easiest to answer because you have a 50 percent chance (one in two) of getting the correct answer. In a multiple-choice question, your chances are reduced to 33 percent (one in three), 25 percent (one in four), 20 percent (one in five), or another percentage based on the number of answers. Use the following strategies to obtain better results on true-false tests.

READ EACH QUESTION CAREFULLY. By reading each question carefully, you will find key words and terms to help you choose your answer. This is the best strategy for taking true-false tests.

LOOK FOR DEFINITES AND ABSOLUTES. How many things in this world are definite and absolute? Not many. In some true-false questions, certain key words tell you that a definite is being included as part of the answer. Most—but not all—definite answers are false. A list of common definite/absolute key words appears in Activity 6.

LOOK FOR THE LENGTH OF THE STATEMENT. The longer a true-false statement is, the more likely it is to be true. If all else fails, take a guess. Read the longest answers in Activity 7 and decide whether they are true. You have a 50 percent chance of getting the answer correct.

ACTIVITY 6

Definite key words are listed in the first column. In the second column, write the exception, or non-definite term, that is related to the key word. Use the examples to help you. Can you think of any others?

Definite/Absolute Terms	Exception Terms
All	Some
Always	Sometimes
Never	_Sometimes_
Everyone	_Some one_
Nobody	_Somebody_
Is/Are	_could/might_
Must	_Maybe_
None	_Some_
Absolutely	_Possibly_

Try your luck on the following true-false questions. Place a "T" for true or "F" for false in the blank next to each statement. State the reason for your answer. Identify any key words that support your reason. Then discuss your answers with a partner or group.

_F_ 1. All people have similar ways of learning.

Reason for my answer: _____

_F_ 2. The best time to begin reviewing for a test is within 24 hours of the test.

Reason for my answer: _____

_F_ 3. Rote memorization is the most efficient way to learn.

Reason for my answer: _____

_F_ 4. All men are created equal.

Reason for my answer: _____

_F_ 5. Men are usually physically stronger than women.

Reason for my answer: _____

_T_ 6. Some birds do not fly.

Reason for my answer: _____

_F_ 7. College is always harder than high school.

Reason for my answer: _____

_T_ 8. For most job interviews, you should wear clean, neatly pressed clothes and look presentable.

Reason for my answer: _____

_F_ 9. Eating oat bran reduces cholesterol.

Reason for my answer: _____

_T_ 10. Most students can benefit from learning active study skills.

Reason for my answer: _____

What have you learned about taking true-false tests?

_____

_____

At this point, we hope you have realized that not only what you study is valuable but the strategies you use when taking the test are equally important. Combining your study knowledge with effective strategies is a sure-fire formula for testing success.

Matching Tests

A matching test, when used, is usually only part of a test, not an entire test itself. Matching is similar to multiple-choice because only the correct response needs to be identified. Matching tests are slightly more challenging than multiple-choice because you must locate matching terms or ideas from lists of information. Some instructors ask for the opposite term or idea, so read the directions carefully! Some chapters of this book contain vocabulary matching exercises in the Review section. If these are challenging for you, use the suggestions below to help make them easier. When taking a matching test, keep several points in mind.

UNDERSTAND THE FORMAT. A matching test is made up of two columns or sets of information. Most often, you are asked to match a piece of information in the left column with a piece of information in the right column. Sometimes the format is reversed, and you are asked to match a piece of information on the right with a piece of information on the left. By reading the directions carefully, you will understand the test format.

COUNT THE POSSIBLE ANSWERS. Suppose you are asked to match the information in two columns. The left column lists 10 vocabulary terms you need to identify, and the right column lists the 12 possible definitions. It is obvious that two of the definitions on the right will not have a matching term on the left. On some tests, you may need to use the same answer more than once. The directions—or your instructor's verbal instructions—may indicate whether or not you can do this. If the directions aren't clear, then ask!

REVIEW ALL POSSIBLE CHOICES BEFORE ANSWERING. The better answer may be at the end of the list. You can make a correct judgment only after reading all the answers.

USE THE PROCESS OF ELIMINATION. If you answer the easy questions first, cross off the used ones. You will have fewer possibilities, which makes the more difficult terms easier to match. This also saves time by forcing you to look at only the unmarked answers.

MENTALLY REPEAT THE CHOICES. Mentally say the term on the left; then go down each possible answer on the right, and fill in the best answer. Mentally talking to yourself helps you focus. And, when you find the correct answer, it will sound right.

■ Focus on Ethics

You are the assistant manager of an office products store. Several of the employees are students at your former high school who are working part-time. You're not much older than they are, and you like them. You often joke around with them and consider them your friends. One day one of them approaches you and tells you that she has a test coming up that she needs to study for, but she also needs the money so she can't take time off work to study. She is normally a very good worker, so you tell her she can sit in the break room and study for a couple of hours during one of her shifts. What is (are) the problem(s) with this? How else could this have been handled?

The left column contains a list of terms from this book; the right column contains a list of definitions. Match the terms by placing the correct letter from the right in the blank on the left. (See page 295 for answers.)

_____ 1. Active learning	A. A reader's road map
_____ 2. Background knowledge	B. Note-taking method best used by a random learner
_____ 3. Cornell Method	C. What you already know
_____ 4. Critical thinking	D. High or fast reading gears
_____ 5. Pre-viewing	E. Learning like a sponge
_____ 6. Passive learning	F. Note-taking method used by the sequential learner
_____ 7. Mind Map	G. Some things that affect your study concentration
_____ 8. Mind wandering	H. Learning like a rock
_____ 9. Learning influences	I. Can only be reduced, not eliminated
_____ 10. Skimming and scanning	J. Listening for instructor clues
	K. Thinking about thinking
	L. An effective means of time management

Fill-in-the-Blank Tests

Usually, fill-in-the-blank questions are one part of a test, not entire tests in themselves. Generally, they ask you to identify the meanings of new words associated with the subject you are learning.

Fill-in-the-blanks are more difficult than multiple-choice, true-false, or matching because you must think of the answer instead of just identifying it. Several guidelines will help you when responding to fill-in-the-blank tests.

COMPLETE FILL-IN-THE-BLANK QUESTIONS LAST. If your test has several parts, leave fill-in-the blank questions until last. You may find the answers in the other sections.

BE SURE YOUR ANSWER MAKES SENSE. If the question asks for more than one item or the verb is plural, the answer is probably plural. If the question asks for one thing or the verb is singular, your answer is probably singular. If the word *an* appears before the blank, the answer must start with a vowel. Above all, your answer must make sense based on the context in which it is written.

CONSIDER THE LENGTH OF THE BLANK. Usually, a short blank means a short answer. A long blank probably means a long answer or a large word. Two blanks usually mean a two-word answer.

Try your skill by answering the following fill-in-the-blank questions based on information covered so far in this book. If you have trouble with an answer, refer to the chapter identified in parentheses after each statement. (See page 295 for answers.)

1. An _____ learner is one who takes responsibility for his or her learning and learns from mistakes. (Chapter 1)

2. A learner who blames others for his or her learning failures doesn't take _____ for his or her own learning. (Chapter 10)

3. A _____ learner is organized and logical, while a _____ learner is more unorganized and creative. (Chapter 2)

4. _____ means putting off doing something unpleasant or burdensome until a future time. (Chapter 4)

5. The best way to build vocabulary is to use your _____ _____. (Chapter 8)

6. The first two things readers should know before they start to read is their _____ and _____. (Chapter 8)

7. All readers should learn to read faster because it increases their _____. (Chapter 9)

8. In order to read faster, you can read _____ _____, _____, or use_____. (Chapter 9)

9. In the Cornell Method of note taking, the _____ of the notes is for your informal outline and the _____ _____ is for key words and questions to study. (Chapter 6)

10. The goal of this book is to help you study _____ not _____. (Chapters 1–13)

Short-Answer Questions

Short-answer questions generally require an answer of only a few sentences. For example, you may be asked to define a vocabulary term or identify a person. Or, you may be required to state the reason for an event or provide the date it took place.

To answer short-answer questions accurately, look for key words. The key words are listed on the left below, and the answers are listed on the right.

Key Words	Best Answer
Who?	Identify the person.
When?	Provide the date.
Where?	Name the place.

Why?	State the reason or cause.
What?	Explain the event.
How?	Describe the method or reason.

When you are unsure of an answer, take a guess as long as there is no guessing penalty. You may be right or get partial credit.

Essay Tests

The essay test is the most challenging type of test because it requires you to understand the material thoroughly. Also, many students believe they are poor writers, so writing anything, especially an essay for a test, makes them feel inadequate and overwhelmed before they start. Putting in more study time over a longer period of time combined with the strategies below will help you feel more confident and capable of writing your essays. You will master the material and prove that mastery to your instructor in your well-thought-out writing.

There are many strategies to keep in mind as you begin the essay part of a test. (Also, see Chapter 13 for more ideas.)

READ THE DIRECTIONS CAREFULLY. Though reading directions is essential in any test-taking situation, essay test directions are especially important. The essay directions will tell you:

1. *How many essay questions you need to answer.* Sometimes you will be given a choice of questions to answer, such as three out of five. In this case, make sure to answer only three. If you answer four, chances are that the instructor will count the first three you wrote, not the best three.

2. *How long the essay should be.* Few instructors enjoy reading long essays. Try to come close to the number of words required, while also answering the question to your satisfaction.

3. *How you should budget your time.* The amount of time you allow for answering an essay question depends on how many points the question is worth, the suggested length of the answer, and how quickly you can develop an answer. This is where pre-viewing the test is very helpful.

4. *What type of answer you should give.* Before you answer any essay question, make sure you understand what the question is asking. Avoid giving your opinion unless you are asked for it. Review Figure 10-4 for additional guidance.

5. *How many components you should discuss.* Some essay questions ask you to respond to more than one question. In the following sample essay question, four responses are required.

Sample essay question: Students benefit from becoming active learners. Define active learner, and compare this person to a passive learner. Discuss the reasons becoming active in the learning process is important. Evaluate your experiences as an active and passive learner.

"Begin with the end in mind."

—**Stephen R. Covey, Author of *The Seven Habits of Highly Effective People***

Success tip

Open-book tests are often harder than closed-book exams, so study and prepare for them as much as you would for any test. Follow these tips to enhance your success:

- Familiarize yourself with your book, notes, and other materials. Be sure to bring all of the allowed materials to your test and be sure you know where key information and concepts can be found.
- If permitted, highlight, underline, or use adhesive tags to mark key concepts on the pages.
- Looking up answers in the book takes up valuable time, so answer the questions you know first. Then, go back and answer the questions that you need to look up in the book.

FIGURE 10-4

Understanding Essay Directions

Below are some common words and related definitions used in essay-test directions. Learn them now so you can respond appropriately and accurately on tests.

Directions	Meanings	Example Questions
Name	List in 1, 2, 3 order.	Name the first five U.S. presidents.
List	Provide the information required.	List three ways to improve listening.
Give	Explain.	Give two reasons for taking notes.
Discuss	Provide a comprehensive answer.	Discuss active learning.
Describe	Illustrate in words.	Describe life in the twenty-first century.
Define	Provide a definition.	Define pre-viewing.
Identify	Give a brief and correct answer.	Identify the parts of a flower.
Explain	Provide clear, complete thoughts.	Explain why procrastination is a student's worst enemy.
State	Explain in your own words.	State why jobs are not for life anymore.
Compare	Discuss similarities and differences.	Compare computers and typewriters.
Contrast	Discuss differences only.	Contrast (or distinguish between) computers and typewriters.
Illustrate	Give examples, or draw a picture labeling the parts.	Illustrate how to use Mind Mapping.
Criticize	Give evidence on both sides.	Criticize the use of force by police in arrests.
Evaluate	Draw conclusions and make judgments.	Evaluate the need for affordable day care.
Comment	Write your reaction to the topic; support your opinion with facts or illustrations.	Comment on the increase of unemployment in America during the 1930s.

WRITE FOR THE INTENDED AUDIENCE. In the case of a test, your intended audience is your instructor, an individual who knows the subject matter. However, to communicate simply, clearly, and completely, write as though the reader knows nothing about the topic.

MAKE YOUR PAPER EASY TO READ. Many students forget that someone has to read their test paper. Follow these guidelines for improving your essays.

- Write neatly and use an erasable pen to correct mistakes.
- Write on the right-hand side of your test booklet, if possible, and leave the left side for writing rough outlines, or making changes and additions.

- Consider leaving a blank line in between written ones in case you want to add more detail or make your writing more legible there.

- Name, date, and number every loose page.

- Substitute synonyms for words you use frequently to reduce repetition.

- Use the vocabulary of the subject area you are being tested on. The more you use it accurately, the more the instructor believes you understand the concepts.

- Use connecting words to make the essay flow. (See Chapter 13.)

USE THE TRIED AND TRUE ESSAY FORMULA. There is an old essay formula that goes like this:

1. *"Tell them what you want to tell them."* In the first paragraph, start with a direct response to the question.

2. *"Then tell them."* In the body paragraphs, mention the topics described in the question. Provide general information and specific examples, using the vocabulary of the course or subject.

3. *"Then tell them what you told them."* In the concluding paragraph, restate your thesis or main ideas.

In this book, chapters are like essays, and they follow this formula. See if you can locate the three parts in at least one of the chapters.

ORGANIZE YOUR IDEAS BEFORE STARTING TO WRITE. Many students begin writing answers to essay questions without thinking about how their ideas will flow. Since one of the grading criteria for papers is organization, organize your thoughts before you begin writing. In Chapter 13, you will learn about Idea Mapping as a prewriting process for essays and papers. Idea Mapping is a way to create a quick outline of what you want to write. It can be written in the margin to guide you while writing. (Turn to Chapter 13 now if you want to learn more.)

PROOFREAD YOUR ANSWERS. Silently reread your answers word for word, pronouncing every word in your head. This will help you catch grammatical mistakes. Also, review your writing for misspellings, flow of ideas, and organization.

■ Focus on Technology

You may be asked to prepare an essay using a word processor. If this is the case, be sure to use the program's Spelling Check ability for checking your work. But, most importantly, use it properly. Make sure to check the spelling and grammar suggestions of your program, as they are not always correct. For example, if you misspell the word "definitely" (meaning with certainty), your program will try to identify the word you were trying to spell and will give you several suggestions from which to choose. Make sure to read through the list rather than select the very first option. Some programs will actually auto-correct and replace your word with a different word. In the case of *definitely*, the word is often *defiantly*. Therefore, you should not only use your Spelling Check function, but also proofread your work, just in case.

Practice taking an essay test by completing the exercise below. Respond to three out of the four items. Each answer should be approximately 100 words.

1. *Define* active learner, and compare an active learner to a passive learner.

_____

_____

_____

_____

_____

_____

_____

2. *Discuss* the reasons why becoming active in the learning process is important.

_____

_____

_____

_____

_____

_____

_____

3. *Evaluate* your experiences as an active and passive learner.

_____

_____

_____

_____

_____

_____

4. For a student to be successful, effective note-taking skills are important. Describe two effective note-taking methods.

_____

_____

_____

_____

_____

_____

_____

Performance Tests

Taking a driving test behind the wheel of a car is an example of a performance test. What other types of performance tests have you taken? What types of performance tests do you expect to take in the future?

Performance tests are sometimes combined with written tests, and sometimes they stand alone. They are different from written tests because they require a performance or demonstration. To prepare for a performance test, first study and understand the information you have to demonstrate. Then, practice until you are sure you can perform the required task well. For example, suppose you are taking a computer repair course; on a performance test, you are asked to add RAM to a computer. To accomplish this, you need to know how to open the computer, locate the memory chip, place the new chip in its correct slot, and close the computer safely. How would you prepare for this test?

You can probably guess that the most effective way to prepare for a performance test is to study, then practice, practice, practice.

ACTIVITY 11

Imagine you are the instructor of a class you are currently taking. Working independently or with others, choose a topic, and create a test worth 100 points. Include at least one section of objective questions and one section of subjective questions. If the content lends itself to a performance test, describe what the learner will be required to do on the test. Once the test is written, decide how you will evaluate the learner's outcome.

Checkpoint

1 Which type(s) of tests do you take most often?

_____

_____

2 Which test strategies work best for you?

_____

_____

3 What new strategies did you learn in this chapter?

_____

_____

CHAPTER SUMMARY

1. Understanding how you react to tests provides important personal information about how you deal with stress.

2. Taking responsibility for your own learning, keeping grades in perspective, realizing you won't know everything, and taking care of your body's needs are ways to reduce test-taking stress.

3. Taking a test is just like playing a game. The object of the game is to get as many points as possible in the time you are given to play.

4. The rules of the game are the important pieces of information you need to know before a game or test begins. The ten rules are as follows: Act as if you will succeed, arrive ahead of time, bring the essential testing tools, ignore panic pushers, pre-view the playing field, write in the margin any information you want to remember, complete the easy questions first, know if there is a guessing penalty, avoid changing your answers, and write clearly and neatly.

5. There are smart strategies you can use for each type of test. Once you learn and use them, they will be essential for more successful testing outcomes.

CHAPTER ASSESSMENT

Terms Review

Match the following terms to their definitions.

_D_ bad stress

_C_ educated guess

_E_ good stress

_G_ multiple guess

_B_ panic pushers

_F_ perspective

_A_ stress

a. Your body's reaction to something that happens.

b. People who ask you for the answers before a test and cause you to lose your confidence.

c. Using strategies to narrow down possible answers.

d. A reaction of fear and worry that undermines you.

e. A reaction that energizes and motivates you.

f. How you personally view things.

g. Not using any strategies when responding to multiple-choice questions.

Concept Review

Fill in the blank with the best word (or words) you can think of based on the content of this chapter.

1. Taking a test is just like playing a _____.

2. To help budget your time during a test, you can pre-view the test, looking for the _____.

3. It is your _responsibility_ to do well; you can't blame others.

4. You can tell yourself you will do well by using daily _____.

5. Attending to your _body's_ needs can give you energy and mental clarity for learning.

6. One _Test_ _____ does not make or break your academic career. This is a good _pers_ _____ to have.

Review

Based on the information you learned in this chapter, answer the following questions using your own words and thoughts.

1. What is stress? Give an example of good stress and bad stress.

_____

_____

_____

_____

2. How might your reaction to taking a test affect your ability to be successful?

_____

_____

_____

_____

3. How can you reduce testing stress?

_____

_____

_____

_____

4. What does "pre-view the playing field" mean?

_____

_____

_____

_____

5. What do you think "pretend as if" means in relation to test taking?

_____

_____

_____

_____

6. Of the ten rules for test taking, which ones are easiest to remember?

_____

_____

_____

_____

7. What did you learn about taking multiple-choice tests?

_____

_____

_____

_____

8. What did you learn about taking true-false tests?

_____

_____

_____

_____

9. What is the most important thing to know when taking a matching test?

_____

_____

_____

_____

10. Name at least three things you learned about essay tests.

_____

_____

_____

_____

_____

_____

11. Searching on the Web for test-taking strategies, find at least one more testing strategy not mentioned in this chapter.

_____

_____

_____

_____

12. Searching on the Web for tests and stress, find at least one more stress management strategy not mentioned in this chapter.

_____

_____

_____

_____

13. While searching on the Web for questions 11 and 12, what else did you find of interest about test taking?

_____

_____

_____

_____

_____

_____

CASE STUDIES

for Creative and Critical Thinking

ACADEMIC CASE—Connecting to Culinary Arts and Testing

Jamal has been taking classes at the local culinary art school for eighteen months. Next month is his "final" exam, which is in two parts. A written section consists of multiple-choice questions about general kitchen concepts and fill-in-the-blank vocabulary terms. He will also have to create a menu, list the ingredients, and write the recipes. In a performance section, he will have to cook a main course using the recipe he wrote. Jamal is a good chef but a nervous test-taker. He is worried and certain he is going to fail.

1. What do you think is Jamal's biggest problem?

   _____

   _____

   _____

2. What advice would you give Jamal to help him mentally prepare for his test?

   _____

   _____

   _____

3. How do you suggest Jamal "study" for this type of test?

   _____

   _____

   _____

WORKPLACE CASE—Connecting to Computerized Testing

Blanca is preparing to take her state's teacher certification test on the computer, which she has already failed once. Her state requires that she wait three months before repeating the exam, and she is hoping to graduate with her certification so she can get a teaching position in the fall. During her previous testing experience, she felt nervous and rushed due to the timed nature of her exam. She knew that her trouble area was mathematics, and she lost a great deal of time on a particular type of problem.

1. Which of the "rules of the game" would be most useful for Blanca to use to improve her performance?

   _____

   _____

   _____

2. What can Blanca do to be more calm, confident, and prepared the second time around?

   _____

   _____

   _____

Activity Answer Keys

Answers to Activity 5 (pages 278–279)

1. C—Both Paris and London are mentioned twice in the answers, while the other cities are only mentioned once. If you only remembered one of the two cities, you had to make a choice.

2. C—Using background knowledge, you might know that Italy is a peninsula surrounded by water on three sides, thus making "a lack of adequate ports" not possible.

3. D—First, use the process of elimination. By looking at the five answers, you will see three that are similar (C, D, E). This could indicate that the right answer is one of these three choices.

   If you didn't know the math for figuring out the answer, at least you could narrow down the possibilities. Knowing that the answer is probably in sixteenths, and then figuring one-third into sixteenths, would seem an efficient use of your test-taking time.

4. B—The key word is *mismatched*. In order to find the answer, you first need to find the matching items. This can help eliminate some of your choices. By matching the city correctly to its state, you can then see that A, C, and D are not mismatched. Letter B is the mismatched one.

5. A—Because "cluss" is in the answer.

6. B—There are two reasons why letter B appears to be the correct choice.

   1. It is the longest answer.
   2. It satisfies the condition presented in the question (... is true when...) because it includes the word *if*.

7. C—Letters A, B, and D use definite terms such as *all*, *always*, and *no*. The question uses the word *frequently*, making letter C, which contains the word *usually*, a better answer.

8. D—Letter D best satisfies the grammar rule that the article *an* is used before words beginning with a vowel, not with a consonant. Most instructors don't make it this easy for you, but if they do, be aware of it.

9. A—Letter A is the only answer that agrees with the plural form of *conditions* used in the question.

10. B—The key word is *always*. Vost is "always" present in all of the answers.

11. C—The answer is given in question 8. (Remember that pre-viewing the playing field can help find answers within a test!)

12. C—According to studies of instructor-created exams (not standardized tests), this is the most common answer given on multiple-choice exams, followed by B, then A, then D. When all else fails, a "C" guess is better than no answer at all!

Answers to Activity 8 (page 283)

E. 1. Active Learning (Learning like a sponge)
C. 2. Background Knowledge (What you already know)
F. 3. Cornell Method (Note-taking method best used by sequential learners)
K. 4. Critical Thinking (Thinking about thinking)
A. 5. Previewing (A reader's road map)
H. 6. Passive Learning (Learning like a rock)
B. 7. Mind Mapping® (Note-taking method best used by a random learner)
I. 8. Mind-wandering (Can only be reduced, not eliminated)
G. 9. Learning Influences (Those things that affect your study concentration)
D. 10. Skimming and Scanning (High/fast reading gears)

Answers to Activity 9 (page 284)

1. *an* active

2. passive

3. sequential; random

4. procrastination

5. background knowledge

6. purpose and responsibility

7. concentration

8. key words, phrases, pacers

9. body, recall column

10. smarter, harder

11

Using Your Critical and Creative Mind

Chapter Goals

After studying and working with the information in this chapter, you should be able to:

- Define critical thinking and creative thinking and describe the differences between these types of thinking.
- Identify situations that require critical thinking and use appropriate techniques.
- Identify situations that require creative thinking and use appropriate techniques.
- Use the problem-solving model to improve the quality of your thinking.

Angel is a high school senior who has applied to three colleges for the coming fall. He has dutifully completed all of the college applications, including the ones for financial aid. He isn't sure exactly what he wants to study yet so he is looking at schools that provide a strong and broad liberal arts education.

During his winter vacation, he and his parents are planning a car trip to visit the three colleges. Angel wants to see the campuses and get a feel for the schools before deciding on where he wants to go.

The first school he visits is in a big city. It's a relatively small school with a population of about 1,500. The classroom buildings have old world charm but the dorms look old and don't have modern amenities like Internet access. It is only two hours from home, and one of his best friends has already been accepted there.

The second school is located in a rural area with farmlands surrounding the campus. It has a large population of over 10,000 students. The buildings are very modern and up-to-date with all the latest technology. It is four hours from home, and Angel doesn't know anyone going there, yet.

His third choice is a state college located only 30 minutes from his house. The student population is over 20,000. The campus is in a country-like setting but is very close to a busy town. It's an old campus, but the buildings are being upgraded as state funds become available. Angel likes the sports program here and thinks a few friends will end up here as well.

Angel has much to consider. If you were in Angel's situation, what factors would you focus on? Why?

Think about an important purchase you have made, such as a car, a bicycle, a digital music player, or other big-ticket item. What did you do to consider the cost, size, and the best value? The thinking you use when considering these factors is both creative and critical—creative, in that you come up with many choices, and critical, in that you finally make one decision.

You use your thinking all the time, such as when you discuss a problem with a trusted friend, decide which school to attend or which organization to join, solve a problem at your job, or even when you just need to figure out what to eat or where to go for dinner. You use thinking when you get up every day and decide what you will do first, second, and third. You use thinking when you decide to delete junk e-mails without opening them or not to download songs from the Internet illegally.

Sometimes, your thinking will be positive; other times, negative. *Positive thinking*, or thinking that improves your situation, helps you move in the direction of success in whatever task you are doing. For example, if you are trying to approach an instructor about what you believe is an unfair test grade, you can think positively that you will state your case as calmly as possible and hope she or he will see the situation in your favor. Even if your grade isn't changed, at least you made an effort. If you think negatively in this situation, you might blame the instructor or not even attempt to meet with her or him because you are sure your grade won't be changed. This *negative thinking*, or thinking that weakens your situation, moves you in the direction of failure and is not productive.

Being consciously aware of the thinking you do will improve your ability to think effectively. You will learn to look at making choices as something that is necessary to come to a smart conclusion.

Thinking critically and creatively is as natural for the mind as movement is for the body. Both are improved with know-how, practice, and good coaching.

This is a know-how, practice, and coaching chapter for improving your critical and creative thinking. By studying the material, you will better understand how you think, and you will gain confidence in your thinking ability. In addition, you will learn to appreciate the importance of effective thinking in today's fast-paced world.

©Digital Vision

Time for thinking is necessary for considering options and making smart decisions. The more aware you are of your thinking, the better your thinking will be.

> Thinking critically and creatively is as natural for the mind as movement is for the body. Both are improved with know-how, practice, and good coaching.

The following self-evaluation will give you an idea of how familiar, or unfamiliar, you are with some of the topics and terms discussed in this chapter. After reading each statement, circle the letter Y, S, or N to indicate the answer that is most appropriate for you. Answer honestly. Rate yourself at the end; then complete the information on your Self-Check Progress Chart.

Y = yes; frequently   S = sometimes   N = no; never

1. I am consciously aware of my thinking process.   Y   S   N

2. I can define critical thinking and creative thinking.   Y   S   N

3. I know what metacognition means.   Y   S   N

4. I know the difference between divergent and convergent thinking.   Y   S   N

5. I know at least four guidelines for critical thinking.   Y   S   N

6. I can identify common thinking errors in advertising and political speeches.   Y   S   N

7. I can recognize the difference between facts and opinions.   Y   S   N

8. I take time to use thinking skills when I solve problems.   Y   S   N

9. I know the four rules of brainstorming.   Y   S   N

10. I realize that know-how and practice can improve my thinking.   Y   S   N

Rate Yourself:

Number of Ys _____ × 100 = _____

Number of Ss _____ × 50 = _____

Number of Ns _____ × 0 = _____   **Total** _____

What Are Critical and Creative Thinking?

The use of critical- and creative-thinking skills is an important and natural part of learning and living. In the past, most work was done by hand, and individuals followed their boss's instructions. Today, employers look for workers with good thinking skills. People work in teams and use highly technical equipment, such as computers, robots, and communications technology. They are often called upon to make important decisions that would have been assigned to supervisors only a few years ago.

This new workplace requires brainpower; that is, employees who have skills in critical and creative thinking—people who can decide what needs to be done and create ways to do it. When you use critical and creative thinking, you *think* about your thinking. This is called **metacognition**. Critical and creative thinking are similar yet different. The following explanations will help you understand the difference.

1. **Critical thinking** means *thinking about thinking in order to decide what to believe and how to behave.*

2. **Creative thinking** means *thinking about thinking in order to bring something new into existence, such as an idea, event, or object.*

"*I have a theory about the human mind. A brain is a lot like a computer. It will only take so many facts, and then it will go into overload and blow up.*"

—**Erma Bombeck, Writer and humorist**

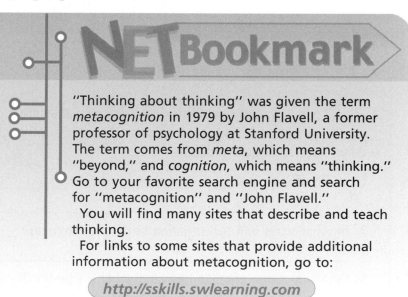

NETBookmark

"Thinking about thinking" was given the term *metacognition* in 1979 by John Flavell, a former professor of psychology at Stanford University. The term comes from *meta*, which means "beyond," and *cognition*, which means "thinking." Go to your favorite search engine and search for "metacognition" and "John Flavell."

You will find many sites that describe and teach thinking.

For links to some sites that provide additional information about metacognition, go to:

http://sskills.swlearning.com

Both types of thinking ask you to stop, reflect, and plan before you act. When you use *critical thinking*, you think about things that *already* exist, and you wonder how to react to them. For example, when a doctor decides which critically ill heart-transplant patient should get an available heart, he or she uses critical thinking. When you *think creatively*, you think about the need for something that *doesn't yet exist*. Inventors are good examples of people who use creative thinking.

Common Characteristics of Critical and Creative Thinking

Critical and creative thinking share five attributes. Knowing these common characteristics will be helpful.

1. Both critical and creative thinking are processes (ways of doing things) that are used to solve problems.

2. Both critical and creative thinking are time-consuming.

3. Both critical and creative thinking aim for solutions or outcomes.

4. Both critical and creative thinking can be improved through knowledge, practice, and coaching.

5. Critical and creative thinking work together for effective problem solving.

Angel, at the beginning of this chapter, has to decide which college he wants to attend. He needs to know what his options are and what his needs will be in the future, which requires *creative thinking*. To make his decision, Angel needs to think about what he believes will be the best option, choosing the school he ultimately wants to attend. That is *critical thinking*.

ACTIVITY 1

Angel's case shows how critical and creative thinking work together for effective problem solving (Attribute 5 above). Take a few minutes to write your thoughts below about the other four attributes as they relate to Angel's problem.

1. In what ways is Angel's situation a process? _____

_____

2. In what ways will the situation be time-consuming? _____

_____

3. What are some possible outcomes of this situation? _____

_____

4. What skills might improve Angel's ability to handle this situation? _____

_____

Now think about tasks in your own life that require critical and creative thinking. List two tasks below; then analyze each to determine when you would use critical thinking and when you would use creative thinking. Examples of tasks include planning your course of study, writing a paper, giving a party, accomplishing a work task, and organizing a political campaign.

Task 1: _____

1. Processes—What do you have to do? _____

2. Time—How much time do you estimate it will take? _____

3. Products—What are some possible outcomes? _____

4. Skills—What skills are needed? _____

_____

5. Critical Thinking—Which aspect of the task requires critical thinking?
(Hint: decision making) _____

6. Creative Thinking—Which aspect of the task requires creative thinking?
(Hint: being open to possibilities) _____

ACTIVITY 1 (continued)

Task 2: _____

1. Processes—What do you have to do? _____

2. Time—How much time do you estimate it will take? _____

3. Products—What are some possible outcomes? _____

4. Skills—What skills are needed? _____

5. Critical Thinking—Which aspect of the task requires critical thinking?
   (Hint: decision making) _____

6. Creative Thinking—Which aspect of the task requires creative thinking?
   (Hint: being open to possibilities) _____

Thinking Takes Time

As you can see from Angel's and your own examples, thinking is a time-consuming process. Effective thinking often takes time, yet you are probably used to things happening quickly in life. Because technology allows the events of everyday life to move at a fast pace, you usually get fast results. Stopping to think can feel dull and boring at first.

Metacognition can help you here. When you are involved in tasks requiring critical and creative thinking and you get feelings of "too slow," "boring," or "too much trouble," use these feelings as signals that you need to mentally slow down. Be metacognitive, and tell yourself that your reactions are normal. When you need to solve a complex problem or reach a difficult decision, it _will_ take time so make the time to think.

Success tip

When was the last time you had a big problem that needed to be solved? Did you secretly wish it would just go away? Unfortunately, problems don't just disappear. To be solved effectively, they need to be picked apart and thought through. Using your thinking can work and so can adding the thoughts of a trusted friend or relative. Remember, two heads really are better than one!

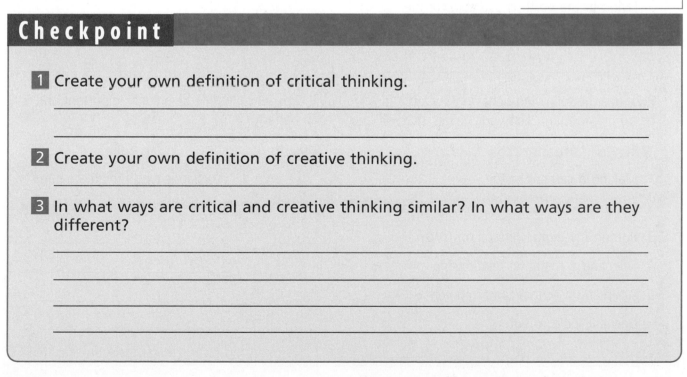

Checkpoint

1 Create your own definition of critical thinking.

_____

_____

2 Create your own definition of creative thinking.

_____

3 In what ways are critical and creative thinking similar? In what ways are they different?

_____

_____

_____

_____

Your Critical Mind

Critical thinking focuses on the here and now. When you think critically, you concern yourself with what you think is happening and how you will deal with a given situation. How you behave depends on your beliefs. Critical thinking deals with beliefs and behaviors.

Beliefs are interpretations, evaluations, conclusions, and predictions you consider to be true. If you believe that your sister is mechanically inclined, you may think she can change your car's spark plugs. If you have failed mathematics in the past, you may have mistakenly concluded that you can't do math.

Your beliefs guide your behaviors. The physical and mental skills you've acquired, such as driving a car or reciting the multiplication tables, were influenced by your belief that they were important. The only behaviors not influenced by beliefs are those that are automatic, such as bodily functions and reflexes.

ACTIVITY 2

Write possible behaviors related to the beliefs listed below. Add a few beliefs and behaviors of your own to the list.

Belief	Possible Behaviors
1. I'm not a great golfer. I doubt I'll ever play better than John can.	_____
2. I'm a good cook.	_____
3. I don't understand what's going on, so I must not be smart.	_____
4. I've worked hard for my money, so I can spend it however I want.	_____
5. Living in the north is too cold for me.	_____
6. _____	_____
7. _____	_____

Prioritize the following behaviors (or situations) you may experience, with 1 being very important and 5 being unimportant. List your beliefs that will guide each behavior.

Behavior (Situation)	Priority	My Belief
1. Making a career change	_1_	If I change jobs, I might be happier.
2. Deciding what to wear to your graduation party	____	_____
3. Putting my digital photos on DVDs	____	_____
4. Selecting a romantic relationship	____	_____
5. Attending a school/camp reunion	____	_____
6. Deciding how to vote	____	_____

Why and When to Think Critically

You need critical thinking to help you solve problems or make decisions that are important to you. Many common behaviors, such as bathing and eating, don't require daily critical thinking. You perform them based on previously established beliefs.

New situations and new information call for critical thinking. Seeing new products, hearing dramatic news stories, and experiencing personal or work problems all require you to decide what you believe. For example, the media frequently reports health findings, such as "Chocolate really is good for you" or "A low-carb diet will help you lose weight." Depending on your beliefs and the evidence presented, you will need to think critically about what you choose to believe. Just because something is printed or broadcast doesn't mean the information is 100 percent accurate or complete.

You might trust your instructors because they are experts in their fields. You might trust a local restaurant to make your favorite dish taste the same way every time. When you read, however, you must decide whether to believe the author.

- Is the author a recognized authority on the subject?
- Are the author's credentials cited?
- Is the work of other experts referenced in the material?

When you do research on the Web, you ultimately have to decide what to believe because it can be difficult to judge the credibility of the source. (See Chapter 12 for more information.)

How Do You Think Critically?

While you can't be sure critical thinking will provide correct answers, you can avoid obvious mistakes in thinking. First, metacognate.

When you have a problem to solve or a decision to make, think about your thinking. Sleep on it, count to ten, or use some other method to give yourself time to think. You need to be able to calm your brain because many situations that require critical thinking are emotionally upsetting. The part of the brain that thinks critically does not function at its best under stress, time pressure, or emotional shock.

The following six guidelines can help you develop your critical-thinking ability. They were adapted by Louise Loomis of The New England Cognitive Center from material written by Anita Harnadeck.

1. *Be open-minded about new ideas.* The world is changing rapidly and a lot of ideas are floating around. Resistance to new ideas is natural, so being open-minded takes practice.

2. *Know when you need more information.* Do you ever feel incompetent or inadequate? Chances are you just need more information. Locate the background knowledge you need and eliminate the negative self-talk.

3. *Be aware that different people have different ideas about the meanings of words, gestures, expressions, and other*

communication signals. This guideline is known as "different strokes for different folks." It's easy to get angry when others see things differently from you. Just be open-minded to new ideas, count to ten, and hear the speaker out. This is a heavy-duty metacognitive guideline. Use it to avoid unpleasantness, arguments, and violence.

4. *Know the difference between something that* must *be true and something that* might *be true.* This helps you separate facts (must be's) from opinions (might be's). This is a useful technique for dealing with rumors, gossip, and information you find on the Web.

5. *Separate emotional and logical thinking.* Research about the brain has revealed that people have emotional responses to all situations in their lives. Good critical thinking invites you to combine emotions and logic to make decisions and solve problems. Acknowledging and managing feelings is called "emotional intelligence" and is commonly talked about in schools and the workplace.

6. *Develop your vocabulary in order to understand others and to make yourself understood.* Chapter 8 discusses how to build vocabulary. Use its tips and guidelines to enjoy the power of a large vocabulary. The brain loves words. Feed it!

By using these six guidelines, you can increase your self-esteem because you will feel mentally competent in many situations. The guidelines will be helpful for:

- Identifying situations that can be improved by critical thinking.
- Developing conscious attention to your thinking.
- Increasing your confidence about your thinking.
- Avoiding harmful gossip and futile arguments.

ACTIVITY 3

Review the descriptions of the six critical-thinking guidelines given above. Discuss them with your classmates and relate them to examples from real life. Answer the questions that follow each guideline.

1. Be open-minded to new ideas.

   Learning is the continuous exposure to new ideas by breaking old habits and ways of thought. What new ideas or information have you learned recently? _____

   _____

   _____

ACTIVITY 3 (continued)

2. Know when you need more information.

   When was the last time something didn't make sense to you? How did you feel? What did you do? What will you do in the future? _____

   _____

3. Be aware that different people have different ideas about the meanings of words, gestures, expressions, and other communication signals.

   a. Think of a time when someone disagreed with you. What happened? How did you feel? What did you do?_____

   _____

   b. Think of a time when you were with people who dressed or acted differently from you. What happened? How did you feel? What did you do? _____

   _____

   _____

   c. How can this guideline help you deal with other people? _____

   _____

4. Know the difference between something that must be true (fact) and something that might be true (opinion).

   Decide which of the following statements are facts and which are opinions.

   a. Albany is the capital of New York State. _____

   b. New York City should be the capital. _____

   c. Newton is a great scientist because he discovered the law of gravity. _____

   d. The woman behind me in line must be upset about the wait because she looks angry. _____

   e. My friend is always late when we meet; I must not be important to him. _____

5. Separate emotional and logical thinking.

   This guideline suggests that you are constantly collecting both logical and emotional information in situations that require critical thinking. For example, your logic may tell you that the red shirt is a better buy than the blue one. But if you don't like the red shirt (an emotional response), purchasing it will be a waste of time and money and a source of regret if you never wear it. What are your emotional and logical thoughts about the following situations?

	Emotional	Logical
Writing a long paper or document	_____	_____
Preparing for an oral presentation	_____	_____
Making plans for a vacation	_____	_____
Telling your boss about a mistake you made	_____	_____

6. Develop your vocabulary in order to understand others and make yourself understood.

   How do you keep track of new words? _____

   _____

By being aware of how others influence your thinking process, you will be able to judge situations more clearly and come to better decisions.

Mistakes in Critical Thinking

So many mistakes in critical thinking are made by people that numerous books have been written about the topic. Though you will make mistakes on your own, the actions and words of other people often contribute to your mistakes. By being aware of how others influence your thinking process, you will be able to judge situations more clearly and come to better decisions.

Mistakes in thinking are called **fallacies**. The factors that influence fallacies in thinking range from your trusted friends and work colleagues to television ads and newspaper articles. They distract you from making decisions based on critical thinking. Some of the most common fallacies are described below.

PEER PRESSURE. **Peer pressure** causes you to go along with the crowd in order to be accepted or popular.

> *Example:* "Ling and I are skipping class tonight to go to the hockey game. Aren't you coming with us?"

HORSE LAUGH. **Horse laugh** refers to making fun of someone or something when you disagree. This fallacy is best communicated by one's tone of voice or body language.

> *Example:* Wallie is talking to a coworker, and the coworker says, "You're doing *that* project?"

TWO WRONGS MAKE A RIGHT. **Two wrongs make a right** refers to returning an insult with an insult.

> *Example:* "My coworker didn't invite me to her party, so I'm not going to help her with her project."

HASTY GENERALIZATION. **Hasty generalization** refers to making a decision too quickly.

> *Example:* "I know I just met him, but I don't like him," or "I tried playing tennis once, and I'm not any good at it."

NAME-CALLING. **Name-calling** substitutes a personal insult for a direct response.

> *Example:* Joe says, "Being metacognitive about studying is a great help." Pat responds, "That's a typical nerd statement if I ever heard one."

SCARE TACTICS, APPEALS TO PITY, AND APPLE POLISHING. These fallacies all focus on emotional thinking and ignore logic. These fallacies use intimidation, pleas for sympathy, and compliments, respectively.

> *Example of* **Scare Tactics***:* "We, the membership committee of the Sigma Club, see in your application that you've been very active

with the student newspaper. Did you know that our club president was kicked off your paper's editorial board last year?"

*Example of **Appeals to Pity***: "Professor Amato, please let me hand in my paper tomorrow. I had to take care of my sick grandmother last night. Then, when I finally got to work on my paper, my printer ran out of toner, and it was too late to buy any because the stores were all closed. If you accept my paper late, I'll be able to stay off academic probation."

*Example of **Apple Polishing***: "Hannah, please let me photocopy your notes to study for the exam. Your handwriting is so much neater than mine, and you always get more out of Professor Smith's lectures than I do."

FALSE DILEMMA. People use a **false dilemma** to make you think there are only two choices in a situation—the one they favor and an unappealing alternative.

Example: The statement "Strong men watch wrestling on TV, so what's the matter with you?" is intended to make you think you aren't strong if you don't enjoy professional wrestling. Actually, one has little to do with the other; there are many ways to be strong. People often combine peer pressure, mentioned earlier, with the false dilemma tactic.

SLIPPERY SLOPE. People tend to use **slippery slope** thinking in situations involving change. Claims are made that the change being requested or considered will lead to many more changes and that the end result will be bad.

Example: "If we let you have two excused absences, then you'll want three. Before we know it, all of our absentee standards will have disappeared."

BEGGING THE QUESTION. Begging the question is also known as "circular reasoning." The same statement gets repeated with different words, but nothing is added to the meaning. This is very popular in advertisements.

Example: "Athletes need a good, healthy diet. Therefore, it's important to pay attention to what you eat if you want to perform well in sports."

STRAW PERSON. Have you ever had someone disagree with you by changing your statement? The changed statement is the "**straw person**." In the following example, notice how the brother changes the one time clean-up request to a daily one.

Example: You ask your brother to help you clean the bathroom. He says he can't clean it every day. It's too much work and a waste of time.

TESTIMONIAL. Using someone of status to convince others of the "right" thing to do is one of the most common fallacies used in advertising and political campaigns.

Example: Using someone famous to sell life insurance to elderly people is an example. They believe the life insurance is a good product because the famous person says so. (But it doesn't mean it really is!)

ACTIVITY 4

Review the examples of the thinking mistakes listed below. Match each fallacy with its example by placing the correct letter on the answer line.

Fallacy

Example

_____ 1. Two wrongs make a right

a. One look at that woman's clothes, and I knew we had nothing in common.

_____ 2. Hasty generalization

b. I'd like to have you on my committee. You're always on time, you have lots of ideas, and you are great on the phone.

_____ 3. Peer pressure

c. José, tell me how to do this assignment. I need to get a good grade. If you help, I won't tell your girlfriend I saw you out with Susannah.

_____ 4. Apple polishing

d. After Iman ruined my dress and made no effort to replace it, I had no problem borrowing her cashmere sweater without asking her permission.

_____ 5. Horse laugh

e. I don't know if we should admit anyone under 25 to this club. The next thing you know, they'll be running everything their way and older people won't come.

_____ 6. Scare tactics

f. Recycling in this town? You've got to be kidding. What a joke!

_____ 7. Slippery slope

g. Antonio says that regular planning helps him keep on top of his studies. That's too much work for me. I can't be bothered jotting things down every five minutes.

_____ 8. Begging the question

h. You don't have a laptop computer? Everyone I know owns one.

_____ 9. Straw person

i. That's just like a freshman to ask the way to the bookstore.

_____ 10. Name-calling

j. Keeping an up-to-date assignment book helps you remember your assignments. You won't forget your homework if you write your assignments all in the same place.

Point of View

The fallacies you've been learning are frequently used by people who want to persuade you to believe or do something. They have a particular point of view, and their message to you is tilted to favor that point of view. That tilt is called **bias**. Two common groups of persuaders in American society are politicians and advertisers. Politicians want you to vote for them. Advertisers want you to buy their products or support their cause.

In order to influence you, a persuader only shows you a part of the picture (that's the bias) or a point of view he or she thinks you will like. Presenting part of a picture is called **card stacking**. The persuader only shows you the cards he or she has chosen instead of the full deck.

Several of the critical-thinking guidelines can help you with bias. *Know when you need more information* (Guideline 2) is something to keep in mind when you suspect the persuader is stacking the cards. *Separate emotional and logical thinking* (Guideline 5) when you sense that the persuader is appealing to your emotions—greed, fear, pity—and is omitting a logical approach. *Know the difference between something that must be true and something that might be true* (Guideline 4) when the persuader is making statements that are not backed by any proof. *Build up your vocabulary* (Guideline 6) when the persuader uses unfamiliar words and terms.

Looking for points of view is a critical-thinking strategy. While it is easy to believe people who share your point of view, *remember to be open-minded to new ideas* (Guideline 1). Consider using other points of view and accepting people who have them.

Points of view connect with what you believe is important in life. Because what's important carries feelings, part of your critical thinking is always connected to your feelings. Your brain has emotional and logical responses. A careful thinker notices how feelings are involved in problem solving and decision making.

Most sources of information have points of view. This book, for example, is biased in favor of studying and learning. The author values learning and believes that education is important and that everyone can learn how to learn. Radio talk-show hosts usually have a bias toward a certain political party or social agenda. Fashion magazines have a bias toward the claims their advertisers make about their products' ability to enhance beauty and style. What's your point of view?

> *"You cannot teach a man anything; you can only help him find it within himself."*
>
> **—Galileo Galilei, Italian astronomer and physicist**

Politicians often tell you what they think you want to hear, not necessarily what they believe. Listen and look for any fallacies in their thinking—they will be framed in their public point of view.

©Digital Vision

1. Describe the point of view of a person who would not want to use this book.

_____

_____

_____

2. Describe the points of view of someone who pierces parts of his or her body and someone who does not.

_____

_____

_____

3. Describe the points of view of an employee who feels he or she deserves a raise and the boss who disagrees.

_____

_____

_____

4. Watch a commercial on television and describe the point of view of the company selling the product or service and the possible point of view of the consumer.

_____

_____

_____

Checkpoint

1 In what situations might you think critically?

_____

_____

2 List as many of the six guidelines for critical thinking as you can remember.

_____

_____

3 Describe at least three fallacies, and explain their role in critical thinking.

_____

_____

_____

Your Creative Mind

As you might recall from earlier in this chapter, creative thinking means "thinking about thinking in order to bring something new into existence." This new thing can be something like an idea, a plan, an event, an object, a book, a play, a research paper, or a process. It's important to know that:

- You are a natural creative thinker because creative thinking is part of being human.
- You can improve your creative thinking by learning about it.
- You don't have to be artistic to be a creative thinker.

If you don't see yourself as creative, you might see yourself in these other similar terms:

- Innovative
- Imaginative
- Inventive
- Resourceful

There are many ways to think creatively, and you will learn some of them in this section.

Why and When You Need Creative Thinking

You use creative thinking when you need new choices for solving a specific problem. A few examples include:

- When something you care about isn't working out the way you want
  Example: You haven't found enough reference material for your research paper.
- When you want to do something, but find you don't have enough time, money, or resources to do it
  Example: You want to take a vacation on a cruise ship.
- When you want to think of ways to deal with bad situations
  Example: You have a flat tire on your way to class.
- When you want to change the way you are doing something
  Example: You are president of the class and you aren't happy with the way the planning committees are doing their work.

Creative thinking and critical thinking are similar. You use them in daily life to assist in problem solving and decision making. Critical thinking leads to creative thinking, and creative thinking leads to critical thinking. For example, your critical thinking tells you that you need to study more to get better grades. Your creative thinking comes up with ideas for increasing your study time. Then your critical thinking selects the best ideas. Finally, your desire for success (or fear of failure) drives you to do the necessary work.

|Success tip

You don't have to be artistic to be creative. Many students who do not excel in art classes truly believe they are not creative—just because they aren't good in art. However, some of the most creative people in the world can't draw to save their lives! So don't make the mistake of confusing creativity with artistic talent. Creativity is a way of thinking that anyone can learn and develop.

Many common daily activities that engage you in creative thinking are listed below. Describe why they might require creative thinking. Can you list more?

Driving in heavy traffic _____

_____

Deciding what to cook or eat for dinner_____

_____

Allocating time for studying and reading _____

_____

Responding to criticism _____

_____

Playing a strategic game such as chess or checkers _____

_____

_____

Success tip

Important scholars are often awarded sabbaticals and grants for time and support while they study and complete research in preparation for writing a book or carrying out a project. Often this is the only way they can do the preparation part of their creative work.

How Do You Think Creatively?

You can do creative thinking alone or with others. In either case, your goal is to bring something new into existence, such as an idea, an event, a plan, an object, or a process. Creative thinking consists of five stages. Knowing about these stages can help you improve your creative thinking.

STAGE 1. *Insight*—Insight occurs when you realize you need to think creatively about something in your life that isn't working right. You want or need to do something about it. Insight can come from within ("My study skills need improvement") or from outside ("My psychology paper is due next week").

STAGE 2. *Preparation*—Preparation refers to naming or identifying your specific problem and gathering information. Preparation time varies based on available resources.

STAGE 3. *Incubation*—Incubation is the mulling-things-over stage. For example, you may have researched a paper or project and are now thinking about how to organize all the information and present the topic. What are its main ideas? What important points should be included? What can be omitted?

For scientists, incubation is a period of puzzling over the meaning of new evidence gathered during the preparation stage that doesn't fit previous explanations. Incubation time varies from a few minutes or days to many years in some instances. "Sleep on it" is an incubation term. Often when you wake up, you have a solution or an inspiration.

STAGE 4. *Inspiration*—Inspiration often comes in a quick flash of knowing. Suddenly you "see" a way to solve your problem. It's frequently called the "Aha!" experience. Your inspiration makes you feel good because you realize you can solve your problem.

Inspiration doesn't produce a psychology paper, nor does it complete a work project. Instead, inspiration tells you how to approach the paper (what the theme will be, what you should include, and the sequence of thought) and how to proceed on your project (calling those who can help, getting a boss's support, researching additional information). The next step, actualization, actually gets the paper written and the project completed.

STAGE 5. *Actualization*—Actualization is the heavy-duty work that makes your inspiration a reality. It can be very time-consuming and is often accomplished in long intensive hours of continuous work called massed practice. You get all your research together and work through the process. In school, writing marathons are often called *"all-nighters."* At work, getting a project realized can mean hours of overtime.

ACTIVITY 7

Below are examples of the stages in the creative process as they relate to writing a paper. Read each example and write in the name of the stage it represents.

1. _____ You're stuck. You have found a lot of information about American women in World War II, but you can't decide which aspect to focus on.

2. _____ Your sociology instructor has assigned a paper on World War II. You realize you want to write about American women in World War II because you've heard about them from your grandmother.

3. _____ You've got it! Your grandmother was a WAC (Women's Army Corps). You're going to write about women in the Army in World War II. You'll use anecdotes and other materials from your grandmother in addition to information from library and Internet research.

4. _____ You are gathering information for a paper about the role of American women in World War II.

5. _____ Now the process of writing the paper has begun. You select information from your original research, determine what additional information you need, and organize your findings into an outline. You also assemble a bibliography.

"*You see things and you ask, 'Why?' But I dream things that never were and ask, 'Why not?'*"

—**George Bernard Shaw, Irish playwright**

Divergent and Convergent Thinking

Both convergent and divergent thinking are necessary for real-life problem solving and decision making. **Divergent thinking**, mostly related to creative thinking, is thinking aimed at finding many possible answers. **Convergent thinking**, mostly related to critical thinking, looks for correct answers or guides us toward making a selection from many possible answers.

The answer to the question, "What work did American women do during World War II?" requires divergent thinking, while the answers to "What does WAC stand for?" and "Which aspect of American women shall I write about?" require convergent thinking.

In Chapter 2, you identified your learning style as leaning toward either sequential or random learning. A preference toward random learning generally means you find strength and comfort in divergent thinking (more creative), while a preference toward sequential learning generally means you find strength and comfort in convergent thinking (more critical). Since everyone possesses qualities of both types of learners, everyone is able to think both creatively and critically.

ACTIVITY 8

Write six questions that require divergent thinking and six that require convergent thinking.

Divergent Thinking Questions

1. _____

2. _____

3. _____

4. _____

5. _____

6. _____

Convergent Thinking Questions

1. _____

2. _____

3. _____

4. _____

5. _____

6. _____

The Brainstorming Process

Brainstorming, one of the oldest and most widely used divergent thinking skills, is an open-minded process of coming up with as many ideas as possible on a topic as quickly as possible. Many people enjoy brainstorming and often do it just for fun.

Brainstorming's inventor, Alex Osborn, is one of the great names in the field of creativity and creative thinking. He and J. Guilford, creator of the concepts of divergent and convergent thinking, are considered founding fathers in this field.

Many people are familiar with the term brainstorming but don't really know how to do it correctly. You can do brainstorming alone or with others. Here are four guidelines for brainstorming:

1. *Defer any kind of judgment.* This is the most important guideline. When coming up with possible ideas, don't judge them. Doing so slows things down and inhibits the production of ideas. Accept *all* ideas to let them flow.

2. *Aim for quantity, not quality.* Try to get at least 20 ideas. The first few ideas will be the most familiar. Pressure to produce more ideas forces new ways of thinking, which is what you're after.

3. *Accept wacky ideas.* These ideas often open the way to new insights and lead to practical adaptations.

4. *Piggyback.* Build on your own and others' ideas. This is not copying. If an idea comes up twice, make no comment. Just record it. The person you presented it to may be on a train of thought that will lead to new ideas.

Establishing the right environment for brainstorming is just as important as following the guidelines. Here are some tips:

- Review the four guidelines with everyone before starting.
- Set an established time and place.
- Plan to brainstorm for 15 to 30 minutes.
- Set up groups of no more than seven so everyone can talk. Permit no interruptions and no socializing.
- Work rapidly, with one participant recording the ideas. (Note: This person can also receive ideas from people *after* the session.)
- Set up the room so people can sit comfortably in a circle.
- Value the process, and thank participants for their help.
- Report later to participants on the outcomes of the brainstorming session.

■ Focus on Ethics

You have a job as a network administrator. This position gives you access to the e-mail accounts of other employees, one of whom is notorious for blaming others for his mistakes. No one, including you, likes this person. Several employees have been encouraging you to read his e-mails in the hopes that you will find something that could be used to cause the company to fire him.

You want the other employees to like you, but you don't feel it is right to read someone else's e-mails. Will you read his e-mails? Why or why not? (Hint: Is this an example of a critical-thinking fallacy?) What are some other options for handling the situation?

ACTIVITY 9

On separate pieces of paper, practice brainstorming, using the activities listed below. If possible, work with a group, following the tips described on the previous page. Otherwise, write your own brainstorming ideas.

1. Warm up with these three ideas by separately naming ten things that:

   a) are green.   b) have wheels.   c) have push buttons.

2. Now, list ten uses for:

   a) a paper clip.   b) a plastic bag.   c) an aluminum pie plate.

3. List as many ways as possible to use:

   a) a stack of wire coat hangers.   b) a water bottle.   c) a T-shirt.

ACTIVITY 10

Using the four brainstorming guidelines, practice brainstorming ideas for the following problem. Write down your brainstorming ideas on a separate piece of paper.

Tamika, Keisha, Nadia, and Jin are working together on a research paper for their history class. They have agreed to split the project into these four equal parts: Tamika is responsible for the library research; Keisha is responsible for the research on the Web; Nadia is responsible for gathering the ideas and creating the outline for writing; Jin is responsible for creating the first draft. Everyone will then review it and make changes together. The problem is Jin is too busy with his job, so he hasn't been attending their meetings. He isn't prepared to write the first draft and hasn't made the time. The other three are upset. The project is now due in five days. What can they do?

Checkpoint

1 What is creative thinking?

_____

_____

2 What are the five stages in the creative-thinking process?

_____

_____

3 What are the four guidelines for brainstorming?

_____

_____

_____

Improving Your Life with Thinking

All of the thinking skills you've learned and practiced in this chapter can improve your life by helping you solve problems, make decisions, and accomplish tasks. Which of the thinking skills did you already use, and which ones were new to you when you began this chapter? By becoming conscious of the thinking you do, you will be prepared to meet life's challenges, come up with creative options, and make smarter decisions.

The 20-Minute Problem-Solving Model

Now it's time to play with your thinking skills using the 20-Minute Problem-Solving Model. You just may get some inspirational solutions and come up with a pleasing result.

Many people who work in companies use this process with work issues. Since everyone involved with the issue participates in solving the problem, everyone buys into the options and can make smarter choices.

You can use this model by yourself, but it is easier to learn the process by working with one or two other people. One person identifies a problem and the others help solve it. If you have enough people, assign someone as the timekeeper and another as the scribe. Follow these steps to solve a problem in 20 minutes—or less!

STEP 1. Describe the problem to the other people for five minutes. Say everything you can about the problem. Remember the 5Ws and H: Who? What? When? Where? Why? and How? What led to the problem? What are the consequences? What are your feelings? What are the feelings of others? If you run out of things to say, start repeating things you said before. Just keep talking for five minutes. The scribe writes the information on a flip chart, white board, or other writable wall surface so others can see it. If it's just you and another person, a piece of paper will suffice. Everyone else's job is to just listen.

STEP 2. Allow the others to ask you questions for five minutes; then answer their questions. Many times, the questions that are asked give you insights into possible solutions or make you think of things you haven't yet considered. Your answers will then help the questioners come up with even smarter questions. Some suggested questions: What do you really want? Is this a new problem? If the problem occurred before, how did you and others react? How has it worked out?

STEP 3. In the group, brainstorm ideas for solutions for five minutes. The scribe records the ideas for you.

STEP 4. Select the ideas that seem best to you. If you want, you can ask the others for suggestions, but you don't have to. If you don't ask them, they are not allowed to volunteer their ideas. As a group, develop a plan of action.

People are always amazed at what they can accomplish with this 20-minute creative problem-solving process. The most difficult part is

> By becoming conscious of your thinking, you are better prepared to meet life's challenges, come up with creative options, and make smarter decisions.

the first five minutes. It's often hard for the problem owner to talk for five minutes and for the listeners to stay quiet! But it keeps everyone focused, and no time is wasted on socializing.

Seven Thinking Skills that Improve Your Life

The following seven ideas summarize the focus of this chapter. Use them and apply the information to improve the quality of your thinking and your life. As you read them, stop for a moment and think about what they personally mean to you. If you need a refresher about any of these ideas, review them in the chapter before going on to the next idea.

1. Be metacognitive in difficult situations.
2. Use the guidelines for critical thinking.
3. Avoid mistakes in thinking.
4. Find reliable resources on the Internet.
5. Honor the stages of the creative process.
6. Brainstorm.
7. Give yourself time to think.

■ Focus on Technology

If you don't already know about your school library's digital content, find out about what they have and how you can access it—both on and off campus. Most schools allow students automatic access to digital content when using a computer on campus, but require a password for access from an off-campus site. Make sure to find out early what you need to do to access library content from off campus; it could save you a lot of time.

Checkpoint

1 Describe the 20-minute Creative Problem-Solving Model.

_____

_____

2 What are the seven thinking skills that improve your life?

_____

_____

_____

_____

3 What have you learned about your thinking?

_____

_____

_____

CHAPTER SUMMARY

1. Critical and creative thinking are important because they help you with the decision-making and problem-solving tasks of your life.

2. Critical- and creative-thinking skills are important because they force you to slow down when you need to solve a difficult problem or make a difficult decision. When you slow down, your brain is more at ease and can do its best work for you.

3. You need to use critical and creative thinking for success in school and at home. In addition, you need these skills in your career because today's workplace requires people who are effective thinkers and effective problem solvers.

4. When you are mindful of your thinking (metacognitive), you can improve the quality of your thinking.

5. Critical thinking asks you to stop and think, especially when you need to make important decisions. Not necessarily believing everything you read and hear, using the guidelines for critical thinking, and being aware of fallacies and points of view can help you think clearly and effectively.

6. Creative thinking goes through five stages: insight, preparation, incubation, inspiration, and actualization.

7. Divergent thinking asks you to find choices for solving problems, while convergent thinking asks you to make a decision from among the choices.

8. Brainstorming is an open-minded process of coming up with many ideas on a topic as quickly as possible. The four brainstorming guidelines lead you through the process.

9. You can use the 20-minute Creative Problem-Solving Model to help you solve problems.

CHAPTER ASSESSMENT

Terms Review

Match the following terms to their definitions. Match the terms within each category.

Critical and Creative Thinking

_____ creative thinking

_____ divergent thinking

_____ brainstorming

_____ critical thinking

_____ beliefs

_____ convergent thinking

_____ bias

_____ card stacking

_____ metacognition

a. An open-minded process to come up with as many ideas as possible on a topic as quickly as possible.

b. Thinking aimed at finding many possible answers.

c. Thinking about thinking in order to bring something new into existence, such as an idea, an event, or an object.

d. Interpretations, evaluations, conclusions, and predictions you consider to be true.

e. Thinking about thinking in order to decide what to believe and how to behave.

f. Looks for correct answers or guides us toward selecting from many possible answers.

g. Thinking about thinking.

h. A tilted point of view.

i. Presenting a partial picture to influence your point of view.

Mistakes in Critical Thinking

_____ fallacies

_____ peer pressure

_____ horse laugh

_____ two wrongs make a right

_____ hasty generalization

_____ name-calling

_____ scare tactics

_____ appeals to pity

_____ apple polishing

_____ false dilemma

_____ slippery slope

_____ begging the question

_____ straw person

_____ testimonial

j. Asking someone to feel sorry for you is an example of this thinking.

k. Trying to convince others by complimenting them.

l. Also known as "circular reasoning," the same statement gets repeated with different words, but nothing is added to the meaning.

m. Makes you think there are only two choices in a situation—the one you favor and the other is unfavorable.

n. Mistakes in thinking.

o. Making a decision too quickly.

p. Making fun of someone or something when you disagree.

q. Substitutes a personal insult for a direct response.

r. Causes you to go along with the crowd to be accepted or popular.

s. Make you emotional and fearful without using logic.

t. Claims are made that the change will lead to many more changes and that the end result will be bad.

u. Someone disagrees with you by changing your statement.

v. Using someone of status to convince others of the "right" thing to do.

w. Returning an insult with an insult.

Review

Based on the information you learned in this chapter, answer the following questions using your own words and thoughts.

1. In your own words, what is critical thinking?

_____

_____

_____

_____

_____

2. What are beliefs, and how are they important to critical thinking?

_____

_____

_____

_____

3. What is the relationship between metacognition and critical thinking?

_____

_____

_____

4. Why is point of view important?

_____

_____

_____

_____

5. Describe a situation in which you did some critical thinking.

_____

_____

_____

_____

6. Describe a situation in which you did some creative thinking.

_____

_____

_____

_____

7. Give several examples of mistakes in thinking you have seen or heard.

_____

_____

_____

_____

8. When might you use brainstorming? List at least three situations.

_____

_____

_____

_____

9. Explain how creative and critical thinking can improve your life.

_____

_____

_____

_____

10. What have you learned from this chapter?

_____

_____

_____

_____

CASE STUDIES

for Creative and Critical Thinking

 ACADEMIC CASE—Connecting to Collaborative Assignments

Hector, Gabriela, and Ty are classmates in an architectural drawing course. As a group, they have been given the task of designing a high-end home with a required square footage and a minimum number of bedrooms and bathrooms, all under a strict budget. This project presents several challenges and decision points that have to be considered thoroughly. The variables considered in this assignment include cost of materials, labor, and market conditions in the building area. The solution is to be presented in two weeks.

1. Why are critical- and creative-thinking strategies important to the success of this project?

   _____

   _____

2. What are the five stages of critical thinking, and how will they be applied to this project?

   _____

   _____

   _____

   _____

   _____

3. Could Erik, Jessica, and Ty benefit from the 20-Minute Creative Problem-Solving Model? Explain.

   _____

   _____

   _____

 WORKPLACE CASE—Connecting to Budgeting and Planning

Jaleel and Ana are coworkers in an office supply store. Their manager has asked them to come up with a budget for how much they think the store will need to spend to expand its handheld computer products section. This requires moving other products to other parts of the store and also purchasing the display cases and products to showcase in the new area.

1. What type of thinking do Jaleel and Ana need to do first? Where might they go to get information?

   _____

   _____

   _____

2. What are some considerations that Jaleel and Ana need to think about when making their product choices for display in the new area?

   _____

   _____

   _____

Reading and Researching Online

Chapter Goals

After studying and working with the information in this chapter, you should be able to:

- Understand the Internet and the World Wide Web.
- Learn how to search for information on the Web.
- Read on screen more efficiently and effectively.
- Understand how to be efficient when conducting research online.
- Evaluate and validate web sites and understand the challenges and risks of gathering information from the Web.
- Define *wikis*, *blogs*, *RSS feeds*, and *podcasts*.

Terms

- blog
- browser
- download
- hyperlink
- Internet
- ISP
- metasearch engine
- podcast
- post
- protocols
- RSS feed
- search engine
- subject directory
- URL
- wiki
- World Wide Web

Quinesha and Kai are both taking an English Composition class. In the first week of classes, they are assigned a research paper that is due at the end of the semester.

At the end of the first week of classes, Quinesha goes to the college library and activates her library access. She also fills out a form that allows her to access all of the online library resources when she is working off campus. This means that Quinesha can research the online library database content—including full-text journal articles, newspaper articles, and other research materials—when she is off campus, using a computer with Internet access. Quinesha has a very busy work and family schedule and does not have time to stay on campus after classes, so having off-campus access to research materials allows her to do research from home throughout the semester. She writes her first draft two weeks before the paper is due and asks the instructor for feedback before writing the final draft.

Kai, on the other hand, does not set up his off-campus access. He relies on the Google search engine for all of his research. Even though he has the whole semester to do the paper, he has not planned his time effectively, so he writes his entire paper the night before it is due. **Who do you think did a better job on the paper? What are the benefits of having off-campus access to your library's online content?**

Knowing how to use the Internet is a key intellectual skill for now and the future. It is a powerful tool for conducting research and gathering information on any topic imaginable. The information you used to look for in a library is now available to you anywhere there is a computer with an Internet connection—on your desktop at work or at home; via your laptop in public libraries, restaurants, hotels, and airports; and even on your cell phone.

You can use the Internet to read Homer's *Odyssey* in Greek, trade stocks, find a job anywhere in the world, compare car prices, get the latest news and weather around the world, take a course in German, view a podcast of your niece's second grade science project, or locate and contact a long-lost relative, but you have to know *how*. With so much information available in this rapidly changing world, finding the information we need, *when* we need it, and knowing *how* to use it are some of the most important skills we can develop for our personal and professional lives.

Major technological changes tend to make people nervous, and the Internet is no exception. It has been blamed for all types of problems from eyestrain to high blood pressure to anti-social behavior. Given our real-world need for information, however, it seems clear that the Internet offers far more benefits than risks. We can use the Internet:

- as an interactive and comprehensive source of information combining text, images, and sound in a way no other medium can.

- as a means for developing problem-solving skills by requiring us to think logically and critically about content and search methods.

- as a communication tool second to none.

- to find and use information that once was obscure and difficult to locate.

- to foster computer literacy and technology skills.

- 24 hours a day, 7 days a week.

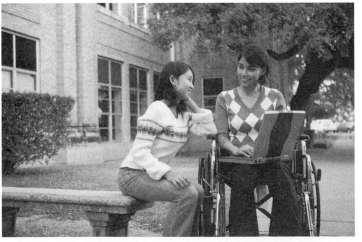

©Getty Images/PhotoDisc

Access to the Internet doesn't have to be just at home or at work anymore. You can bring it with you and connect almost anywhere.

> With so much information available in this rapidly changing world, finding the information we need, *when* we need it, and knowing *how* to use it are some of the most important skills we can develop for our personal and professional lives.

Self-Check ✔

The following self-evaluation will give you an idea of how familiar, or unfamiliar, you are with some of the topics and terms discussed in this chapter. After reading each statement, circle the letter Y, S, or N to indicate the answer that is most appropriate for you. Answer honestly. Rate yourself at the end; then complete the information on your Self-Check Progress Chart.

Y = yes; frequently   S = sometimes   N = no; never

1. I understand what the World Wide Web is and what kind of information can be located on it.   Y   S   N

2. I know the difference between a search engine and a directory.   Y   S   N

3. I know how to use the basic search features of the Web.   Y   S   N

4. I know how to refine searches to locate exact information.   Y   S   N

5. I am able to read online text quickly and comfortably, without printing materials unnecessarily.   Y   S   N

6. I understand the copyright restrictions of downloading text and images from web sites.   Y   S   N

7. I know how to evaluate the validity of web sources.   Y   S   N

8. I know how to create reports using web sources.   Y   S   N

9. I know about wikis, blogs, feeds, and pod casts.   Y   S   N

10. I feel confident that I know how to find information on the Web.   Y   S   N

Rate Yourself:

Number of Ys _____ × 100 = _____

Number of Ss _____ × 50 = _____

Number of Ns _____ × 0 = _____   **Total** _____

"*The Web today is a medium for communication between people, using computers as a largely invisible part of the infrastructure.*"

—Dr. Tim Berners-Lee, Developer of the World Wide Web

The Internet and the World Wide Web

In the early 1970s, the U.S. Department of Defense commissioned a study on computer technology. The goal of the study was to develop a secure computer-to-computer communication system that would allow information to be sent along a complex network of electronic paths. If one path or computer system was destroyed or unavailable, the information could still continue to travel along alternate paths to reach its intended destination. This early Internet was used for 20 years almost exclusively for research purposes by military, university, and scientific communities.

By the mid-1990s, the business community had embraced the widespread use of personal desktop computers for workplace tasks, including communication via e-mail. It was at this time that the Internet started to become the sophisticated information tool we know it to be.

The **Internet** today is an expansive worldwide electronic network that is made up of thousands of smaller networks, including governmental, commercial, and educational networks. The Internet uses standard **protocols**, or languages, to allow large computer networks to interconnect and communicate with one another.

Scientist Dr. Tim Berners-Lee made the navigation easier by letting users move from document to document by clicking on highlighted words or phrases, known as **hyperlinks**. From this, attractive graphics and mouse technology have been developed to provide a way to access information, known as the **World Wide Web**. The World Wide Web, or the Web, is a huge system of linked resources on the Internet that contain hyperlinks to other resources or web sites. The Web is a way of accessing information over the Internet and utilizes browsers such as Netscape® and Internet Explorer® to locate web pages.

Getting Connected

You may already be well versed in how to connect to the Internet, but you may not fully understand how it all works. To access information on the Web, you use two main things:

1. An Internet Service Provider (**ISP**), a company through which you access the Internet on a paid subscription basis and

2. A web **browser**, a software program that is used to view web pages (such as Netscape® and Internet Explorer®).

Using an e-mail program and a file transfer protocol (ftp) program, you are able to send messages and transfer files over the Internet. With a site's unique address, you can access a single page of information, or web site. That address, known as the **URL**, or Uniform Resource Locator, can be keyed into an address or location box in your browser software. For instance, if you wanted to visit the web site for the publisher of this textbook, you would need to key the URL *http://www.thomsonedu.com* into the address box. To visit the web site of the author of this book, you would key the URL, *http://www.TheCorporateEducator.com*.

Search Engines and Subject Directories

Once you are connected to the Internet, you have access to billions of pages of information, so it is impossible to know *all* the URLs. This is where search engines and subject directories are needed.

A **search engine** is a computer program that recognizes the entered keywords to locate specific web pages. It checks the complete text of web pages for the keyword or words. When you use a search engine, you are not searching the entire Internet; rather you are searching the pages in that database. Also, many search engines have pay-per-click advertising programs that allow companies to pay to list their product or service on the first few pages of results. Companies pay every time someone clicks on their ads.

There are thousands of search engines. Some popular ones include:

- Alta Vista
- Google
- MSN
- Yahoo!
- Ask.com
- AOL Search

Some search engines like Dogpile, Vivisimo, Metacrawler, and KartOO are known as **metasearch engines**. They query multiple search engines at once and give you the results. Some metasearch engines separate the results, showing you the results of each search engine separately; others compile the results and present one list of links based on the frequency of occurrence, among other criteria. Either way, it can save you a lot of time jumping from search engine to search engine looking for the same information. Think of it as one-stop shopping.

A **subject directory** is a database of hand-chosen sites that have been reviewed and selected by people rather than by a computer program. The sites are organized into subject categories such as Arts, Science, Entertainment, Reference, News, Government, and Business. Many directories also contain a search engine. Some popular subject directories include:

- Yahoo!
- Google
- Infomine
- AlltheWeb
- Lycos
- About

Think about what you have done or can do on the Web. Maybe you have bought gifts, searched for a job, obtained driving directions, found a book you wanted, or learned about a new place. Maybe you frequently **download** songs by transferring audio files from a web site to a digital music player. Knowing how and where to search allows you to take advantage of the amazing resources available at your fingertips.

Success tip

If you really want to explore search engines, check out *Search Engine Colossus*, an international online directory of search engines that includes search services from hundreds of countries, including those in languages other than English.

Select your favorite search engine for resolving the following issue. You can use a metasearch engine to compare results from several search engines.

Textbooks are essential, but they can be a significant investment for students. For some students, the convenience of buying high-quality, unmarked textbooks in the campus bookstore can be cost prohibitive, so they look for cheaper alternatives.

1. Where can you find used textbooks online? What search terms did you use? What are the risks of buying and using used textbooks?

   _____

   _____

2. Where can you find the best price for new textbooks online? What did you do to modify your search?

   _____

   _____

3. How can you sell your used textbooks online? What sites pay the most for used textbooks?

   _____

   _____

4. Find information about eTextbooks. What are some of the benefits of eTextbooks?

   _____

   _____

Checkpoint

1 Where and when did the Internet begin?

_____

2 What is the difference between a search engine, a metasearch engine, and a directory?

_____

_____

3 How is the Web helpful to you?

_____

_____

_____

Search Techniques

The biggest problem with the Web as an information resource is its sheer size. If, for example, you perform a search on Google using "ice" as the query term, you will get about 422 million links. No matter what kind of information you need, not all of these 422 million links are going to be useful to you. For effective searching, you need a way to define your search clearly.

Search engines have different methods for ranking web sites. If you conduct searches on four different engines: Google, Alta Vista, Excite, and HotBot with the same search query terms, it is unlikely that the first ten links will be the same. People and their businesses are lucky to be listed on the first page of results because people click-through to them the most, hence, more potential buyers or visitors. Many users think the best links are on the first page, which is not true. Those on the first page have just found a way—usually through paid advertising or excessive linking with other web sites—to be listed at the top. (Note that even if the service gives you just a tiny box for typing your query, you can still type in the whole query, and the space will scroll to accommodate the words.)

Designing the Search

Knowing about search design can help you find what you are looking for quickly. For example, suppose you need to find pictures of the famous Leonardo da Vinci painting, the *Mona Lisa*. If you go to the Google home page and type in *Mona Lisa*, you will get millions of hits with the top link being image results. If you click the "image" button for your search, you will get a list of thumbnail photos of over 50,000 images of the *Mona Lisa*. Some of the images will be of the actual painting, but the results will also include parodies and high school art projects. If you click the "news" button, your top links are likely to contain book and movie references, and even restaurant names.

Designing a quick and effective search, therefore, involves knowing what you are looking for as well as knowing how to use the various search options available on your particular search engine. For example, some services, without telling you, take the terms in your search query and connect them with OR, which broadens the search instead of narrowing it. It might return any page with *Mona* OR *Lisa*. That would be a lot of useless links for your purpose. You can use "+" symbols between your terms, such as +Mona+Lisa. This would return pages that include "Mona" AND "Lisa" somewhere on the site, but not necessarily next to each other.

Clarifying the Search

Typically, you can clarify your search even further by typing your search words within quotation marks. The quotation marks mean the results will include pages with the exact phrase only. In the above *Mona Lisa* example it might be best to use the Advanced Search function. Using the advanced search function on Google (located

"*The ultimate search engine would basically understand everything in the world, and it would always give you the right thing. And we're a long, long ways from that.***"**

—Larry Page, Google co-founder

Success tip

The expression "surfing the net," a term coined by Jean Armour Polly in 1992, perfectly captures the idea of skimming across an ocean of information. Once you catch an "e-wave," you can ride it as far as you want. Be aware, though, that sometimes your ride on the Internet will take you to places you didn't intend to go. So, when surfing the Web, stay focused on what YOU are searching for so you avoid getting wiped out or submerged in distracting and unrelated information.

"Almost overnight, the Internet has gone from a technical wonder to a business must."

—Bill Schrader,
CEO of PSINet

next to the search bar) and other search engines will allow you to specify the exact search you want without using +, −, or quotation marks. Instead, menu options will help you define your search by using what is essentially a *Boolean* (or logical) search and can include such choices as:

Search term	Represents
with **all** of the words	Plus (+) symbol or AND
with the **exact phrase**	Using "quotation marks" or AND
with **at least one** of the words	OR
without the words	Minus (−) symbol or NOT

The advanced search page might also allow you to choose:

    Language (other than English)
    File format (word document, PDF, PowerPoint, etc.)
    Date (a site was last updated)
    Domain (results ONLY from a certain domain)
    Usage rights

An even better option for finding authentic images of the Mona Lisa might be a search engine's advanced image search. If you type in *Mona Lisa* on the Google homepage, click on "Images," and then click on "Advanced Image Search," not only will you have the main search options but you also might have menu options for:

    Image size
    File types (JPEG, GIF, etc.)
    Coloration (black and white, grayscale)

If you find all this business about file formats and exact phrases and quotes baffling, you might want to try your luck on the search service Ask.com. This service lets you ask an ordinary English-language question. Often, it finds just what you are looking for, but sometimes it produces strange results based on the vagueness of your question. It's worth a look, though, because it can also find pages that a straight logical search might miss.

ACTIVITY 2

To get you started using search techniques, see if you can find the answers to these questions using a search engine. Write down what search term(s) you used next to your answer.

1. What is the population of New York City?_____

2. What team won the 1949 World Series (baseball)?_____

3. What is the average winter temperature of Juneau, Alaska?_____

4. Who discovered penicillin?_____

5. Who is Steven Jobs?_____

Using the grid below as your guide, create searches that will return useful results quickly. Think carefully about the design of your search and make sure to try some of the suggestions in the "Designing the Search" section. Use a separate sheet of paper if you want to compare the results of different search engines.

Sites that provide...	Search Terms and Number of Hits	Best Two Listings on the First Page (How can you tell?)	How effective was your search? How could you improve it?
Free, easy-to-search databases of phone numbers and e-mail addresses of U.S. citizens			
Free, easy-to-search databases of phone numbers and e-mail addresses of international citizens			
Information about finding jobs advertised in your area			
Job interview and resume tips			
Information about saving for retirement			
Where to find maps and driving directions			
Free, full-text access to literature that is no longer under copyright protection			
Free clip-art and graphics			

ACTIVITY 3 (continued)

Where you can access academic journal articles, newspaper articles, and other research-related information			
Where to find weather forecasts of major cities			
The ten most affluent people in the country			
Top salaries of football players (or all sports figures)			
What research databases are available through your school's library			

Checkpoint

1 Why is it helpful to understand search design?

_____

_____

2 What does designing a search involve?

_____

_____

3 What are some options for clarifying your search?

_____

_____

Reading on Screen

Once you have found the information you are looking for, how are you going to read it? You may tend to print it out because you feel more comfortable reading a paper document than reading on screen. However, learning to read more on screen will not only save trees, but will also save you time.

If you learn to read more on screen, you won't have to make decisions about what to do with the paper because you will store the material in files in your computer. You can easily search the document for keywords and skip to the material you are most interested in. If you have a portable device to which you can download your material, you can carry it with you without the weight of paper.

Chapter 9, Revving Up Your Reading, will come in handy, as you can use many of the same faster reading strategies on screen. Reading key words and/or phrases helps move your eyes across the lines more easily. Though you can't easily use hand or card pacers, you can use the screen pacers on pages 334–336. In addition, there are ways to make the text easier to read on-screen.

Physical Appearance of Text

The following suggestions offer general guidelines for improving the appearance of the text to make your on-screen reading easier and more comfortable. Follow these guidelines when you design electronic documents. If after using these suggestions you still find the screen difficult to read, consider asking your doctor about computer glasses. These offer a special prescription that accommodates the unique distance from your eyes to the screen.

DENSITY OF TEXT. In this paragraph you will likely notice that the use of white space and the overall density of text can play an important role in the legibility of computer-displayed text. Having letters and/or lines of text too close together can make reading text from a screen more difficult. Having more space between letters, words, and lines on a screen of text can make the text easier to read. When reading on-screen, change your font format to normal character spacing.

MARGIN ALIGNMENT. How the margins are lined up can also affect how we read. *Fully justified* text (both left and right margins in line, like this paragraph) tends to look better, but it can be more difficult to read because it can distort the amount of white space in a line. *Left justification* (where the left margin of text is all in line) with a ragged right margin (like the Focus on Technology on page 335) may be easier to read. To read faster on-screen, create double or 1.5 spacing between lines.

ALL CAPS VS. MIXED CASE. When reading continuous text, you will read easier and faster if the text is in upper and lower case letters instead of ALL CAPITALS. It is more efficient because mixing

> Learning to read more on screen will not only save trees but will also save you time.

"With so much information now online, it is exceptionally easy to simply dive in and drown."

—Alfred Glossbrenner, Author

cases creates a more distinctive word shape. When it comes to writing e-mails or other electronic communication documents, using all capital letters is just bad manners. Readers often feel as though the author is yelling.

TYPES OF FONTS. Font refers to the size and shape of letters of text. One of the most frequently encountered fonts is the one you are reading now, called Times New Roman. It is also the font used regularly for newspapers and other printed materials. Fonts primarily consist of *serif* or *sans serif* characters. This means that the letters have little lines as a part of the letters such as in the "serif" example here, or they do not (**sans serif**), such as in the Arial font. The most readable fonts on screen are typically sans serif because they present a more clear and robust letter. Microsoft has created ClearType fonts, which are more readable on a screen and appear to be helping screen reading comfort.

SIZE OF FONTS. The font size that is most readable depends on several factors—your vision, your angle to the screen, and the font itself. In general, anything under 10 points is too small to read at a comfortable distance from the screen. Anything over 18 points may be too large and give the reader a sense that they are being shouted at. On average, 12-point font is the most widely used and preferred.

USE OF COLOR. Colors can be used quite effectively to aid the reading process; however, what is pleasing to one reader may not be pleasing to another. Typically, dark text on a light background, such as black or navy on white or gray tends to be more readable. Any background with a texture makes any text placed on it less readable. You can experiment with this in your word processing program to find the most readable option for you.

Pacers

Remember the hand, pen, or white card pacers from Chapter 9? They act as guides for your eyes to follow while you are reading. When reading from a computer screen, you may find that using a pacer can be challenging. You can't comfortably hold your hand, pen, or white card up to the screen to follow the text. Instead, try the following techniques that rely on computer technology for pacing.

HIGHLIGHTING PACER. The following suggestion works best with documents in "Read Only" mode. It is particularly useful for helping you keep your place when you are tired. To use this pacer:

1. Direct your cursor to the far left or right of the target text.
2. When the cursor turns into an arrow, click and hold your left mouse button, and slowly drag your mouse down as you read.

The text will continue to be highlighted as long as you hold the button.

3. Move your mouse down as you finish reading a line of text, keeping the mouse button pressed in to keep highlighting the text.

Because you are highlighting all of the text in your document, there is a danger of accidentally deleting it all. Use this strategy carefully—and know how to use your UNDO command!

SCROLLING PACER. Another pacing method is made possible with Microsoft's Intellimouse or similar devices with scroll-wheel capabilities. There is a scrolling feature available on this mouse that is controlled by a roller ball. You simply need to roll the ball to advance the text. If you want to set the text to scroll automatically, simply click the ball (you will see up and down directional arrows) and move your mouse down or up to control the speed and direction of the scrolling text.

CURSOR AS A PACER. Using your cursor as a pacer is like running your fingers under a line of text as you are reading. It is important to hold your mouse gently and keep your arm supported in some way, such as with a wrist support, and then try the following:

1. With your mouse, guide your cursor directly under the line of text that you are reading.

2. "Underline" by moving the cursor only under the center two thirds of the line of text—especially when the line is long.

3. Read the text, using your peripheral vision to read the parts to the left and right of the text you are "underlining" with the cursor.

4. When you move your cursor to the next line, you can move your eyes faster because the cursor acts as a guide.

5. When you have finished reading the screen of text, use your "page down" button on your keyboard. This will advance you to the next full screen of text.

LINE-BY-LINE PACERS. The *line-by-line* pacing method is similar to the paper pacing method of placing a white card above or under the line of text you are reading. Line-by-line on your computer screen provides a "straight edge" that will serve as a guide for your eyes. There are two ways you can use this method: line-by-line "top" and line-by-line "bottom."

The *line-by-line "top"* pacing method is like placing a white card *above* a line of text in a book you are reading. The card helps block out text that you have *already* read, while the *line-by-line "bottom"* pacing method is like placing a white card *below* a line of text. The card helps block out *upcoming* text while helping keep your eyes focused on the text you *are* reading. On the computer screen, you can

> ■ **Focus on** Technology
>
> This whole chapter focuses on technology, but here's another idea to help you read better: If you are interrupted when you are reading online or in a word processing document, double-click on the word where you stopped reading before you turn away from the screen. The word will be highlighted, and you will have saved your place until you are able to return to your screen reading.

use the top or bottom of your electronic page as your straight edge or guide for your eyes.

For the line-by-line methods, you want to:

1. Position the text you are reading at either the "top" or "bottom" of the screen, depending on the method you choose.
2. Advance through the text by either:
   a. Clicking with your mouse in the scroll bar.
   b. Using the down arrow on your keyboard.

It takes some practice because the scrolling may not advance exactly one line at a time. Using this "straight edge" as a guide helps you keep your place in your reading.

Using pacers effectively when reading on screen can take some practice, but will significantly increase your reading speed as well as your concentration and comprehension. It can feel a little awkward at first, but the advantages are well worth the effort.

ACTIVITY 4

Go to the web site of a newspaper or magazine you know. Locate an article of interest to you that is at least one full screen in length. If there is a printer-friendly option, click on it.

Using each of the on-screen pacers, read a section of the article. Decide which one(s) might work best for you. Describe below your experience with using on-screen pacers.

_____

_____

_____

_____

Checkpoint

1 What do you think makes reading on screen different from reading from paper?

_____

2 What can you do to make your on-screen reading easier?

_____

_____

3 Describe two on-screen pacers.

_____

_____

Researching Online

When you seek any information online, including the hours of a local restaurant, the address of a business, or directions to a new location, you are conducting online research. You might even turn to the Web for these answers on a daily basis. However, research of an academic or professional nature, such as for essays, term papers, projects, or reports can prove more challenging.

When doing this kind of research, you could spend hours or even days trying to find *all* the information about your topic on the Web. Finding it all, however, should not be the goal; rather, your goal should be to find the *right* information in a timely fashion and to know what to do with it. This section offers strategies for finding the information you need quickly, and organizing the information once you have found it.

Avoiding Online Distractions

One of the biggest challenges when conducting research online comes from the probability of being sidetracked. It is very easy to get lost in the vast amount of information available on the Web. Following link after link can take you farther and farther away from your topic and makes it easy to lose sight of your original research goal. It can also become quite addicting. Here are some strategies you can use to help keep you focused on your research tasks.

DEFINE YOUR PURPOSE AND TIME FRAME. If defining your purpose when reading a *printed* document is valuable, it is even *more* important to define *why* you are reading an *online* document. It helps to answer the question "Why am I here?" to keep you focused specifically on what *you* need while researching online.

After you identify your purpose, it is a good idea to establish a time frame for your project. Larger research projects require more time and will likely involve several sessions. Therefore, not only do you want to determine how long the entire research project will take, but also you want to decide how much time you will spend during each individual session. People tend to work better when working to a deadline.

HAVE A PLAN. Having a clear purpose in mind will help you create and follow a plan or strategy for your online reading. When you research online and come across a link you are tempted to follow, ask yourself the following two questions in order to make your decision whether "to follow or not to follow" the link:

> **Question #1:** *How sure am I that the link WILL bring me closer to my purpose?* If I am pretty sure, I will stay with the link. If you are reading an article that is definitely meeting your purpose, but there is also a link that you are pretty sure will be useful, it's a good idea to finish one article before jumping off to

"*Literacy in the 21st Century includes more than the ability to read and write; it also includes the ability to search, locate, and use digital information in a meaningful way.***"**

—Pam Mullan, Author, *Read More, Faster ...On-Screen*

another—even if you only pre-view the initial article (see Chapter 8 for pre-viewing).

Question #2: *How sure am I that the current link will NOT bring me closer to my purpose?* If I am sure the link doesn't contain what I need, I will consider following another link.

A second strategy might be to look for a "print" version of your target document. If you click on "print version," but do not print it, you will have the same information, but the document will not contain the distracting advertisements associated with online documentation.

ORGANIZE. Whether you are accessing online newspaper-style articles, academic or professional journal articles, or longer documents, creating folders to effectively store the information you want to keep is incredibly useful. Creating folders on a computer is just as purposeful as using folders in a filing cabinet. If you stored all of your paper documents in a filing cabinet without putting them in folders, it could be quite difficult to locate information you need quickly and easily. If you store all of your computer documents in your "My Documents" folder, it can be equally difficult.

Therefore, it is important to learn how to create folders, and then to think carefully about what you will name them. It can be as simple as having folders named "Home," "School," and "Work." You can then create subfolders within each of those broad categories.

For example, let's say you are taking a World Religions course. You notice on the syllabus that you will have three different writing assignments and a presentation, all requiring online research. It will help you organize your semester if you create a file with the semester name "Fall, 2008." Inside that folder, create a subfolder entitled "World Religion." This is where you would store course information. With several research assignments in the course, you should create another level of subfolders for essays and presentations. For example, you would create a subfolder entitled "Essays" and include your Compare and Contrast essay, Dietary Laws essay, and Roles of Women essay. Spending a little time creating and labeling folders means you will be able to store and locate the information easily.

Your folder hierarchy would look something like this:

FALL 2008 (main file)
World Religion (folder)

- *Essays* (subfolder)
  - Compare and Contrast (inside Essays subfolder)
  - Dietary Laws (inside Essays subfolder)
  - Roles of Women (inside Essays subfolder)
- *Presentations* (subfolder)

When you find a document you think you might use for your essay or presentation, save the entire document (or relevant section), in the appropriate folder, rather than just copying sentences or paragraphs. It is easy to inadvertently plagiarize something when you take sentences and even paragraphs out of context.

TAKE NOTES. Taking notes on material while reading from a computer screen can be tricky. The biggest question, as with taking notes from printed material, is "What do I keep?" It is not enough to save documents to your folders; you must also read and synthesize the information. To fully understand a topic, it is useful to interact with the information by taking notes.

If you like using the Cornell Method of note taking, you can set up your word processing document with a three-inch margin line indented from the left to give you a recall column and body. The Table and Columns functions in a word processor are also useful for setting up a recall column and body area.

If you want to avoid printing, you can take notes electronically. One strategy is to keep your original document intact and save a second copy where you can highlight selected passages, write your comments, and generally respond to the material. This way you can keep track of what information you want to use and how you want to use it, while also avoiding inadvertent plagiarism. You can also use the "Track Changes" functions to take notes and interact with the text, while still maintaining the original text.

Pre-Viewing Online Documents

Having a strategy for reading your online documents and the tools to speed up your reading are two of the best ways to stay motivated and focused when reading longer documents from a screen. Therefore, before reading any article, make sure to evaluate the source of the information given and, if reliable, pre-view the material by following these steps:

Success tip

Besides using the Cornell Method, consider the following tips for taking notes while working online or on screen:

- Use abbreviations (B4, w/, w/o, mgmt).
- Add color to highlight important points.
- Use symbols in place of words (<, >, =, @, #, Σ).
- Use bullet points.
- Change to different styles and sizes of text.
- Use underscoring.
- Use numbers (1., 2., 3.).
- Use letters (A., B., C.).
- Make boxes or circles.
- Create diagrams. (Try using the table function of your word processing program to set up a grid for information of a compare/contrast nature.)

When doing research online, be sure to gather all of the relevant source information from any source you review.

"*I agree completely with my son James when he says 'The Internet is like electricity. The latter lights up everything, while the former lights up knowledge.*'"

—Kerry Packer, Australian media and business tycoon

1. Look at any preliminary information about the source and the author, the title, date, and any introductory material.
2. Read the first paragraph, which is typically the introduction.
3. Read the first sentences of each subsequent paragraph.
4. Read the last paragraph, which is typically the conclusion.
5. Avoid advertising and unrelated links.
6. Note anything that is highlighted, bold, italicized, or in some way made to stand out from the rest of the text—but only if it has to do with the immediate topic (not links or advertisements).

These steps will give you the main points of the article and help you decide if you need to read the whole article.

Saving Search Results

Once you pre-view a document and decide it is worth keeping, there are a variety of ways to save it for future reference for your research papers and projects. The material you save should be used for note-taking purposes; it should not be re-pasted into your final paper and used word-for-word. If you do quote another source, make sure to document and cite the source completely.

TEXT BY SELECTION. The simplest way to extract text from a web page is to select it by clicking and dragging and then selecting "Copy" from the Edit menu. Then, in your word processing document, select "Paste" from the Edit menu to insert the text. (See the Success Tip on this page!)

The only problem with this method is that the text you selected might have some unwanted formatting. It might contain hard returns making each line a half-page wide. To use the material, you will have to edit it one line at a time, which can be very time-consuming.

TEXT BY PAGE. Another tactic for adding web information to your document is to save the whole web page as a separate file. All common browsers allow this choice under the File menu. You can typically "Save As Web Page" or "Save As Text."

When you open the web page in your word processor, you will see a fairly close representation of the page as it appeared in the browser. But, now, when you select and copy text, and paste that text into a document, the lines are set to the page width automatically. If you are going to be clipping quotes from a dozen different sources, this simplifies things greatly.

USING IMAGES. For some projects you may want to include a chart or graphic with your text. When you have located the image you want to use, select and save it. Then, use the word processor's "Insert" command to place the image in your document. Note that this is acceptable for nonprofit or educational purposes, but if you were preparing a document for publication, the copyright rules would apply: get permission for *everything* from the original source.

Success tip

Before you copy text or images from the Internet, be aware of the "fair use" guidelines for copyrighted work. This fair use provision of copyright law permits copyrighted material to be used within limits—AND with proper source citation—for nonprofit educational purposes only. The copyright laws are applied very differently to commercial products, however. Never use a copyrighted image without receiving written permission and following the guidelines set by the copyright holder.

CITING SOURCES. Though the content of web sites change rapidly, you should *always* cite the web page as a source when you use *any* web material in your own reports. Knowing what documentation style (MLA, APA, etc.) your teacher requires will help you organize your research and document it properly. Different styles require different information and formats, but the following is typical:

- Author, date, and title of the work
- Name of the web site (if it has one) or title of journal, book, and/or article (if needed)
- Date *you* retrieved the information from the Web
- URL of the web site where you found the information

APA Style Example: Smith, J. (2006). *Online research*. Retrieved May 15, 2007, from http://www.thomsonedu.com.

MLA Style Example: Smith, Jane. "Online Research." *Thomson*. 1 Oct. 2006. 15 May 2007. <http://www.thomsonedu.com>.

Much material on the Web is taken from print sources (*Business Week Online* is based, naturally enough, on *Business Week*), so reference the print original, as well. For more detailed examples of online sources (and proper formatting), search online for "citing web sources" and the name of the style format you prefer.

Be careful to gather all of the relevant source information from every source you look at (even if you don't use it later) because it will help you avoid re-researching. Include this information with each document you save, and also copy it into a separate document that can become your "Works Cited" page.

Success tip

During online research, it is easy to find some text you want to keep, and copy and paste it into a word processing document. (Always remember to document where it came from!) This practice is fine when you just need to refer to the text later to form your thoughts for your paper, BUT it is NOT appropriate to cut and paste the text into your paper. In fact, it is illegal and is also considered *plagiarism*.

Checkpoint

1 Why is it important to define your purpose and time frame for research?

_____

_____

2 What are the steps for pre-viewing an online document?

_____

_____

3 Why is it important to document your online sources when doing research?

_____

_____

Evaluating Online Sources

If there is something you want to know about, chances are *someone* has posted a web page providing the information you seek. The good thing about this is you will find some sort of answer; the hard part is figuring out what to believe.

Despite the amazing benefits of researching online, there are risks online users can easily avoid by making sure to evaluate the validity of web sites. Unlike printed documents, such as textbooks and most magazines, which are professionally written and checked for accuracy, information on the Internet may be posted by anyone. No one is the designated gatekeeper to make sure online information is correct. You may not know whether a seventh grader or a national expert has written the site you visit. Consequently, you must learn to evaluate any source you find.

The Web may house hundreds of thousands of valuable research and sales sites, but it is also home to a good deal of inaccurate and potentially dangerous information. Hate groups recruit new members online. Con artists have created fake charity sites to swindle people out of their money. Chat room rumors have spread inaccurate information about a company, resulting in a significant drop in its stock value. Basically, it is your job to figure out who is telling the truth, and who is not.

Whether you are reading short articles or conducting detailed research online, it is important to know whether the information is credible. Consider using the following acronym in order to evaluate an online source. The acronym spells out D – SOURCE to help you remember to evaluate the source before accepting the accuracy of information gathered online.

D = Dependable

S = Says Who?

O = Objective

U = Understandable

R = Recent

C = Complete

E = Evidence

D = Dependable

As with any source of information, and particularly with web resources, you must ask yourself about the *dependability* of the source. Unlike paper publications that are more likely to have editors

---

NETBookmark

It is very easy for anyone researching on the Web to copy and paste text from an online article or other resource. To use this information appropriately—without plagiarism or copyright penalties—it MUST be referenced accurately and in correct form according to the writing style your instructor prefers you to use. Some common styles are *APA Style, MLA Style, Turabian Style,* and *Chicago Manual of Style.* Search online for examples of these styles using terms such as "Electronic References" and "Citing Web Sources."

For links to some sites that provide additional information about appropriate referencing of web sources, go to:

http://sskills.swlearning.com

and fact checkers, anyone can publish pretty much anything on the Web. There are no web standards for accuracy or validity of information. That is why it is essential to be a critical and questioning reader when reading any online documentation. Ask yourself these important questions to test the dependability of an electronic source:

Is the information located on a site created by a known entity? For example, is an article from a printed national, international, or local newspaper or magazine?

Is there a non-web equivalent of the material that would provide a way of verifying its legitimacy?

Does the source contain spelling, typographical, or grammatical errors? If so, this indicates the information is not being properly edited and brings the quality of the information into question, though one or two typos here and there can be just simple and unintentional human errors. Too many of these types of errors can also result in incorrect information.

S = Says Who?

Ask *"Says who?"* of all online documents. *On whose authority is the information being presented?* Sometimes you will need to search for the information about the author. It may be contained within the article, at the beginning or the end of the article, or you may have to refer to another resource in order to gather more information to verify the author's credentials. Look for the following information about the authors:

> *Who wrote it?*
>
> *What are their credentials?*
>
> *What else have they written on the topic?*
>
> *What are the authors' affiliations (university department, organization, corporate title, etc.)?*
>
> *Is contact information provided?*

If you cannot find any information about the authors or cannot find sufficient credibility in the authors' backgrounds, consider disqualifying them as a source.

O = Objective

Ask *"How objective is this?"* Practically everything that you read will have some sort of bias or particular personal slant. This is not necessarily "bad," but in order to interpret any information accurately, you need to be aware of the level of bias. To determine the level of bias, you must think critically about the information the author or site provider provides as well as the information NOT provided. In any product web site, you will find factual information, but it certainly won't be objective. It will tell you the product is the best and explain how it will benefit you—whether it really will or not. It's good to be a little skeptical. If the article provides opinion or an editorial, be aware that it is designed to show a particular point of view, but should not be accepted as fact.

U = Understandable

Ask *"Is this information easy to understand?"* You want to make sure the information is presented clearly and you have enough background knowledge to make sense of it, even if the reading is challenging. If you find that the material uses very difficult vocabulary or a lot of jargon, you might want to find material targeted to a different audience.

R = Recent

Ask *"How old is this information?"* Most articles will provide a date, but a date could have different meanings. It may mean:

- when the article was first published
- when it was first placed on the Web
- when the most recent revision was done

Timeliness will have more importance for some topics than others. For example, marketing trends, technology, science, and business are topic areas that age quickly. Information from social sciences and the humanities tend to stay relevant longer. Old information can still be perfectly relevant—your goal is to ask the questions and make the decisions about the relevance of the information.

Dates aren't always provided, in which case you may need to search a bit more, find a different source for the information, or contact the author for the date. If there are references, looking for the most recent publication date in the references can help you narrow the time frame. When dealing with financial information, such as with a company's annual report, the date is extremely important. For online newspaper articles, check for the date and for the edition in which the article was published. Any statistical data presented in charts or graphs should give clear information about when the data was gathered.

C = Complete

Ask *"Is that all there is?"* Some online information will be a "work in progress" or will be somewhat incomplete. Look for:

- How thoroughly the author deals with the topic
- A sense of completeness
- The depth of the material
- New information (or is it a summary of other research?)
- An "under construction" icon that indicates a work in progress
- A printed equivalent

■ Focus on Ethics

You've been assigned to write a research paper on a topic that you don't know much about. In doing research on the Web, you come across several articles that cover the topic quite well. You realize that the authors have managed to convey their ideas more clearly and concisely than you believe you could do. You know that your friends all download material from the Internet. So, you decide to cut and paste sentences and paragraphs from different articles and use your own words to tie the pieces together. Is there anything wrong with doing this? How about if you use quotation marks for the sections you copy—does that make it OK to use the material?

E = Evidence

Ask *"Where's the beef?"* Some online materials can appear quite flashy but contain very little valuable substance. Look for whether or not:

- The author referred to other sources to substantiate claims.
- The sources used are noteworthy.
- The material contains a bibliography.
- The material contains footnotes.
- The references within the text are reliable.
- The hyperlinks are to credible sources.

Looking questioningly and critically at any written source is a valuable part of research reading; however, it becomes even more important for online sources because they are often not scrutinized by editors and publishers to the same degree that print sources are.

ACTIVITY 5

Using the **"D-SOURCE"** acronym, evaluate *at least* two web sites on the *same* subject. Explain your answers with details and examples from the site.

Web Site 1 _____ Web Site 2 _____

D = Dependable What aspects of this site make it appear dependable? In what ways is it lacking dependability? Is information professionally and accurately written, with very few grammar and spelling errors?

_____

_____

S = Says Who? Does the site appear to have the authority to present the information? What evidence on the site (or elsewhere) gives the author authority?

_____

_____

O = Objective What appears to be the bias of this source? How can you tell? Are there multiple perspectives for the topic? What are they?

_____

_____

U = Understandable Is the material readable? What might make you choose a different source?

ACTIVITY 5 (continued)

_____

_____

R = Recent When was the site last updated? Is the information appropriately current?

_____

_____

C = Complete Does the site appear complete? Are there topics that should be covered but aren't? Are there a variety of external links that supplement the information given in the site? Are these links well maintained, and are they helpful and insightful?

_____

_____

E = Evidence Does the author of the site substantiate claims with reputable sources? What sources—experts, scientific studies, statistics, and so on—does the site use? Can any of this be verified?

_____

_____

Checkpoint

1 Why is it essential to evaluate the web sites you visit?

_____

_____

_____

_____

2 From the D-SOURCE acronym, which concepts do you think are most important?

_____

_____

3 What did you learn from doing Activity 5?

_____

_____

Wikis, Blogs, Feeds, and Podcasts

The rate at which technological advancements are being made is surpassed only by the rate at which the terminology and jargon to describe that technology is created. In other words, new technology requires a lot of new words; we need words to describe the technology and words to describe how that technology is used. Google was originally a noun describing a search engine; it has now become a verb to describe how we use the search engine, for example, "I'll just Google it." We began using "text messaging" or "texting" with our friends. As technology became faster, the terminology came to be known as "*instant* messaging" or simply "IM," as in "I will IM you." In the following section, you will find a very brief introduction to some of the more recent technologies being used on the Internet and the jargon used to describe their usage.

Wikis

As Wikipedia (the free encyclopedia web site that anyone can edit) tells us, a **wiki** (Hawaiian for quick or fast) is a type of web site that allows users to easily add and edit content. The Wikipedia site, started in 2001, contains millions of pages of information on topics ranging from geography to health, all of which have been created by its visitors.

There are thousands of wiki sites available, most allowing unrestricted or limited-restriction editing. The drawbacks are obvious; misleading, incorrect, and even dangerous content can be easily added by anyone, and thus evaluating online sources becomes more relevant than ever. Supporters of the media form suggest that eventually all inaccurate information will be corrected.

While wikis appear to be around to stay, using Wikipedia as a resource for academic writing is discouraged, but it can be an interesting starting point. And, even though Wikipedia is considered a free resource, if you use the information found there, you must document it as a source.

Blogs

A **blog**, shortened from "web log" or "weblog," is just that: a log or journal-type series of entries displayed on the Web. Blogs are web sites located on blog-specific hosting services, or, with special blog software, they can be supported by regular web-hosting services. Typically, blog entries are posted on a regular basis, such as every Wednesday, and appear on the site in reverse chronological order (the most recent first).

When you create a piece for a blog, which might contain text, hypertext, images, links, or audio or video files, it is called a **post**, a *blog post* or an *entry;* when you add or edit a post, you are a *blogger;* and when you are creating it you are *blogging*. The whole process can become mind-*bloggling*, but it has become a fast-growing

> **"***When I started eBay, it was a hobby, an experiment to see if people could use the Internet to be empowered through access to an efficient market. I actually wasn't thinking about it in terms of a social impact. It was really about helping people connect around a sphere of interest so they could do business.***"**
>
> **—Pierre Omidyar, Technologist and founder of eBay**

form of communication on the Web and is used more and more frequently in the classroom as a means for journaling and peer-group communicating.

RSS Feeds

An **RSS feed**–an acronym for "Rich Site Summary" or for "Really Simple Syndication"–does just what the name implies: it sends news feeds or brief summaries (with links to full versions) of a site's new content to users. Instead of surfing several favorite news sites daily, the information you want comes to you at intervals defined by you. And, because the feeds are brief (usually headlines, summaries, and links), they can easily be sent to and downloaded on any compatible device, including a cell phone, a handheld computer, or a pager.

But the biggest advantage of RSS feeds may not be what the technology provides, but in what it doesn't require of a user; subscribers do not need to provide an e-mail address as required when subscribing to an online newsletter. Reducing unwanted e-mail is a clear benefit to most users.

Podcasts

If you visit news sites like MSNBC, you have probably seen the little orange buttons labeled "POD." This indicates that an audio or video file, such as a radio interview or a video of a weather storm, is being circulated on the Internet utilizing RSS technology. Like the text example above, **podcasts** allow subscribers to view or listen to new audio or video content that is automatically delivered where and when specified by the subscriber.

Success tip

Because technology allows us to create and pass along all kinds of information quickly, it sometimes feels like we are literally being dumped upon. One way to receive useful information about topics you have interest in is to subscribe to either RSS feeds or search engine alerts. Go to your favorite search engine and look for "RSS feeds" and "alerts" for the web sites that interest you.

ACTIVITY 6

1. Look up a topic or person on Wikipedia. Compare the Wikipedia entry to information from two other print or online sources. How accurate did you find the wiki entry? How do you know?

   _____

   _____

   _____

   _____

2. Find and visit three blog sites. What do they have in common? How are they different?

   _____

   _____

   _____

ACTIVITY 6 (continued)

_____

3. Find three news sites that offer RSS feeds, podcasts, or web alerts/updates. Name the sites and explain the type of content that is available through these services.

_____

_____

_____

_____

_____

4. Locate some examples of hoaxes circulated via e-mail or web postings. (Some examples are shampoo, anti-perspirant, and artificial sweetener warnings. Are the warnings valid? How do you know? How difficult is it to find information on the Internet that contradicts the warnings?)

_____

_____

_____

_____

Checkpoint

1 What is a wiki? Why do you need to be skeptical about using one?

_____

_____

2 What are blogs? If you have ever posted to one, what do you like/dislike about them?

_____

_____

3 What is an RSS Feed? How might you use it?

_____

_____

CHAPTER SUMMARY

1. The Internet is an expansive worldwide electronic network. The World Wide Web is a huge system of linked resources on the Internet that contain hyperlinks to web sites. You connect to the Internet through an ISP or web browser.

2. Search engines help you locate specific information based on keywords you input. A metasearch engine queries multiple search engines to come up with its results. A subject directory is a database of web sites reviewed and hand picked by people instead of computers.

3. To search effectively and efficiently on the Web, you need to define and clarify your search to locate the most useful web sites for your interests.

4. The faster reading strategies learned in Chapter 9 can help you to read faster on screen. In addition, learning to change the physical appearance of the text for improved readability and using pacers specifically for on-screen reading will help you read better and faster on screen.

5. When doing research online, it helps to define your search to avoid distractions, to organize your findings so you can access them later, and to take notes for reference. Pre-viewing online articles will help you spend your time on the most useful information. Learning how to effectively save your search results will save you time when writing your paper or doing a project.

6. Because anyone can post a web site on the Internet, it is important to evaluate each one using the D-SOURCE acronym: Dependable, Says Who?, Objective, Understandable, Recent, Complete, Evidence.

7. There are new terms being created all the time because of technological advances. Wikis, blogs, RSS feeds, and podcasts are some recent examples.

CHAPTER ASSESSMENT

Terms Review

Fill in the blanks with the appropriate key terms on the left.

blog

browser

download

hyperlink

Internet

ISP

metasearch engine

podcast

post

protocols

RSS feed

search engine

subject directory

URL

wiki

World Wide Web

1. A(n) _____ is a journal-type entry on the Web. When you create a(n) _____ for it, you are adding an entry.

2. What you key into an address box in your browser software is called a(n) _____.

3. To connect to the Internet, you need a(n) _____ and web _____, such as Netscape or Internet Explorer.

4. A(n) _____ is a computer program that recognizes the entered keywords to locate specific web pages. A(n) _____ queries multiple search engines at once and gives you the results.

5. The _____ is an expansive worldwide electronic network that is made up of thousands of smaller networks, including governmental, commercial, and educational networks. It uses standard _____, or languages, to allow large computer networks to interconnect and communicate with one another.

6. A(n) _____ allows Internet users to move from document to document by clicking on a highlighted word or phrase.

7. The _____ is a huge system of linked resources on the Internet that contain web sites.

8. Many students _____ music and other audio files to their computers and iPods.

9. A(n) _____ is an online encyclopedia that anyone can make changes to.

10. A(n) _____ provides you with information you want from news, sports, and entertainment web sites.

11. A(n) _____ allows subscribers to view or listen to new content posted to the Web that is automatically delivered where and when specified by the subscriber.

12. A(n) _____ is a search engine created by people, not computers.

Review

Based on the information you learned in this chapter, answer the following questions using your own words and thoughts.

1. In your opinion, why should you learn how to use the Web?

_____

_____

_____

_____

2. What is the basic difference between a search engine and a subject directory? Why should this matter?

_____

_____

_____

_____

_____

3. What type(s) of information might a chef look for on the Web?

_____

_____

_____

_____

_____

4. What type(s) of information might a doctor look for on the Web?

_____

_____

_____

_____

5. What are some things to consider and use when reading on screen?

_____

_____

_____

6. How can you be responsible and truthful in your web research for reports or projects?

_____

_____

_____

_____

7. How can you take notes from research you read online?

_____

_____

_____

_____

8. Why is it a good idea to evaluate web sites?

_____

_____

_____

_____

9. What other ways might the Web help you personally, academically, or professionally?

_____

_____

_____

_____

10. What have you learned from this chapter?

_____

_____

_____

_____

CASE STUDIES

for Creative and Critical Thinking

ACADEMIC CASE—Connecting to Consumer Economics

For her Consumer Economics course, Dora needed to research buying a car. She was given a hypothetical household's family needs and budget and was assigned to come up with a car to purchase that would fit within the household budget and needs. She was also to suggest the best financing option based on the family budget. Dora had never done this type of research before, and she was concerned about finding a dependable car that would be affordable. A friend suggested she do some research on the Web, checking out types of cars, their cost, and finance options before visiting dealerships for more information. Though she felt overwhelmed by the task, she started searching by name brands of cars she had heard about. She found several cars she liked, but the prices were higher than she expected.

1. Where on the Web would you recommend Dora search for car models and features?

   _____

   _____

   _____

2. From what you found, what financing options do think Dora should consider?

   _____

   _____

WORKPLACE CASE—Connecting to Vacation Planning

Vacation time was coming up in a month and Deion wanted to go somewhere new and different. Sitting on his kitchen table were some brochures about the Caribbean. As he thumbed through them, he realized they had great photos but not much detailed information about the various locations shown. Some travel packages included airfare; others did not state whether it was included or not. Also, there were different price levels for each travel package but no clear explanations about what exactly was covered. Deion realized he needed more detailed information in order to have the vacation he wanted.

1. Name five or six sources of travel information Deion could research before making his vacation plans.

   _____

   _____

   _____

2. How will Deion know that the travel web sites you suggest are reputable? (Hint: Remember D-SOURCE!)

   _____

   _____

   _____

   _____

13 Writing in the Real World

Terms

- body (of a paper)
- brainstorming
- conclusion
- editing
- introduction
- issue
- KISS
- mapping
- plagiarism
- position
- rough draft
- thesis
- thesis statement
- writing process
- 5Ws and H

Chapter Goals

After studying and working with the information in this chapter, you should be able to:

- Describe the importance of writing and identify the types of real-world materials people write.
- Describe the writing process for essays, papers, and reports, using the 5Ws and H to create an organized outline.
- Write effective e-mails.

Marcus has worked for ten years in a company that manufactures athletic equipment. Recently, the company was sold, and Marcus's new boss asked him to prepare a report to be presented at the next meeting of the company's board of directors in two weeks. The report needs to describe the duties of each person in Marcus's department and the reasons to keep the department intact rather than consolidating duties or laying off the employees.

Because he has been the department supervisor for four years, Marcus feels confident that he can describe the department's functions and its benefits in a way that convinces the board to keep all the employees. His only problem about writing the report is knowing how to do it. Though Marcus writes e-mails and brief reports all the time for his job, he doesn't have a lot of experience writing large reports—especially one as important as this.

Between his fear of writing such an important report, and not knowing where to start, he puts off doing it until the night before the board meeting. He pulls an all-nighter and is happy to have finished it.

Unfortunately, Marcus's report didn't persuade the board to keep his department. They were now all without a job.

What could Marcus have done to increase his chances of keeping his job?

Learning how to communicate effectively on paper IS an important part of the world you live and function in, of the jobs or careers you choose, and of your interactions with other people. Learning to communicate effectively in this real world means that you are not only able to be heard, but also able to be understood.

Perhaps up until now, you have not done a lot of writing. You may not have confidence in your writing ability or maybe you just do not know how to get started. This chapter provides information that will help you become a better writer for both academic tasks, like essays and papers, and real-world ones, like writing e-mails and work reports.

Do you feel intimidated or overwhelmed with the idea of having to write a college entrance essay, a detailed report for your boss at work, or an e-mail asking for a refund? This is a feeling shared by many others; but if you reflect on it, it is the thinking that is intimidating. Actually doing the writing task is empowering.

Getting started is probably the most challenging part of any writing task. This chapter will provide strategies for getting started and a writing process to follow that will make getting started easier.

This one chapter does not contain all you need to know about writing. Many books are devoted to the topic, and courses are designed to help you develop your writing fully. But the chapter will certainly give you some important tools for writing short essays, longer papers, reports, and e-mails. In the bibliography located at the back of this book, you will find other resources for improving your writing. In addition, you can find a lot of information on the Web as well as in your school or local library.

> Learning how to communicate effectively on paper IS an important part of the world you live and function in, the jobs or careers you choose, and the people with whom you interact.

Writing is something that you will do every day of your life. What writing activities are required in your world?

The following self-evaluation will give you an idea of how familiar, or unfamiliar, you are with some of the topics and terms discussed in this chapter. After reading each statement, circle the letter Y, S, or N to indicate the answer that is most appropriate for you. Answer honestly, and rate yourself at the end; then complete the information on your Self-Check Progress Chart.

Y = yes; frequently   S = sometimes   N = no; never

1. I know that writing is an important part of school, work, and personal life.   Y   S   N

2. I understand that good writing follows a process.   Y   S   N

3. I schedule time ahead for my longer writing projects.   Y   S   N

4. I know how to use the Internet for research.   Y   S   N

5. I know how to decide on a topic.   Y   S   N

6. I know how to write a good thesis statement.   Y   S   N

7. I can create an organized outline for my writing by using the mapping process.   Y   S   N

8. I can describe the three parts of most written communication.   Y   S   N

9. I know how to effectively present the final draft of my writing.   Y   S   N

10. I know how to write effective e-mail.   Y   S   N

Rate Yourself:

Number of Ys _____ × 100 = _____

Number of Ss _____ × 50 = _____

Number of Ns _____ × 0 = _____   **Total** _____

Writing for School, Work, and Personal Life

"*A pen is the tongue of the mind.*"

—**Miguel Cervantes, Author of *Don Quixote***

Communicating your thoughts effectively on paper or on a computer screen is very important to your success in school, at work, and in your personal life. When you write essays and papers for an academic assignment, write e-mails, or submit information on a blog, you are learning how to effectively talk on paper. These writing activities are the training ground for writing tasks in the workplace and for personal use. Developing this ability enables you to communicate your thoughts and ideas more easily, both on paper and orally. Those who write well have greater job success rates, including the possibility of increased income, than poor writers. See Figure 13-1 for just some of the possible writing tasks you will perform in your work and personal life.

Since writing is such an important part of life, it is not only essential that you learn how to write, but that you learn how to write well. In this chapter, you will learn many valuable writing strategies for writing essays, papers, reports, and e-mails.

FIGURE 13-1

Types of Writing

In the working world, writing is essential for doing a job. Here is a partial listing of the types of workplace writing:

✓advertisements	✓job descriptions	✓policies/procedures
✓annual reports	✓lab reports	✓press releases
✓cover letters	✓letters of complaint	✓product reviews
✓customer service logs	✓letters of inquiry	✓progress reports
✓diaries/journals	✓letters of recommendation	✓reports
✓directions	✓magazine articles	✓research reports
✓e-mail	✓meeting minutes	✓resumes
✓financial statements	✓memos	✓service reports
✓instruction manuals	✓newsletters	✓speeches
✓job applications	✓phone messages	✓technical reports

Writing is often needed in your personal life. A partial list of personal writing follows:

✓bank loan solicitation	✓e-mail	✓mortgage documents
✓billing questions	✓instant messaging	✓notes to your child's teacher
✓complaint letters	✓job hunting cover letters	✓thank you notes

Think about people you may know who do the jobs listed in the left column. In the right column, list some of the writing activities these people do. You may use the lists in Figure 13-1 for reference.

Profession	Writing Activities
Nurse	Medical chart updates, patient reports
Business professional	E-mails, letters, reports, meeting minutes, presentations
Electrician	
Office assistant	
Auto mechanic	
Teacher	
Job seeker	
Parent	
Computer technician	
Police officer	
Lawyer	
Pharmacist	
Doctor	
News reporter	
Salesperson	
Other	

Checkpoint

1 What is the primary purpose of writing?

_____

_____

2 At what writing activities are you already skilled?

_____

_____

3 What writing activities would you like to do better?

_____

_____

Writing Essays, Papers, and Reports

Writing a good short essay or longer research paper or report involves following a **writing process**, or series of related steps. Doctors follow a process when they operate on a patient, and mechanics follow a process when they repair a car. Travel agents follow a process when arranging vacations for their clients, and event planners follow a process when setting up special events and parties. A process is not just one action, but a series of steps or procedures that enables these individuals to do their jobs. By understanding that writing is also a process with a series of essential steps, you will be better equipped to handle any writing task.

The process of writing takes time. Though some learners try to skip steps or cram them all into one night, it is NOT easily possible to do a good job without spending quality time in each part of the process. If you can plan some time away from your writing in between drafts, you will return to your writing with a fresh perspective to make it even better. Understanding this will encourage you to plan your time in small timeframes over a period of time instead of one very large block of time all at once.

There are eight detailed steps in the writing process. Lengthy research papers and reports require all eight steps, while shorter essays, papers, or letters require only a few steps. Once you learn the steps, you will be able to use them for all kinds of school writing as well as workplace writing, such as reports, policy manuals, performance reviews, and so on.

Before completing any of the activities in the eight steps of the writing process, you will benefit from pre-viewing each step *before* reading them in detail. (See Chapter 8 for more information on pre-viewing.) This will help you understand how each step flows into the next and leads to a quality piece of writing. The eight steps are shown in Figure 13-2.

> *"By writing much, one learns to write well."*
>
> **—Robert Southey, English poet**

FIGURE 13-2

Eight Steps of the Writing Process

Step 1: Creating Time to Write

Step 2: Deciding on a Topic

Step 3: Doing Research

Step 4: Creating a Thesis Statement

Step 5: Creating an Outline

Step 6: Writing the Rough Draft

Step 7: Revising the Rough Draft

Step 8: Creating the Final Draft

Step 1 Creating Time to Write

Creating time for writing is the first step in the writing process. While any process, especially writing, takes time, the length of time depends on the task. If you are asked to write an essay in class, you have to complete it in the time allowed, but if you are asked to write a one- or two-page report for your boss, you may have several days to prepare it. If you are asked to write a five- to ten-page research paper, you might need to schedule six to eight weeks for the task.

Working on a research paper for six to eight weeks does not mean that you write for six to eight weeks; it means you work on the paper a little at a time over a six- to eight-week period. Trying to write a paper without making adequate time for it can cause unnecessary stress. Planning for this in advance ensures that you still have enough time for both the paper and your other responsibilities, especially homework, work, and family obligations.

Effective writing occurs step by step over a period of time, not all at once. Even for essay tests and letters, you need time to create an outline, do the actual writing, and revise and edit. Research papers and long reports require more development, such as a thesis statement, research, a rough draft, and a final draft.

The following guide will help you schedule the writing of a lengthy research paper. Since this is only a guide, you can adjust the time frame according to your task. It is always wise to plan a little extra time, just in case unexpected events get in the way. (See Chapter 4, Learning Time Management, for more information on scheduling time for papers.)

Decide on a topic (may include some research)	1 week
Research time	2 weeks
Creating a thesis statement and outline	1 week
Writing your first draft	2 weeks
Revision	1 week
Final draft	1 week

Breaking your writing project into tasks and writing them on your calendar will help you schedule the time you need for the project and will help ensure that you have the time available to do it. If you are going to Cousin Sally's wedding next weekend, that is not the best time to plan to do any part of your writing. But, if you don't work on Friday night until 6:00 p.m., you can schedule some writing time in the afternoon after classes.

Follow the writing process for longer papers and reports shown in Figure 13-3. Notice that some of the more time-consuming tasks are repeated several times instead of being shown as a one-time activity. The breaks you schedule between writing activities allow you to think, so that you bring a fresh perspective to your process when you do the next activity.

FIGURE 13-3

The Writing Process for Longer Papers and Reports

Step 2   Deciding on a Topic

After you schedule your time, you must decide on a *topic* (if you don't already have one), such as global warming, gardening, pollution, music, or some other subject. Some topics can be covered in only a few paragraphs, while others require many pages.

If you are assigned the topic, obviously, you must write about that topic. If you have a choice, you may become overwhelmed by the options. The best topic is one that interests you, so that the time and effort you put into it will be more satisfying.

You can use the Internet, encyclopedia indexes, book tables of contents, and periodical indexes to look for possible topics. If you are writing for a class, it is always a good idea to get your instructor's approval of a topic *before* spending time on research.

The following is a list of considerations for choosing a topic:

- Does it *interest* you? (If so, then use it; if not, don't.)

- Is there *enough* information to write the appropriate amount of material?

- Is the subject *very new*? (If so, you may have trouble finding enough published research material.)

- Is there *too much information* available? Can you narrow the topic and still report on it effectively?

For the purpose of practicing this writing process, choose a topic. You can use one that has been assigned by an instructor or one you

"Have something to say, and say it as clearly as you can. That is the only secret."

—Matthew Arnold, English poet

just want to know more about. Review the previous recommendations before you make your final decision, then write your topic below.

My topic is: _____

Step 3   Doing Research

Doing research means locating usable information about the topic or learning about something you want to know. Refer to Chapters 7, 8, and 11 in this book to help you take effective notes, read thoroughly, skim and scan, and critically evaluate your sources. If you have not already read Chapter 12, Reading and Researching Online, do so now. It provides you with information about how to use the Internet for research. Your local or school library is also a great source for information. Ask the librarian to help you locate the best materials on your topic.

Compile your research neatly on individual sheets of loose-leaf paper or 3 × 5″ index cards, so you can easily re-order your notes and refer to them during your writing. Remember to *always* document all of your sources—both electronic and paper. Avoid plagiarism by *paraphrasing* your research material (saying it in your own words) as you write your notes. **Plagiarism** is using another person's words or ideas without giving proper credit. In many schools and courses, it is cause for a failing grade. Any material that comes word-for-word from your sources must be in quotes in your paper and documented as such.

Step 4   Creating a Thesis Statement

A *topic* is what you study, while a **thesis** is the main point of your writing or the conclusion you draw from what you learn. Creating a thesis statement narrows your topic down so you can focus on one issue surrounding the topic.

A **thesis statement** is a summary of your thesis. *Every essay and research paper must have a thesis statement because it tells the reader what you are going to prove. Though business reports generally do not require thesis statements, a statement may add to the effectiveness of your writing.*

Creating a thesis statement requires a two-step process. First, you must identify the issues that surround your subject. Then you must state your position on the **issue**—the unresolved question. Your **position** is your point of view on an issue.

Topic	Issue
Global warming	■ whether global warming is a threat to people and the environment
	■ whether global warming should be stopped
	■ whether global warming is caused by industrial pollution
	■ whether global warming should be discussed as an international issue

Success tip

1. Understand the definition of *plagiarize:* to steal and pass off the ideas or words of another as one's own; to use another's production without crediting the source.
2. Don't do it! ALWAYS document your sources.

Every essay and research paper must have a thesis statement because it tells the reader what you are going to prove.

Albert Einstein	■ whether Albert's childhood affected his view of the world
	■ whether religion played a role in Albert's upbringing
	■ whether Albert was influenced by Germany at the turn of the century
Gardening	■ whether planting too early in the year affects plant height
	■ whether gardening is therapeutic
	■ whether gardens can help the quality of the earth's air

ACTIVITY 2

Write two issue statements for each topic listed below. Remember to include the topic you listed earlier in this chapter.

Topic	Possible Issues
Pollution	_____
	_____
Music	_____
	_____
The Internet	_____
	_____
School uniforms	_____
	_____
Your topic	_____
	_____
	_____
	_____

Once you have identified several issues, you can begin to identify your position. By identifying your position, you create a statement that you will argue in your writing. Your *position*, or point of view on an issue, can also be considered a *thesis statement*.

Possible Topic	Thesis Statements
Global warming	Global warming is a threat to people and the environment.
Albert Einstein	Albert's childhood affected his views on the world.
Gardening	Planting a garden can improve the earth's air quality.

Note that a thesis statement does not give any explanation or reason *why* you think the way you do. You will provide your explanation in your writing.

ACTIVITY 3

Try to come up with thesis statements based on the issues you listed in Activity 2. Remember to include the topic you listed earlier in this chapter. Though you will come up with a thesis statement before you write, you may change it as you develop additional ideas. This is all right as long as your paper or essay proves your position.

Topic   **Thesis Statements**

Pollution   _____

Music   _____

The Internet   _____

School uniforms   _____

Your topic   _____

"*My most important piece of advice to all you would-be writers: When you write, try to leave out all the parts readers skip.*"

—**Elmore Leonard, Popular American novelist and screenwriter**

Step 5   Creating an Outline

Now it is time to organize your thoughts and information. By the time you get to this step, you will have already written some material. If you researched a long report, you should have plenty of information. If you are writing a short essay or letter, your writing process may start at this step.

Organized writing helps the reader understand what is being said and receives a higher grade than unorganized writing. If your writing is unorganized or confusing, readers will have a difficult time understanding your thoughts. If, on the other hand, your writing is organized and flows smoothly from one idea to the next, you will have succeeded in communicating your thoughts effectively. Organizing your thoughts is accomplished easily by using a pre-writing process called mapping.

Mapping is a pre-writing process that helps you organize your thoughts and information on paper and results in an informal outline. The informal outline is a writer's road map—the same one you follow for pre-viewing. (See Chapter 8 for more information on pre-viewing.)

It is similar but not the same as the note-taking method of Mind Mapping explained in Chapter 6.

Success tip

There are software programs on the market that guide you through this mapping and brainstorming process for writing. To find out more, go to your favorite search engine and conduct a search for "brainstorming software" to find the most up-to-date versions available.

1. ***Set-Up.*** Mapping begins when you draw a circle or cloud shape in the middle of a blank piece of paper and write the thesis statement inside it. You proceed by drawing about ten lines coming out from the circle. The picture will look similar to a spider or a cloud with rays of sun coming out of it, as in the example in Figure 13-4.

2. ***Brainstorm with 5Ws and H.*** Once you have written your thesis statement, it is time to brainstorm questions. **Brainstorming**, which is described in more detail in Chapter 3, is a random, unorganized thought-generating process that results in new ideas. For writing, brainstorming is guided by using the same 5Ws and H introduced in Chapter 1. To refresh your memory, the **5Ws and H** are: Who?, What?, When?, Where?, Why?, and How?. Write each of the 5Ws and H across the top left of your sheet of paper with the thesis statement in the middle.

   Using the global warming example from Figure 13-4, the questions in Figure 13-5 can be generated from the 5Ws and H and written on the paper. There are no rules to follow for which of the 5Ws and H you use or how often. Though your paper or essay may not answer all of these questions, you are beginning to think actively and creatively about the paper's contents and organization *before* you write.

3. ***Organize the Outline.*** You now have many good questions about the thesis statement, but they are not organized. To organize them, first review all of the questions. Then decide which question your reader should learn about first. On a separate blank piece of summary paper, write your first choice question in the recall column. Place a check mark next to this question on your brainstorm sheet, indicating that the question has been used. Then continue evaluating your questions to decide which question would make the most sense for the reader to read about next. *Leave at least five blank spaces between each question.* If you see a question that does not relate well to the thesis, cross it off your brainstorm sheet. If you think a question should be reworded or added, then make the appropriate changes.

   By the time you finish this process, you will have a much clearer idea of what you can cover in your paper or essay. It should help you feel more confident that you already know some of the content and are now aware of what you need to find. Since getting started is the hardest part of any writing project, this brainstorming and organizing process makes it possible to get started without being overly concerned about correctness. The best parts about this are that it is easy to do and it doesn't take a lot of time!

FIGURE 13-4

Beginning the Mapping Process

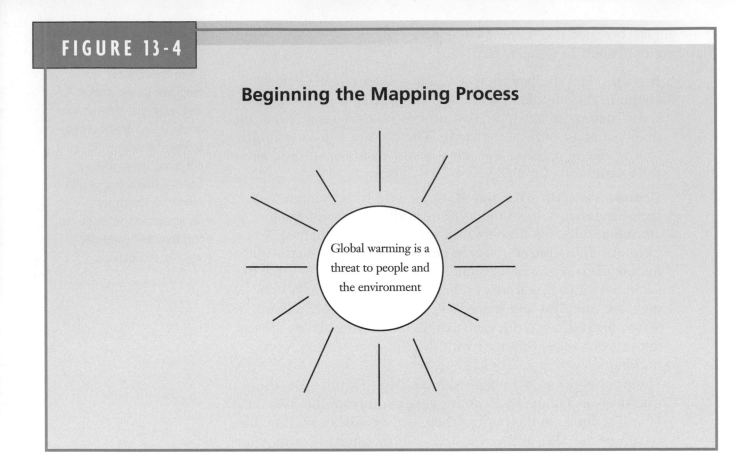

FIGURE 13-5

Mapping: Brainstorming with the 5Ws and H Example

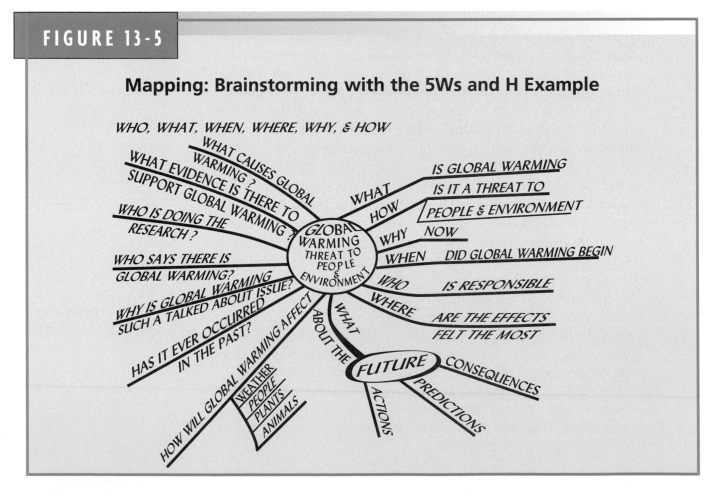

Figure 13-6 on the next page is just one suggested way of organizing the questions for the global warming example. Notice that the question "When did global warming begin?" was changed to "When was it first noticed as a problem?" The revised question communicates the message better. The question "Has it ever occurred in the past?" can be used as a detail to answer "When was it first noticed?" The question "Who says there is global warming?" was not selected. If this was your paper, you might prefer a different question arrangement. As long as the answers to the questions flow from one to the next, then the map will work.

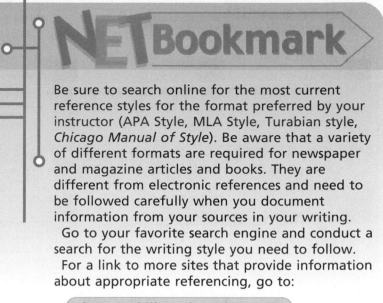

Be sure to search online for the most current reference styles for the format preferred by your instructor (APA Style, MLA Style, Turabian style, *Chicago Manual of Style*). Be aware that a variety of different formats are required for newspaper and magazine articles and books. They are different from electronic references and need to be followed carefully when you document information from your sources in your writing.

Go to your favorite search engine and conduct a search for the writing style you need to follow.

For a link to more sites that provide information about appropriate referencing, go to:

http://sskills.swlearning.com

Mapping with the 5Ws and H is also very effective for quickly organizing your thoughts for essay tests. You can create your spider map in the margin or on a separate piece of paper. This does not take long and is well worth the benefit of having your thoughts organized before you begin writing.

4. ***Check for Idea Flow.*** When you have finished using, changing, or eliminating your questions, read them to see if your order makes sense. If you can easily see the organization of your paper in your questions, then you have succeeded in creating the framework of your outline. Does rearranging the questions help? Does adding more questions or removing some help? Make changes as you see fit.

5. ***Fill in the Details.*** Once the flow of ideas is established, then it is time to fill in the details. Using the body of the summary paper and key words, fill in the details that answer each question. Include any statistics, names, quotes, or important dates—along with the sources. If you did not do any research, fill in any details you would want to include in your writing.

If you do not have enough information to answer a question and the question is important to your paper, then do a little more research to look for the answer. Figure 13-7 on the next page shows some details for each of the questions asked in the global warming example.

After filling in the details, you may need to reorganize their order. In the end, you will have completed your writer's road map. Make changes to the map as you develop the paper. Now you are ready to begin writing your rough draft.

FIGURE 13-6

Organizing Questions from Your Map

8. How is ti a threat to people and the environment?	
9. How will global warming effect:	
* weather	
* people	
* plants	
* animals	
10. Where are the effects felt the most?	
11. Why Now?	
12. What about the future? * consequences * predictions * actions	

Thesis Statement	Global Warming is a threat to people and the environment
1. What is global warming? (GW)	
2. Why is GW such a talked about issue?	
3. When was it first noticed as a problem?	
4. What causes GW?	
5. Who is responsible?	
6. What evidence is there to support GW?	
7. Who is doing research?	(GW)

FIGURE 13-7

Filling in the Details

8. How is ti a threat to people and the environment?	- breathing disorders/asthma - skin cancer from sum exposure - increase in diseases carried by animals - food supply contaminated
9. How will global warming effect:	temp's up 9° fareinheit from 25 & water supply upply arth theory R flooding (rising sea levels) pply

Thesis Statement	Global Warming is a threat to people and the environment	
1. What is global warming?	- also known as "Greenhouse Effect" - depletion of ozone layer.	
2. Why is GW such a talked about issue?	- effects on people - effects on environment - effects on layer shrinking	
3. When was it first noticed as a problem?	- ozone layer & sun harmfulness - warmer night temperatures - changing weather patterns - has it ever occurred in the past	on of causes on dioxide causing change phere ppers no more ric bills up ather in New England.
4. What causes GW?	- chemicals in environment/factor - aerosol cans - cutting down of trees in rainforest - car emissions	
5. Who is responsible?	- those involved in the cause: - others: - - - - - -	
6. What evidence is there to support GW?	See #5 - use some examples:	
7. Who is doing research-	- scientists - environmentalists - of public health/gov't - Earth summit 1992 in Rio de Janiero	

Using the topic and thesis statement you chose earlier in this chapter, proceed through the five steps for mapping with the 5Ws and H. You can work independently or solicit the help of a partner. Partners are especially helpful in the brainstorming process. When you finish, you should have an outline of questions and some details for your writing task.

Topic:_____

Thesis Statement:_____

Who?, What?, When?, Where?, Why?, and How?

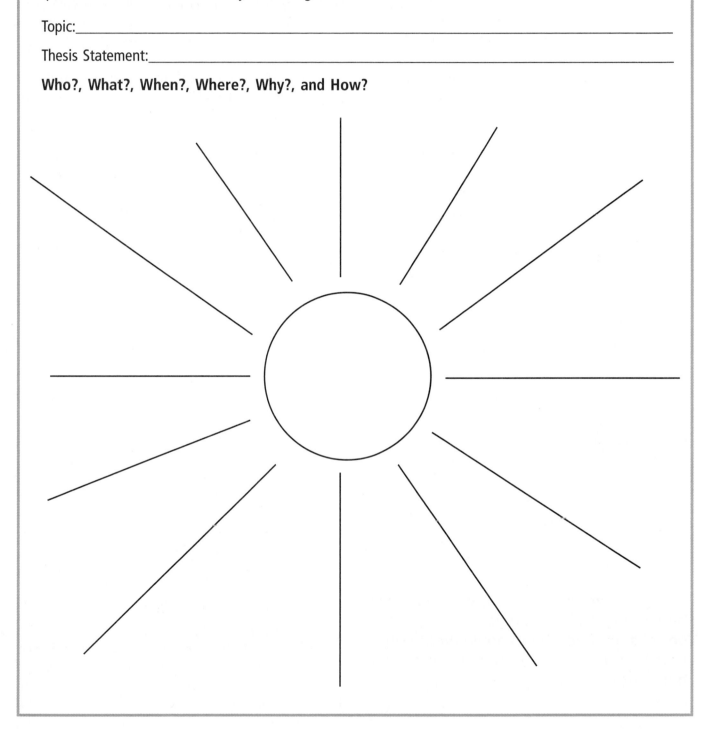

Step 6   Writing the Rough Draft

The **rough draft** of your paper is just that: rough. It is your first attempt at getting your ideas down on paper. This means you should not expect to have a finished smooth-flowing paper ready to hand in after this step, even though many students try to pass off their rough draft as their final copy. You need not worry about making mistakes, including spelling and punctuation, at this time. This draft is not supposed to be perfect. You will have an opportunity to revise your rough draft in the next step. Some people call it their "sloppy copy," which makes them feel better about allowing themselves to have mistakes in their work at this stage.

When writing your rough draft, make sure to leave a double or triple space between each line you write. This will give you room for making changes and revising later.

Every essay or paper you write should have three parts: an *introduction*, a *body*, and a *conclusion*. Each of these parts serves a specific purpose.

■ Focus on Ethics

You have worked really hard researching and writing a particular paper. Your best friend is very impressed and asks if he can share your paper with another friend. Of course, you say yes. A couple of months later, your cousin calls to tell you that she has just read an article in a magazine that sounds exactly like the paper you wrote. You get a copy of the magazine, and sure enough, there is your material, but the article has been submitted by your best friend under *his* name. Your name is not mentioned anywhere in the article. You ask your best friend about it, and he tells you that you had given him permission to use your material, so there is nothing wrong with what he did.

Is there something wrong with what your best friend did? Would you have given permission if you had known what your best friend planned to do with what you had written?

THE INTRODUCTION. The **introduction** tells a reader what the paper is about. Though many writers begin with phrases like "In this essay, I will discuss…," it is much more appealing and engaging to the reader to be more creative and interesting. The use of questions, statistics, personal points of view, and strong statements are just some options for beginning your writing.

The introduction includes a thesis statement and identifies what will be proved or discussed. If you are writing an essay, the introduction can be a paragraph or so in length. If you are writing a ten-page paper or report, the introduction should be at least several paragraphs long and total at least a page or more.

Using stories, analogies, personal examples, or interesting information you found while researching will help in forming your introduction. Using the global warming example, here's a possible introduction to a short essay:

Imagine that every year the summer season will be a little hotter than the summer before. Imagine that it no longer snows in the United States. Imagine that going outside with skin exposed to the sun increases the chances of getting cancer by 25 percent. Imagine having to wear an oxygen mask every day just to survive. Why would anyone want to imagine these situations? Probably because this could happen. Global warming is the cause of each of these problems and is a threat to people and the environment.

Now it is your turn to write a possible introduction for your essay or paper. Think about how you can make it interesting for the reader. (Use additional paper if you need more space.)

_____

_____

_____

_____

_____

_____

_____

THE BODY. The **body** of your paper is the place where you support and document your position. This is where you discuss your point of view and back up your thesis with facts and specific information. The body of a paper should contain background information about your topic, including important points, historical information, and definitions of key words relating to the topic. In addition to your own point of view, the body is where you state other possible points of view. Most of the material you created in your informal outline should be used in the body. Use the following information to create the body of your paper.

1. ***Remember to write for your audience.*** Your audience may be an instructor, a boss, or a work team. Though your audience may be familiar with your topic, it is sometimes helpful to assume that they know nothing. Write as if you were an instructor providing the information to a student. This forces you to communicate clearly and fully. For example, if you were writing a paper on global warming, you might know that your instructor is familiar with the term "ozone layer." By pretending he or she is not, however, you are forced to define the term, making the paper easier for the reader to understand. (For workplace writing, though, be careful not to waste your readers' time by unnecessarily explaining information that they already know.)

2. ***Write freely and simply.*** While writing your rough draft, don't worry about grammar, spelling, or punctuation. It is more important to get your ideas on paper and revise them later. The following acronym is used by many writers as a reminder to avoid long sentences with big words.

     KISS = Keep It Simple and Short

> Things to remember about the body of your paper:
>
> 1. Write for your audience.
> 2. Write freely and simply.
> 3. Use connecting words.
> 4. Document your sources.
> 5. Keep your research notes.

3. ***Use connecting words.*** Connecting words help to bridge the relationship between sentences. For instance, the word "however" means you are making an exception to something you just said. The words "in addition to" mean you are adding more to what is already said.

ACTIVITY 6

Below is a list of common connecting words. Try to figure out what they mean and how they are used. Use the right side for your suggestions.

Connecting Words	Suggestions for Usage
however	making an exception
in addition to	adding more to what was just said
in other words	restating to explain better
most of all	pointing out the most of something
furthermore	
consequently	
on the other hand	
as a result	
therefore	
to sum up	
for example	
first, second, third	
for this reason	
above all	
in conclusion	
although	
because	
since	
previously	
ultimately	
afterwards	
meanwhile	
presently	
subsequently	

4. ***Document your sources.*** Documenting where you found your information is required for academic papers and other lengthy writing. This lends credibility to your words and recognizes others whose information you used. Simply include the author's last name and the pages where you found the specific information when quoting paper resources. Then, in the bibliography include the remaining information. For electronic resources, you document your sources differently depending on if the material is based on a paper article, if it is a standalone web site (not based on a paper document), or if there is more than one author. Since the referencing guidelines change often, it is suggested to consult the web site of your instructor's preferred referencing style.

You may be asked to document your sources according the guidelines of the American Psychological Association (APA), the Modern Language Association (MLA), Campbell's, or some other documenting source. Your school or local library will have the information you need. Three examples of documenting a book source in the body of a paper according to *A Guide to MLA Documentation Style for Research Papers* are shown in the lettered items below. The source would be shown as follows in the Works Cited or Bibliography section at the end your paper:

Brooks, John. *Telephone: The First Hundred Years*. New York: Harper, 1976.

a. Cite the author's last name and page number(s) in parentheses. For example:

One historian argues that the telephone created "a new habit of mind—a habit of tense alertness, of demanding and expecting immediate results." (Brooks 117-18)

b. Use the author's last name in your sentence and place only the page number(s) of the source in parentheses. For example:

Brooks points out that the telephone created "a new habit of mind—a habit of tense alertness, of demanding and expecting immediate results." (117-18)

c. Give the author's last name in the sentence when you cite the entire work. For example:

Brooks argues that the history of the telephone is characterized by innovations that have changed public attitudes toward technology.

5. ***Keep your research notes.*** When you finish using the research notes for your rough draft, do not throw them away. You may need them for checking a source or making sure you wrote the right information. Sometimes instructors want to see your notes to make sure your writing is authentic (created by you), and not picked up from the resources you used. The only way to prove this is to keep your notes.

"There is no such thing as good writing; there's only good rewriting."

—Ernest Hemingway, American novelist and short story writer

Success tip

Even though it is easy to cut and paste text for your paper from a web site *without documenting your source*, **don't do it!** Instructors know when this has been done and even have software to detect it. If you are caught plagiarizing someone else's writing, you can fail the paper, the class, or in some cases, be expelled from the school. Keep your work as your own to stay in school and avoid the shame and embarrassment.

THE CONCLUSION. The **conclusion** is a summary of your important points. It lets readers know you are finished with your argument. The conclusion also allows you to restate your position and to explain why you believe what you believe. When you read longer newspaper or magazine articles, notice how the writers make their conclusions. Their examples may give you some creative ideas for how to end your writing. The conclusion for a five- to ten-page paper is usually more than one paragraph, while shorter papers may be just one paragraph.

ACTIVITY 7

On your paper, begin writing the rough draft of your paper using the information in the preceding section. If you have done some research on the topic, make the paper at least three pages long. If you have not completed the research, then make your paper one to two pages long.

Step 7   Revising the Rough Draft

At this point in the writing process, the hardest work is done. You have decided on a topic, completed your research, created a thesis statement and outline, and written the rough draft. Now is the time to prepare the final draft. People who try to cram their writing in the day or night before it is due miss out on this valuable part of the writing process.

Before beginning to revise your rough draft, set it aside for a day or more. Getting away from it for a while refreshes your thought process and allows you to continue with a new perspective.

Revising your rough draft means editing it. **Editing** is the process of correcting, adding, eliminating, or rearranging your information so that it makes sense to the reader. This also includes changes in grammar, spelling, and punctuation. Fix the errors identified by your computer's spelling and grammar checkers, but do *not* rely only on these programs because they do *not* catch all mistakes. One way to find mistakes is to read your writing aloud. It helps to identify quickly what doesn't sound right and what isn't spelled correctly. Another method for checking spelling is to read your sentences backwards. Reading sentences backwards allows you to focus on each word individually without thinking about the content.

If, during the time between your rough draft and final draft you had another idea to add, now is the time to do it. Or, maybe you reconsidered what you already wrote and want to omit something. The final draft stage allows you to form your writing into the quality piece it should be.

■ Focus on Technology

Remember to use technology to help you schedule and manage your writing time. Most word processing and e-mail programs, as well as cell phones, contain a calendar or scheduling function. Make sure you learn how to use it and decide if digital time management is right for you. You may still scribble things down on paper from time to time, but sticky notes can't ring you when it's time for you to go to class.

The questions below are provided as a guide for revising your paper. Read each question; then go back to your paper, and check for the answer. If the answer to any question is "no" (which many will be), you need to correct, add, eliminate, or rearrange the information. If the answer to a question is "yes," then you have completed the revision for that question.

For the Introduction:

Is the thesis statement included? _____

Is the thesis statement interesting or catchy? _____

Is the thesis statement long enough or complete enough? _____

Is the thesis statement clear? _____

Am I happy with my introduction? _____

For the Body:

Does the body follow an outline or writer's road map? _____

Is the first sentence of every paragraph a main idea (topic sentence)? _____

Does each paragraph support the main idea? _____

Are the ideas easy to follow? _____

Are each of the main ideas backed up by research, quotes, or other experiences?_____

Are the sources quoted properly? _____

Are the key points clearly stated? _____

Is the content specific enough? _____

Are the examples appropriate to the topic? _____

Did I avoid using the same word over and over again? _____

Is the grammar correct? _____

Is the spelling correct? _____

Is the punctuation correct? _____

Am I happy with the body content? _____

For the Conclusion:

Is the thesis restated in the summary? _____

Does the conclusion summarize my point of view? _____

Am I happy with the conclusion? _____

If you think of your paper as a work of art and present it that way, others will see it that way also.

Step 8   Creating the Final Draft

Creating the final draft is the easy part. This is where you format the paper for its final readers. Review the following guidelines for preparing a research paper and adapt them to your needs.

- Leave a one-inch margin on the top, bottom, and sides of your paper. Double-space and paginate the paper.
- Create a cover sheet or title page. Key your title in the middle of a blank piece of paper. Then, for school papers, on the bottom right side, include your name, the class number and name, your instructor's name, and the date (see Figure 13-8).
- If you have a color printer, consider adding a bit of color to your paper's cover or headings. (Keep it professional and tasteful.)
- Use a clean, readable font, such as 10- or 12-point Times Roman or Arial.
- Start the first page of a paper after the cover sheet approximately three inches from the top.
- Indent the first line of every paragraph.
- Indent and single-space any quotes.
- Prepare the bibliography and works cited list on separate pages with appropriate headings.

Now that you have typed your paper, read it aloud, either to yourself or to someone else, to quickly find anything that does not make sense. Listen for grammatical problems and look for incorrect spelling and punctuation. Your final draft should be clean, neat, and free of typographical and mechanics errors—including incorrect spelling and punctuation. Make changes as needed.

Neatness counts as much as organization. If you think of your paper as a work of art and present it that way, others will see it that way also. This means the final draft should be clean, with no smudges, coffee stains, or fingerprints. Find ways to add color and interest to your paper by adding appropriate, topic-related clip art or photos or by changing the font color. Avoid using correction fluid unless absolutely necessary. Use a report cover, or staple the pages together in the upper left-hand corner.

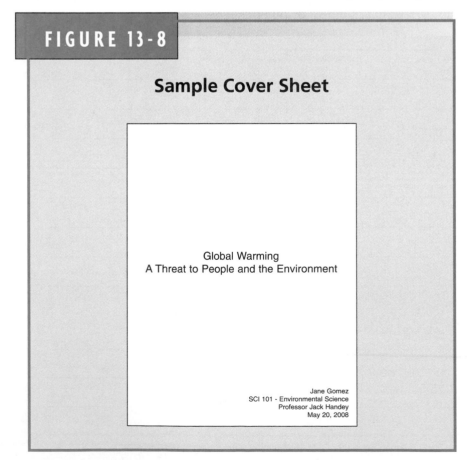

FIGURE 13-8

Sample Cover Sheet

Global Warming
A Threat to People and the Environment

Jane Gomez
SCI 101 - Environmental Science
Professor Jack Handey
May 20, 2008

Prepare the final draft of your paper now. When you finish, reward yourself for a job well done!

Checkpoint

1 Describe the three parts of any essay, paper, or report.

_____

_____

2 What are the eight steps in the writing process?

_____

_____

_____

_____

3 What is the easiest part of the writing process for you? The hardest?

_____

_____

Let others' writing inspire and guide you to create your own quality writing.

"*The volume of interactions is headed toward infinity, and infinity is winning.*"

—McKinsey & Company

Writing E-mail

E-mail is one of the most common and important writing activities for computer users including professional workers, online learners, and other Internet users. It is THE preferred mode of communication over face-to-face meetings, telephones, and faxes. E-mail messages are expected to reach 2.6 trillion in 2007 in the U.S. alone.

E-mail connects you to people, information, and the Internet. It allows you to send a short message quickly and effectively to many people at once, especially to people who are far away. E-mail can help you manage your time better by limiting time-consuming phone conversations and face-to-face meetings.

Because facial expressions, body language, and tone of voice are missing from e-mail, though, you lose valuable clues to the message. Therefore, the words you choose, and the way you use and present them, are extremely important. Misusing words leads to a misunderstanding of the message by the reader, which can lead to a situation you never intended.

ACTIVITY 10

Research news magazines to find at least one story reported in the press about the misuse of e-mail. You may be shocked at what you find. Share the stories with others so they may avoid making e-mail mistakes!

_____

_____

_____

_____

_____

_____

_____

_____

_____

_____

_____

_____

_____

_____

_____

Wilma Davidson, author of *Business Writing*, suggests the following e-mail writing guidelines. Review them and identify which ones you already use and which you might want to use in the future.

Send E-mail to the Right People

For the primary recipients of your message—people from whom you want action—key the receiver's address in the To: field.

For people who are to be courtesy copied—meaning they are not expected to take action—use the Cc: field for the address. To: and Cc: recipients can see all the names and addresses in the To: and Cc: fields.

If your program has the Bcc: option (blind courtesy copy), use it to share information with a recipient from whom you do not expect a response. Some believe Bcc: hints that a message is being sent behind someone's back, since all the recipient addresses are not listed. Many spammers—those who send junk e-mail—use the Bcc: field.

Write an Informative, Specific, and Engaging Subject Line

An e-mail should prove to the receiver as quickly as possible why it should or should not be read. When people look at their e-mail in-box, one way they decide which ones to read first are those with the most informative, specific, and engaging subject lines. Which subject line tells you more or gets your attention first?

a. Meeting Info   a. Thurs. meeting postponed 'til Tues.

b. I have a question   b. What's the dress code for Jo's party?

c. (no subject)   c. *Any* subject

ACTIVITY 11

Revise these e-mail subject lines to make them more informative and engaging. Invent a context for the message as needed.

Original Subject Line	Revised Subject Line
1. FYI	_____
2. It's Late	_____
3. Thoughts	_____
4. Tires	_____
5. The New Year	_____
6. Are You Free?	_____

"*As e-mail has become more entrenched, the people that use e-mail effectively tend to wield more influence than those who write badly or annoy people with their messages.*"

—Joan Tunstall, Author of *Better Faster E-mail*

Bottom-Line Your Message

Place the key point or question first in the e-mail communication. Too many people ramble, explaining why they need what they want, and don't come to the point until the end. To be a good e-mail writer, help the reader get your message sooner.

Be Brief

When writing e-mail, longer is not better. Ideally, e-mail messages should resemble a postcard more than a letter. Keep the KISS rule in mind (Keep It Simple and Short).

Use Spaces and Paragraph Breaks for Readability

Many people write lengthy e-mails using one long paragraph. This makes the message difficult to read. Though the format options are limited on e-mail, try creating smaller paragraphs and putting a line space between each one. The reader will thank you. Never use all capital letters to emphasize an entire paragraph. This is difficult to read and is interpreted as "yelling."

Provide the Reader with an Easy Way to Reply

This means being specific in your request, whenever possible, with a yes or no response.

Be as Personal as the Situation Allows

When communicating with a professor, boss, or coworker, you might need to be more formal than writing to a friend or relative. Use your judgment. It is always in good taste to start your e-mail with the person's name—first name if you know it, or formal name, like "Mr. Jones," if you don't.

Avoid Sarcasm

Remember, you only have your words to communicate. Sometimes your words can be misinterpreted and the reader thinks something you didn't intend. Only use *emoticons,* or "smiley faces," in informal communications with people you know well. Be as straightforward as you can, especially with people you don't know well.

Proof It

Making a keying error or spelling mistake is easy with e-mail. This makes your communication look sloppy and gives the reader the wrong impression. How you look on screen is a direct reflection of you. Always spell check *and* proof your messages before sending.

Wait a Moment Before Pressing Send

Double-check your message before you send. Also, make sure you have attached any documents that are needed. Make sure the tone, topic, and appearance of your e-mail won't embarrass you.

Success tip

Always use discretion with your e-mail messages. E-mail should *not* be used for

- lengthy or complicated messages.
- indiscreet messages.
- sensitive topics that are better resolved in person.
- confidential or private messages.
- angry responses.
- any message you wouldn't want to be made public or have forwarded to others.

At work, use e-mail only for business purposes.

With a partner, create a situation where you need to communicate with each other by e-mail, such as for planning a party, getting together to study, proposing ideas for a work project, or another reason. Have one person begin by writing the first e-mail message according to the guidelines described above. The message can be written on paper, or online if you have access to e-mail. Print your messages out for later use in this activity. Ask the second person to reply and continue with at least three communications each. When you complete the e-mail chain, share your messages with others in your class. Discuss how the messages are effective and how they can be improved. You may use the space below to draft your first two exchanges.

First message _____

_____

_____

Reply _____

_____

Second message _____

_____

_____

_____

Reply _____

_____

_____

Checkpoint

1 How is writing an e-mail message different from writing a letter?

_____

_____

2 Why is writing an informative subject line important?

_____

_____

3 Which of the e-mail writing guidelines makes the most sense to you?

_____

_____

CHAPTER SUMMARY

1. Communicating your thoughts on paper effectively is very important for your success in school, at work, and in your personal life.

2. Writing long essays, papers, and reports requires an eight-step process. Shorter writing will use fewer steps. The more experience you have writing, the better writer you will be.

3. The first steps of the eight-step process include finding time to write, deciding on a topic, doing research, and creating a thesis statement. The next steps include creating an outline using the 5Ws and H and writing a rough draft to include an introduction, the body, and a conclusion. The final steps include revising the rough draft and creating your final draft.

4. When starting any writing process, scheduling the time to write at various times is necessary for being able to complete the assignment and create a quality result.

5. Writing effective e-mail correspondence enhances your position with others. E-mail carries its own set of guidelines that, when followed, make for effective written communication. Since you only have your words to make your impression, it is in your best interest to proof your e-mails before sending.

CHAPTER ASSESSMENT

Terms Review

Match the following terms to their definitions.

___body
___brainstorming
___conclusion
___editing
___introduction
___issue
___KISS
___mapping
___plagiarism
___position
___rough draft
___thesis
___thesis statement
___writing process
___5Ws and H

a. A pre-writing process that helps you organize your thoughts and information on paper resulting in an informal outline

b. The main idea of your writing

c. Summarizes your main points

d. An unresolved question you will discuss in your writing

e. Your point of view about the topic of your paper

f. The unauthorized copying of material and calling it your own. It is not tolerated in the academic community.

g. Coming up with a lot of random thoughts that generate new ideas

h. Questions that help you generate and narrow down your ideas

i. First attempt at writing your paper

j. The process of correcting, adding, eliminating, and rearranging your writing so it makes sense to the reader

k. Reminder to keep your paper simple and short

l. Part of a paper that tells the reader what your writing is about

m. Part of a paper where you support and document your position

n. Part of a paper that summarizes your important points

o. Has eight steps; all are used for longer papers and reports while only a few are used for shorter essays

Review

Based on the information you learned in this chapter, answer the following questions using your own words and thoughts.

1. Pick an occupation—one in which you currently work or one in which you want to work—and describe the types of writing you think will be required in this job.

   _____

   _____

   _____

   _____

2. Describe the writing process in your own words without looking back at this chapter.

   _____

   _____

   _____

   _____

   _____

3. What can you do to select a topic for a paper? What are some points to consider?

   _____

   _____

   _____

   _____

4. What is a thesis statement? How do you create a thesis statement?

   _____

   _____

   _____

   _____

5. What are the 5Ws and H? How can they be used to generate ideas for your essay or paper?

   _____

   _____

   _____

   _____

6. Describe mapping in your own words.

   _____

   _____

   _____

   _____

   _____

   _____

7. What are the three parts of any essay or paper? What purpose does each part serve?

_____

_____

_____

_____

_____

8. What is involved in revising a rough draft?

_____

_____

_____

_____

9. Why do you need to make a plan for the writing process? What if you don't have a plan?

_____

_____

_____

_____

10. What area in writing is the most challenging for you? What might you do to make it easier?

_____

_____

_____

_____

11. Why is writing effective e-mail important?

_____

_____

_____

_____

12. How can you use the e-mail guidelines in this chapter to write better e-mails?

_____

_____

_____

_____

13. How will learning to communicate well on paper benefit you?

_____

_____

_____

_____

CASE STUDIES

for Creative and Critical Thinking

Jaxon was surprised when he received his final grade for the accounting course he had just completed. His instructor, Dr. Sarah Kwan, gave him a "C-" for his efforts, but he was expecting at least a "B" based on his own calculations. He quickly decided to send an e-mail to Dr. Kwan explaining his side of the situation. The subject of the e-mail read "Wrong Grade," and the lengthy text of the message included the phrase "You obviously made a mistake when calculating my grade." He immediately sent the e-mail and regretted this action the next day after reading in the syllabus that the class would be graded on a curve.

1. What fundamental rules for writing an e-mail did Jaxon break when he sent his message to Dr. Kwan? Explain.

_____

_____

_____

2. How would you change Jaxon's e-mail to better serve his purpose?

_____

_____

3. While writing effective e-mail is an important skill, sometimes it is not the best form of communication for every situation. Since he wants to become an accounting major, Jaxon will likely have Dr. Kwan for more advanced accounting courses. How could he have better managed this situation?

_____

_____

WORKPLACE CASE—Connecting to Small Business and Community Concerns

Art, the owner of a small ice cream shop, was writing a letter to a newspaper to complain about a local trucking service. He felt that the trucks roared down his street faster than the speed limit. Often, several trucks traveled together, which created dust in the summer and bothered his customers. He thought that, occasionally, they did not come to a full stop at the stop sign, and most recently, he had found tire marks on the newly seeded lawn in front of his shop. He was also afraid for the safety of his young customers who had to cross the street to get to the shop.

1. Which of Art's concerns should he research to be sure his observations and statements are accurate before he writes the letter?

_____

_____

2. What might Art write in a letter to get the newspaper's attention about his problem with the trucks?

_____

_____

_____

Recommended Reading

Getting Motivated

Baldoni, John. *Great Motivation Secrets of Great Leaders*. New York, NY: McGraw-Hill, 2005.

Brim, Gilbert. *Ambition: How We Manage Success and Failure Throughout Our Lives*. New York, NY: Basic Books, 2000.

De Bono, Edward. *Serious Creativity: Using the Power of Lateral Thinking to Create New Ideas*. New York, NY: Advanced Practical Thinking, 1993.

McWilliams, Peter. *Do It! Let's Get Off Our Buts*. Los Angeles, CA: Prelude Press, 1997.

Ottens, Allen J. *Coping with Academic Anxiety*. New York, NY: Rosen Publishing Group, 1991.

Robbins, Anthony. *Awaken the Giant Within: How to Take Immediate Control of Your Mental, Emotional, Physical & Financial Destiny*. New York, NY: Fireside, 1993.

Saftlas, Zev. *Motivation That Works: How to Get Motivated and Stay Motivated*. Brooklyn, NY: Coaching With Results, Inc., 2004.

Samuel, Mark and Sophie Chiche. *The Power of Personal Accountability*. Katonah, NY: Xephor Press, 2004.

Waitley, Denis. *The Psychology of Human Motivation*. Chicago, IL: Nightingale-Conant, 1991. (Cassette recording. Includes a workbook entitled *Psych Up!*)

Self-Esteem and Positive Thinking

Anthony, Robert and Joe Vitale. *Beyond Positive Thinking: A No-Nonsense Formula for Getting the Results You Want*. Newport News, VA: Morgan James Publishing, 2004.

Helmsteter, Shad. *The Self-Talk Solution*. New York, NY: Dove Audio, Inc., 1998. (Audiocassettes.)

Martarano, Joseph T. and John P. Kildahl. *Beyond Negative Thinking: Breaking the Cycle of Depressing and Anxious Thoughts*. Cambridge, MA: Da Capo Press/Perseus Book Group, 2001.

McKay, Matthew and Patrick Fanning. *Self-Esteem*. Oakland, CA: New Harbinger Publications, 2000.

Peale, Norman Vincent. *The Power of Positive Thinking*. Philadelphia, PA: Running Press/Perseus Book Group, 2002.

Reaching Your Goals

Carnegie, Dale. *How to Win Friends and Influence People*. New York, NY: Simon and Schuster, 1998. (Also available on audio CD.)

Covey, Stephen R. *The Seven Habits of Highly Effective People*. New York, NY: Simon and Schuster, 2004. (Also available on audio-cassette and CD.)

Lakein, Alan. *How to Get Control of Your Time and Your Life*. New York, NY: Signet Books, The New American Library, 1996.

Leonard, George. *Mastery: The Keys to Success and Long-Term Fulfillment*. New York, NY: Plume, 1992.

Pincott, Jennifer (Editor). *Success: Advice for Achieving Your Goals from Remarkably Accomplished People*. New York, NY: Random House, 2005.

Exploring Careers and Aptitude

Bolles, Richard Nelson. *What Color Is Your Parachute 2006: A Practical Guide for Job-Hunters and Career Changers*. Berkeley, CA: Ten Speed Press, 2005.

Farr, J. Michael and Laurence Shatkin. *Best Jobs for the 21st Century*. Indianapolis, IN: JIST Works, 2003.

Farr, J. Michael and Laurence Shatkin. *50 Best Jobs for Your Personality*. Indianapolis, IN: JIST Works, 2005.

Likoff, Laurie (Editor). *Encyclopedia of Careers and Vocational Guidance*. New York, NY: Facts On File, 2005.

Tieger, Paul D. *Do What You Are: Discover the Perfect Career for You Through the Secrets of Personality Type*. Boston, MA: Little, Brown, 1995.

U.S. Department of Labor. *Occupational Outlook Handbook 2006–2007*. Indianapolis, IN: JIST Works, 2006. (Also available online at http://www.bls.gov/oco.)

Improving Your Writing

(Also, ask your writing instructors for their personal favorites.)

Davidson, Wilma. *Business Writing: What Works, What Won't*. New York, NY: St. Martins Press, 2001.

Humphrey, Doris and Robert Conklin. *Connections: Writing for Your World*. Mason, OH: Thomson South-Western, 2005.

Kirszner, Laurie G. and Stephen R. Mandell. *Holt Handbook*, 6th Edition. Boston, MA: Heinle, 2003.

Larocque, Paula. *The Book on Writing: The Ultimate Guide to Writing Well*. Oak Park, IL: Marion Street Press, 2003.

Strunk, William, E. B. White, and Roger Angell. *The Elements of Style*, 4th Edition. Boston, MA: Allyn & Bacon, 2000.

Troyka, Lynn Quitman and Douglas Hesse. *The Simon & Schuster Handbook for Writers*, 8th Edition. New York, NY: Simon & Schuster, 2007.

Improving Your Reading Speed

Marks Beale, Abby. *10 Days to Faster Reading*. New York, NY: Warner Books, 2001.

Mullan, Pam. *Read More, Faster . . . On-Screen.* 2005 (e-book available from TheCorporateEducator.com).

Timed Readings Series. New York, NY: Jamestown Education/Glencoe McGraw-Hill, 2003. (Call 1-800-USA-READ for a Jamestown catalog.)

Internet Research and Sources

Hock, Randolph. *The Extreme Searcher's Internet Handbook: A Guide for the Serious Searcher*. Medford, NJ: CyberAge Books, 2004.

Li, Xia and Nancy Crane. *Electronic Styles: A Handbook for Citing Electronic Information*. Medford, NJ: Information Today, 1996.

Schlein, Alan. *Find It Online: The Complete Guide to Online Research*, 4th Edition. Tempe, AZ: Facts On Demand Press, 2004.

Walker, Janice R. and Todd Taylor. *The Columbia Guide to Online Style*. New York, NY: Columbia University Press, NY, 1998.

BIBLIOGRAPHY

Apps, Jerold W. *Study Skills for Today's College Student*. New York, NY: McGraw-Hill, 1990.

Andrews, Robert. *Cassell Dictionary of Contemporary Quotations*. London: Cassell/Orion, 1997.

Baugh, L. Sue. *How to Write Term Papers & Reports*. Columbus, OH: Glencoe McGraw-Hill, 2001.

Bennett, Deborah J. *Logic Made Easy: How to Know When Language Deceives You*. New York, NY: W. W. Norton & Co, 2005.

Burrow, James L. *Marketing*. Mason, OH: Thomson South-Western, 2002.

Buzan, Tony. *Use Both Sides of Your Brain*, 3rd Edition. New York, NY: The Penguin Group, 1991.

Christie, Chris. *Aha!: CPS Process Concepts*. Syracuse, NY: Challenge Institute, 1989.

Coman, Marcia and Kathy Heavers. *How to Improve Your Study Skills*. Columbus, OH: Glencoe McGraw-Hill, 2001.

Davidson, Wilma. *Business Writing: What Works, What Won't*. New York, NY: St. Martins Press, 2001.

Donnelly, Mary Queen. *Skills for Consumer Success*. Mason, OH: Thomson South-Western, 2005.

Fobes, Richard. *The Creative Problem Solver's Toolbox*. Corvallis, OR: Solutions Through Innovation, 1993.

Fry, Ron. *How to Study (Book Series)*, 5th Edition. Hawthorne, NJ: Career Press, 2000.

Galica, Gregory S. *The Blue Book: A Student's Guide to Essay Exams*. San Diego, CA: Harcourt, Brace, Jovanovich, 1991.

Gibbs, J. J. *Dancing with Your Books: The Zen Way of Studying*. New York, NY: Penguin Group, 1990.

Goleman, Daniel. *Emotional Intelligence, 10th Anniversary Edition*. New York, NY: Bantam Books, 2005.

Gross, Ronald. *Peak Learning*, Revised Edition. Los Angeles, CA: Jeremy P. Tarcher, Inc., 1999.

Guilford, J. P. *The Analysis of Intelligence*. New York, NY: McGraw-Hill, 1971.

Hermann, Ned. *Creative Brain*. Lake Lure, NC: Brain Books, 1989.

Jensen, Eric. *Student Success Secrets*. New York, NY: Barron's, 2003.

Jensen, Eric. *Brain-Based Learning: The New Science of Teaching and Training*. Thousand Oaks, CA: Corwin Press, 2000.

Kanar, Carol C. *The Confident Student*. Boston, MA: Houghton Mifflin Company, 2003.

Kerley, Peggy, et al. *Civil Litigation for the Paralegal*. Clifton Park, NY: Thomson Delmar Publishers, 2000.

Kesselman-Turkel, Judi and Franklynn Peterson. *Secrets to Writing Great Papers*. Madison, WI: University of Wisconsin Press, 2003.

Kesselman-Turkel, Judi and Franklynn Peterson. *Research Shortcuts*. Madison, WI: University of Wisconsin Press, 2003.

Kesselman-Turkel, Judi and Franklynn Peterson. *Test-Taking Strategies*. Madison, WI: University of Wisconsin Press, 2003.

Kleindl, Brad Alan and James L. Burrow. *E-Commerce Marketing*. Mason, OH: Thomson South-Western, 2005.

Knowles, Elizabeth. *The Oxford Dictionary of Modern Quotations*. New York, NY: Oxford University Press, 2004.

Lakein, Alan. *How to Get Control of Your Time and Your Life*. New York, NY: Signet Books, The New American Library, 1996.

Langer, Ellen. *Mindfulness*. Reading, MA: Perseus Books, 1990.

Levitt, Julie Griffin. *Your Career: How to Make It Happen*. Mason, OH: Thomson South-Western, 2006.

Media Matters: Critical Thinking in the Information Age. Cincinnati, OH: South-Western Educational Publishing, 2000.

Moore, Brooke Noel and Richard Parker. *Critical Thinking*. New York, NY: The McGraw-Hill Companies, 2004.

Mullan, Pam. *Read More, Faster… On-Screen*. 2005 (e-book available from TheCorporateEducator.com).

North, Vanda and Tony Buzan. *Get Ahead*. Riverton, NJ: Oakdale Printing, 1996.

Olney, Claude Dr. *Where There's a Will There's an "A."* Chesterbrook Educational Publishers, 1988. (Audiotape and videocassette.)

Osborn, Alex. *Your Creative Power*. West Lafayette, IN: Purdue University Press, 1999.

Parnes, Sydney, Editor. *Source Book for Creative Problem Solving*. Buffalo, NY: Creative Education Foundation Press, 1992.

Parnes, Sydney. *Optimize the Magic of Your Mind*. Buffalo, NY: Creative Education Foundation Press, 1997.

Patterson, Becky. *Concentration: Strategies for Attaining Focus*. Dubuque, IA: Kendall-Hunt, 1993.

Pauk, Walter and Ross J. Q. Owens. *How to Study in College,* 8th Edition. Boston, MA: Houghton Mifflin Company, 2004.

Paul, Richard and Linda Elder. *Critical Thinking: Learn the Tools the Best Thinkers Use*. Old Tappan, NJ: Prentice Hall, 2006.

Rockowitz, Murray, et al. *How to Prepare for the GED High School Equivalency Exam*. New York, NY: Barrons, 2004.

Ruchlis, Hy and Sandra Oddo. *Clear Thinking*. Buffalo, NY: Prometheus Books, 1990.

Ruggiero, Vincent R. *Beyond Feelings: A Guide to Critical Thinking*. New York, NY: McGraw-Hill, 2003.

Schlein, Alan. *Find It Online: The Complete Guide to Online Research,* 4th Edition. Tempe, AZ: Facts On Demand Press, 2004.

Trimmer, Joseph. *A Guide to MLA Documentation Style: With an Appendix on APA Style*. Boston, MA: Houghton Mifflin Company, 2003.

VanGundy, Arthur B. *Brain Boosters for Business Advantage*. San Diego, CA: Pfeiffer & Company, 1995.

Wlodkowski, Raymond J. *Enhancing Adult Motivation to Learn*. San Francisco, CA: Jossey-Bass Publishers, 1998.

Wyckoff, Joyce. *Mindmapping: Your Personal Guide to Exploring Creativity and Problem Solving*. New York, NY: Berkeley Books, 1991.

Zorn, Robert. *Speed Reading*. New York, NY: HarperCollins Reference, 1995.

GLOSSARY

A

abridged dictionary a shorter version of an unabridged dictionary (a book that contains words and their meanings listed in alphabetical order), smaller in size because some words are omitted

academic calendar monthly calendar, from September to August, used by individuals attending school or taking training courses

acronym a memory device; word or words formed from the first letters of words or groups of letters in a phrase

active doing something; being conscious and mindful

active reader a reader who uses pre-reading strategies, continually builds strong vocabulary, and uses background knowledge to create understanding

alphabetical information arranged in order from A to Z

antonyms words that are opposite in meaning

appeals to pity critical-thinking fallacy; soliciting sympathy from others

apple polishing critical-thinking fallacy; complimenting another person to get something that is desired

arm-swing rule gently sweeping a semi-circle of clear desk space to allow a clutter-free area for your elbows, reading material, a notebook, and other necessary study items

auditory learner a person who prefers to learn by hearing information, listening, or speaking

B

background knowledge what you already know based on your previous experiences and learning; long-term memory, where learning is permanently stored

bad stress stress that makes performing well or achieving goals challenging because of fear or worry

balanced learner a learner who has an equal preference for sequential and random learning

begging the question critical-thinking fallacy; when a statement is repeated with different words, but nothing is added to the meaning; also called "circular reasoning"

beliefs interpretations, evaluations, conclusions, and predictions a person considers to be true

bias a tilted point of view

bibliography tells what reading resources the author used in writing the book

blog short for "web log" or "weblog"; a log or journal-type series of entries displayed on the Web

body (of a paper) the main part of a paper where you support and document your position

body (of summary paper) the right-hand side of summary paper, used for writing the bulk of your notes

body language the postures, gestures, and expressions we use to communicate without words

brainstorming widely used divergent thinking skill; an open-minded process to come up with as many ideas as possible on a topic, as quickly as possible

browser a software program that is used to view web pages

C

caption text above, below, or next to an illustration or graphic that explains its content or purpose

card stacking presenting only part of the picture in order to influence or persuade others

category a non-alphabetical method of classifying information by items that are similar

cause the reason something happens

CEUs Continuing Education Units, credits required for many certified professionals

chronological order information arranged in time or numerical order

classification the category, class, or group a subject falls into

column width how wide or narrow the printed text is on a page

compare look at things to emphasize their similarities

concentration the art of being focused and the ability to pay attention

conclusion a summary of the important points in your paper; it lets readers know you are finished with your argument and allows you to restate your position and to explain why you believe what you believe

conscious aware and mindful

context clues the word clues or hints that lead to the meaning of the vocabulary word

contrast a way to look at things that emphasizes their differences

convergent thinking related to critical thinking; looks for correct answers or guides a person toward selecting from several answers

coping attitude neither positive nor negative, an attitude that helps a person cope with the work or situation

cramming trying to memorize a lot of information in a very short period of time

creative thinking thinking about thinking in order to bring something new into existence

critical thinking thinking about thinking in order to decide what to believe and how to behave

D

daily activity log a list of the activities you do from the time you get up until you go to sleep; a simple way for individuals to see how they spend their time

dictionary a book that contains words and their meanings listed in alphabetical order

divergent thinking related to creative thinking; thinking aimed at finding many possible answers

download save text, image, or media files from the Internet to a computer

E

editing the process of correcting, adding, eliminating, or rearranging information so that it makes sense to the reader

educated guess a guess based on good information and test strategies

effect what happens as a result of a cause

effective being capable of producing a desired result

effective highlighting reading a complete paragraph or section before highlighting anything; never highlighting more than a few words or phrases at a time, deciding what is important

effective learning space an environment where concentration comes easily and learning occurs

effective recall level the memory level at which you can recall, or remember, studied information in a variety of appropriate ways

efficient accomplishing a job with a minimum amount of time and effort

empowered feeling confident and capable of learning something by using good study habits

eye span the amount of information a person sees at a time when looking down at a page

F

fallacies mistakes in thinking

false dilemma critical-thinking fallacy; creating a dilemma where one does not exist to make someone think there are only two choices in a situation

fiction reading material that is imaginative in nature and composed of invented ideas

5Ws and H Who?, What?, When?, Where?, Why?, and How?; questions to answer when studying and generating ideas

flexible reader a reader who knows how to skim and scan and can adjust his or her reading techniques according to the reading purpose, difficulty of material, and background knowledge

footnotes explanatory comments or reference notes that relate to a specific part of text on a page

full notes taking all of your notes on paper, not in the textbook; reducing the text back into the author's outline using summary paper

G

goal something that a person wants to have or do or hopes to be

good stress stress that helps with motivation and energy

H

hasty generalization critical-thinking fallacy; making a decision too quickly

headings provide specific information about the chapter as well as the outline of the information

hemisphericity a learning styles theory that suggests the brain has two hemispheres, left and right, with each representing certain qualities

highlighting using a colored marker to underline the important information in reading material

horse laugh critical-thinking fallacy; making fun of someone or something when you disagree

hyperlink highlighted words or phrases containing an address or URL that links one web site to another

I

independent learner a person who prefers to learn alone

ineffective learning space an environment that makes learning difficult and results in wasted time

inefficient anything that wastes time and effort

intellectual capital a smart work force that is able to continuously learn and improve

Internet an expansive worldwide electronic network that is made up of thousands of smaller networks, including governmental, commercial, and educational networks

introduction beginning of a paper that tells the reader what the paper will be about

ISP Internet Service Provider; company through which access to the Internet is gained on a paid subscription basis

issue an unresolved question about a topic

J

just reading the most passive reading method; reading from the beginning to the end of the material without pre-viewing the material or taking notes

K

key words the bigger, most important words in text

KISS Keep it simple and short; a reminder to writers avoid long sentences with big words

L

learning acquiring knowledge through systematic, methodical study or frequent review; a natural and constant process of gathering and processing information

learning environment the combination of learning influences that are present while a person learns or works

learning goal completing projects and assignments in a reasonable time frame and on time

learning influences things that affect how well you concentrate while trying to learn

learning styles how people prefer to gather information and what they do with it

long-term goal a goal that takes longer than six months to a year to achieve

M

mapping a pre-writing thought process that helps a writer organize thoughts and information on paper and results in an informal outline

margin notes summary notes or questions you create in the margin of reading material; notes located in the blank space outside the printed text on a page

memorizing trying to commit information to memory by rote or mechanical repetition

memory devices techniques to help you recall the information you need to study

mental learning environment what your mind thinks about while you are learning

metacognition conscious attention to thinking; thinking about your thinking

metasearch engine search programs that query multiple search engines at once and provide the results

mindful aware and conscious

mindless unconscious and passive

Mind Mapping® a creative way to take notes that organizes ideas through visual patterns and pictures

mind wandering a momentary lack of concentration or focus; daydreaming

mnemonic sentence memory device; an aid to organizing ideas in which people make up a sentence using their own words

monthly calendar month-long calendar used to keep track of and plan assignments and work projects

multiple guess taking a wild guess on a multiple-choice question when the answer is unknown

multiple intelligences learning theory that suggests people can be strong in one or more of eight natural intelligences: logical/mathematical, visual/spatial, body/kinesthetic, musical/rhythmic, interpersonal, intrapersonal, verbal/linguistic, and/or naturalist

N

name-calling critical-thinking fallacy that substitutes a personal insult for a direct response

nonfiction reading material that is factual in nature

O

objective test test made up of questions that have a single correct answer, such as multiple-choice, matching, true-false, or fill-in-the-blank

observers people who learn by paying careful attention to what they see

osmosis a passive process by which a person learns information or ideas without conscious effort

P

pacer a person's hand or a white card that is used to keep a reader's place while reading and can be used to force a reader's eyes to move down the page faster

palmtop calendar electronic handheld organizer

panic pushers nervous or unprepared test takers who should be avoided before a test because they ask questions and cause others to panic and lose confidence

participants people who learn by getting involved in the learning process

passive doing nothing; being unconscious and mindless

passive reader a reader who does not use comprehension strategies when reading and learning

peer pressure critical-thinking fallacy; something that causes a person to go along with the crowd in order to be accepted or popular

performance test test that measures how well a person can execute, or perform, a certain task or activity

peripheral vision the wide distance a person is able to see on the left and right while staring straight ahead

persistence continuing until you succeed; refusing to quit

perspective a person's point of view; how a person views things, based on his or her background and expectations

phrase a group of words that expresses a thought

physical learning space the place where a person chooses to read or study

physiology generally, the way a body feels

plagiarism using another person's words without giving proper credit

podcast utilizes RSS technology to allow web site subscribers to view or listen to new audio or video content that is automatically delivered where and when specified by the subscriber

position a writer's point of view on an issue

post an entry of text, hypertext, images, links, or audio or video files on a blog

prefix a part of the word that is added to the beginning

pre-viewing using pre-reading strategies; examining nonfiction reading material to discover the writer's outline *before* reading in detail

procrastination putting off doing something unpleasant or burdensome until a future time

productive time time spent in an activity that leads to a goal

protocols standard "languages" used by the Internet that allow large computer networks to interconnect and communicate with one another

publisher a person or company whose business is to reproduce books and periodicals, for sale

purpose the reason why you read or do an assignment

R

random learner a learner who has a less logical, more haphazard approach to taking in information (compare to sequential learning style)

reading actively using reading strategies, such as pre-viewing, reading key words, reading phrases, and using pacers

reading purpose the reason why a person reads

reading responsibility how you are accountable for the information you read

recall column (of summary paper) the left-hand side of a summary paper, used for information you want to recall or remember

research locating usable information for a paper or project

responsibility how a person is accountable for reading, learning, or an assignment

reward something you give yourself in return for your effort

root word the basic part of a word that conveys the word's foundation or origin

rough draft a writer's first attempt at getting ideas down on paper

RSS feed Rich Site Summary or Really Simple Syndication; offers news feeds or brief summaries of a web site's new/updated content to users

S

scanning looking only for a specific fact or piece of information without reading everything

scare tactics critical-thinking fallacy; using intimidation to cause fear in another person

search engine a computer program that recognizes keywords then locates specific web pages

sensory learning preference visual, auditory, and tactile preferences for learning

sequential learner a person who learns in a logical, step-by-step way while taking in information (compare to random learning style)

short-term goal something you want to achieve within the next six months to a year

skimming reading in high gear; looking only for the general or main ideas

slippery slope critical-thinking fallacy; when a claim is made that one change will lead to more changes and end in a bad result

social learner a person who prefers to learn in a group

straw person critical-thinking fallacy; disagreeing by changing a person's statement

stress the body's reaction to something that happened or is about to happen

subject directory a database of hand-chosen sites that have been reviewed and selected by people rather than by a computer program

subjective test a test made up of questions that evaluate overall understanding of material by requiring the test taker to write opinions or comments, such as short-answer or essay

suffix the part of a word added at the end

summary a brief statement or restatement of main points

summary paper special paper with a 3-inch left margin, used for the Cornell Method of Note Taking

syllabus a schedule of assignments for a course

symbolism in fiction, something that represents and stands for something else

synonyms words that are similar in meaning

T

tactile learner a person who prefers to use the body to learn and to be involved physically in the learning

testimonial critical-thinking fallacy; convincing others by using a quote or endorsement from someone of status

testing success factor something that contributes to a successful test result

textual information located within the paragraphs of the text

thesaurus a type of dictionary that contains only synonyms and antonyms

thesis the conclusion you draw from what you study; the main point of a paper

thesis statement a summary of the thesis that tells the reader what you are going to prove or argue in your paper

topic sentence the main idea of a paragraph, usually the first sentence of every paragraph

two wrongs make a right critical-thinking fallacy; returning an insult with an insult

U

unabridged dictionary the most complete type of a dictionary (a book that contains words and their meanings listed in alphabetical order) because it includes all words and definitions

unconscious mindless and passive

unproductive time time spent in an activity that does not lead to a goal

URL Uniform Resource Locator; the address of a web site

V

visual learner person who prefers to use the eyes to learn, by seeing information via demonstration or in the mind's eye

visualization creating or recalling mental pictures relating to what you are learning

W

weekly activity log similar to a daily activity log list of activities, but completed for a full week, or seven days in a row

weekly project planner a detailed assignment pad that contains a to-do list specific to one day; divided into five, one-day periods with plenty of space to write; an effective way to keep track of assignments and plan study time according to a term calendar

wiki a type of web site that allows users to easily add and edit content; Hawaiian for "quick" or "fast"

word structures prefixes, roots, suffixes, and other parts of words

World Wide Web a huge system of linked resources on the Internet that contain hyperlinks to other resources or web sites

writing process a series of related writing steps to follow during a writing task: 1) creating time to write, 2) deciding on a topic, 3) doing research, 4) creating a thesis statement, 5) creating an outline, 6) writing a rough draft, 7) revising the rough draft, 8) creating the final draft

INDEX

Note: **Boldface** numbers indicate illustrations.

C